SPENSER STUDIES

XVIII

SPENSER STUDIES

A Renaissance Poetry Annual XVIII

Volume XVIII edited by

THERESA KRIER JOHN WATSON
PATRICK CHENEY

AMS PRESS
NEW YORK

SPENSER STUDIES
A RENAISSANCE POETRY ANNUAL

edited by

Anne Lake Prescott, William A. Oram, and Thomas P. Roche, Jr.

is published annually by AMS Press, Inc. as a forum for Spenser scholarship and criticism and related Renaissance subjects. Manuscripts must be double-spaced, including notes, which should be grouped at the end and should be prepared according to *The Chicago Manual of Style.* Authors of essay-length manuscripts should include an abstract of 100-150 words and provide a disk version of the article, preferably in a Windows-compatible format. One copy of each manuscript should be sent to Thomas P. Roche, Jr., Department of English, Princeton University, Princeton, NJ 08544, one copy to Anne Lake Prescott, Department of English, Barnard College, Columbia University, 3009 Broadway, New York, NY 10027-6598, and one copy to William A. Oram, Department of English, Smith College, Northampton, MA 01063.

Please send inquiries concerning subscriptions or the availability of earlier volumes to AMS Press, Inc., Brooklyn Navy Yard, Bldg. 292, Suite 417, Brooklyn, NY 11205, USA.

Manufactured in the United States of America

ISSN 0195-9468
Volume XVIII, ISBN 0-404-19218-1

Contents

Part I
Spenser Fashioning a Past: Nostalgia and Irony

THERESA KRIER, JOHN WATKINS,
AND PATRICK CHENEY

Introduction

THIS SPECIAL ISSUE OF *SPENSER STUDIES* traces its origin to an international conference, "The Place of Spenser: Words, Worlds, Works," held at Spenser's own Pembroke College in Cambridge, England, July 6–8, 2001, sponsored by the International Spenser Society. By "the place of Spenser," the conference organizers aimed to evoke both the geographical site of the New Poet's late-sixteenth-century university education and an occasion for an early twenty-first-century academic conference seeking to locate Spenser's poetry and prose historically.

The conference brought together over 200 Spenserians from around the world, including scholars from the United States, Canada, England, Ireland, Wales, Scotland, Japan, Sweden, Russia, and China. The three-day event featured plenary lectures by Margreta de Grazia, Louis Montrose, and Richard McCabe, and included panels, workshops, and a concluding roundtable that cast a retrospective eye over the conference and what it might suggest about trends in work on Spenser. Special highlights included a hearty dinner in the Pembroke dining hall (a portrait of Spenser looking on), with entertainment by distinguished poets Eiléan Ní Chuilleanáin from Trinity College, Dublin, and Paul Muldoon, the Oxford Professor of Poetry, who read from their poetry on Spenser; an exhibit of rare Spenser books in the Old Library, Christ's College; and a reception in the University of Cambridge Bookshop on Trinity Street, celebrating the timely publication of *The Cambridge Companion to Edmund Spenser*, edited by Andrew Hadfield.

No one was more aware than Spenser of the failure of even the most carefully crafted language to encompass the richness of a memorable social occasion. If he lamented his inability to "count the seas abundant progeny" in the River Marriage, we follow him in awareness of the capacity of any one collection to encompass all that was read, discussed, debated, and thought at Cambridge. When John Watkins organized the closing roundtable, he made one gesture toward the totality of our critical vision: he tried to make sure that at least one member of the seven-member roundtable attended every paper session and workshop. After the conference was over, he asked each roundtabler to submit nominations for the best papers that he or she heard during our three days together at Pembroke.

The results of this poll were as humbling as they were rewarding. Each roundtabler named five or six papers, far too many to fill one volume. Luckily, the tree of Spenserian publication has many branches, all flourishing. Papers by Margreta de Grazia, Jeff Dolven, Richard McCabe, Louis Montrose, Maureen Quilligan, Jennifer Summit have appeared in print elsewhere. Papers by Linda Gregerson, Marshall Grossman, and Laura Knoppers from the session on "Spenser and Death" will appear in a Palgrave collection on death in Spenser and Milton, and Dorothy Stephens' paper will become an essay in a new volume of essays on Irigaray and premodern cultures. Some of the potential authors whom we contacted felt that their ideas were still developing; like so many of the papers we heard in Cambridge, they will appear in future volumes destined to shape the way we and our students will read Spenser over the next several decades.

One of the great pleasures of "Words, Worlds, Works" was the de facto presence of several conferences-within-the-conference that gave Spenserians with focused interests a chance to share their work. Two sessions devoted to Elizabeth I featured papers by Bill Oram, Roger Kuin, and Donald Stump with responses by Leah Marcus and Carole Levin. Elizabeth also featured prominently in Kim Cole's paper on chastity in Book III. As Richard McCabe's haunting and provocative plenary reminded us, Spenserians continue to wrestle with the questions of Spenser's place in Ireland, and of Ireland's place in Spenser's imagination. Scholars offering exciting new perspectives on these questions included Thomas Herron, Maryclaire Moroney, David Baker, Chris Ivic, and Willey Maley. The historicist interest of these papers complemented work delivered in other sessions by Samuel Kessler, David Wilson-Okamura, Bradin Cormack, William O'Neil, Gary Schmidt, Chris Warley.

One of the conference's highlights, the book exhibit in the Old Library of Christ's College, occasioned papers on the materiality of the book and on Spenser's reading habits by Carol Kaske, Harold Weatherby, Jim Shiavoni, and Lee Piepho. A session entitled "Texts," which rounded off the concern with the materiality of *The Faerie Queene* and other works in the Spenserian canon, featured memorable papers on the contrast between modern and early modern reading practices (Joseph Loewenstein), the new Longman text (Toshiyuki Suzuki), and the publication history of *The Faerie Queene*'s dedications (Jean R. Brink).

As Jennifer Summit's paper on the pathos and politics of book collecting following the Protestant iconoclasts' decimation of medieval libraries reminded us, a commitment to political and cultural history has never compromised the Spenserian's abiding interest in Spenser's text. We remain profoundly attentive to the poetic histories inscribed in his play of intertexts and in his verbal play. For reasons perhaps yet to be more fully explored by future critics, many of the papers most devoted to neoformalist work focused on Book III. Judith H. Anderson returned to Amoret's plight, about which she had written a well-known and moving essay, in her conference paper "Busirane's Place: The House of Rhetoric." Ken Gross also returned to a passage on which he had already eloquently written to consider the Gardens of Adonis less as a meditation on cosmology than as an allegory of human consciousness. Like many of the essayists in this volume, he seemed attracted to the Spenser who specializes in representing phenomena and conditions all but impossible to verbalize, conditions of which we are hardly aware until he delineates them.

Readers of this volume will find essayists' fresh engagements with inexhaustible Spenserian questions of literary genre, mode, and discourse. How various are the kinds of allegory and the work they do, how various need our definitions of allegory be, in reading Spenser? These questions are implied by the pieces of Elizabeth Bellamy on Edgar Wind on Isis Church, John Watkins on the multiple versions of pride in *The Faerie Queene* I, Theresa Krier on Stoic allegory in *Mutabilitie* and *The Tempest*, Galina Yermolenko on the troubled dreams of Redcrosse and Scudamour, Elizabeth Harvey's examination of Helkiah Crooke's 1615 medical anatomy *Microcosmographia*, and her suggestion that Crooke makes manifest principles of Spenserian allegory which in turn come to underpin early modern medical understandings of the body. Or again, do we ever come to the end of the minutely calibrated levels of irony and commitment in the Spenserian narrator? In this question Bellamy and Yermolenko are joined by Harry Berger, who revisits *The Faerie Queene* II nearly half a century after his book on Spenser's book, *The Allegorical Temper*, and charts his shifts in thinking about narrative and representation. How do genres meet and transform one another in Spenser's hybrid works, and how do other discourses—medical, political philosophy, historiography, religious polemic—cross-hatch and infuse poetic genres? Clare Kinney, on *Troilus and Criseyde* and *The Shepheardes*

Calender, works on the relationship of lyric and epic; Andrew King shows how Spenser's appropriation of Galfridian history complicates and even thwarts, as much as it seems to promise, a smooth narrative of royal genealogy; Mary Ellen Lamb offers new hope for articulating how, precisely, popular practices of mumming and its figures like St. George work in *The Faerie Queene*; Graham Hammill draws together several works by Spenser to trace his thinking on republics, and the implications for his poetics; Bart Van Es raises questions of both temporality and polity in his essay on chorography and Spenser's English and Irish rivers. Patrick Cheney reveals multiple discourses on death jostling in *Daphnaida*, generating new and open-ended ways of reading this often frustrating poem and others of Spenser's shorter works. Gordon Braden's essay on the *Amoretti* and female pride within Petrarchan discourse is perhaps the elegant exception that proves the rule about this volume's interest in hybrid or mongrel forms: by sticking with the poet/lover who persists in the folly of his own narrow representation of Petrarchan sonneteering, he shows how the lover might become wise.

Newly articulated issues arise as well, both in the Cambridge conference and in this issue of *Spenser Studies*. Gordon Teskey, Theresa Krier, Graham Hammill, Grant Williams—and, at the conference, Kenneth Gross, Katherine Eggert, and many members of the memory workshop and the allegory workshop—are thinking about how thinking itself is assayed and represented in Spenser's work, what form it takes from moment to moment, what sort of thinking is linked to, say, romance, or to allegory. In this, we are all indebted to Angus Fletcher's work, especially but not solely his *Colors of the Mind: Conjectures on Thinking in Literature*. But thinking also becomes a topic opened up by Foucauldian developments of the ways that discourses function, the slant ways they are imbricated with the category of genre, the perspectives and internal distantiation they provide a writer—as in Watkins's deductions about Spenser's degree of commitment to Protestantism in *Faerie Queene* I. Grant Williams brings to this volume haunting concepts of forgetting, remembering, and trauma in his discussion of the House of Alma as a transformation and enlargement of the arts of memory tradition; Gordon Teskey describes some of Heidegger's most enigmatic sayings on thinking, and links them to Spenserian romance. One conference member mentioned in our concluding plenary that very few speakers had discussed neoplatonism, the long-lived workhorse of Spenser studies. On the other hand, various philosophical materialisms drawn from ancient sources have received a fresh burst of interest in the wake of critical interest in the materiality of human bodies, and in this volume both Elizabeth Harvey and Theresa Krier work with relationships between philosophical materialism and allegory. In light of the conference's engagement with the topic of thinking, we are especially grateful to be able to publish here the memoirs of A. C. Hamilton and Thomas Roche, Jr., who give us a little of the flavor of thinking in literature in the middle of the twentieth century. We hope that their pieces will lead to more remembering, for Spenserians owe enormous gratitude to the critical and historical labors of literary scholars when the profession was young.

Heidegger makes much of the fact that "thinking" and "thanking" share a common root in Germanic languages, and we editors take this opportunity to thank all our contributors, who let us think with them. Thanks go to Andrew King, who permitted us to use a phrase from his essay for the middle section of this volume. To get us to the place of Spenser in Cambridge, the International Spenser Society received a good deal of collective help during the past few years: from Caroline Adams, who served as the conference planner at Pembroke; from Lauren Silberman, who initially chaired the conference organizing committee; from Elizabeth Fowler, who joined volume editors Patrick Cheney and John Watkins as conference organizers; the organizing committee itself: Colin Burrow, who served as faculty contact in Cambridge; Roland Greene, who organized the opening panel that featured Thomas P. Roche, Jr., A.C. Hamilton, and Harry Berger, Jr.; Andrew Hadfield, who arranged the reception with Cambridge University Press; Willy Maley, who penned much of the lively discourse about the conference, and who is solely responsible for authoring its subtitle, "Words, Worlds, Works;" Richard McCabe, who served as faculty contact with Pembroke from beginning to end; and to Jerome Dees and Theresa Krier, who, in their roles as successive editors of *The Spenser Review*, devoted space for publicizing the conference, and then for reporting on its contents and results. Finally, special thanks goes to Andrew Zurcher, of Gonville and Caius College, Cambridge, who performed the heroic activity of making the entire conference available, combining astonishing skills, at once electronic, managerial, personal, and—as one of the singers of Elizabethan airs at the banquet—vocal.

We are grateful to the editors of *Spenser Studies*, William A. Oram, Jr., Anne Lake Prescott, and Thomas P. Roche, Jr., for kindly making their journal available for these essays on the place of Spenser.

ELIZABETH J. BELLAMY

Wind in Spenser's Isis Church

This essay revisits *The Faerie Queene*'s Isis Church episode via a look back at Edgar Wind's *Pagan Mysteries in the Renaissance.* Upon recently rereading his book and encountering the intriguing embeddedness of Spenser within his foray into the symbolic worlds of the likes of Michelangelo, Veronese, Botticelli, and others, I wondered why Wind overlooked the Isis Church episode when expanding on his core concept of "pagan mysteries in the Renaissance." In general, Spenserians have not found Wind's intellectual-historical presuppositions and methods especially congenial. But a return to Wind's study can actually serve as a kind of wake-up call for readers of the Isis Church episode. Should we conclude that Isis Church is best read, in a Windian framework, as a "failed mystery?" To what extent is Wind's non-mention of Isis Church a spectral absent presence that should haunt any reading of the episode? My essay contends that a more positive outcome of Wind's non-mention of Isis Church is its uncanny suggestion of new protocols for rereading this episode.

Introduction

THIS ESSAY RETURNS TO THE OFT-VISITED ceremonial mysteries of *The Faerie Queene's* Isis Church episode (V.vii) by way of a look back at Edgar Wind's *Pagan Mysteries in the Renaissance*, that hoary, landmark study in Neoplatonism from the Warburg group, now some forty-five years old. Wind's examples of "pagan mysteries" in the Renaissance are taken almost exclusively from Italian paintings, woodcuts, engravings, emblems, and medals. Thus, it is all the more noteworthy when at one point in his study, Wind momentarily turns his gaze from the Continent to England—specifically, to *The Faerie Queene* and the Mt. Acidale episode's mysterious dance of the graces witnessed by Calidore (VI.x.24). Here, our "sage and serious" Spenser, when viewed through the scholarly lens of the Warburg school, becomes transformed into a Neoplatonic hierophant whose piping Colin presides over what Wind perceives as an authentic "pagan mystery in the Renaissance."

For Spenserians, stumbling across Spenser in the dense, esoteric, and far-reaching terrain of Wind's Continental philology is rather like unexpectedly meeting up with an old friend. As I recently reread his book and encountered the intriguing embeddedness of Spenser within his foray into the symbolic worlds of the likes of Michelangelo, Veronese, Botticelli, Titian, I asked: why did Wind overlook or exclude so many of *The Faerie Queene*'s other visionary riches from his core concept of "pagan mysteries in the Renaissance?" As his privileged example of a Spenserian pagan mystery, why did Wind choose Mt. Acidale's Irish and English fairies over, say, the seemingly more obvious Isis Church episode, where Faerie Land intersects with the pagan mysteries of ancient Egypt?

This question seems all the more compelling in light of Wind's own engagements with the myth of Isis and Osiris throughout his study. He addresses Osiris as the prototypical dismembered god, as well as the centrality of the Isiac and Osirian mysteries for the Orphic *prisci theologi*. At one point, Wind quotes Pico's paraphrase of Plutarch on the now clichéd ciphers of ancient Egyptian wisdom: " 'That is why the Egyptians had sculptures of sphinxes in all their temples, to indicate that divine knowledge, if committed to writing at all, must be covered with enigmatic veils and poetic dissimulation.' "[1] And Wind further alludes to what he terms the "verbal juggling" of Apuleius describing his experience as a neophyte in the spring festival rites of Isis: " 'Behold, I have conveyed to you what you must not know although you have heard it' " (*Metamorphoses* [*The Golden Ass*] XI.23; quoted in Wind, 11). Thus, given that the Temple of Isis figures fairly prominently in Wind's exposition of pagan mysteries, and given Wind's interest in Spenser, why didn't *The Faerie Queene*'s Isis Church episode, unlike the Acidale episode, fail to merit so much as a passing glance in a footnote?[2]

A return to Wind's study might serve as a kind of wake-up call for readers of Spenser's Isis Church. Should we conclude that Isis Church is best read, in a Windian framework, as a "failed mystery"? To what extent is Wind's non-mention of Isis Church a spectral absent presence that should haunt any reading of the episode? I contend that a more positive outcome of Wind's non-mention of Isis

Church is its uncanny suggestion of new protocols for rereading this episode. In the first half of my essay, I review how Wind defines a pagan mystery, and speculate on why he may have been disinclined to view the Isis Church episode as a "pagan mystery in the Renaissance." In the essay's second half, I consider the question of whether Spenser knowingly presented Isis Church as a kind of failed mystery, a claim that necessarily entails investigating some of the implications of his choice of Plutarch as a source for Isis Church. My argument unfolds as less an answer to this question than, I hope, a pertinent posing of additional questions, many of which will remain rhetorical because I think we are ultimately better off not so much talking about Isis Church as *circling around* it. Thus, my goal is not so much to provide a reading of Isis Church as to demonstrate how Wind's study can be a productive backdrop for any revisiting of this episode. In the final analysis, the most intriguing "wind" blowing through Isis Church may be not the "hideous tempest" that fans the embers of Isis's altar but the breezes emanating from *Pagan Mysteries in the Renaissance*.[3]

RAGING CORRECTLY IN NEOPLATONISM

At this juncture, it is worth rehearsing the exotic particulars of the Isis Church episode, during which Britomart experiences "strange visions" of the "antique world" of the Egyptians. The temple at which she arrives "with great humility" (V.vii.3.7), following her defeat of Dolon, is "Borne vppon stately pillours, all dispred/With shining gold" (V.vii.5.4–5); and unlike the iron man Talus, who is not admitted into the temple, Britomart prepares for initiation into the Isiac mysteries by priests "duely attend[ing]/Vppon the rites and daily sacrifize,/All clad in linnen robes" and wearing "rich Mitres shaped like the Moone" (V.vii..4.2–6).[4] The statue—the "Idoll"—of Isis, who "had powre in things diuine" (V.vii.6.7), is adorned in a silver-fringed linen stole and, in one of *The Faerie Queene*'s more vivid iconographic moments, stands with one foot on a crocodile. "All that night," Spenser narrates, Britomart sleeps "Vnder the wings of Isis" (V.vii.12.2), dreaming that she has become her priestess, or even Isis herself.

Britomart dreams "a wondrous vision"—and a highly erotic vision—in which Isis's linen stole turns "scarlet red," and a "hideous tempest" fans the embers of the altar into "outragious flames," at which point Isis's awakening crocodile "did streight deuoure/Both flames and tempest," threatening the goddess who beats him back with her rod (V.vii.13–15).[5] The crocodile "so neare her drew" that Britomart-as-Isis "soone enwombed grew," giving birth to a regal lion (V.vii.16.4–5). Upon awakening, she is "full of fearefull fright,/ And doubtfully dismayd" by her dream-vision, and seeks guidance from a priest of Isis to lead her "out of errour blind" (V.vii.16–19). The priest offers the following interpretation: Britomart is an Isis-figure, and Arthegall, her imperial lover, is the Crocodile Osiris, the Osirian god of Justice "of the race/Of th'old Aegyptian kings, that whylome were" (V.vii.2.5–6). Together, they represent the union of justice and equity and will continue the British nation. Britomart is "eased in her troublous thought" (V.vii.24.2) and leaves an offering of gold and silver to the goddess-Idoll before resuming her search for Arthegall.

Spenser's Isis Church episode is, to be sure, one of *The Faerie Queene*'s crucial prophetic moments, a major phase in its evolution as a dynastic epic that looks back at the mysteries of pagan Egypt, even as it looks ahead to Troynovant. Yet the episode's manifest paganness seems not to have worked in its favor as any kind of Windian "pagan mystery." In general, Spenserians have not found Wind's intellectual-historical presuppositions and methods especially congenial.[6] But I suggest that we can use Wind's highly motivated, if brief, turn to *The Faerie Queene* as the occasion for a valuable review of the now largely forgotten Neoplatonic protocols of his discourse: what exactly *is* a Renaissance "pagan mystery?" What *does* the "pagan" in "pagan mystery" mean? And how crucial is Wind's concept to ongoing readings of the paganness, and apparent lack of mystery, of Spenser's Isis Church episode? We can look a bit askance at what may now strike us as the Orientalism of the title of Wind's study. But this should not deter us from closely examining Wind's programmatic attempt, as he puts it, to "penetrate the pagan mysteries of the Renaissance" (1), for reading Isis Church with and against the grain of Wind's study yields an additional perspective on the vexed question of how Spenser thinks about, indeed *thinks*, inspiration.

Among other things, Wind's study of Neoplatonic allegory is just such an attempt at thinking inspiration. Wind's pagan mysteries are not so much aesthetic as they are philosophical; his study opens with Plato's declaration in the *Phaedrus* that philosophy itself was a kind of mystical initiation. The essence of a pagan mystery is the ability, in Wind's succinct echoing of the *Phaedrus* 244 E, to "rage correctly," the power to enter into communion with the Beyond (3). Thus, the "pagan mysteries of the Renaissance" centered on how the soul could be induced by a certain kind of poetic hymn to rise to a state of philosophic enthusiasm. In short, for Wind the "pagan mysteries" of the Renaissance celebrated meditation as a philosophical discipline.

In Neoplatonic allegory, it is important to note that this disciplined purging of the mind, or *askesis*, always involves motion—specifically, motion around the One. Thus, in his *Enneads* (6.9.8), Plotinus argues that the soul's natural motion "is circular, as around some inner object, about a center, the point to which it owes its origin"; and Ficino claims that there exists "a certain continuous attraction (beginning from God, emanating to the World, and returning at last to God), which returns again, as if in a kind of circle, to the same place whence it issued" (*De Amore*, II.ii).[7] Raging correctly, then, is highly dependent on the interpreter's ability to enter into these cosmic rhythms of emanation and reversion. To rage correctly is to be attuned also to the motion of the deities. To successfully interpret a deity is to understand that no deity can be locked into a one-to-one correspondence of signification: rather, the interpretive goal of the so-called Orphic theology is to locate the deity within a dynamic network of associations, a swirling system of analogies and correspondences. The Neoplatonic hierophant must absolutely refuse to limit the essence of the gods to anything less than a simultaneous and dispersed network of images and associations. "With every shift of argument," writes Wind, "a new harmony or discord may thus be discovered between the gods" (198).[8]

Why was Wind moved to include Spenser's Acidale in his study of pagan mysteries? Because, much like Botticelli's eminently philosophical *Primavera*, whose secretive art was, as Wind points out, "designed for initiates, hence requir[ing] an initiation" (15), Spenser's Acidale episode relies on what Wind marvelously terms a "perilous alchemy" of the graces to *animate* its mysteries and set in motion the correspondences among the gods (26). In such a scheme, Colin Clout rages correctly as he pipes to the Fourth Grace-as-Venus: Colin enters into the circular motion of the maidens and apprehends the unnamed "Damzell" as Acidale's hybrid Venus—not a fixed goddess but rather a movable part, always hinting at the other gods (i.e., the dual deities of Venus-Diana, Venus-Jupiter, Venus-Juno, and Venus-Saturn).[9] Early in his book, Wind writes elegantly that philosophical interpretation of the mysteries of the ancients depends "on that altogether indefinable but unmistakable sense of pitch" (16n.47). For Wind, Spenser's Acidale episode is just such a pagan—that is, *philosophical*—mystery, a *thinking* of inspiration that attains an "indefinable sense of pitch" found in the greatest Renaissance paintings.

Now we can more readily see why Wind did not single out the Isis Church episode as the essence of a Spenserian pagan mystery. To be sure, on the surface, the episode would seem to meet all the requirements for a mystery. In Neoplatonism, Isis was often associated with Venus: like Venus, Isis was a hermeneutically powerful, hybrid goddess of whom all the other gods are aspects. Britomart, moreover, is explicitly prepared for a kind of mystical initiation by the linen-robed priests. But Wind, a reader of Porphyry's *Life of Plotinus*, might have been tempted to unfavorably compare Britomart's Isis Church initiation with Porphyry's story of having been visited by an Egyptian priest who wished to display his power by summoning up Plotinus's presiding demon in the Temple of Isis. When not a lowly demon but a divinity apeared, the priest exclaimed: " 'You are singularly graced; the guiding-spirit within you is not of the lower degree but a God.' "[10] For Wind, Britomart's encounter with the high priests of Isis clearly did not possess the same mysterious and alchemizing potential as Plotinus's inspired sojourn in his Temple of Isis. For that matter, the priests of Spenser's Isis might have struck Wind as little more than warmed-over Plutarch: "They wore rich Mitres shaped like the Moone,/To shew that Isis doth the Moone portend;/Like as Osyris signifies the Sunne" (V.vii.4.6–8). The heavy-handed, bookish obviousness of this passage's lunar and solar symbolism hardly achieves Wind's "unmistakable sense of pitch": it hardly promises an ecstatic access to the gods, or the divine seizures necessary to set in motion the Neoplatonic rhythms of procession, rapture, and return that constitute a pagan mystery.[11]

Commenting on Botticelli's *Primavera*, E. H. Gombrich nicely perceives that the "haunting character of Botticelli's physiognomies not only permits but *demands* interpretation."[12] But apparently Wind perceived no such demand for interpretation in the empty hermeticism of Isis Church. In fact, Wind offers a salutary note of caution that should be heeded by anyone tempted to overread the mysteriousness of Spenser's Isis Church episode: "It would be absurd to look for a mystery behind every hybrid image of the Renaissance" (25). Thus, we can easily imagine Wind dismissing Spenser's unanimated Isiac High Priest, "stifly star[ing]" at Britomart "Like one adawed with some dreadful spright," as a risible mystagogue—closer to the Egyptian Busyrane than "that altogether indefinable but unmistakable sense of pitch" generated, if only momentarily, by Colin on Acidale. For Wind, the very argument to *Faerie Queene* V.vii, narrating with bland efficiency that "Britomart comes to Isis Church," might have resonated unfavorably with his own quoting of Plotinus: " 'The gods must come to me, not I to them' " (5). In other words, one does not so much come to a Temple of Isis as wait for the right moment to be embraced by its uncanny mysteries.

Wind's non-mention of Isis Church poses a bit of a problem for Spenserians. To return to the question I posed earlier in my essay: is Spenser's Isis Church episode best read as a kind of failed pagan mystery? Is Britomart a mere parody of a true initiate into the Isiac mysteries? It is impossible to negotiate these questions before tackling another pragmatic and nagging question: when do we *know* whether a painting or a poem has attained Wind's "altogether indefinable but unmistakable sense of pitch," thereby attaining the status of a pagan mystery? Wind himself is acutely aware of this authenticity question, conceding from the very outset of his study that "any attempt to penetrate the pagan mysteries of the Renaissance should perhaps begin with the admission that the term "mysteries" has several meanings, and that these already tended to become blurred in antiquity, *to the great enrichment and confusion of the subject*" (1; emphasis added). In the *Republic* 365 A, Plato mocked mysteries as fit for the vulgar. But, as we have seen, it is also the case that in his *Phaedrus*, philosophy itself is the ability to rage correctly. Wind alludes to Porphyry's *Life of Plotinus*, where Porphyry writes that he himself once recited an enthusiastic hymn to members of Plotinus's school assembled to celebrate the birthday of Plato—a performance not well received by the fastidious audience: Porphyry, they observed, " 'is off his head.' " Plotinus, however, rose to his pupil's defense, declaring: " 'You have shown yourself a poet, a philosopher, and a hierophant' " (5).

But how do we know, as both Plotinus and Wind seem to, when hierophants are raging correctly? How can we be as sure as Wind that Colin has achieved that unmistakable sense of pitch, while Spenser's "stifly star[ing]" Isis-priest might be, echoing Porphyry's detractors, merely "off his head," merely a participant in what Plotinus termed "the lesser spectacles" (*Enneads* 6.9.11)? *Or* are these questions poorly framed—limiting our interpretive options by forcing the premature conclusion that the peculiarly static nature of Spenser's Isis Church ceremonies does indeed constitute a kind of failed mystery? After all, as we have seen, Wind's own concession that the term "mysteries" had already "tended to become blurred in antiquity" complicates any such distinction between "raging correctly" and being "off one's head." So let us pause to look at how Wind expands on this "blurring" process in the Renaissance; to do so is to begin, I hope, to clear a subtler and more productive space for approaching the Isis Church ceremonies.

Wind argues, "Whenever 'the mysteries of the ancients' were invoked by De Bussi, Beroaldo, Perotti, or Landino, not to mention

Ficino or Pico della Mirandola, their concern was less with the original mystery cults than with their philosophical adaptation" (7). In other words, Landino or Ficino or Pico read Plotinus, Iamblichus, Porphyry, Proclus, et al., as lenses through which to view the mysteries of antiquity; and they were less intrigued with the particulars of these mysteries than with how the Neoplatonic philosophers of late antiquity raged correctly in their exegetic adaptations of the mysteries. Wind contends that the pagan revival to which Ficino and Pico adhered was, therefore, "less 'a revival of the classics' than a recrudescence of that ugly thing which has been called 'late-antique syncretism' " (22), when mysteries were finally recorded in script. Wind does not further comment on or explain his provocative description of late-antique syncretism as an ugly thing. But we should fill in the blanks, as his term will have large implications for my rereading of Spenser's Isis Church. Late-antique syncretism was an ugly thing, for Wind, insofar as it was complexly *mediated*: in the final analysis, the appeal for Renaissance Neoplatonism of the likes of Plotinus and Porphyry was the exegetical ingenuity of their mediating philosophical adaptations, their inspired methods for attaining that "unmistakable sense of pitch" as the very core of raging correctly. In order to fully understand a classical author, claims Wind, a Ficino, for one, "would always turn to a Hellenistic commentary" (23). And this turning to a Hellenistic commentary *itself* replicated the source commentary's own syncretism—hence, Wind's designation of Ficino's and Pico's indulgences in Neoplatonic allegorizing as a "recrudescence," a breaking out anew after a dormant period.

To return to my earlier nagging question: when do we *know* when hierophants are "raging correctly"? The answer, picking up on the discussion of the previous paragraph, is that a pagan mystery in the Renaissance "rages correctly" when it deploys a Hellenistic commentary to generate a "philosophical" (i.e., Neoplatonic) adaptation of a mystery of antiquity: a "pagan mystery" in the Renaissance has achieved an "unmistakable sense of pitch" when it successfully mediates its Hellenistic source. Although I have no ill-advised intention here to follow Wind into the thorny linguistic and philological thickets of syncretism, in my essay's final section, I would like to investigate further some of the implications of what it might mean to label *The Faerie Queene*'s Isis Church ceremonies as syncretic. Or, more precisely, I want to investigate the extent to which Isis Church can be productively read not as a failed mystery, but as Spenser's own strange recrudescence of "that ugly thing which has been called 'late-antique syncretism.' " Finally, I will speculate on why, in the particular case of Spenser's turn to Plutarch's Hellenistic commentary on the ancient Osirian and Isiac mysteries, Wind evidently perceived no moment of raging correctly.

PLUTARCH, WIND, AND THE "CHATTERING" OF MYSTERIES

To enter into the task of talking about the syncretism of Isis Church, we must first fully contextualize Spenser's use of Plutarch as a source by pondering the self-conscious Egyptianness of the poet's static Isis Church ceremonies. There are many valuable points of entry into discussing Spenser's representation of Egypt in the Isis Church episode.[13] But perhaps most relevant for my purposes is Angus Fletcher's observation in his *The Prophetic Moment*, spurred by Frances Yates's *Giordano Bruno and the Hermetic Tradition*, that the Isis Church episode reflects a vogue of Egyptian iconography in the latter half of the sixteenth century: that is to say, the Isis Church episode, more than merely iconographic, is conspicuously voguish in its iconography, an especially exotic example of the sixteenth century's veneration of Egyptian learning.[14] The episode's lavish apparatus of shining gold temples, flaming altars, and linen-robed priests performing sacrificial rites to an idol surely ranks among *The Faerie Queene*'s most Orientalist performances. And indeed Upton's 1758 commentary on *The Faerie Queene*, intriguingly anticipating Said's axiomatic claim that the "Orient" of the West has less to do with the real Orient than it does with the West's own cultural imaginary, insists that in the Isis Church episode, "Spenser does not carry you to Aegypt; you stand upon allegorical and Fairy Ground."[15]

Upton's claim that Spenser does not really carry readers of *The Faerie Queene* to Egypt invites further nuancing: if Upton is right, then is this despite the episode's manifest Egyptian voguishness—or *because* of it? The later sixteenth-century vogue of Egyptian high antiquity (i.e., Egypt as the source of true hieroglyphics and the fount of all wisdom, as opposed to the decadent, doomed Egypt of Shakespeare's *Antony and Cleopatra*) was, of course, largely fueled by Plutarch's vastly influential second-century essay in comparative religion, *De Iside et Osiride*.[16] As Upton himself and many others have noted, Britomart's stay in Isis Church relies primarily on Plutarch's exotic accounts of the ancient Osirian rites, replete with secret initiations, mysteries presided over by strictly chaste priests, and crocodile cults. Thus, we could say that the Isis Church episode is Spenser's attempt to carry us not so much to Egypt as to Plutarch's Egypt.[17]

But what are the precise implications of labeling Plutarch as a source for the Isis Church episode? Identifying Plutarch as Spenser's source often seems to be accompanied by a kind of comfort level, as if this gesture towards Plutarch somehows anchors our understanding of the episode's pagan mysteriousness. But identifying Plutarch as Spenser's source, rather than simplifying, further complicates our reading of Isis Church. I suggest that any reading of the episode would do well to keep in mind Wind's contention that whenever a Renaissance painter, philosopher, or poet turned to Hellenistic commentary, the result was so often to stir up "that ugly thing which has been called 'late-antique syncretism.' " In the case of Spenser's Isis Church episode, where the reader views the Isiac ceremonies through a distinctly Plutarchan lens, the task of interpretation becomes uglier (i.e., considerably more complex and mediated) when we bear in mind that Plutarch's treatise was itself burdened with the heavy weight of the historical fact that Isis and Osiris had been worshipped for nothing less than two and a half millennia.

Plutarch's treatise is an ambitious adaptation of Egyptian theology to Platonic philosophy. But if we begin to reflect on Plutarch's *own* mediate sense of the exotic otherness of the Isiac/Osirian mysteries, the question arises: to what extent does Plutarch himself, to echo Upton, really "carry [us] to Aegypt?" That the Isiac/Osirian mysteries reported by Plutarch so readily offered Spenser fertile opportunities for his allegory—and that England's imperial future is foreseen by an Isiac/Osirian priest who all too speedily "eases" Britomart "in her troublous thought"—might give us pause when we consider Plutarch's own ambivalence toward these ancient priestly rituals. This ambivalence stems from his drawing a major distinction between Osirian myth as accessible to all and the sacred rituals, which are available to the initiated only. (We could say that this distinction constitutes Plutarch's own wrestling with the problem of the "blurring" of mysteries in antiquity.) Readers of Plutarch's *Of Isis and Osiris* are not immediately carried to Egypt, for time and again throughout his work, Plutarch, perhaps more than Plotinus or Proclus, seems determined to preserve a certain fastidious distance between himself and the sacred priestly mysteries: "Let us leave the sacred rites unmentioned" or "I pass over the cutting of wood, the rending of linen and the pouring of libations, because much mystery-lore is involved." He refers to aspects of the Osirian cults which are "preserved by being clothed in mystic rites, although they are not divulged by initiates or seen by people at large."[18] Catch-phrases such as "as the initiates know," "most of the priests say," "the Egyptians relate," "Thus the Egyptians believe and say," are repeated throughout, as if Plutarch is signaling his reluctance to further probe the knowledge of the initiates. Phrased broadly, there are discernible limits to Plutarch's curiosity about Egypt's ancient, exotic Isiac/Osirian cults—and unlike Spenser's Britomart, who eagerly seeks Isis's "powre in things diuine" and becomes an initiate literally overnight, Plutarch himself (who may or may not have been an initiate) is reluctant to cross over the threshold of any of the Osirian temples he writes about.

Interestingly, despite his treatise's valuable window into the Osirian and Isiac cults, it is worth noting that Plutarch's hellenized Isis and Osiris have often been a source of frustration and confusion for the discipline of Egyptology. As classicist and Egyptologist John Gwyn Griffiths observes in his edition *Of Isis and Osiris*, "[T]he question arises whether in fact his study of the Egyptian gods is not more marked by a desire to explain their nature and myths in Hellenic terms than to record the native explanations and the striking ways in which Egyptian religious thought differed from the Greek."[19] We could say, though, that Egyptology's disciplinary frustration with *Of Isis and Osiris* marks the precise boundaries of Plutarch's Neoplatonism as, in a Windian framework, a mode of allegorizing less interested in the original mysteries themselves than in raging correctly as it seeks, what Michael J. B. Allen calls a "mythological grammar" for interpreting the gods.[20] Thus, Griffiths' objection to what he terms Plutarch's "desire" (i.e., his desire to explain the Egyptian gods in Hellenic terms) can be intriguingly juxtaposed with Wind's willing "desire" to confront that "ugly thing which has been called 'late-antique syncretism.' "

From his disciplinary stance within Egyptology, Griffiths himself, to one degree or another, comes close to acknowledging the ugly thing of the syncretism of late antiquity: "[H]ow far was the subject matter of Plutarch's treatise in vogue among adherents of the Osirian religion in his day? Only a very cultured élite, one can imagine, would have thought like this, and they would have been nurtured in Neo-Platonism before being converted to Isis and Osiris" (74). As a document of comparative religion, Plutarch's treatise falls short of the philosophical enthusiasm that sustains Plotinus or Proclus. But when we recall Plutarch's main intention of carrying his readers not to Egypt, but rather to the complex intersection of Egyptian theology and Plato's philosophy, then we can appreciate the extent to which *Of Isis and Osiris* is a disciplined exercise in applied Platonism—a careful *reworking* of the Osirian mysteries. Indeed, we could say that

Plutarch's ambivalence toward the original Osirian cults *is* the philosophic space of Neoplatonism, not to mention an exemplary performance of that "ugly thing" known as late-antique syncretism. Bluntly put, in Plutarch's late antiquity, if the Osirian initiates thought they could, in effect, return to Egypt without first going through the rigors of Neoplatonism's own initiation rituals, they were merely "off their heads."

We can readily grant that Spenser's pressing the Osirian crocodile into service for the ends of nation building constitutes a bold and highly original use of Plutarch (and provides Fletcher with much food for thought for his tracing of *The Faerie Queene*'s "Galfridean" matrix). But the reader should nevertheless not be too hasty in overlooking the fact that the poet's gesture is in violation of every Neoplatonic protocol. Thus, had Plutarch read the Isis Church episode, he almost certainly would have cautioned that in Arthegall's association with a crocodile, there is not so much an engine of imperial allegory as a deep mystery—a mystery that the priest must not be too quick to interpret or impatient to unfold. And one can imagine Wind, in the process of reading *The Faerie Queene* with an eye to locating its authentic mysteries, dismissing Britomart as insufficiently nurtured within Neoplatonism prior to her speedy conversion, not properly hellenized in an episode where Plutarch's exegetical ingenuity ossifies into Spenser's "stifly star[ing]" and *incorrectly* raging Isis priest. However, to turn the screw even further, what I would really like to know is the extent to which Spenser *himself* was attuned to the rhetorical repetitions of Plutarch's ambivalent, distancing caveats about the Osirian mysteries. If Spenser was so attuned, then his fashioning a Britomart who rushes in to receive an Osirian prophecy where Plutarch fears to tread—the alacrity with which he overcomes Plutarch's reluctance to bridge the gap between Osirian myth as accessible to all and the sacred ritual as available to the initiated only—may constitute less a resonant prophetic moment than a quintessential moment of Spenserian wit and irony, a calculated subversion of the very concept of a pagan mystery.

Plutarch, of course, had not read Spenser. But Spenser had read Plutarch, and Wind had read both Plutarch and Spenser—an intertextuality that makes it all the more compelling to read the Isis Church episode alongside *Pagan Mysteries in the Renaissance*, enabling, as it does, a way of further pursuing a possible Spenserian irony in Isis Church. Wind's most intriguing observation about Plutarch renders the task of reading *Of Isis and Osiris*, and, by extension, Isis Church, even more complex. Near the conclusion of his study, Wind almost coyly brings up the danger of "misjudg[ing] altogether the atmosphere in which the pagan mysteries were revived. They were sponsored by men of letters who had learned from Plato that the deepest things are best spoken of in a tone of irony . . . . [E]ven Plutarch had chattered of mysteries in a mocking tone" (236). Wind's readers might justifiably view this admission as badly belated. It is interesting that Wind slips in this caveat only at the conclusion of his study; and, to be sure, the easily misjudged "mocking tone" that often accompanied the description of these otherwise solemn mysteries is another major reason why late-antique syncretism was such an "ugly thing."

Wind does not offer a specific example of Plutarch's mocking "chattering" of mysteries, but we would do well to ponder the tone of Plutarch's cautionary claim, "[F]or it is not the cultivation of a beard and the wearing of a threadbare cloak that make a philosopher, nor does dressing in linen . . . make an Isiac devotee; the true devotee of Isis is he who, whenever he hears the traditional view of what is displayed and done with regard to these gods, examines and investigates rationally what truth there may be in it" (3). Spenser surely read this passage, which makes it all the more intriguing that in his writing of Isis Church, he does precisely what Plutarch warns against—that is, he writes an episode in which the mere fact of "dressing in linen" is sufficient to create an Isiac devotee. Thus, to rephrase my essay's recurrent question: should we read the Isis Church episode as a failed mystery—or rather as Spenser's sly take on Plutarch? Given Spenser's own indulgences in *serio ludere*, the mock somberness of Plutarch's chattering of mysteries would have appealed to the poet's sense of humor and tendency to "play/With double senses" (III.iv.28). Put another way, Spenser may have been less interested in presenting a pagan mystery of correct raging than in experimenting with that easily misjudged tone of mock chattering.

In sum, taking our cues from Wind, we should not mistake the Isis Church episode for a Renaissance pagan mystery. But if Spenser did encode Plutarch's ambivalence toward the Osirian mysteries, then the Isis Church episode is perhaps best read as *The Faerie Queene*'s performance of Wind's own methodological concern over the blurred meanings of the term "mysteries" in antiquity. Where is Egypt to be found in *The Faerie Queene*? Wind would argue that Egypt is found not in Isis Church, but on Acidale in the "perfect pitch" and exegetic ingenuity of Neoplatonism's interpretation of the three graces. But rather than dismissing Isis Church as a failed mystery or an empty hermeticism, perhaps we would do better to read the Egypt of Isis Church as Spenser's deliberate plunge into the scholarly mess resulting from, in Wind's phrase, "the recrudescence of that ugly thing called 'late-antique syncretism' "—to the great enrichment and confusion of our ongoing reading of *The Faerie Queene*.

NOTES

1. Pico, *Commento sopra una canzona de amore composta da Girolamo Benivieni* (III.xi); quoted in Edgar Wind, *Pagan Mysteries in the Renaissance* (New York: W. W. Norton & Co., 1958), 17. Of Wind's reading of Plutarch, I will have more to say near the end of my essay.

2. Wind also briefly lingers awhile in Book 4 of *The Faerie Queene*, alluding to the brothers Priamond, Diamond, and Triamond, as well as the veiled statue of Venus in Spenser's "Great Venus Temple" (210–11). This latter mention signals Wind's familiarity with Spenserian "temples," rendering the absence of Isis Church from his study even more conspicuous.

3. I hope the reader will permit this play on words, even though the *w* in Wind's name is pronounced as a *v*.

4. All references to *The Faerie Queene* are taken from A. C. Hamilton, ed., *Edmund Spenser: The Faerie Queene* (London: Longman, 1977).

5. For an account of "the strange shapes of sexual violence and orality" that permeate this episode, see Kenneth Gross, *Spenserian Poetics: Idolatry, Iconoclasm, and Magic* (Ithaca: Cornell University Press, 1985): 178–80. Gross's account of Britomart's dream was perhaps the first significant gender reading of the Isis Church episode.

6. I am thinking here of Alastair Fowler's critique of Robert Ellrodt for "distinguish[ing] 'orthodox' Renaissance Neoplatonism from the more diffuse Neoplatonism that had been assimilated to Christian and even perhaps to Judaic thought forms at a very early date. Robert Ellrodt has made this distinction acutely and learnedly; but it often seems unnecessarily sophisticated from a literary-critical point of view." See Fowler, "Emanations of Glory: Neoplatonic Order in Spenser's *Faerie Queene*," in *A Theatre for Spenserians*, ed. Judith M. Kennedy and James A. Reither (Toronto: University of Toronto Press, 1973), 53. My guess is that Fowler is also pointing in the direction of the Warburg school and Wind here, as well.

7. *The Essential Plotinus*, trans. Elmer O'Brien (Indianapolis: Hackett Publishing, 1964), 84; Marsilio Ficino, *Commentary on Plato's Symposium on Love*, trans. Sears Jayne (Dallas: Spring Publications, 1985).

8. For more on this method of "Orphic" reading as perceived by the Warburg school, see E. H. Gombrich, "Botticelli's Mythologies: A Study in the Neoplatonic Symbolism of his Circle," *Journal of the Warburg and Courtauld Institutes* 8 (1945): 38. For a more recent account of what he refers to as Neoplatonism's "mythological grammar," see Michael J. B. Allen, *The Platonism of Marsilio Ficino: A Study of His "Phaedrus" Commentary, Its Sources and Genesis* (Berkeley: University of California Press, 1984), 114.

9. For a further elaboration of Spenser's "hybrid" Venus on Acidale, see my essay "Colin and Orphic Interpretation: Reading Neoplatonically on Spenser's Acidale," *Comparative Literature Studies* 27:3 (1990): 182–86.
10. *Plotinus: The Enneads*, trans. Stephen MacKenna (London: Faber and Faber, 1962).
11. Spenser's "Idoll" Isis could serve as a prime example of Gross's elegant account of the idol as "the truth that has collapsed into a lie, the urgent, mythopoeic cipher converted into a vacant myth" (*Spenserian Poetics*, 27).
12. "Botticelli's Mythologies," 11; emphasis mine.
13. The most thorough study of the iconography of Book 5 is Jane Aptekar, *Icons of Justice: Iconography and Thematic Imagery in Book V of The Faerie Queene* (New York: Columbia University Press, 1967). See also T. K. Dunseath, *Spenser's Allegory of Justice in the Faerie Queene* V (Princeton: Princeton University Press, 1968). On the cosmic symbolism of Book 5 in general, see Alastair Fowler, *Spenser and the Numbers of Time* (New York: Barnes & Noble, 1964).
14. Angus Fletcher, *The Prophetic Moment: An Essay on Spenser* (Chicago: University of Chicago Press, 1971), 124.
15. *The Works of Edmund Spenser: A Variorum Edition*, ed. Edwin Greenlaw, et al., 11 vols. (Baltimore: Johns Hopkins University Press, 1932–57), 5: 217.
16. The early modern period harbored an intriguing ambivalence toward Egypt. Its vogue of Egyptian and hermetic wisdom, its celebration of exotic Egyptian customs and religious practices, was largely influenced by the second book of Herodotus' *Histories*, translated into English in 1584. But when this Herodotean matter became inmixed with late sixteenth-century travel accounts that often viewed Egyptians as racial "others," Egypt was depicted as "whorish" and "decadent." This "decadent" Egypt of the travelogues is perhaps reflected in Spenser's depiction of the "fertile slime"of the Nile's "fattie waues" (I.i.21), and the fact that Book II's Castle of Alma is made of "Aegyptian slime" (II.ix.21). Interestingly, Cleopatra is imprisoned in Lucifera's dungeon (I.v.50). For a recent, useful overview of what he calls "the unstable early modern discourse about Egyptian antiquity," see John Michael Archer, *Old Worlds: Egypt, Southwest Asia, India, and Russia in Early Modern English Writing* (Stanford, CA: Stanford University Press, 2001).
17. Additional sources are Diodorus Siculus and Apuleius. On the importance of Apuleius as Spenser's source, see Stella P. Revard, "Isis in Spenser and Apuleius," in *Tales Within Tales: Apuleius Through Time: Essays in Honor of Professor Emeritus Richard J. Schoeck*, ed. Constance C. Wright and Julia Bolton Holloway (New York: AMS Press, 2000).
18. Plutarch's "De Iside et Osiride," ed., intro., trans. John Gwyn Griffiths (Cambridge: University of Wales Press, 1970), 35, 21, 28.
19. Griffiths, ed., *Plutarch's "De Iside et Osiride,"* 31. Griffiths also quotes from Henri Frankfort's 1950 *The Problem of Similarity in Ancient Near Eastern Religions*: " 'Even Plutarch, who was well informed, has hellenized Isis and Osiris so thoroughly that his book has long been a source of confusion to Egyptologists' " (31).
20. One such example of "raging correctly" is Plutarch's asserting the identity of Osiris and Dionysus.

CLARE R. KINNEY

Marginal Presence, Lyric Resonance, Epic Absence: *Troilus and Criseyde* and/in *The Shepheardes Calender*

The Shepheardes Calender suggests a conscious dialogue with Chaucer's *Troilus and Criseyde* in Immerito's echo of the envoy of the *Troilus* in his dedicatory poem and Epilogue and in E.K.'s (mis)quotation of Pandarus's admonition to Troilus ("Uncouthe, unkiste") as he introduces the New Poet. These marginal allusions invite a larger consideration of Spenser's relations with the *Troilus*. Colin Clout, as well as Immerito, is "uncouthe, unkiste," and the Petrarchan impasse which threatens his artistic career resonates interestingly against lovelorn Troilus's own rehearsal of the first English translation of a Petrarchan sonnet. *The Shepheardes Calender* provides an alternative to Colin's narcissistic lyricism in its anticipation of a "famous flight" to epic; this enacts a telling revision of Troilus's very different, post-mortem "flight" (which triggers Chaucer's epilogue). Chaucer's *roman antique* teases the proto-Virgilian Spenser with an English epic precursor that never was—and perhaps renders all the more significant his later enfolding and completion of another Chaucerian romance within Book IV of his "poem historicall." *The Faerie Queene*'s reinvocation of the English Tityrus revises, furthermore, E.K.'s brokering of Immerito: Spenser now recanonizes an alienated, "uncouthe, unkiste" Chaucer.

CHAUCER IS AN OMNIPRESENT AND REMARKABLY mutable ghost in the machinery of *The Shepheardes Calender*. He is the English Tityrus invoked in E.K.'s prefatory letter and glosses to authorize Spenser's attempt to restore the dignity of the mother tongue, but he is also the dead father whose wellspring of poetry fails to refresh Colin Clout in the "June" eclogue. Thanks to the sixteenth-century ascription of anti-ecclesiastical satires such as *The Plowman's Tale* and *Jack Upland* to his authorship, he is the proto-Protestant reconstructed and lauded by John Foxe and other contemporary commentators—the homely homilist whom various critics have argued shapes Spenser's putatively "Chaucerian" manner in the religious debates of the "May," "July," and "September" eclogues.[1] At the same time, *The Shepheardes Calender* presents Chaucer as a precursor who is as much a popular entertainer as a sage and serious poet: he is invoked by Colin as the singer who would proffer "mery tales, to keepe us wake,/The while our sheepe about us safely fedde" ("June," 87–88).[2]

Spenser's reinscription of his predecessor within the book which announces his own ambitious entrance upon the English literary scene is teasingly multivalent; there is, however, one Chaucerian work which *The Shepheardes Calender* invokes more directly than any other. This essay will try to tease out some of the larger implications of the striking allusions to *Troilus and Criseyde* which frame Spenser's pastoral experiments. *The Shepheardes Calender*'s dialogue with some of the lyric discourses within Chaucer's romance speaks interestingly to certain aspects of Colin Clout's poetic practice; furthermore, the *Calender*'s specific but selective echoes of the ending of the *Troilus* offer their own oblique commentary upon the more ambitious projects foreshadowed within Spenser's text and paratext. Even as *Troilus and Criseyde* offers the Elizabethan poet a suggestive model for the Petrarchism of his unhappy swain, Chaucer's idiosyncratic treatment of potentially "epic" material in his generically hybrid encounter with the Matter of Troy represents a charged moment within the vernacular literary tradition which is of particular interest, I would argue, to an artist whose pastoral debut explicitly anticipates a classically grounded and officially Virgilian career trajectory.

The starting point for my own exploration of the "*Troilus* connection" is on the margins of the eclogues, at the beginning of E.K's prefatory epistle to Gabriel Harvey:

> Uncouthe, unkiste, Sayde the olde famous Poete Chaucer: whom for his excellencie and wonderfull skil in making, his scholler Lidgate, a worthy scholler of so excellent a maister, calleth the Loadestarre of our Language: and whom our Colin clout in his Æglogue calleth Tityrus the God of shepheards, comparing hym to the worthines of the Roman Tityrus Virgile. Which proverbe, myne own good friend Ma. Harvey, as in that

> good old Poete it served well Pandares purpose, for the bolstering of his baudy brocage, so very well taketh place in this our new Poete, who for that he is uncouthe (as said Chaucer), is unkist, and unknown to most men, is regarded but of few. But I dout not, so soone as his name shall come into the knowledg of men, and his worthines be sounded in the tromp of fame, but that he shall be not onely kiste, but also beloved of all, embraced of the most, and wondered at of the best.
>
> (p. 13, ll. 1–17)

The passage offers us some rather mixed signals about the "olde famous Poet." E.K. invokes him (via Lydgate) in terms which recall Caxton's encomium of Chaucer as "worshipful fader & first foundeur & embelissher of . . . eloquence in our englissh."[3] In the very same sentence, he draws the reader's attention to *The Shepheardes Calender*'s internal equation of Chaucer with Virgil as the new poet's model and mentor: the fledgling author's ties to the vernacular tradition are emphasized as his proto-Virgilian career is announced, and Chaucer becomes an authorizing original for Immerito's originality. However, E.K.'s actual paraphrase of Pandarus's snappy advice to Troilus, not to mention the epistle's explicit aligning of Pandarus's "bawdy brocage" with E.K.'s brokering of what he will later describe as the "maydenhead" of the new poet, has a much less elevated resonance (203).[4] Chaucer's Pandarus is a rather dubious figure of the artist, a slippery manipulator of language whose opportunistic deployment of proverbial wisdom does not exactly reflect the high *sentence* of a Virgilian maker. He presides over and shapes a secret romance in which he takes a consuming and voyeuristic interest (E.K. perhaps becomes a version of the go-between and confidant when he tells his readers that he is "privie" to Immerito's "counsell" and the "secret meaning" of his poems [188–89]). The allusion frankly speaks to E.K.'s own advocacy of the unknown author and anticipates his fulsome glosses of the eclogues; it also potentially alerts the reader to the fact that all the speakers within the eclogues who rehearse, mediate and praise Colin Clout's songs in his absence are playing Pandar to some degree as they proffer Colin and Colin's author to the reader's embrace.

I should note at this point that I am very much persuaded by Louise Schleiner's arguments that the E.K. epistle and the E.K. glosses are a joint production of Spenser and Gabriel Harvey, in which Spenser has the lion's part—although often adopting or pastiching his friend's highly recognizable style.[5] E.K.'s quotation of the *Troilus* is thoroughly tangled up in the reconstruction of Chaucer as the English Tityrus and the laureation of the New Poet made manifest within both the text and the glosses of the *Calender*. But the work's deployment of this particular Chaucerian intertext in its framing material has additional ramifications which are worth exploring at some length. E.K.'s preliminary allusion is of course complemented by Immerito's own echo of the envoy to *Troilus and Criseyde*—"Go, litel bok, go litel myn tragedye" (5.1786)—in the "Goe little booke, thy selfe present" of his dedicatory poem to Sidney, as well as in his Epilogue's instruction: "Goe lyttle Calender, thou hast a free passeporte" (Epilogue, l. 7). Immerito's subsequent command that his *Calender* the "high steppes adore" of nobler writers (including Chaucer himself) echoes the Chaucerian narrator's own command that his little book "kis the steppes where as thow seest pace/Virgile, Ovide, Omer, Lucan, and Stace" (*Troilus and Criseyde*, 5.1791–92). Previous discussions of the import of these allusions have tended to concentrate either on E.K.'s Pandaric role as go-between or on the differences between the poetic trajectories of the Chaucerian and Spenserian envoys. I will be returning, eventually, to the latter, but I want to look rather more closely at just why Spenser suggests that he is keenly aware of *this particular Chaucerian poem* as he frames *The Shepheardes Calender*.[6]

When Pandarus begins to woo his niece for his friend in *Troilus and Criseyde*, the narrator cheers him on: "Now Janus, god of entree, thow hym gyde!" (2.77). There is thus a certain felicity in E.K.'s choosing to invoke Pandarus directly as he first announces the entrance of the New Poet and afterwards lectures his reader on the propriety of Immerito's making January the starting point of his calendar ("The generall argument of the whole booke," p. 23, ll. 40–96). Yet on the face of it, the pairing of these two works is an unlikely one: what exactly has Spenser's complicated experiment in remodeling Virgilian pastoral in the form of a homegrown classic, complete with scholarly apparatus, got to do with Chaucer's romancing of the Trojan war? On closer inspection, some similarities emerge. Both works are much concerned with questions of literary authority, but tend to mystify as much as elucidate the role of their own *auctors*: Chaucer's narrator puts his Boccaccian source under erasure, claiming to be transcribing the work of a Latin writer called "Lollius"; E.K. situates the first flight of his poet in the tradition of Virgil, Mantuan, Petrarch, Boccaccio, Marot and others, but his endnotes are prone to misidentify the authors who are being imitated at particular moments in the eclogues or to misquote their texts.[7] In both works the figure of the author is elusive: there has been a good deal of discussion of the feints and dissemblings of Chaucer's "unreliable narrator," and in *The Shepheardes Calender* the voice of Spenser is dispersed among those of Immerito, Colin, E.K. and all of the pastoral speakers of his open-ended dialogues.[8] Both works are indeed strikingly dialogic, heteroglot texts: in *Troilus and Criseyde* the vision of no one of its speaking subjects is absolute or unchallenged, and the proverbs and aphorisms with which all of Chaucer's characters (and in particular Pandarus) intermittently attempt to fix experience prove as unstable as the teasing and teasingly glossed emblems that follow the eclogues of *The Shepheardes Calender.*[9]

Which brings me back to E.K.'s own rehearsal of Pandarus's admonition—an admonition whose original Chaucerian context is certainly suggestive. In Book 1 of *Troilus and Criseyde,* when he has learned of his friend's love for his niece, Pandarus offers to plead Troilus's cause to the lady; when the young man insists that his case is hopeless, Pandarus berates him for pining over a woman who knows nothing of his feelings: "Unknowe, unkist, and lost that is unsought" (1.809). E.K.'s (mis)quotation positions the new Poet, in the prefatory epistle, as the Troilus whose worth he is brokering to Gabriel Harvey in particular and to his readership in general.[10] Of course, the real Troilus of *The Shepheardes Calender* is Spenser's (or Immerito's) troubled alter ego, the lovelorn Colin Clout.[11]

There is an obvious parallel between Troilus the betrayed lover, displaced by the scheming Diomede, and the Colin who reports in "June" that his Rosalind's faith has been subverted by the "trecheree" of one Menalcas. But the likeness runs deeper. As John Watkins points out, "[e]rotic impasse leads to artistic stagnation" in the Colin plot of *The Shepheardes Calender*: the promising would-be laureate becomes lost in the funhouse of Petrarchan complaint and cannot enact any larger agenda than the reflection upon and of his own woes.[12] Chaucer's Troilus is not, officially, a novice poet, but his own agency is certainly undermined by a version of the same phenomenon; moreover, when Pandarus first finds him locked in solipsistic despair, frozen in the posture of the despondent lover, the reader has already seen him woefully composing a love lyric. The poem in question, Book 1's "Canticus Troili" (ll. 400–420), does not appear in Boccaccio's *Il Filostrato,* Chaucer's main source for *Troilus and Criseyde,* but is Chaucer's own translation—the very first English translation—of a Petrarchan sonnet. Beginning "If no love is, O God what fele I so?" it offers a close rendering of poem 132 of the *Rime sparse,* "*S'amor non é. . . .*"[13] Troilus will take up the Petrarchan posture again in the later stages of Chaucer's narrative:

after the departure of Criseyde from Troy, and even before he learns of her failure of faith, he delivers a second "Canticus Troili," beginning "O sterre, of which I lost have al the light" (5.638–44). Although Chaucer is here translating neither Petrarch nor Boccaccio, Book 5's lyric of privation reprises Petrarch's image of the storm-tossed lover from the previous song (11. 415–18) as Troilus insists once more, "Toward my deth with wynd in steere I saille" (5.641). Spenser's Colin and Chaucer's Troilus indeed end up enacting comparable death drives: once Criseyde's betrayal is revealed, we hear that "after deth, withouten wordes moore,/Ful faste [Troilus] cride, his reste hym to restore" (5.1671–2); Colin punctuates his "December" eclogue with wretched self-apostrophes: "Why livest thou stil, and yet hast thy deathes wound?/Why dyest thou stil, and yet alive art founde?" (ll. 96–97) and, "weary of this stounde" (l.140), anticipates the "timely" death hastening towards him in the winter of his discontent (ll. 144–50).

I am not seeking to claim that the *Troilus* is the absolute or exclusive source for Colin's Petrarchism—the Petrarchan experiments of Wyatt, Surrey and their followers were obviously available to Spenser. I am more interested in the fact that, given *The Shepheardes Calender*'s singling out of Chaucer as its father-figure within the vernacular literary tradition, certain aspects of Colin Clout's lyric performance might be aligned with the particular dynamics of the very early translation (in every sense of the word) of Petrarch to be found in the Chaucerian poem which haunts the margins of Spenser's poetic beginning. There is real evidence, moreover, that late sixteenth-century readers and writers were quite aware that Chaucer was a translator of Petrarchan lyric. In a headnote to his translation of "*S'amor non é*," in *The Ekatompathia or Passionate Centurie of Love* (1582), Thomas Watson remarks that his own rendering of the poem "varieth from that sense, which Chawcer useth in translating the selfe same."[14] (We might also note that Roger Ascham strikingly couples Chaucer and Petrarch in *The Schoolmaster* [1570], as he criticizes the lack of discrimination among "those who make Chaucer in English and Petrarch in Italian their Gods in verses."[15]) In *The Shepheardes Calender*'s "August" eclogue, Colin Clout's woeful sestina of erotic privation is recited by Cuddie in a Petrarchan performance which suggests that Spenser is emulating Chaucer's own innovatory lyricism. If the earlier poet gives us the first English translation of a sonnet from the *Rime sparse*, Spenser gives us the first published English sestina in the Petrarchan mode.[16] E.K., uncharacteristically, offers not a word of commentary on Colin/Cuddie's sestina: he does not address its form in his notes or provide any glosses upon its language. His surprising silence—this is, after all, the rhetorician who will wax enthusiastic over "a prety Epanorthosis . . . and withall a Paronomasia"—suggests another variation on Chaucerian practice. Just before we read Chaucer's translation of Petrarch's "*S'amor non é*," the narrator of *Troilus and Criseyde* devotes a whole stanza to declaring that he is translating Troilus's first song word for word from his "auctor," Lollius (1.393–97): the author of *Troilus and Criseyde* makes a point of muddying the intertextual waters by having this mediating voice honor an imaginary and non-existent source. Spenser doesn't even bother to do this: at the conclusion of "August," Perigot's exclamation, "Oh Colin, Colin, the shepheards joye,/How I admire ech turning of thy verse" (ll. 190–91), makes Colin/Immerito/ Spenser the only begetter of the sestina form.

Colin's sestina does not only rehearse a Petrarchan form; it also speaks suggestively to the narrative and lyric content of the *Troilus*. Describing the departure of Rosalind from his vicinity, and his consequent misery, Colin declares, "Thus all the nights in plaints, the daye in woe/I vowed have to wayst, till safe and sound/She home return" (ll. 179–181). His lamentations recall those of Troilus as he awaits Criseyde's promised return to Troy and contemplates her deserted palace (5.540–53; 565–616): he, like Colin, hopes for a reunion that is not to be; he, like Colin, can only resort to Petrarchan complaint in the song which begins "Oh sterre, of which I lost have al the light . . . ." But it is important to emphasize that Troilus's complaints comprise only one of many discourses in circulation in *Troilus and Criseyde*, just as Colin's complaints constitute only one of many discourses in circulation in *The Shepheardes Calender*: both works ultimately offer alternatives to the claustrophobic perspective of the Petrarchan lyricist, and one may usefully compare the different escape trajectories they project.

The Shepheardes Calender generates its own counterpoints to Colin's more narcissistic makings within the rather different lyric space constituted by the pastoral singer's celebration of Eliza in "April" and his elegy for Dido in "November;" it also canvasses the possibility of Colin's self-transcendence in the "October" dialogue between Piers and Cuddie. The maker may be borne on the wings of Poesy's "aspyring wit" to achieve a higher and specifically epic vision (ll. 83–84), in which, as Piers suggests, the Muse may "display her fluttryng wing" and "sing of bloody Mars, of wars, of giusts" (ll. 37–44): this is the "famous flight" that Cuddie argues would be attainable by Colin were he not "with love so ill bedight" (ll. 88–90). It is also the "greater flyght" that E.K. intimates is anticipated by the poetry authored by Immerito (Epistle, 158), the poetry which suggests that even if its maker is now the "bird, whose principals be scarce growen out," he will "in time . . . be hable to keepe wing with the best" as he pursues the Virgilian trajectory (Epistle, 165–67).[17] It is not clear that the much complaining Colin completes the famous flight, and I am personally drawn to Harry Berger's suggestion that he does not so much move "toward increasing spirituality as toward increasing petulance, which by *December* attains to heaven only in the sense that it assumes cosmic proportions."[18] What we have instead are some very strong suggestions, not only that Colin's maker is ready to abandon his lowly shepherd's weeds for trumpets stern but also that Immerito has already produced (in the work of art that both introduces and leaves behind Colin Clout) a modestly monumental classic.

The final stanzas of Chaucer's *Troilus* would have offered Spenser something rather different from the flight from Petrarchan pastoral to epic. (We should perhaps remember that Chaucer's nearest approach to imagining a "famous flight" of his own occurs when he is hauled off by a very chatty eagle to survey the House of Virgil's Fama.) When Troilus dies in battle, his spirit ascends to the eighth sphere and, looking down upon "this litel spot of erthe," laughs at humanity's vicissitudes in general and the pains of love in particular (5.1808–25): his new found detachment from his own hurt ushers in the Christian epilogue in which Chaucer invokes and celebrates the divine love that will "falsen no wight" (5.1835–48).[19] *Troilus and Criseyde's* fusion of *roman antique* with *de casibus* tragedy gives way to divine comedy and its secular discourses of love—Petrarchan and otherwise—defer to a higher object of desire. The epilogue to *The Shepheardes Calender* actively invokes the ending of the *Troilus* in its modesty topos: Immerito despatches his "lyttle Calender" to go with a "lowly gate" to follow Chaucer and other noble predecessors at a distance "and their high steppes adore." (Chaucer's narrator despatches his own "litel bok" to "kis the steppes" of his classical predecessors well before he actually gets around to despatching his hero.) But as David Lee Miller points out, Spenser's rehearsal of Chaucerian humility is complicated by the Ovidian echoes to be found in Immerito's earlier claim to have made a Calender "[t]hat steele in strength, and time in durance shall outweare," a work that "shall continewe till the worlds dissolution" (Epilogue, 2, 4).[20] If Chaucer's Troilus takes flight and achieves a new vision, Spenser's Immerito makes his *Calender* announce its own poetic apotheosis.

The secular and metapoetic emphases that adumbrate the modesty of Immerito's final words diverge quite sharply from the particular form of self-abnegation figured forth in the concluding stanza of

Troilus and Criseyde. Chaucer fittingly enough brings his divine comedy to a close by offering his readers a Dantesque prayer to the Trinity:

> Thow oon, and two, and thre, eterne on lyve,
> That regnest ay in thre, and two, and oon,
> Uncircumscript, and al maist circumscrive,
> Us from visible and invisible foon
> Defende . . . .
>
> (5.1863–67)

In the Spenserian work, by contrast, E.K. has already hinted, in his gloss to the missing emblem for the "December" eclogue, that it is the *Calender* which will be "eterne on lyve:" "all things perish, and come to theyr last end," he writes, "but workes of learned wits and monuments of Poetry abide for ever" (p. 212). (The very "monumentalization" of *The Shepheardes Calender* in its first edition, furnished as it is with all the scholarly apparatus its readers would associate with a canonized work of classical antiquity, actually anticipates by twenty years the first thoroughly "monumental" scholarly commentary upon Chaucer's poems represented by Thomas Speght's 1598 and 1602 editions of his *Works.*)[21] The contrast between the two endings offers an almost textbook medieval/Renaissance opposition: the earlier poet defers to the divinity which circumscribes the work of mortal auctors and emphasizes the contingency and imperfection of all "olde clerkis speche" (5.1854); the later one asserts the transcendent power of human art. But it would over-simplify matters to stop here, for the suggestively different emphases of the two poetic epilogues also invite us to recognize that Immerito's pursuit of the Virgilian trajectory will very specifically supply what his English Tityrus refused to offer in *Troilus and Criseyde,* namely, a vernacular epic.

The references to *Troilus and Criseyde* in the text and paratext of the first flight of the New Poet are especially suggestive, I would propose, because the Chaucerian narrative would indeed be the nearest thing Spenser could find in English literary history to epic.[22] Chaucer takes up the matter of Troy, invokes various Muses, and intermittently displays a striking consciousness that he is writing a "poem historicall" as he meditates upon diachronic language shifts and issues of literary transmission and reception—but he ultimately undoes the authority of "payens corsed old rites" (5.1849). Although he despatches his book to kiss the feet of Virgil, Ovid and company, he refuses, at the last, to canonize "the forme of olde clerkis speche/ In poetrie": the penultimate stanza of *Troilus and Criseyde* replaces the poem under the correction of the emphatically unclassical "moral Gower" and "philosophical Strode" (5.1856–59). One should note, moreover, that well before the reader reaches the revisionary perspective of *Troilus and Criseyde*'s epilogue-cum-palinode, it has become clear that Chaucer has carefully distinguished his concerns from those of epic. Even if the Trojan war ultimately determines the fate of Chaucer's lovers (who are separated when Calchas, invoking his foreknowledge of the Greek victory, persuades the Greeks to retrieve his daughter from the doomed city by way of an exchange of prisoners), the conflict for the most part lurks on the margins of a romance narrative whose action unfolds in private spaces and secret bowers: the lover's time of happiness is stolen from history. Chaucer's poem explicitly refuses to be "heroic." His narrator declares that if he had chosen to write of the deeds of Troilus, he could relate his feats in battle, but "for that I to writen first bigan/Of his love" (5.1768–69), he is not interested in arms and the man, and he instructs us to seek out Dares if we want to read the epic details of his prowess (5.1770–71).

And yet I do not think it would be sufficient to say that Spenser invokes Chaucer's not-quite-epic poem in the margins of *The Shepheardes Calender* (and partially reconstructs its author as the English Tityrus) only to imply its deficiencies and to demonstrate the necessity of overgoing his predecessor in his fidelity to his own Virgilian model. We do, of course, have some hints that Colin may become the new Tityrus: although Immerito's alter ego laments his alienation from the Chaucerian source in "June," wishing that "some little drops would flowe,/Of that the spring was in his learned hedde" (ll. 93–94), his pessimism is qualified within "November." Thenot, requesting to hear Colin's songs, speaks of the poet-swain as one who has been "watered at the Muses well" and is himself the source of poetic nourishment: "The kindlye dewe drops from the higher tree,/And wets the little plants that lowly dwell" (ll. 30–32). But within the larger design of *The Shepheardes Calender*, the achievement of "November's" virtuoso elegy to Dido does not seem to impinge upon "December's" complaints.[23]

In the final eclogue, just before he hangs up his pipe, Colin laments that his wellspring has run dry: "The fragrant flowres, that in my garden grewe,/Bene withered, as they had bene gathered long. / Theyr rootes bene dryed up for lacke of dewe" (ll. 109–11). His flowers of Petrarchan rhetoric will yield no first fruits. Colin's creator, however, will not only go on to pursue the Virgilian epic project but will also mark out a space within his own capacious reconception of it for Chaucerian romance. Indeed he will not only find room for Chaucerian romance within his epic, he will also discover epic possibilities within Chaucerian romance. When, in Book IV of *The Faerie Queene*, Spenser revisits the "well of English vndefyled," the Chaucerian source, to reprise and complete *The Squire's Tale*, he furnishes it with his own epic machinery in his depiction of Agape's *descensus* into the infernal region to learn the future of her progeny.[24] *He* becomes the scriptor (or deus artifex) who circumscribes both the classical and the native tradition.

When Spenser reinvokes Chaucer's ghost in Book IV, he couples his praise with a lament for the maker which seems somewhat at variance with Immerito's (and E.K.'s) optimism at the end of the *Calender* about the eternizing power of art. Time, he claims, has "quite defaste" the "famous moniment" of his predecessor: the poet's works are "brought to nought by little bits" (IV. ii. 33). Chaucer himself, it seems, is now in danger of being "uncouth, unkiste." It is certainly true that sixteenth-century celebrations of Chaucer have a defensive tone to them and are likely to acknowledge that there are already readers and critics who find his English too alien, too antique, too barbaric. About seventy years before Spenser's debut, we find the speaker of John Skelton's "Phillipe Sparrowe" lamenting that despite the "delectable" and "comendable" matter of Chaucer's poetry, "Now men wold haue amended/his english, where at they barke,/And mar all they warke"—a sentiment which somewhat anticipates the fear Immerito articulates in his dedicatory envoy to Sidney that Envy may barke at *his* book ("To His Booke," p. 12).[25] Sidney himself gives rather double-edged praise to *Troilus and Criseyde* in *The Defence of Poesy*: admitting that Chaucer performed "excellently" in the writing of that poem, he adds, "I know not whether to marvel more, either that he in that misty time could see so clearly, or that we in this clear age go so stumblingly after him. Yet had he great wants, fit to be forgiven in so reverend an antiquity."[26] By the seventeenth century Chaucer is being saved from his own uncouthness (in all senses of the word) by translators like Jonathan Sidnam (who "modernizes" the English of the first three books of *Troilus and Criseyde* circa 1630) and Sir Francis Kynaston (who publishes a Latin version of its first two books in 1635).[27] One of the prefatory encomia to Kynaston's volume observes that "Time can silence Chaucer's tongue" and goes on to declare that Kynaston will preserve Chaucer's "witte" in the Latin translation that will now become "Th'Originall," even as the vernacular text "growes dumbe."[28]

Spenser himself takes a rather different tack. In his pastoral debut, his re-citation of the text of *Troilus and Criseyde* invites our awareness of the *translatio studii* Chaucer enacted (in the *Troilus*'s first run at "Englishing" the Petrarchan model of lyric complaint) and the *translatio studii* he refused to embrace (in the *Troilus*'s swerve from the epic possibilities of its "matere"). When Spenser revisits the poetry of his predecessor within the epic framework of *The Faerie Queene*, his idiosyncratic work of "translation" does not concentrate upon rehabilitating Chaucer's ostensibly uncouth language—indeed his own poem's conscious archaism, its refusal to jettison entirely the linguistic eccentricities of *The Shepheardes Calender*, suggests rather a continuing declaration of solidarity with the idiolect of the English Tityrus. Book IV offers instead a reinflection of a fragmentary "lost" text in terms of genre. Reprising E.K.'s brokering of Immerito, Spenser plays Pandarus for Chaucer in his own manner, recanonizing, reclassifying and reclassicizing him within his poem historicall's Legend of Friendship.

NOTES

1. See, for example, Alice S. Miskimin, *The Renaissance Chaucer* (New Haven: Yale University Press, 1975), 286; John A. King, *Spenser's Poetry and the Reformation Tradition* (Princeton: Princeton University Press, 1990), 26–28. For Foxe's comments (which appear in "A Protestation to the whole Church of England" in the 1570 edition of his *Ecclesiasticall history, contaynyng the Actes and Monumentes of thynges passed in every Kynges tyme in this Realme*), see Caroline Spurgeon, *Five Hundred Years of Chaucer Criticism and Allusion,* 3 vols. (New York: Russell and Russell, 1960), I:105.

2. Edmund Spenser, *The Shepheardes Calender*, in *The Yale Edition of the Shorter Poems of Edmund Spenser*, ed. William A. Oram et al. (New Haven: Yale University Press, 1989), "June," ll. 85–86. Future citations of the poems or the prefatory prose texts will be indicated parenthetically by line number, citations of the glosses by page number.

3. William Caxton, Epilogue of *Boethius de Consolacione Philosophie* (1.497), cited in Spurgeon, I.58.

4. The Chaucerian line in question is "Unknowe, unkist, and lost that is unsought," *Troilus and Criseyde*, in *The Riverside Chaucer*, ed. Larry D. Benson et al., 2nd ed. (Boston: Houghton Mifflin, 1987), 1.809. Subsequent references to this edition will be noted parenthetically by book and line number. Spenser himself would almost certainly have read Chaucer in William Thynne's edition; the only differences between Thynne and the Riverside text in the material I quote occur at 5.641 (which Thynne gives as "To warde my deth with wynde I stere and sayle") and 5.1809 (where Thynne follows an alternative MS tradition in making Troilus ascend to the *seventh* sphere).

5. Louise Schleiner, "Spenser's 'E.K.' as Edmund Kent (Kenned/of Kent): Kyth (Couth), Kissed, and Kunning-Conning," *English Literary Renaissance* 20 (1990): 374–407.

6. On E.K. as Pandar, see, for example, Sherri Geller, "You Can't Tell a Book by Its Contents: "(Mis)Interpretation in/of Spenser's *The Shepheardes Calender*," *Spenser Studies* 13 (1999): 23–64, here, 31–33; David Lee Miller, "Authorship, Anonymity and *The Shepheardes Calender*," *Modern Language Quarterly* 40 (1979): 219–36, here 222; Anthony M. Esolen, "The Disingenuous Poet Laureate: Spenser's Adoption of Chaucer," *Studies in Philology* 87 (1990): 285–311, 296; Lynn Staley Johnson, *The Shepheardes Calender: An Introduction* (University Park: Pennsylvania State University Press, 1990), p. 27ff; on the envoys see, for example, Miskimin, 282–86; Miller, 222–25; A.C. Spearing, *Medieval to Renaissance in English Poetry* (Cambridge: Cambridge University Press, 1985), 332.

7. For example, E.K.'s notes wrongly claim that the "October" eclogue is written in imitation of Theocritus' *Idyll* 16.

8. For a concise summary of critical discussions of Chaucer's narrator in *Troilus and Criseyde* (and of the relationship between poet and narrator), see C. David Benson, *Chaucer's Troilus and Criseyde* (Cambridge, Mass.: Unwin Hyman Inc., 1990), 112–19. On the dialogic nature of Spenser's text and "dialogic exchange" within it, see Roland Greene, "*The Shepheardes Calender*, Dialogue and Periphrasis," *Spenser Studies* 8 (1990): 1–33. On the "scattered self" of the author in *The Shepheardes Calender* (and its relationship to medieval representations of the poetic subject), see Spearing, "The Poetic Subject from Chaucer to Spenser," in *Subjects on the World's Stage: Essays on British Literature of the Middle Ages and the Renaissance*, ed. David G. Allen and Robert A. White (Newark: University of Delaware Press, 1995), 12–37.

9. For a particularly good discussion of Chaucer's deployment of proverbial material in his poem, see Karla Taylor, "Proverbs and the Authentication of Convention in *Troilus and Criseyde*," in *Chaucer's "Troilus": Essays in Criticism*, ed. Stephen A. Barney (Hamden, CT: Archon Books, 1980), pp. 277–96.

10. Geller (p. 31) aligns the New Poet not with Troilus but with Criseyde as a feminized object of display whose maidenhead is being brokered; the problem with this reading is that Criseyde, who is a widow, does not have a maidenhead.

11. Louis Adrian Montrose suggests that we might think of Colin as the persona of Spenser's Immerito persona: "Interpreting Spenser's February Eclogue," *Spenser Studies* 2 (1981): 67–74; here 71.

12. John Watkins, *The Specter of Dido: Spenser and Virgilian Epic* (New Haven: Yale University Press, 1995), 71.

13. For the Petrarchan sonnet, see *Petrarch's Lyric Poems: The Rime sparse and Other Lyrics*, ed. and trans. Robert M. Durling (Cambridge, Mass.: Harvard University Press, 1976).

14. Thomas Watson, *Poems: Viz. The Ekatompathia or passionate centurie of love [1582]; Meliboeus, sivè Ecloga inobitum, &c. 1590; An eglogue upon the death of Right Honorable Sir Francis Walsingham. 1590; The teares of fancy, or Love disdained*, ed. Edward Arber (Birmingham, 1870), 41.

15. Roger Ascham, *The Schoolmaster*, ed. Lawrence V. Ryan (Ithaca: Cornell University Press, 1967), 147. One of *The Shepheardes Calender's* versions of Chaucer

includes an oddly Petrarchan reconfiguration of the poet himself: in "June," Colin declares of the English "Tityrus," "Well couth *he* wayle his Woes, and lightly slake/ The flames, which love within his heart had bredd" (85–86, emphasis mine), a rather surprising description, as Spearing points out, of a poet who so often presents himself as an outsider in matters of love (*Medieval to Renaissance*, 330). The description may be influenced by Spenser's acquaintance with William Thynne's edition of Chaucer's works, which included such pseudo-Chaucerian love complaints as "La Belle Dame Sans Merci." For an account of Thynne's edition and its pseudo-Chaucerian inclusions, see James E. Blodgett, "William Thynne," in *Editing Chaucer: the Great Tradition,* ed. Paul Ruggiers (Pilgrim Books: Norman, Oklahoma, 1984), 35–52.

16. Thomas Cain offers a brief discussion of Spenser's innovation in his introduction to "August," *Yale Edition of the Shorter Poems*, 136. Petrarch himself did not, of course, invent the sestina, although his series of sestinas in the *Rime sparse* offer particularly highly developed versions of the form; it originated in Provençal poetry and had previously been deployed by Dante. See Durling's introduction to *Petrarch's Lyric Poems*, 16–17.

17. For a very full discussion of the "famous flight" motif in Spenser's poetry, see Patrick Cheney, *Spenser's Famous Flight: A Renaissance Idea of a Literary Career* (Toronto: University of Toronto Press, 1993). Cheney's discussion of the Spenserian career trajectory differs in emphasis from my own and although he discusses some of the Chaucerian intertexts within the poet's oeuvre, he makes no mention of Troilus's ascent at the conclusion of *Troilus and Criseyde.*

18. Harry Berger, Jr., "The Mirror Stage of Colin Clout," *Revisionary Play: Studies in the Spenserian Dynamics* (Berkeley: University of California Press, 1990), 331.

19. For a particularly detailed account of the significance of Troilus's "flight," see John M. Steadman, *Disembodied Laughter: Troilus and the Apotheosis Tradition* (Berkeley and Los Angeles: University of California Press, 1972); Steadman specifically discusses the differences between Troilus's ascent and comparable episodes in classical epic (42–65).

20. Miller, 222.

21. On Speght's editions, see Derek Pearsall, "Thomas Speght," *Editing Chaucer,* 71–92.

22. For discussions of the epic aspects of the *Troilus*, see Morton W. Bloomfield, "Distance and Predestination in *Troilus and Criseyde,*" *PMLA* 72 (1957): 16–17, John P. McCall, "The Trojan Scene in Chaucer's *Troilus,*" *ELH* 29 (1962): 263–75 and Christopher Baswell and Paul B. Taylor, "The 'Faire Queene Eleyne,' in Chaucer's *Troilus,*" *Speculum* 63 (1988): 293–311.

23. Miller suggestively describes the progression from "January" to "December" as the "negative bildungsroman" of Colin Clout (233).

24. Edmund Spenser, *The Faerie Queene*, ed. A. C. Hamilton, text edited by Hiroshi Yamashita, Toshiyuki Suzuki (New York: Longman, 2001), IV. ii. 32 and (for Agape's descent) IV. ii. 46–53. Future citations of this work will be indicated parenthetically. For particularly rich and helpful discussions of Spenser's completion of *The Squire's Tale*, see Cheney, "Spenser's Completion of *The Squire's Tale*: Love, Magic and Heroic Action in the Legend of Cambell and Triamond," *Journal of*

Medieval and Renaissance Studies 15 (1985): 135–55; Craig Berry, " 'Sundrie Doubts': Vulnerable Understanding and Dubious Origins in Spenser's Continuation of *The Squire's Tale*," in Theresa M. Krier, ed., *Refiguring Chaucer in the Renaissance* (Gainesville: University Press of Florida, 1998), 106–127; Krier, *Birth Passages: Maternity and Nostalgia, Antiquity to Shakespeare* (Ithaca: Cornell University Press, 2002), 204–25. Berry's claim (115) that Spenser very specifically reconstructs Chaucer as an *epic* poet in the course of paying his respects at IV.iii.32 is particularly suggestive.

25. "Phillipe Sparrowe" (c.1507), ll 783–803; see Spurgeon, I:69. Interestingly, where Spenser fears the envy of others, Chaucer instructs his "little book" not to envy the "makings" of others (5.1789–90).

26. Sir Philip Sidney, *The Defence of Poesy*, in *Sir Philip Sidney*, ed. Katherine Duncan-Jones (Oxford: Oxford University Press, 1989), 242.

27. For Sidnam's translation, see *A Seventeenth Century Modernisation of the First Three Books of Chaucer's "Troilus and Criseyde,"* ed. Herbert G. Wright (Bern: A. Francke Verlag, 1960). For Kynaston's Latin version, see *Amorvm Troili et Creseidae libri duo priores Anglico-Latini* (Oxford, 1635).

28. Edward Foulis, "Upon that worthy Poet Sir Geofrey Chaucer & Sir Francis Kinastons Translation," *Amorvm Troili et Creseidae*, sign. 4[v], lines 11–12 and 15–16.

JOHN WATKINS

Polemic and Nostalgia: Medieval Crosscurrents in Spenser's Allegory of Pride

This essay recasts the perennial question of Spenser's Protestantism as a question of literary influence: how does *The Faerie Queene*'s nostalgia for medieval representational systems qualify its effectiveness as Reformation polemic? Book I's sequential anatomies of pride in Redcrosse's encounters first with Lucifera and then with Orgoglio suggest the inadequacy of pre-Reformation confidence in human striving. Redcrosse more or less escapes the threat posed by the Seven Deadly Sins—a topos that would have already looked antiquated to Spenser's late sixteenth-century readers—but falls captive to a more comprehensive, ultimately more Protestant, figuration of pride as a misguided trust in the natural man. Yet this is only the first half of a complex intertextual story. As the second section of the essay suggests, the diptychal analysis of pride is itself sufficiently indebted to pre-Reformation commentaries to qualify Book I's denigration of the medieval past as a period of unmitigated error.

NO WRITER IS HARDER TO SITUATE in the history of early modern dissent than Edmund Spenser. Scholars attempting to define his religious and political orientations have assigned him contradictory roles in a master-analysis of politics as an opposition between a dominant absolutism and an emergent constitutionalism. For some critics, *The Faerie Queene* epitomizes the aesthetics of the absolutist state. Characterizing Spenser as a writer who "worships power," Stephen Greenblatt hailed him as "our originating and preeminent poet of empire."[1] For readers like Greenblatt, Spenser's imperial commitments ultimately co-opted whatever gestures he made toward more critical views of the Elizabethan state. Other readers, however, have contested the extent of Spenser's moral and aesthetic allegiances with the regime he ostensibly celebrated. Richard Helgerson, for example, finds in the centrifugal movements of the individual knights from Gloriana's court an image of neo-feudal resistance to the absolutism figured in Gloriana herself, a queen from whom all authority flows hierarchically to the realm.[2] Along with David Norbrook, Michelle O'Callaghan, and others, Helgerson situates Spenser at the beginning of a dissenting tradition that culminated in Milton.[3] For such critics, *The Faerie Queene*—a poem whose exalted titular heroine never actually appears—marks a paradoxical but unmistakable stage on the path to regicide.

This contradictory reception predates contemporary scholarship. As early as the seventeenth century, both supporters and opponents of the Stuarts claimed a Spenserian origin for their politics. Well before Milton hailed Spenser as his "great original," Wither, Browne, and the Fletchers transformed his pastoral songs into the basis of anti-Stuart satires. But at the same time, royalists recalled Spenser as a staunch defender of monarchy and of the Elizabethan state Church. In 1648, a royalist printer issued a short quarto edition of Arthegall's encounter with the Giant as *The Faerie Leveller: or, King CHARLES his Leveller descried and deciphered in Queene ELIZABETHS dayes*. The introduction, which treats the episode as a prototype of Charles I's struggles against Oliver Cromwell, reminds its readers that Elizabeth and her "Poet Laureat" were fully committed to the extermination of radical sectarianism.[4] Spenser's canonization as the "prince" of English poets was inseparable from this appeal to readers across a wide political spectrum. The more *The Faerie Queene* could be read as a foundational text for royalist and Parliamentarian, Whig and Tory sympathies, the more it could be revered as the expression of fundamentally English values that transcended the political fray.

Spenser's orchestrations of divergent intertextual voices within *The Faerie Queene* itself contributed to such divergent views of its political significance.[5] Few early modern works exhibit such tension between their avowed ideological commitments and the political valences of their sources. Spenser characteristically based his poetry on modes and representational schema associated with writers, nations, institutions, ceremonies, and cultural practices that he ostensibly repudiated in his more propagandistic moments as the champion of an ongoing Reformation. Several critical generations ago, C. S. Lewis tried to explain this tension away on the grounds that allegory always looked somehow Catholic in its external manifestation of inner moral states.[6] More recent scholars have qualified this judgment by emphasizing a long alliance between allegory and dissent, and by linking Spenser's archaism to the Tudor reception of Chaucer, Langland, and other medieval writers as proto-Protestants.[7] Nevertheless, despite current emphasis on *The Faerie Queene*'s place in a Foxean tradition of advanced, even dissident Protestant thought, Spenser sometimes seems strangely attached to outward ceremonies—"housling fire" and "holy water" (I.xii.37), elaborate temple services, and ostentatious penances—as well as to scholastic and patristic modes of thought more characteristic of the books spewed out in Errour's vomit than of the Protestant gospel in all its imagined purity.[8] Although Thomas Greene may have overstated the case when he proclaimed Spenser a poet "whose loyalty to his own medieval roots limits his room for poetic maneuver," Spenser's nostalgia complicated his legacy as a propagandist.[9] The same poet who denounced the idolatries of Duessa and Archimago built his poetry around the discredited vestiges of late medieval sacramentalism.

By focusing on Book I's transformation of the medieval anatomy of pride into Redcrosse's encounters with Lucifera and Orgoglio, I want to suggest that current approaches to the Reformation as a point of emphatic rupture have underestimated the complexity of Spenser's response to religious and cultural transformation. While Anthea Hume, John King, Richard Mallette, and others have demonstrated how Spenser reworked his sources to express central Protestant teachings, they have not addressed the complementary question of just how much of the older representational order Spenser left intact.[10] Although his poetry attests to a new religious vision, it also tries to reconcile that vision with older, stabilizing depictions of humanity's encounter with the divine. Despite episodes like Arthur's stripping of Duessa and Guyon's destruction of the Bower of Bliss, Spenser was not a thoroughgoing iconoclast. As Kenneth Gross has noted, a strongly anti-iconoclastic, anti-apocalyptic undercurrent tempered his hostility toward idolatry and false religion.[11] That more conservative strain proved no less influential on later writers than his more radical diatribes against superstition.

Nowhere in *The Faerie Queene* does Spenser's characteristic ambivalence toward older iconographies manifest itself so strongly as in his treatment of the Seven Deadly Sins, one of the poem's most frequently excerpted, anthologized, and imitated passages. My inquiry into the episode focuses on three interlocking interpretive problems. The first is primarily a formalist question that figured prominently in Spenserian scholarship a couple of generations ago: why does Spenser introduce two distinct allegories of pride in narrating Redcrosse's quest for holiness? What is the relationship between Orgoglio and Lucifera, or between the Luciferan pride that Redcrosse successfully evades and the Orgoglian pride that overwhelms him? This formalist line of inquiry leads to a more complicated question about poetic history. To the extent that the House of Pride advertizes its debt to a medieval allegorical tradition and the Orgoglio episode draws on a significantly later body of Italian romance, what does the formal relationship between the two episodes say about Spenser's commitment to the Middle Ages imagined as a discreet cultural moment? Does the greater danger that seems to be posed by Orgoglio suggest an inadequacy in medieval representational paradigms that Spenser must overgo in allying himself with Ariosto and the Italians? Or does it uphold medieval *allegoria* as a necessary stage through which Redcrosse, poet, and reader alike must pass before they can begin to interpret the darker, more complicated, and more Italianate allegories of Book I's central cantos? Finally, I want to consider how Spenser's medievalism qualifies Book I's commitment to apocalyptic historiography. Some of the best recent scholarship on *The Faerie Queene* has situated Spenser in an apocalyptic tradition that leads through Wither, Browne, and the other seventeenth-century Spenserians to Milton. But by ignoring Spenser's continual dialogue with older, medieval voices, it overlooks more conservative elements that temper the stridency of his Reformation polemic. We usually read Duessa's reappearance in those final stanzas as a commentary on the persistence of evil in a pre-apocalyptic, unregenerated world. Yet it may also suggest a fundamental ambivalence about discarding an older representational order.

Critics have traditionally glossed the distinction between Lucifera and Orgoglio as a more or less self-evident distinction between two different moral states. But when they begin to distinguish one species of pride from another, their consensus breaks down. M. Pauline Parker, for instance, treats Orgoglio as an embodiment of "spiritual pride, the pride of the pharisee who is not as other men are."[12] Parker contrasts him with Lucifera, a lesser, "worldly pride, showing itself in ostentation, the flaunting of position and wealth" (84). For other readers, however, Orgoglio is just too earthy to suggest anything spiritual, even spiritual pride. He may be more effective than Lucifera in subduing Redcrosse, but he just isn't as classy. In a commentary endorsed by many later critics, John Ruskin declared Orgoglio a type of "Carnal Pride . . . the common and vulgar pride in the power of this world." He contrasts Orgoglian pride with "the pride of life, spiritual and subtle," presumably represented by Lucifera.[13] The rifts between Ruskin's and Parker's commentaries typify the disagreements—sometimes explicit, but more often implicit—that characterize numerous other critical discussions of Orgoglio's relationship to Lucifera.[14]

Given the text's resistance to totalizing claims about its moral allegory, I want to take one step back from Spenser's concern with virtues and vices per se and focus instead on an intertextual problem that underlies it: Spenser's concern with the representation of virtues and vices by earlier writers. The contrast between Lucifera's House of Pride and Orgoglio's Castle is synecdochic of a larger, encompassing contrast between the respective aesthetic cultures from which Spenser has drawn his materials. Lucifera's pageant of the Seven Deadly Sins derives from a late antique analysis of the moral life that flourished especially during the later Middle Ages, when it served as a basis for countless sermons, treatises, dream visions, morality plays, paintings, tapestries, and bas-reliefs. The Seven Deadlies figured at every level of medieval religious preoccupation, from Latin treatises for learned readers to vernacular popularizations. The topos was so familiar to western Europeans that no one could possibly identify any individual source or groups of sources for Spenser's version.

Redcrosse's encounter with Orgoglio, on the other hand, owes much to sixteenth-century Italian romance, especially to the skeptical comedy of Ludovico Ariosto. Immediately following Redcrosse's fornication with Duessa, a conspicuous replay of Astolfo's affair with the sorceress Alcina in *Orlando Furioso*, the Orgoglio episode typifies the urbane intertextual play that was the hallmark of Ariosto's style. In contrast to the moral allegory of the Sins, which was available even to the illiterate masses in stageplays and countless pictorial representations, Ariostan romance assumed an elite, well-educated audience that could appreciate its tongue-in-cheek allusions to classical literature. Its sardonic stance toward the classics paralleled an equally ironic attitude toward the older moral allegories. Ariosto may have been born in Catholic Italy, but his skepticism was part of a pan-European mistrust not only of the Church as an institution but also of the Church's basic moral theology. North of the Alps, the same mistrust laid the groundwork for the Reformation, and for Ariosto's surprising popularity among sage and serious Protestants.

The movement from Lucifera to Orgoglio figures a passage not only from one kind of pride to another, but from one way of thinking about the moral life to another, from an optimistic belief in human perfectability and perseverance to a skepticism about humanity's ability to achieve anything of moral value through its own efforts. In creating the House of Pride, Spenser thus transformed the procession of the Sins into the first term of a longer commentary on the passing of a medieval allegorical tradition. Critics, anthologists, and teachers have often cited and excerpted the episode as one of the *The Faerie Queene*'s best passages. Ruskin hailed it as "one of the most elaborate and noble pieces in the poem," and students who know *The Faerie Queene* only in its sophomore-survey digest version often think that its highly patterned, schematic allegory is the essence of Spenserian writing. In general, readers have spent so much time admiring how Spenser transforms his medieval materials into a self-contained masterpiece that they have never fully accounted for an eerie fact about its place in literary history. The topos of the Seven Deadly Sins, which had flourished throughout the fourteenth and fifteenth centuries, entered a period of abrupt decline by the middle of the sixteenth century.[15] Several decades separate the procession at Lucifera's house from the last significant English example of the topos, Dunbar's 1509 *Dance of the Seven Deadly Sins*. Dekker's *The Seven Deadly Sinnes of London* appeared in 1606, but it replaced the traditional medieval catalogue with a new list better suited to the sins of an urban, proto-capitalist economy: politic bankruptism, lying, candlelight (carousing at night), sloth, apishness, shaving (cheating and extortion), and cruelty. Along with Marlowe's version in *Doctor Faustus*, Spenser's procession stands in stark isolation as the last representative of the topos in its basic medieval guise before its twentieth-century revival in works like Brecht's *Die Sieben Todessunden*.

But if Spenser retains the old sins, he presents them in a novel way. In contrast with its medieval analogues, his procession is heavily disciplined and self-contained. The sheer perfection of his writing in this passage, with its elaborate connections between each sin and its respective costume, animal, and corresponding disease, is also a sign of its belatedness. Within its tightly arranged stanzas, Spenser freezes a system for analyzing human behavior that had been evolving for over a thousand years into a museum-piece. In earlier formulations, the sins typically confronted seven virtues in full-blown psychomachia. In a fifteenth-century work once attributed to Lydgate, the *Assembly of the Gods*, for example, Vice leads the Seven Deadlies into battle against Virtue, who triumphs over them by enlisting the aid of Perseverance. An early fifteenth-century morality, *The Castle of Perseverance*, includes a similar confrontation between the Sins and their corresponding virtues. "Pride with Mekenes is for-schent," Charity's "fayre rosys" break Envy's head, Wrath finds himself "betyn blak & blo" by Patience, Abstinence leaves Gluttony quailing in a privy, Chastity defeats Lechery, and Industry bashes Sloth's skull with her "pytyr-patyr."[16] In this play written in response to the market expansion that followed the great death, Covetousness alone triumphs temporarily over Generosity, only to be defeated in the end by God's supremely generous act of mercy. Here and in numerous other medieval examples, the Sins are the major hurdle, the supreme manifestation of the infernal trio of World, Flesh, and Devil that Mankind must overcome in his quest for salvation.

In *The Faerie Queene*, on the other hand, the Sins never confront their corresponding virtues, and they do not engage in battle. Something of the old morality tradition persists in the Vice-like figure of Satan standing "vpon the wagon beame/ . . . with a smarting whip in hand,/With which he forward lasht the laesie teme" (I.iv.36). But his role, like that of everything else in the pageant, is conspicuously reduced. Spenser's depictions of the Sins rest on longstanding iconographic precedents. Medieval writers frequently associated individual Sins with particular animals, costumes, and diseases. In the *Assembly of the Gods*, Wrath rides into battle on a wild boar, Pride on a roaring lion, and Envy on a wolf. Spenser's Sins ride similar animals, but no one gets to fight. They retain nothing but their iconography, which Spenser so foregrounds that it almost eclipses their identity as Redcrosse's moral antagonists. Instead of fighting them, he merely watches them: "But that good knight would not so nigh repaire,/ Him selfe estraunging from their ioyaunce vaine,/Whose fellowship seemd far vnfit for warlike swaine" (iv.37). The psychomachia that marked the climax of the medieval sinner's struggle for salvation resolves into mere pageantry.

Medieval moralists typically concluded their presentations with a discourse on Despair as sin's inevitable end.[17] In a sense, Despair brought the cycle of the concatenated Sins back to its beginning, since Despair—the belief that one's sinfulness exceeded the scope of Christ's atonement—was itself a species of Pride. Spenser first recalls this moralizing tradition when Sans Joy challenges Redcrosse one stanza after the Sins' procession. This time, Redcrosse finally gets to fight. But Sans Joy is only a minor version of the more full-blooded Despair characterized by Langland and other medieval writers, or that Redcrosse himself will finally encounter not in the House of Pride but after his captivity in Orgoglio's dungeon. Compared with other Spenserian fights-to-the-death, moreover, the battle with Sans Joy is strikingly indecisive. Redcrosse wounds his enemy, but not mortally. While Sans Joy is whisked away in a Virgilian cloud, Redcrosse is treated by many "skilfull leaches," but not cured. In contrast to his later hospitalization in the House of Holiness, the regimen he undergoes in the House of Pride is palliative—"him to beguile of griefe and agony"—rather than truly corrective or restorative.

Even the moral lesson of his departure is strangely inconclusive, an effect compounded in part by a signature instance of Spenserian pronoun ambiguity. His dwarf may have figured out the connections between Pride, the other Deadlies, and the fate of the men and women imprisoned in Lucifera's dungeons. But the text raises more questions than it answers about the extent to which Redcrosse has truly freed himself from Lucifera's contaminating influences. As the narrator darkly observes, Redcrosse leaves, "albe his woundes wide/ Not throughly heald, vnreadie were to ride" (v.45).

Like everything else in the episode, Redcrosse's battle with Sans Joy and his subsequent escape from Lucifera's wiles recall medieval conventions but drain them of their moral force and representational vigor. Above all, the denouement raises questions about the effectiveness of the older moral allegory. Redcrosse escapes, but despite a long tradition of reading Book I as a *Bildungsroman*, he has learned nothing from his experiences there. As Mallette notes, the narrative ultimately "underscores Redcrosse's widening separation from the saving power of words (and the Word)."[18] He soon falls back into Duessa's hands in an episode based largely on that ultimate early modern critique of allegorical learning, Ariosto's *Orlando Furioso*. The one lesson that the *Furioso* teaches again and again is the futility of any moral education. Heroes and heroines pass through allegorical houses only to repeat their former errors. This is especially true in the sequence of episodes that leads up to Ruggiero's encounter with the suspiciously phallic orc, a drama whose general narrative, moral, and psychological development underlies Redcrosse's encounter with the equally phallic Orgoglio.

As Albert Russell Ascoli has suggested, the cycle of Ruggiero's recurrent lapses undermines the confidence in art's didactic effectiveness that figured in myriad Renaissance defenses of poetry.[19] Rescued from the voluptuous sorceress Alcina, Ruggiero presumably steels himself against further sensual temptations through the lessons conned in Logistilla's allegorical palace of reason, a prototype for such Spenserian venues as the Houses of Holiness and Temperance. Shortly after graduating from this anti-sensualist academy, however, he discovers the naked Angelica chained Andromeda-like to a rock as a sacrifice for the Orca, a creature whose "huge mass that writhed and twisted" ("ch'una gran massa che s'aggiri e torca") provides a graphic image of Ruggiero's own arousal.[20] According to the logic of Logistilla's palace, his subsequent rescue of Angelica from the monster ought to allegorize his mastery over his own passions: a truly temperate hero ought to be able to carry a naked maiden in his arms without succumbing to his baser desires. But Ariosto undermines this confidence in the duration of Logistilla's anti-sensualist teachings when Ruggiero loses control of himself and tries to rape the woman he has just rescued.

This sequence, which only occupies a fraction of Ariosto's massive narrative, had a profound impact on Spenser, who recycles its motifs throughout *The Faerie Queene*. It is a principal source, for example, of Florimell's pyrrhic rescues and of Amoret's sexually charged bondage in Book III. But Spenser seems to have been especially drawn to it in his account of Redcrosse's surrender to Duessa and ultimately to Orgoglio. Numerous features link the two romances: the hero's stripping of his armor as a sign of his sensual abandonment, the sudden appearance of a monster who serves as a projection of his carnality, and the monster's defeat by a magically blazing shield. Spenser based the grove where Redcrosse lies "pourd out in loosnesse on the grassy grownd" (*FQ* I. vii. 7) on Ariosto's description of the *locus amoenus* where Ruggiero surrenders to lust:

> Sul lito un bosco era di querce ombrose,
> dove ognor par che Filomena piangna;
> ch'in mezzo avea un pratel con una fonte . . .
> On the shore was a grove shadowed with oak,
> where Filomena always mourned,
> where in the middle was a grassy spot with a fountain.
> (*OF* 10.113)

Shortly after Angelica disappears from this landscape—with its anticipations of Duessa's well, the grassy bed of Redcrosse's fornication, and even Spenser's moralization of places and events "in the middest" —Ruggiero suddenly hears a great noise and sees "a proud-looking giant" ("gigante, alla sembianza fiero" [*OF* 11.16]) locked in battle with a knight. The giant dazes his victim with a club and only fails to kill him because Ruggiero steps in to fight the giant himself. Ultimately undaunted, the giant escapes from Ruggiero and carries his prey back to an enchanted castle.

This proud-looking giant who batters people with his massive club is the obvious model for Spenser's Orgoglio, who combines his pride with the Orca's specifically sexual associations. The intertextual trajectory from Ruggiero's intervention on behalf of the giant's victim both to Duessa's intercessions for Redcrosse and to Redcrosse's definitive rescue by Arthur is more tortuous. In the rapid movement from Ruggiero's fight with the Orca, to his assault on Angelica, to his attempt to rescue the giant's victim, we see him in numerous and conflicted moral lights. The hero is at once a rapist and a savior. Spenser clarifies some of these ethical boundaries by turning the rape into an act of consensual fornication and by displacing Ruggiero's sexual violence entirely onto Orgoglio. But if Redcrosse is less menacing than Ruggiero, he is also less resilient. In Spenser's most striking revision of his subtext, the errant hero becomes the giant's prey rather than the champion who prevents another knight's demise. The battles with the Orca and the giant, which in the *Furioso* attest to a valor that remains in Ruggiero's character despite his vulnerability to desire, become a single encounter with Orgoglio, one that marks the final depletion of Redcrosse's powers.

In combining the Orca and the "gigante, alla sembianza fiero" into Orgoglio, Spenser creates an allegory of pride that overgoes even Ariosto in its pessimism about humanity's ability to redeem itself through its own efforts. Ruggiero's partial victories over his monsters suggested the persistence of moral powers that might be eclipsed, but never fully extinguished. Distancing himself from the optimism of humanist education theories, Ariosto insists on the limits of his hero's ethical schooling. But if Ruggiero displays a carnality that compromises his nobler aspirations, Redcrosse experiences total moral paralysis from the moment he succumbs to Duessa. As a revision of the Gigante episode from the *Furioso*, Redcrosse's appearance as victim rather than challenger exorcizes the remaining traces of faith in human goodness from Ariosto's already darkened vision. Incorporating the local allegory of pride into an overarching allegory of poetic relationship, Spenser writes as if Ruggiero's partial victories and self-prompted recuperations sustained a flickering Pelagian hope that he was determined to squelch in transforming the *Furioso* into a stronger testimony to humanity's dependence on God. When Arthur succeeds in freeing Redcrosse from Orgoglio's dungeon, Spenser prevents the episode from reaffirming natural moral enterprise by closely identifying the hero with Providence.

My suggestion that Spenser revises Ariosto along anti-Pelagian lines in itself hardly qualifies the received view of him as a champion of the Reformation. But I now want to look more closely at the ideological implications of the sequential arrangement of Redcrosse's encounters with these two embodiments of pride—Lucifera presiding over her conspicuously medievalized pageant and the conspicuously Italianate Orgoglio. The question of their relationship is bound up with a larger question about the way Spenser structures allegorical narrative: does sequential juxtaposition necessarily imply supersession? In one sense, the episodes are two variations on a single theme.

Translated into an Italian representational mode, Lady Pride becomes the monster Orgoglio. But what does this juxtaposition say about the merits of the respective modes, medieval and contemporary Italian, that dominate the two episodes? In the movement from Pride's House to Orgoglio's dungeon, does Spenser "overgo" or reaffirm his medieval roots?

Critics have traditionally read the Lucifera and Orgoglio's juxtaposition as a supersession. Since Redcrosse escapes more readily from Lucifera, they have generally agreed that Orgoglio represents a darker, more dangerous kind of pride, one that can only be overcome through the direct intervention of grace. Hugh Maclean suggests in *The Spenser Encyclopedia*, for example, that "the intoxicating glorification of worldly advancement that pulses through Lucifera's palace springs from, and masks, a self-absorbed and overweening aspiration (anticipating that of Milton's Satan) against which Redcrosse is not entirely proof."[21] To the extent that I accept this reading, I am tempted to see this development in the poem's moral allegory as a kind of evaluative statement about literary history. The more Spenser casts Orgoglian pride—whatever exactly it entails—as more dangerous and irresistible than its Luciferan counterpart, the more he associates the medieval schema on which the earlier episode rests with a kind of representational inadequacy. In medieval formulations, the seven deadlies offered a kind of totalizing analysis of sin: they were the "capital" sins not just in the sense that they were deadly, but also in the sense that they were the basic faults from which all other sins arose. Spenser deprives them of their primacy and replaces the old medieval etiology with an Italian one in which sins stem from one single source: a basic propensity for evil that is inseparable from human nature.

With certain qualifications, Ariosto's moral skepticism complemented the more pessimistic aspects of Spenser's Protestantism more readily than the older opposition between sins and virtues. The taxonomies of the medieval penitentials, with their penances scaled according to the relative gravity of specific offenses, yielded to a single opposition between sin and righteousness.[22] Everyone was equally guilty and equally dependent on Christ's atonement for salvation. The Protestant hermeneutic of salvation thus discounted as works righteousness the psychomachiac opposition between virtues and vices that figured in so many medieval representations of the Seven Deadlies. For the Protestant penitent, the answer to pride was not humility; to envy, charity; or to wrath, patience. In the struggle against Sin *in toto*, grace alone was the only remedy, not human virtue.

On one level, Redcrosse's encounter with Orgoglio parodies the older psychomachia to reveal the insufficiency of the virtues touted in the penitentials as an answer to the Seven Deadlies. In revising his medieval sources, Spenser casts this exaggerated confidence in natural virtue as the kind of pride that leads its victims ultimately to despair and from which they can only be redeemed by grace. Orgoglio's identity as the embodiment of a Pelagian trust in natural virtue underlies his association with Duessa in the ecclesiastical satire that follows his victory over Redcrosse. His triumph predicates her unveiling as the Whore of Babylon, since Protestant thinkers typically cited Pelagianism as the chief error of the medieval Church.

With Duessa mounted upon her seven-headed Beast and holding her chalice of fornications, Spenser seems to commit himself as fully as possible to an apocalyptic narrative of history. The oppositions between Una and Duessa, Arthur and Orgoglio, light and darkness, truth and falsehood, time fallen and time redeemed, that shape the episode implictly discount pre-Reformation teaching as Error. But having just made the case for a reading of Lucifera's relationship to Orgoglio in terms of Book I's apocalyptic theology, I want to end by suggesting why I do not fully believe it. Just when Spenser seems most stringent in his rejection of the Middle Ages, his persistent indebtedness to medieval models resists such a disjunctive historical narrative. Spenser, for example, was not the first moralist to distinguish between two kinds of pride. The opposition between Lucifera and Orgoglio, which I have addressed in terms of Reformation theology, draws on a distinction between *superbia* and *vana gloria* that is at least as old as the topos of the Seven Deadly Sins. Many early moralists insisted that there were in fact eight rather than seven capital sins, because the pride in one's status and achievements—the Luciferan pride of vainglory—differs from *superbia* proper, an inflated sense of one's own natural righteousness that obviates the need for Christ's atonement.[23]

In their diatribes against this darker, more Orgoglian pride, writers like John Cassian, St. Raymund of Pennaforte, Alcuin, Aldhelm of Malmesbury, and numerous other exegetes anticipate the anti-Pelagian diatribes of Luther and Calvin.[24] In one of the earliest and most influential commentaries on the Sins, for example, Cassian draws on the same Pauline scriptures that dominated later Protestant thought in stressing humanity's dependence on grace:

> If we consider also the beginning of the call and salvation of mankind, in which, as the Apostle says, we are saved not of

> ourselves, nor of our works, but by the gift and grace of God, we can clearly see how the whole of perfection is "not of him that willeth nor of him that runneth, but of God that hath mercy," who makes us victorious over our faults without any merits of works and life on our part to outweigh them, or any effort of our will availing to scale the difficult heights of perfection, or to subdue the flesh which we have to use . . . for the performance of everything good flows from His grace, who by multiplying His bounty has granted such lasting bliss, and vast glory to our feeble will and short and petty course of life.[25]

Spenser incorporated the same biblical language in his declaration, "If any strength we haue, it is to ill,/But all the good is Gods, both power an eke will," a phrase that critics have typically glossed as evidence of a distinctly, even militantly Protestant sensibility (*FQ* I.x.1). Yet Cassian wrote in the fourth century, eleven hundred years before Luther. Nor was Cassian the kind of Church Father, like the later Augustine, whom Protestants admired for the thoroughness of his anti-Pelagian vision. Throughout his commentary on the Sins, Cassian portrays the Christian in proto-Erasmian terms as an "athlete who strives lawfully in the spiritual combat and desires to be crowned by the Lord," a phrase that would have seemed charged with works righteousness to Spenser and his Protestant contemporaries (*Institutes*, 290).

In order to grasp the complexity of Spenser's relationship to his medieval precursors, we need to read such passages—not only in Cassian but also in dozens of other pre-Reformation texts that had a direct or indirect influence on *The Faerie Queene*—in terms of their writers' full and ultimately dialectic ethical vision. As Cassian champions the Christian athlete in struggles against gluttony, lust, avarice, wrath, sadness, sloth, and vainglory, he often sounds like the stereotypical Pelagian of Protestant diatribes. But in the athlete's encounter with the eighth and greatest sin, Cassian and writers in the Cassianic tradition turn that apparent confidence in human agency back on itself. The "most fierce beast" embodies nothing less than the arrogant trust in natural powers of resistance that befalls the hero once he has prevailed in every other carnal and spiritual struggle. Like the protagonists of *The Castle of Perseverance*, Cassian's hero vanquishes all the sins but one. That final struggle brings him to the inescapable, and ultimately saving, realization that "all the good is Gods, both power an eke will."

Although we can read the movement from Lucifera to Orgoglio as a Protestant critique of pre-Reformation allegories, it can also be read as a reaffirmation of a moral dialectic that began with Cassian and the Latin fathers and persisted throughout the Middle Ages and well into the early modern period. The medieval distinction between vainglory and superbia paradoxically offered Spenser a schema for defining himself against his Catholic precursors. But I am finally not convinced that the Orgoglio episode necessarily implies something erroneous about the moral assumptions underlying the House of Pride or even about the medieval allegories on which it rests. Spenser was at his most medieval, and most conspicuously indebted to medieval habits of thought, in his ostensible rejection of the Middle Ages. My apocalyptic reading began not so much with Spenser's poetry as with a critical consensus, one that is frankly hard for me to imagine fully discounting, that Orgoglian pride is somehow graver and more threatening than its Luciferan prelude. If their relationship is one not of supersession but of complementarity, and Spenser does not fully discount the Pelagian implications of the older allegorical tradition, he may be less of an ideologue than our current critical climate sometimes suggests. Protestantism certainly modifies his reading of pre-Reformations texts, but those older texts also modify his Protestantism in ways that challenge readings of his poetry as sectarian propaganda.

Although I am close to entering the old fray over whether or not Spenser was a Puritan, my ultimate concern is not with the author's personal beliefs but with the composite effect of his poetry. As Michelle O'Callaghan has recently observed, for later readers, Spenser "was simultaneously the laureate poet gloriously serving his monarch and the oppositional poet, the persecuted critic of the corrupted times."[26] In recent years, professional readers have emphasized the oppositional side of Spenser's writing over its conformist, or even conservative valences. I think their interpretations are in one important sense clearly right: Edmund Spenser the man probably did see ecclesiastical history in sharply apocalyptic terms. But his poetry has origins and ends that complicate his avowed commitments. As a community of scholars, we have done a superb job of explaining why an apocalyptic Spenser mattered so much to dissenting poets from Milton to the romantics. But we have not done such a good job of explaining why he mattered to writers like Pope and the Augustans, who recoiled from the radicalism they associated with Milton and the English Civil War. To reclaim the Spenser that informed their writing, we will need to engage an anti-apocalyptic Spenser, one whose "loyalty to medieval roots" may not have limited his room for poetic maneuver, but certainly complicated his ideological allegiances.

The interplay of polemic and nostalgic voices within *The Faerie Queene* engendered the contradictions of its post-Elizabethan reception history. Spenser's poetry serves as a timely reminder that a work's final ideological significance can never be equated with its author's ostensible polemic project. *The Faerie Queene* clearly reinforced an apocalyptic historiography that provided radicals like Milton a pretext for their attacks on the English monarchy just four decades after Spenser's death. But that is only one side of Spenser's legacy. One could argue just as well that his nostaglia for medieval decorums, and his poem's engagement with figurations of Christian belief that long pre-dated the Reformation, also established a pre-condition for the Restoration. It is finally pointless and distorting to try to map *The Faerie Queene*'s shifting balance of polemic and nostalgic discourses onto a Williamsonian analysis of culture, as if the nostalgic side of his imagination were part of a residual monarchical order soon to be swept away in the emergent apocalypse Spenser heralds in his more polemic moment. Like the English nation with whose fortunes his poetry was so intimately linked, Spenser may have dallied with an apocalypse in which bishops and kings might be no more. But like England itself, he retreated from that apocalyptic vision into a quasi-medieval world of ceremony, sacrament, and incarnational ideals of monarchy.

NOTES

1. Stephen Greenblatt, *Renaissance Self-Fashioning: From More to Shakespeare* (Chicago: University of Chicago Press, 1980), 174.
2. Helgerson, *Forms of Nationhood: The Elizabethan Writing of England* (Chicago: University of Chicago Press, 1992), 49–59.
3. Norbrook, *Poetry and Politics in the English Renaissance* (London: Routledge, 1985), 195–214; O'Callaghan, *The "Shepheards Nation": Jacobean Spenserians and Early Stuart Political Culture, 1612–1625* (Oxford: Clarendon, 2000).
4. *The Faerie Leveller: or, King CHARLES his Leveller descried and deciphered in Queene ELIZABETHS dayes*, Preface (London, 1648).
5. For discussion of seventeenth-century political factors that influenced Spenser's reception, see John Watkins, " 'And yet the end was not': Apocalyptic Deferral and Spenser's Literary Afterlife," in *Worldmaking Spenser: Explorations in the Early Modern Age*, ed. Patrick Cheney and Lauren Silberman (Lexington: University Press of Kentucky, 2000), 156–73.
6. Lewis, *The Allegory of Love: A Study in Medieval Tradition* (London: Oxford University Press, 1936), 321–22.

7. See especially John King's comments on Chaucer, Langland, and pastoral satire in *Spenser's Poetry and the Reformation Tradition* (Princeton: Princeton University Press, 1990), 14–46.

8. *The Works of Edmund Spenser: A Variorum Edition*, ed. Edwin Greenlaw et al., 9 vols. (Baltimore: Johns Hopkins University Press, 1932–49). All references are to this edition and are cited in the text.

9. Greene, *The Light in Troy: Imitation and Discovery in Renaissance Poetry*, The Elizabethan Club Series 7 (New Haven: Yale University Press, 1982), 274.

10. Hume, *Edmund Spenser: Protestant Poet* (Cambridge: Cambridge University Press, 1984); King, *Spenser's Poetry and the Reformation Tradition*; Mallette, *Spenser and the Discourses of Reformation England* (Lincoln: University of Nebraska Press, 1997). Like all readers interested in Book I's theology, I am indebted throughout to Darryl Gless's reminder that "Protestant doctrine" was itself a complicated, richly contradictory body of opinion. See *Interpretation and Theology in Spenser* (Cambridge: Cambridge University Press, 1994). In this essay, I try to extend Gless's line of questioning to the problems of ecclesiology and confessional identity itself. I regret that the valuable essays on Spenser and religion in *Reformation* 6 (2002) did not appear until my present essay was already in press. The essays by Darryl Gless, Clinton Allen Brand, and H. L. Weatherby are particularly relevant to the issues that I raise here. Like me, all three writers recognize the way that Spenser's poetry resists reductive equation with Protestant polemic.

11. Gross, *Spenserian Poetics: Idolatry, Iconoclasm, and Magic* (Ithaca: Cornell University Press, 1985). See also Gless's critique of historical and political interpretations of Spenser's apocalypticism in *Interpretation and Theology*, 118–26.

12. Parker, *The Allegory of* The Faerie Queene (Oxford: Clarendon, 1960), 85. Rosemary Freeman makes a similar point in The Faerie Queene: *A Companion for Readers* (Berkeley: University of California Press, 1970), 100–101.

13. Appendix 2 to *The Stones of Venice*, vol. 3. Quoted as "the classic exposition of the allegory of Book I" by Graham Hough in *A Preface to* The Faerie Queen (New York: Norton, 1962), 147.

14. Harry Berger stands out from many other critics in noting the difficulty of pinpointing Lucifera's relationship to Orgoglio, and more generally, of the Seven Deadlies to Spenser's mythmaking elsewhere in Book I. See *Revisionary Play: Studies in the Spenserian Dynamics* (Berkeley: University of California Press, 1988), 79–80.

15. For a historical survey of the *topos*, see Morton W. Bloomfield, *The Seven Deadly Sins* (1952; rpt. East Lansing: Michigan State University Press, 1967).

16. *The Castle of Perseverance*, in *The Macro Plays*, ed. F. J. Furnivall and Alfred W. Pollard, Early English Text Society, Extra Series, 91 (London: Kegan Paul, Trench, Trübner, 1904), ll. 2202, 2212, 2220, 2399.

17. See Joan Heiges Blythe, "Spenser and the Seven Deadly Sins: Book I, Cantos IV and V," *English Literary History* 39 (1972): 342–52; Susan Snyder, "The Left Hand of God: Despair in Medieval and Renaissance Tradition," *Studies in the Renaissance* 12 (1965): 18–59; see especially 32, 46–47.

18. Mallette, *Spenser and the Discourses of Reformation England*, 34.

19. Ascoli, *Ariosto's Bitter Harmony: Crisis and Evasion in the Italian Renaissance* (Princeton: Princeton University Press, 1987).

20. Lodovico Ariosto, *Orlando Furioso*, ed. Cesare Segre, 2 vols. (Milan: Arnoldo Mondadori, 1976), X.101, trans. mine.
21. *The Spenser Encyclopedia*, ed. A. C. Hamilton et al. (Toronto: University of Toronto Press, 1990) 519.
22. See Blythe's passing remarks on the "Roman Catholic" inadequacy of the *topos* ("Spenser and the Seven Deadly Sins," 347, 351).
23. See Bloomfield, *Seven Deadly Sins*, 69–104.
24. For St. Raymund of Pennaforte's *Summa casuum*, see excerpts in *Sources and Analogues of Chaucer's Canterbury Tales*, ed. W. F. Bryan and Germaine Demptster (Chicago: University of Chicago Press, 1941), 740–41. For Alcuin's *Liber de virtutibus et vitiis ad Widonem Comitem*, see Minge, *Patrologia Latina* (Parisiis: Apud Garnieri Fratres, 1878–), ed. J.-P. Migne and successors, 101:613 ff.
25. *The Twelve Books of John Cassian of the Institutes of the Coenobia, and the Remedies for the Eight Principal Faults*, trans. Edgar C. S. Gibson, in *Nicene and Post-Nicene Fathers, Second Series, vol. 11, Sulpitius Severus, Vincent of Lerins, John Cassian*, ed. Philip Schaff and Henry Wace (1894; rpt. Peabody, Mass.: Hendrickson, 1999), 283.
26. O'Callaghan, " 'The sheapheardes nation,' " 1.

ANDREW KING

Lines of Authority: The Genealogical Theme in *The Faerie Queene*

The genealogical narrative in *The Faerie Queene*, drawing upon the "Brutan" history of Geoffrey of Monmouth and extending the line of British kings down to the Tudor dynasty, is a complex and challenging aspect of the poem that exists in strong relation to Spenser's overall concern with mutability. The genealogical narrative is part of an attempt to define the work as an epic, with a concomitant sense of national destiny and as an emblem for achieved constancy, but that attempt is thrown into the poem's arena and challenged by characters and events. Ideally, royal genealogy should present a rhythmic continuity that opposes and defeats mutability, analogous to the replenishing cycles of the Garden of Adonis. However, Spenser's intellectually honest work admits and explores the problematic nature of the genealogical narrative—in particular, the problematic natures of Arthur and Elizabeth within that narrative. As historical particulars fail to cohere into an idealized providential narrative, the definition of *The Faerie Queene* itself as an epic comes under threat.[1]

POETRY AND GENEALOGY ARE BOTH ABOUT LINES. That sort of pun is particularly Spenserian once we understand the depth of ideas beneath its immediately witty effect. Taking it further, we can say that both poetry and genealogy are made from lines of authority.[2] Genealogical lines, or family-trees, bestow authority upon descendants, and these life-lines are also poetic, or at least literary, in that they construct a narrative for the past that authorizes the present generation. Similarly, poetic lines relate to authority, to their status as authored texts, or literature. These fruitful puns are particularly ripe for picking in relation to epic poetry, in which genealogy, foundation myths, legendary ancestors, and the constructed relationship between the past and the present are, from Virgil onwards, so significant. Genealogical and poetic epic, then, constitutes in all senses lines of authority.

The genealogical theme is at the heart of *The Faerie Queene*, obviously reflecting the influence of Virgil and Ariosto, as well (perhaps less obviously) as the influence of the dynastic Middle English romances still popular in the sixteenth century, such as *Guy of Warwick* and *Bevis of Hampton.*[3] But in Spenser's handling, the genealogical theme is more than simply the standard apparatus of epic. Indeed, this sense of genealogy as standard or conventional to epic is something that Spenser exploits in the context of a poem that is heuristic and questioning rather than widely supportive of Tudor dynastic claims. In fact, genealogy in *The Faerie Queene* struggles for coherence: it struggles to represent persuasively the history of British monarchs as a providential pattern of continuity; and it struggles to represent itself as the organizing narrative of *The Faerie Queene*, the basis of the work's definition as epic. Instead of "struggles to represent," though, it might be more accurate to say that Spenser gives representation to struggle. This essay explores how the genealogical theme in *The Faerie Queene* highlights the tension between mutable historical particulars and the work's aspiration towards achieved virtue and constancy. Each stage of Spenser's handling of this genealogy is arresting because of the difficulties it throws in the way of a patriotic, and therefore in intellectual terms simplistic, reading. Equally, the complexity of the genealogical theme demands our sense that the value of this aspect of the poem involves more than direct political criticism. New Historicism has discouraged readings that move from historical particulars to universals, from moments of politicised response to ideas that are "deeper" or "timeless." Certainly one of the greatest challenges facing critics of *The Faerie Queene* is negotiating the relationship between historical particulars, such as Elizabeth, and their representation within the context of the poem's developed intellectual concerns. This essay seeks to contribute to our understanding of "philosophical Spenser." Certainly the ideas explored here have political implications at all times, but the representation of genealogy within the context of idea-structures such as the Garden of Adonis and the chronicles of Eumnestes' chamber involves a ruminative use of historical particulars in order to explore Spenser's main philosophical preoccupation—mutability. In the process, Tudor genealogy, especially in relation to Elizabeth, emerges as flawed. However, the implications of the issues raised mean that all human institutions, including alternative genealogies and political systems, must be equally flawed. Spenser is not writing political satire or seeking a political fix; the Garden of Adonis is not a blueprint for reform. Rather, the direction of his thinking in relation to the genealogical theme is towards a strong sense of the difficulty inherent in all political and human institutions that seek to represent themselves as constant and grounded in objective authority. Spenser is not agnostic or republican, but he is increasingly aware in *The Faerie Queene* that certain narratives (such as royal genealogy) that presume to derive objective authority from God may be in fact human constructs, and as such mutable and lacking in divine authority. The implications of that insight for his own narrative, *The Faerie Queene*, are equally challenging to the work's authority and generic status as epic.

* * *

The source for Spenser's genealogy is Geoffrey of Monmouth's twelfth-century history of the British (i.e., Celtic and pre-Anglo-Saxon) kings, *Historia regum Britanniae*, as well as later versions and receptions that linked the Tudor dynasty to this ancient Celtic nation. Spenser relates the Galfridian history in three segments: from the settlement of Brutus and the Trojans in Britain to the reign of Uther Pendragon, Arthur's father (II.x.5–68); from the time of Artegall to Elizabeth (III.iii.27–50); and, finally in the poem's narrative sequence, the chronologically prior events of the fall of Troy, the flight of Aeneas, and the early history of Brutus up to arrival in Britain (III.ix.35–51). The remaining narrative of the entire poem is in effect an enlarged examination of one small span within that historical sequence, the reign of Uther Pendragon.[4] But more than that, of course, it is the period of Arthur's youth, before his realization of his true identity. Arthur says to Una:

> For both the lignage and the certein Sire,
> From which I sprong, from mee are hidden yitt.
> For all so soone as life did me admitt
> Into this world, and shewed heuens light,
> From mothers pap I taken was vnfitt:
> And streight deliuered to a Fary knight,
> To be vpbrought in gentle thewes and martiall might.[5]

Here Spenser seems to be aligning his narrative with the received Arthurian tradition, where Arthur will prove to be the son of Uther.

Many readings of *The Faerie Queene* accordingly insist on seeing Arthur as part of the dynastic genealogy and consequently the ancestor of Elizabeth. However, Arthur is in fact absent from the genealogy and his absence entails a strong sense of the difficulty of seeing the historical in terms of the providential—of attaining that epic vision that gives authority to the present. Most responses to Arthur in the poem view him positively, frequently as a flattering ancestor of Elizabeth.[6] Spenser perhaps encourages readers in that direction when tells Ralegh that he "chose the historye of king Arthure" as the "historicall fiction" on which to base his epic narrative because the British hero is "most fitte for the excellency of his person, being made famous by many mens former workes, and also furthest from the daunger of enuy, and suspition of present time" (715). But Spenser was either conscious at the outset of how ironically inappropriate Arthur is as a vehicle to celebrate moral "excellency" in the context of nationhood, or else he allowed the difficulties embedded in the Arthurian history to emerge heuristically as his work progressed. His reference to Arthur "being made famous by many mens former workes" seems to acknowledge that he is constrained by what readers already know of Arthur. He may even be inviting his readers to think of the context of earlier Arthurian "history" and thus consider the significance of his particular manipulations of it. Arthur is in fact a deeply problematic figure in the poem, not through any personal moral failing but through his recalcitrant nature as inherited source material. His story, as Geoffrey of Monmouth and Malory relate it, is a tragic one, and he cannot be manipulated into providential genealogical narratives without heightening awareness of how such narratives are constructed from desire.

* * *

The first section of the genealogy as it is presented in the narrative sequence of *The Faerie Queene* is from the settlement of the Trojans in Britain down to Uther Pendragon, contained in the book, "Briton moniments," read by Arthur in the chamber of Eumnestes, or good memory (II.x-xi). Because Arthur reads this book in memory's chamber, it seems to relate to his past, however novel its contents appear to him at the moment. Equally, because of its subjective relationship to Arthur, this genealogical chronicle breaks off suddenly:

After him Vther, which *Pendragon* hight,

Succeeding There abruptly it did end,
Without full point, or other Cesure right,
As if the rest some wicked hand did rend,
Or th'Author selfe could not at least attend
To finish it.

(II.x.68)

This hiatus is logically necessary because Arthur has read up to the present moment. But the suspension also emphasizes that Arthur and the genealogical narrative are in time—unable to know what happens next. Royal genealogy, in its biological and political succession, should offer an overwhelming sense of continuity, transcending time. Indeed, the predicted patterning generates (in all senses) a narrative that is providential according to the etymology of the word; in short, we can see what's coming. But the abrupt and incomplete ending, in Arthur's reading, conveys more powerfully a sense of temporal constraint and the human experience of uncertainty in the face of time. In the last quotation, "Author," with its upper-case A, is surely a pun on Arthur, and in his inability to "attend/To finish it" Arthur seems not so much a figure of promise as the emblem of time's tyranny, of things cut off. The author/Arthur pun adds another level of word-play to my title—"lines of authority"—and of course this is a severed line. The pun is particularly ironic, because it brings into focus a paradox: Arthur cannot be the author of his line; he lacks authority.

Unlike Aeneas or Ruggiero, Arthur, as traditionally understood, "made famous by many mens former workes," can never be the ancestral hero of a dynastic epic. As noted, the notion of the Tudor myth has led both Early Modern and contemporary readers of *The Faerie Queene* as well as commentators on the figure of Arthur to describe the British king as Elizabeth's ancestor. Spenser may seem to participate in that error when he writes "Thy name O soueraine Queene, thy realme and race,/From this renowmed Prince deriued arre" (II.x.4), but the passage carefully avoids the claim of direct, lineal discent: "name," "realme," and "race" are collective rather than personal legacies. Other sixteenth-century texts and entertainments were less precise in their presentation of royal British genealogy. Arthur Kelton's *A Chronycle with a Genealogie* (1547) represents an unbroken dynastic succession from Brutus to Henry VIII, including Arthur, "Of one dissent, lyne and progeny," "Of the same stocke, lyne and progeny/As by dissent."[7] Kelton also includes a genealogical table in which a direct line is drawn between Arthur and Cadwallader; a marginal gloss ambiguously adds "Betwene Arthur and Cadwalader was .ix. kynges in Britaynge [sic]" ([f.i.r-v]). Thomas Churchyard's *The Worthiness of Wales* (1587) similarly emphasizes that Elizabeth descends "from Arthurs rase and lyne."[8] The Kenilworth pageants of 1575, along with other royal entertainments, also represent Arthur as a direct ancestor of the Queen, and Richard Robinson's 1582 translation of John Leland's *Assertio Arthuri*, or *A Learned and True Assertion of . . . Arthure*, includes a dedicatory epistle which clearly implies an ancestral and biological link between the British king and Elizabeth; Arthur is praised for his "progenie, life, prowesse, prosperitie, and triumphant victories."[9] Responding also to Henry VII's naming of his first-born as Arthur and his adapting Arthur's arms,[10] latter-day historians and Spenserians have tended to view Elizabeth's alleged descent from Arthur as an unproblematic cultural construct and have stressed its centrality to the design and political themes of *The Faerie Queene*. But no narrative account of Arthur from Geoffrey of Monmouth onwards justifies this ancestral view of the British king, and here we come to the principal irony or challenge involved in Spenser's choice of Arthur. Robinson's inclusion of "progenie" in his list of Arthur's achievements is spurious; the fourteenth-century prose *Brut*, later printed by Caxton and drawn upon by sixteenth-century historians, states well the problem with Arthur as a dynastic hero: " he had none heire of his body bigeten: and grete harme was hit that soche a noble Kyng, and so doughty, had none childe of his body bigeten."[11] English sixteenth-century representations of royal genealogy frequently resonate with Old Testament precedents; behind the Tudor descent from the British kings is the providential maintenance of a chosen people. The parallel gained particular force because of the Protestant argument that Apostolic Christianity was established in Britain before the arrival of Augustine of Canterbury in 597.[12] But even if Britain is Israel in the Christian era, Arthur cannot logically be Jesse, the origin of branch and the continuation of stem.[13]

Arthur's lack of direct heirs is viewed as politically calamitous in a number of pre-Spenserian works. In Thomas Hughes's play *The Misfortunes of Arthur* (1588), the king's lack of legitimate progeny is the punishment for deep moral failings; appropriately, his incestuously conceived and illegitimate offspring, Mordred, exploits the weakness of a "Sonnelesse Sire," as Arthur calls himself.[14] Richard Lloyd's *The Nine Worthies* (1584) notes that Arthur's "vnlawfull lust" justly deprived him of "life and kingdome:"

For Mordred his fatall fo, he did beget incestuously,
Vnto his vtter ouerthrow, on his owne sister wickedly:
And thus the father was forlorne, through his sons force in
incest borne.[15]

Malory also includes the incest theme, though other Arthurian texts, such as Geoffrey of Monmouth's *Historia* or John Hardyng's *Chronicle* (pr. 1543), present Mordred as Arthur's nephew. Spenser could therefore have suppressed the element of incest, though the vaunted "excellency of his person" also threatens to sound ironic given the inevitably intertextual nature of the Arthurian reading experience. But what Spenser could not omit is Arthur's death before producing offspring, and here the illogicality of choosing Arthur as an epic hero is striking. The most considered aspect of Arthur's career is his death—"le morte D'Arthur." Caxton, and possibly Malory himself, names Malory's work after the death of Arthur, "Notwythstondyng it treateth of the byrth lyf and actes of the sayd kyng Arthur."[16] Of course, romance heroes eventually die, but not before they have achieved an apparently lasting condition of virtue for their worlds; witness the popular native heroes Bevis of Hampton and Guy of Warwick. For just this reason a number of Arthurian texts suspend the certainty of Arthur's death, hinting instead at his providential healing in Avalon rather than admitting his death and burial at Glastonbury—so famous after the monks' "discovery" of Arthur's and Guinevere's graves in 1191.[17] But Arthur's putative historicity, which is crucial to the dynastic theme of epic, resides in the realism of his death, involving, as Caxton points out, his sepulchre at Glastonbury; the alternative—Avalon and a Messianic second coming—is clearly fantastic, as Gerald of Wales aptly noted.[18] So the problem of *how* he dies—as Hughes' Arthur says, a "Sonnelesse Sire"—remains.

The other chronicle read in Eumnestes' chamber, "Antiquitie of Faerie lond," offers in striking contrast an idealized version of genealogy. Here, there is no sudden breaking off, and Spenser's presentation skilfully suggests timeless constancy rather than the sense of time:

His sonne was *Elfinell,* who ouercame
The wicked *Gobbelines* in bloody field:
But *Elfant* was of most renowmed fame,
Who all of Christall did *Panthea* build:
Then *Elfar,* who two brethren gyauntes kild,
The one of which had two heades, th'other three:

Then *Elfinor*, who was in magick skild . . .

He left three sonnes, the which in order raynd,
And all their Ofspring, in their dew descents.
(II.x.73–74)

The last lines here might remind us of Kelton's emphasis on unbroken linearity, lines of authority: "Of one dissent, lyne and progeny," "Of the same stocke, lyne and progeny/As by dissent." The sense of continuity and permanence, rather than time marked by change, emerges in this passage in the similarity of the names, all beginning "Elf-"; the rulers visually and aurally merge seamlessly into one another. We are given no sense of how one ruler died: merely the appearance of the new ruler, before the demise of the previous one has been noted. And the verblessness of each new ruler's arrival—"Then *Elfar* . . . " , "Then *Elfinor* . . . "—similarly sublimates the sense of time, emphasizing presence and being rather than motion and arrival. This idealized genealogy continues down to Gloriana, but this of course is faerie land, not the history of Britain. It is an ideal pattern that cannot be found in the mutable historical particulars, symbolized in the problematic nature of Arthur. At the end of the first stage of the genealogy, it seems that the best we can do in the historical world is to break off, with anticipation that a providential restoration or solution yet may come.

★ ★ ★

The second section of the genealogy as presented in the narrative sequence of *The Faerie Queene* is Merlin's prophecy to Britomart, concerning her marriage to Artegall and the lineage down to Elizabeth. This too is an interrupted narrative, a broken line that looses its "author-ity" before completion. Merlin says:

Then shall a royall Virgin raine, which shall
Stretch her white rod ouer the *Belgicke* shore,
And the great Castle smite so sore with all,
That it shall make him shake, and shortly learn to fall.

But yet the end is not. There *Merlin* stayd,
As ouercomen of the spirites powre,

> Or some other ghastly spectacle dismayd,
> That secretly he saw, yet note discoure.
>
> (III.iii.49–50)

Both Arthur and Elizabeth are strongly linked by their mutual interrupted genealogies, and thus the problems that we are encountering in the person of Arthur must extend to Elizabeth. Elizabeth is not so much Arthur's descendant as his double; like Arthur, she is a "Sonelesse Sire." We need to return momentarily to Arthur's interrupted reading in the first section of the genealogy:

> After him Vther, which *Pendragon* hight,
> Succeeding There abruptly it did end,
> Without full point, or other Cesure right.

The lack of punctuation in the second line allows the interpretation, at least on the first reading, that it is the line of kings, rather than simply the chronicle, that "There abruptly . . . did end." "Cesure," too, could be a pun on Caesar, or king, again presenting the sense of the complete collapse of the genealogical line; the capitalization of "Cesure" strengthens the significance of this word-play. Building on the links made at the outset between narrative and genealogy, and the deepening of that link in the Arthur/author pun, readers can see that the collapse of the narrative effectively implies or entails the collapse of the British kingship. Elizabeth's situation, at Merlin's moment of breaking off, seems just as anxious; the "royall Virgin" is praised for her reign, but Merlin is by a "ghastly spectacle *dismayd*" —in a characteristically Spenserian pun (e.g., I.i.50), a spectacle that "undoes" the maid, Elizabeth.

It is necessary to return to the beginning of the second section of the genealogical narrative. This section starts with Artegall and Britomart, and the inevitable thing has happened: Arthur's reign has been excised altogether. Despite the anticipation of Arthur's kingship in the *Letter to Ralegh* and the poem, he has no place in the historical British genealogy. Between the end of "Briton moniments" and Merlin's prophecy is one of the "canker holes" which mars Eumnestes' books and scrolls; Arthur *could* be inserted into this space at a later point in the poem, but there would be little point. Genealogically, he is a dead end, and his significance can only be as a symbolic figure, extracted from historical meaning and epic function, in pursuit of Gloriana.

Merlin's prophecy (III.iii.27) and the interpretation of Britomart's dream in Isis' Church (V.vii.21–3) make clear that Artegall, and not Arthur, is the ancestor of Elizabeth. Merlin and Isis' priest prophesy that Artegall and Britomart will produce an (unnamed) child, and Merlin adds that Artegall will shortly after die, perhaps even before the child's birth. Artegall, furthermore, will not be king. Merlin says to Britomart:

> Long time ye both in armes shall beare great sway,
> Till thy wombes burden thee from them do call,
> And his last fate him from thee take away,
> Too rathe cut off by practise criminall
> Of secret foes, that him shall make in mischiefe fall.
> (III.iii.28)

This tragic "morte d'Artegall" recalls Malory's depiction of Arthur's death at the hands of Mordred. But the crucial difference between Artegall and Arthur is that Artegall is allowed to produce a legitimate heir *just* before his death. In that variation, Artegall is a false historical space in which the known historical failing of Arthur can be rewritten in providential terms.[19] Although Artegall appears to epitomize the pressures of history and time, his death is only a diversion that cannot quite distract attention from the fact that he is the means by which Spenser can create a providential romance narrative, similar to the Old Testament, of sustained genealogy. And for all that Arthur seems the character most firmly belonging to the romance mode in the work, his inability to produce that heir and the fundamental need for Artegall remind us of the character's problematic "historical" nature, his chronological limitations. Despite his name, Artegall is *not* "equal to Arthur," and the need to create an unhistorical character to sustain the historical genealogy means that the work's status as epic is questionable. Artegall merely covers another point at which the lines of authority break, and Spenser's use of him rightly feels forced.[20]

In his heirlessness and temporal failure, Arthur is a haunting double for the reader Elizabeth. The heirlessness of queen is not simply matter for political criticism in Spenser's work, however. At the heart of Book III, the book most concerned with Britomart and her dynastic role, is the Garden of Adonis, the great regenerative engine-room of the entire cosmos:

> Infinite shapes of creatures there are bred,

> And vncouth formes, which none yet euer knew,
> And euery sort is in a sondry bed
> Sett by it selfe, and ranckt in comely rew:
> Some fitt for reasonable sowles t'indew,
> Some made for beasts, some made for birds to weare . . .
>
> Daily they grow, and daily forth are sent
> Into the world, it to replenish more,
> Yet is the stocke not lessened, nor spent,
> But still remaines in euerlasting store,
> As it at first created was of yore.
>
> (III.vi.35–36)

This is the image central to Britomart's experience and her dynastic role, and it widens the value in the poem of genealogy and dynastic succession from merely politics to embrace larger philosophical concerns—above all, the concern with time and mutability. In the Garden, reproductive creativity is a solution to the problem of mutability. Ideally, royal genealogy, the Body Politic, presents a system in which, like the Garden, "The substance is not changed, nor altered,/But th'only forme and outward fashion" (III.vi.38). Individual monarchs can come and go, so long as the Body Politic stays constant—like the Garden, where things are "By succession made perpetuall" (III.vi.47).[21] However, the narrator confesses that he does not know where the Garden of Adonis is—"Whether in *Paphos*, or *Cytheron* hill,/Or it in *Gnidus* bee, I wote not well" (III.vi.29)—and its elusiveness as an accessible reality is well reflected in the lack of constancy and regeneration in the real genealogy, particularly in the figures of Arthur and Elizabeth. As an historical particular, Elizabeth fails to embody the regenerative cycles that the Garden of Adonis offers in opposition to mutability. Appropriately, the Garden is the rearing place of Amoret, and not her twin sister Belphoebe, the "Elizabeth" figure.

★ ★ ★

If genealogy is under attack in *The Faerie Queene*—attacked by time and mutability—then the aspiration of the work to be an epic must consequently be threatened. Appropriately, the final section of the genealogy, in III.ix, enacts an attack on the generic definition of the work as epic, threatening to reduce it to parodic fabliau. The last section of the genealogy as it appears in the narrative sequence of the poem takes us to the very origins of Britain, the fall of Troy, connecting Britain to the classical world and Virgil's epic work. However, we find this narrative in the context of subversive irony and parody—specifically, Paridell's seduction of Hellenore. This base sexual act, amidst Book III's focus on chastity, is set against Britomart's presence. What emerges in the handling of the genealogical narrative is effectively a battle of genres—between the epic, championed by Britomart, and the parodic fabliau, deployed by Paridell. Parody is the key notion, as Paridell's name suggests. He entices Hellenore with love messages written in spilt wine, a parody of the Eucharist: "A sacrament prophane in mistery of wine" (III.ix.30). The potentially serious subject-matter of British origins similarly threatens to be overwhelmed by the parodic in the very language that introduces the whole episode. Here, intertextual reference and generic signalling exist in tense relationship with the notion of foundation myth. The narrator begins:

> Then listen Lordings, if ye list to weet
> The cause, why *Satyrane* and *Paridell*
> Mote not be entertayned, as seemed meet,
> Into that Castle (as that Squire does tell.)
>
> (III.ix.3)

The injunction "listen Lordings" is a distinct generic tag that stands out in *The Faerie Queene*, just as it stands out in its most likely immediate source, *The Canterbury Tales*. Chaucer's *Tale of Sir Thopas* similarly begins:

> Listeth, lordes, in good entent,
> And I wol telle verrayment
> Of myrthe and of solas . . .
>
> (VII.711–13)[22]

Chaucer's tale is, among other things, a parody of native romance style.[23] The Host silences Chaucer-the-narrator with the outburst "Namoore of this, for Goddes dignitee / . . . Thy drasty rymyng is nat worth a toord!" (VII.919–930). Spenser has thus teasingly set up the poem's account of the fall of Troy and the origins of Britain with an intertextual reference that deeply ironizes the ensuing narrative.

Paridell's language and motivations as he narrates the fall of Troy further the apparently ironic and parodic treatment of the material.

Overall, the seduction of Hellenore, the young bride of an old husband, recalls fabliaux such as *The Miller's Tale* and *The Merchant's Tale*. The episode begins (III.ix.1–2), reminiscent of the Chaucerian narrator's preface to *The Miller's Tale* (I.3167–86), with apologies for the unseemliness of the ensuing narrative. Malbecco's partial blindness, furthermore, recalls the temporary blindness of January in *The Merchant's Tale*. Just as January keeps May in a locked garden, Malbecco "in close bowre her mewes from all mens sight" (III.ix.5). Chaucer's May willingly cooperates in her own seduction:

> Ther lakketh noght oonly but day and place
> Wher that she myghte unto his lust suffise,
> For it shal be right as he wole devyse.
>
> (IV.1998–2000)

Spenser picks up this line, allowing Hellenore an even more active role than May:

> Nought wants but time and place, which shortly *shee*
> Deuized hath, and to her louer told.
>
> (III.x.11; my emphasis)

The connections between Paridell's account of the fall of Troy and the ironic modes of *Sir Thopas* and Chaucerian fabliaux further emerge in Paridell's narrative and language. Paridell forgets the crucial element of the narrative on which the entire genealogical theme of *The Faerie Queene* rests—that the fall of Troy led to the founding of not only Rome but also "Troynovant," or London. Britomart must remind Paridell that "a third kingdome yet is to arise,/Out of the *Troians* scattered of-spring" (III.ix.44). Genealogy is a definitive element in epic discourse, and Britomart's teleological emphasis places her in the epic mode, just as Paridell's forgetfulness signals his exclusion from that epic theme and genre; by his own admission, his "wits bene light" (III.ix.47). In generic terms, he remains stuck in the world of fabliaux and *Sir Thopas*, as his language, with trite asides undermining his authority, indicates:

> Ah fairest Lady knight, (said *Paridell*)
> Pardon I pray my heedlesse ouersight,
> Who had forgot, *that whilome I heard tell*

From aged *Mnemon*; for my wits bene light.
Indeed he said *(if I remember right,)*
That of the antique *Troian* stocke, there grew
Another plant, that raught to wondrous hight . . .

His [i.e. Brutus's] worke great *Troynovant*, his worke is eke
Faire *Lincolne*, both renowmed far away,
That who from East to West will endlong seeke,
Cannot two fairer Cities find this day,
Except *Cleopolis*: *so heard I say*
Old *Mnemon*.

(III.ix.47, 51; my emphases)

The linguistic tags that here militate against authority recall the narrator's feeble powers in *Sir Thopas*: "as I yow telle may," "I telle it yow," "it is no nay" (VII.749, 758, 766).

Other aspects of this episode are strangely parodic and problematize a sense of providential origins and a politically stable future. Paridell and Hellenore are parodies of Paris and Helen, whose love was the origin of the Trojan war and thus, indirectly, the origin of Britain—since the sack of Troy, in retaliation for Paris' rape of Helen, led to the foundation of Britain. Hellenore parodies the destruction of Troy when she sets fire to Malbecco's treasury:

The rest she fyr'd for sport, or for despight;
As *Hellene*, when she saw a loft appeare
The *Troiane* flames, and reach to heauens hight
Did clap her hands, and ioyed at that dolefull sight.

(III.x.12)

Hellenore is "a second *Hellene*" (III.x.13), and the suffix to her name—"whore"—again points to the parodic nature of the doubling. The Trojan prehistory to Britain is also invoked ironically in Hellenore's erotic interest in Paridell as he tells her about the fall of Troy and Aeneas' journey to Rome. Hellenore here replicates Dido, who fell in love with Aeneas as he recounted the same narrative: "Vpon his lips hong faire Dame *Hellenore* . . . /Fashioning worlds of fancies euermore/In her fraile wit" (III.ix.52). The insubstantial "worlds of fancies" are in pointed contrast to the worlds of Rome and Britain that Aeneas and Britomart prize and seek to achieve. Later Paridell feeds Hellenore's "fancie" with "layes of loue and louers paine,/

Bransles, Ballads, virelayes, and verses vaine" as well as "riddles" (III.x.8). The emphasis here on literary kinds coincides with the generic significance of the echoes of *Sir Thopas* and fabliaux; Paridell, as a parody figure, cannot properly reside in the epic mode.

The character who *is* upholding the epic genre and language in the scene is, of course, Britomart. It is she who remembers the foundation of Britain, and her language is entirely serious and Virgilian:

There there (said *Britomart*) a fresh appeard
  The glory of the later world to spring,
  And *Troy* againe out of her dust was reard,
  To sit in second seat of soueraigne king,
  Of all the world vnder her gouerning.
  But a third kingdome yet is to arise,
  Out of the *Troians* scattered of-spring,
  That is all glory and great enterprise,
Both first and second *Troy* shall dare to equalise.

(III.ix.44)

Britomart upholds epic because she is a crucial part of its genealogical tendency; she will contribute with Artegall to the continuation of the Trojan-British line, leading down to Elizabeth, and in that role she functions, or perhaps fights, to define *The Faerie Queene* as epic. Britomart has access to epic language and narrative because she intends to produce an heir to further the dynasty. Paridell, however, who is himself illegitimate (III.ix.36) and whose affair with Hellenore does not result in progeny, cannot enter into the genealogical narrative of epic. His own status as a bastard limits him to the world of romance-parody and, especially, fabliaux, where encounters are usually sterile or end in illegitimate progeny. Why should Spenser give Paridell a voice at all? Why oppose the epic with parodic and subversive genres? Britomart and Paridell each draw the narrative in different generic and linguistic directions, to some extent reflecting the sixteenth-century debate concerning the historical validity of the Galfridian "British History."[24] But Paridell cannot be lightly dismissed; he is, after all, the only character in Book III who manages to unhorse Britomart, even if he is unhorsed himself in the exchange (III.ix.16). They are in some senses evenly matched characters, and Paridell's fabliau world of parody, illegitimacy, and sterlility poses a serious challenge to Britomart's aims and the entire epic and genealogical impulse of the poem.[25] Paridell's incomplete narrative can be completed only by Britomart, but the threat to continuous narrative, like the threat to genealogical succession, is real. At the end of the Paridell and Hellenore episode, Britomart's epic vision has been seriously challenged, just as *The Miller's Tale* challenges the solemnity of *The Knight's Tale*. And the deceptions involved in Artegall's role in the genealogy, seen in dicussion of Merlin's prophecy, further problematize Britomart's epic ambitions. The "succession . . . perpetuall" must be suspenseful in relation to her, as it is with Elizabeth.

* * *

The challenge in relation to the genealogical theme in the poem is to perceive its philosophical or meditative depth. Equally, the challenge in relation to the poem's reactions to Elizabeth is to see how historical particulars are being worked into a poem that, while deeply political, is more than a work of political satire and complaint. The Garden of Adonis is at the heart of this topic, and in the midst of Book III it is the central image defining Britomart's quest and what her espousal to Artegall will entail. Clearly, the implications of genealogy, especially royal genealogy and reproduction, are cosmic rather than merely political or social. What is said of Adonis in the Garden applies equally to the sense of continuity that should ideally derive from royal succession and the maintenance of the Body Politic:

> . . . for he may not
> For euer dye, and euer buried bee
> In balefull night, where all thinges are forgot;
> All be he subiect to mortalitie,
> Yet is eterne in mutability,
> And by succession made perpetuall,
> Transformed oft, and changed diuerslie:
> For him the Father of all formes they call;
> Therfore needs mote he liue, that liuing giues to all.
>
> (III.vi.47)

That royal genealogy fails to provide that sort of response to mutability seems ultimately less an indictment of the human institution than a moving acceptance of an insoluble condition. The inability of genealogy in the poem to provide an unproblematic sense of the work's epic nature, celebrating nationhood in the context of a confident, providential view of the present and future, reflects above all Spenser's intellectual rigour and honesty. The gaps and patched fissures visible in the genealogy—the broken lines of authority—inevitably imply Spenser's "sacrifice" of his epic, and in the process he creates a more interesting work, one in which readers can experience the implications of the poem's "failure." Spenser's politics have deep roots in his philosophical concerns, namely the opposition of mutability and constancy, and thus the failure of Elizabeth in the poem is also not a point of political attack; rather, it is a way to evaluate the ineluctable mutability of even the most resonant and enshrined of human constructs.

NOTES

1. I am very grateful to Patrick Cheney, Theresa Krier, Helen Cooper, and Matthew Woodcock for reading this work as it developed and offering stimulating criticism.

2. The title of my essay replicates an existing published title, Steven N. Zwicker, *Lines of Authority: Politics and English Literary Culture, 1649–1689* (Ithaca: Cornell University Press, 1993). My opening paragraph explains how my sense and use of this title has developed from puns specifically relevant to the notion of Arthurian genealogy. I admire Zwicker's book on Civil War literature, but I do not intend any comparison or connection between it and my essay, which deals with quite different concerns and employs the conceptual basis of the title differently.

3. On Spenser's assimilation of genealogical and dynastic themes from classical and Italian humanist epic, see Andrew Fichter, *Poets Historical: Dynastic Epic in the Renaissance* (New Haven: Yale University Press, 1982). On Spenser's use of Middle English romance, see Andrew King, The Faerie Queene *and Middle English Romance: The Matter of Just Memory* (Oxford: Oxford University Press, 2000).

4. Wayne Erickson, *Mapping* The Faerie Queene: *Quest Structures and the World of the Poem* (New York: Garland Press, 1996), 72–73 correctly notes that the fifth-century setting exists at the text's literal level, and it competes within the poem with alternative settings, such as sixteenth-century Europe and a classical mythological past, in a narrative that is overall time-inclusive.

5. Edmund Spenser, *The Faerie Queene*, ed. A. C. Hamilton, Hiroshi Yamashita, and Toshiyuki Suzuki, 2nd ed. (Harlow: Longman, 2001), I.ix.3. All further citations will be to this edition.

6. See, for example: Isabel E. Rathborne, *The Meaning of Spenser's Fairyland* (New York: Columbia University Press, 1937); Carrie Anna Harper, *The Sources of the British Chronicle History in Spenser's* Faerie Queene (New York: Bryn Mawr monographs, 1964), 1–2; Charles Bowie Millican, *Spenser and the Table Round* (New York: Harvard University Press, 1967), 16–17; Angus Fletcher, *The Prophetic Moment*

(Chicago: University of Chicago Press, 1971), 108; A. Bartlett Giamatti, *Play of Double Senses* (Englewood Cliffs: Prentice-Hall, 1975), 58–59; David A. Summers, *Spenser's Arthur* (Lanham: University Press of America, 1997), 8, 161; Fichter, *Poets Historical*, 5. Margaret Christian, " 'The ground of storie': Genealogy in *The Faerie Queene*," *Spenser Studies* 9 (1991; for 1988): 61–79 (72) argues that Elizabeth descends from Arthur through a kingly rather than consanguineal lineage; this is true, though Arthur's place even within a kingly lineage in *The Faerie Queene* must be, I will argue, suspect. A noteable exception to the works above that view Arthur as Elizabeth's ancestor is Erickson, *Mapping*, 29, 106. I encountered Erickson's stimulating book after writing the conference papers on which this essay is based. I hope that the present study is complementary with his work, offering a different emphasis by turning attention to the issues of genre and mutability.

7. Arthur Kelton, *A Chronycle with a Genealogie Declaryng that the Brittons and Welshemen are Lineallye Dyscended from Brute* . . . (London, 1547), e.iiii.[r].

8. Thomas Churchyard, *The Worthiness of Wales*, Spenser Society 20 (New York, 1876), 34.

9. John Leland, *The Assertion of King Arthure*, tr. Richard Robinson, in Christopher Middleton, *The Famous History of Chinon of England*, ed. William Edward Mead, EETS 165 (London, 1925), 7.

10. T. D. Kendrick, *British Antiquity* (London: Methuen, 1950), 35–37.

11. *The Brut*, ed. Friedrich W. D. Brie, EETS 131, 136 (London, 1906, 1908), 91.2–4.

12. See King, Faerie Queene *and Middle English Romance*, 179–80.

13. Richard Grafton's *An Abridgement of the Chronicles of England* (London, 1564) is one Elizabethan historical work that emphasizes the significant hiatus in native monarchical lineage; see, e.g., [3.v].

14. [Thomas Hughes and others], *The Misfortunes of Arthur*, ed. Brian Jay Corrigan (New York: Garland, 1992), V.i.98–105, 117–25.

15. Richard Lloyd, *A Briefe Discourse of* . . . *the Nine Worthies* (London, 1584), [f.i.v].

16. Sir Thomas Malory, *The Works of Sir Thomas Malory*, ed. Eugène Vinaver, rev. P. J. C. Field, 3 vols. (Oxford: Oxford University Press, 1990), 1260, footnote to 29. Spenser teasingly anticipates the death of his Arthur: "when he dyde, the Faerie Queene it [his shield] brought/To Faerie lond, where yet it may be seene, if sought" (I.vii.36).

17. See further: Antonia Gransden, "The Growth of the Glastonbury Traditions and Legends in the Twelfth Century," *Journal of Ecclesiastical History* 27 (1976), 337–58.

18. [Gerald of Wales], *Giraldi Cambrensis opera*, ed. J. S. Brewer, J. F. Dimock, and George F. Warner, RS 21, 8 vols. (London, 1861–1891), IV.49.

19. There is a character named "Artgualchar, Earl of Warwick," in Geoffrey's *Historia*, but he in no sense provides an "historical" or narrative model for Spenser's Artegall. For his appearance, see Geoffrey of Monmouth, *The History of the Kings of Britain*, tr. Lewis Thorpe (Harmondsworth: Penguin Books, 1966), 227.

20. It is therefore particularly interesting to consider how ironized Artegall is, especially in Book V; see King, Faerie Queene *and Middle English Romance*, chapter 7.

21. On the notion of the Body Politic, especially in relation to Elizabeth and the pressures placed upon her because of her heirlessness, see: Marie Axton, *The Queen's Two Bodies: Drama and the Elizabethan Succession* (London: Royal Historical Society, 1977).

22. Geoffrey Chaucer, *The Riverside Chaucer*, gen. ed. Larry D. Benson, 3rd ed. (Boston: Houghton Mifflin, 1987). The formula is repeated, with a sense of anxiety at an evidently rustling audience, midway through the tale: "Yet listeth, lordes, to my tale/Murier than the nightyngale" (VII.833–34).

23. The highly popular *Sir Bevis of Hampton*, for instance, begins with the same formula invoked by the Spenserian narrator at the outset of the Paridell episode: "Lystonythe, lording*es*, yf ye will dwell:/Of a doughty man I wyll you tell . . . "(b-text, 1–2). *The Romance of Sir Beues of Hamtoun*, ed. Eugene Kölbing, EETS ES 46, 48, 65 (London, 1885, 1886, 1894). On the continued reading and dissemination of *Bevis* in manuscript and print in the sixteenth century as well as its impact on Spenser, see: Jennifer Fellows, " '*Bevis redivivus*' ": The Printed Editions of *Sir Bevis of Hampton*," in Jennifer Fellows et al., eds., *Romance Reading on the Book: Essays on Medieval Narrative Presented to Maldwyn Mills* (Cardiff: University of Wales Press, 1996), 251–68; King, Faerie Queene *and Middle English Romance*, 126–59. Other romances that begin with the "listen lords" formula are *The Wedding of Sir Gawain and Dame Ragnell* and *Sir Gawain and the Carl of Carlisle*.

24. For an introduction to the debate, see James P. Carley, "Polydore Vergil and John Leland on King Arthur: The Battle of the Books," *Interpretations* 15 (1984): 86–100.

25. Paridell makes later and significant appearances in the work. He, with Blandamour, parodies friendship in Book IV, and in Book V Paridell is identified, during the trial of Duessa, as a conspirator against Mercilla (V.ix.41–2)—which intensifies the sense in which he opposes the interests of Elizabeth.

Part II

Spenser and the Renaissance: Giving Representation to Struggle

HARRY BERGER, JR.

Wring Out the Old: Squeezing the Text, 1951–2001

for Judith Anderson and Angus Fletcher

A profile of fifty years of criticism suggests the importance for Spenser studies of new approaches to questions concerning the repressiveness of allegory, the politics of gender, intertextual relations, and narratorial irony. Foremost among the effects of these changes on the interpretation of Book II of *The Faerie Queene* is an emergent attitude of skepticism toward the traditional reading in which the masculine protagonists of Temperance prove their virtue by defeating the wicked witch. The emergence of feminist and gender-oriented perspectives accompanied by more nuanced conceptions of literary mimesis has made it possible to read the demonization of Acrasia with suspicion and to explore the possibility that the misogynist and gynephobic representation of woman is a target rather a donnée of the second book; the possibility, in short, that Acrasia is a displacement of masculine *akrasia*. If Spenser is the poet's poet whose poetry is about poetry, this may be so in the sense that one of its dominant objectives is to critique—and not merely to emulate—the androcentricism of the epico-romantic discourse it celebrates and continues.

We have nothing to fear but fear itself.
—Franklin Delano Roosevelt

Jeepers [!], Creepers!
—Harry Warren and Johnny Mercer

I BEGAN WRITING THIS ESSAY a year ago, just a half century after I had begun reading Spenser.[1] By the early 1950s, World War

II had turned cold while the intellectual climate of the universities was warming up in the glow of the magisterial studies that lit a fire under all of us in my generation, studies that drove us beyond war-torn Europe, beyond the balkanized precincts of academic disciplines, toward relatively more integrated and global approaches to culture that presaged the future of humanistic curricula. There were the translations of Auerbach, Curtius, and de Beauvoir that appeared in 1953, the books by Kantorowicz and Wind that came out a few years later along with translations of Lèvi-Strauss, followed in the early 1960s by belated translations of Sartre and Merleau-Ponty. Although these authors were changing my view of Spenser, literature, and the world, I remained mired in the practice of close interpretation then being promoted by the New Critics who were my teachers at Yale. At the time, these same New Critics were pushing Metaphysical poetry and not having any truck with *The Faerie Queene*. Consequently, I decided that trying to close-read *The Faerie Queene* would be a way to get in their face, and that is what I proceeded to do, and what I'm still doing, though the critical map has changed in so many ways.

In retrospect, two features of the Spenser sector of the post-war map stand out. First, it was still dominated by the pre-war culture of the *Variorum* edition, a culture steeped (if not drowned) in a more or less pious and genteel ideology produced by an uncritical commitment to the interpretive procedures of the history of ideas.[2] Second, the criticism of my generation, including my own, was sexist and gender-blind. I was aware of the first but had no awareness whatsoever of the second. I made the *Variorum* culture my target, which made me feel hip, and I thought nothing of referring to Frances Yates as Miss Yates, which made me feel courtly. Today I think the classical-to-Christian scenario that informs my account of Book II in *The Allegorical Temper* is about as *Variorum* as you can get, and never more so than when I blame everything on the witch I refer to as a demonic allegorist. Now, as I revisit the scene of my crime, I know that what I should have written was not "demonic," but "demonized."

Between then and now, three convergent public conversations about the politics of reading have profoundly affected Spenser criticism. One concerned orality and literacy; the second concerned feminism, gender, and the role of the reader; and the third concerned the possibility of internal distance and oppositional reading. For me personally, what made the difference was, first, finding my way into a method of reading that emphasized the internal distance of the text from its narrative and, second, discovering the interpretive power of feminist and gender criticism, which was the single most important factor in my critical reorientation between the 1950s and today.

Though feminist criticism started to make a difference in the early 1960s, it didn't really enter Spenser commentary until the late 1970s. But when it did kick in, its impact on me was profound. It provided a viewpoint from which to stand outside and revaluate the traditional account of Spenser as the poet's poet whose poetry is poetry about poetry. I still accept that account, but the revaluation taught me to look at Spenser's poetry as a critique of the poetry it is about, and a critique in a particular sense: it represents the precursors as elements in a pastiche integrated under a single rubric, the rubric of embattled male fantasy and discourse.

As to the change in method of reading, sometimes a single essay will turn your practice around, and this happened to me several times, but what I remember most vividly is the effect produced by an essay John Webster published twenty-five years ago. It taught me to distinguish two different invitations Spenser's poetry sends.[3] The first is to look *through* the language in either or both of two ways: to read as if listening to a story or as if visualizing it; in other words, to treat it as a speaking picture. The second is to look *at* the language, look *into* it, explore "the languageness of language" (as Joel Fineman put it).[4] In simple terms, the first induces you to read more quickly and the second induces you to slow down. The first solicits obedience to the instructions of the allegorical police and promises to lead you to the heaven of official meaning while the second invites you to question or oppose that solicitation. Webster's approach evokes the spirit of Kenelm Digby, who wrote in 1638 that unless Spenser is read with "great attention, rare and wonderful conceptions will unperceived slide by" the reader, who "will think he hath mett with nothing but familiar and easie discourses: But lett one dwell a while upon them, and he shall feele a strange fulness and roundness in all he sayth."[5]

Mieke Bal makes a distinction similar to Webster's between two modes of reading, "reading for the text," which involves the "continual shaping and reshaping of sign events," and the "realist" mode of "reading for a content . . . modeled on reality at the expense of awareness of the signifying system of which the work is constructed."[6] Although these two modes are incompatible, they can, she insists, "be brought to bear on the same work," and in fact exploring the conflict between them is itself an exemplary "critical endeavor" (508). In Spenser, the equivalent of the realist mode is the allegorico-narrative mode that produces speaking pictures and that often seems "countertextual" in that it resists or discourages "reading for the text."[7]

The relevance of such a lectorial dialectic to *The Faerie Queene* has been reinforced by powerful studies of Spenserian allegory. In different ways, for example, both Susanne Wofford and Gordon Teskey have focused our attention not merely on the violence of allegory but on its conspicuously suspect character. As Teskey puts it, "the more powerful the allegory, the more openly violent the moments in which the materials of narrative are shown being actively subdued for the purpose of raising a structure of meaning."[8] It's the very ostensiveness of the violence that calls forth resistance from both characters and readers. One of the important consequences of this view has been to reinforce an older idea of allegory—the idea that allegory battens on the visualizable and audible content of poetry after capturing (or abstracting) it from its textual environment. For allegorical purposes, one picture is worth a thousand words, which is to say, a thousand words is or should be reducible to a speaking picture. This is a countertextual theory, a theory that defends against interpretation.[9]

To shift to the information-theory metaphor Teskey once used, allegory thrives on redundancy, and textuality is the noise it tries to override.[10] Redundancy is the principle on which the speaking pictures called emblems rely for effectiveness. In some brief but excellent comments on Spenser's recourse to speaking pictures, Elizabeth Heale notes that such images "could say much in little because their readers could be relied on to recognize many of the traditional connotations and implications. . . . Spenser uses such traditional images throughout *The Faerie Queene*, but they are particularly frequent and particularly important in Book II." Their conspicuous presence and resonance in the Bower of Bliss, for example, give the episode a "clear moral significance."[11] But just what is that significance? At the end of her absorbing chapter on Book II, Heale suggests two different answers: (1) The whole of the Bower of Bliss episode has made it clear that "the delinquency is Acrasia's: she it is who has perverted nature and art, making their beauty a web to trap men's souls," but (2) "while Acrasia's garden has drawn and seduced the weak and unwary, there are those who willingly seek it out. It is a sign of Spenser's realism that the destruction of the Bower and the action of the Palmer's staff will not free these men from themselves" (72). I return to this passage later but for now it is enough to say that in these two statements Spenser's more "realistic" attribution of delinquency and responsibility is not to Acrasia but to her so-called victims.

The possibility of textual critique or internal distance is promoted by the ambivalent manner in which Spenser's poetry cues readers to respond to the topos as simultaneously a natural place in the mimetic order and a literary place in the intertextual order. By "natural" I mean visualizable (and thus allegorizable). The Bower of Bliss, for example, appears as a topos in the sense of a place the reader is invited mentally to imagine and travel through. Part of the illusion is that this place is created and populated not by poetic art but by independent actors, characters, or persons, figures like Acrasia on whom the power of agency is conferred—in this case the disempowering agency of embowerment.[12] Susanne Wofford registers the power of this invitation in the following comment: "Central to the poetics of the Bower of Bliss . . . is the text's identification of the power that transforms men into animals as female sexuality rather than as its own artistic necessity."[13] Yet the perception of this power can be changed by recognizing that the visualizable Bower is a signifier of the topos as a literary place—a Tasso place, for example, or a Chaucer place, or a Homer place. When *i*llusion gives way to *a*llusion, the mimetic contiguity of the topos as a bower on a "wandring Island" (II.i.51) gives way to the intertextual continuity of a misogynist discourse centered on the figure of Circe: "Acrasia and her bower are themselves new and complex versions of a long tradition of seductive enchantresses and emasculating gardens to which Spenser alludes."[14]

A major feature of Spenserian allusion is the topos of resistance Colin Burrow has found characteristic of "classicizing epics in the romance tradition," a topos in which "authors and heroes alike battle to separate themselves from deceptive women in order at once to obey their rulers, and to replicate the structural unity and animating virtues of Virgilian epic." Guyon's destruction of the Bower is a moment in such a battle and the moment "is acutely awkward: it shows Spenser attempting to exorcise from his hero and his poem a digressive form of romance, in which knights abandon their course to pursue pitiful ladies . . . . Particularly disturbing for contemporary readers is the way issues of gender and questions of genre are interfolded: resisting a woman becomes a means of moving closer to Virgilian heroism."[15]

What makes Acrasia and the Bower different and new in this respect has been brilliantly characterized by Mary Ellen Lamb: Spenser, she argues, tweaks "assumptions about masculinity codified as the virtue of Temperance" by constructing Acrasia as the product of effeminizing poetry and as the embodiment of "gendered fictions" calculated to unman the male reader.[16] Spenser, in other words, tweaks Heale's "long tradition," the diachronic series of poems by male authors about male warriors and wanderers and the women who try to lead them astray. "Tweaking" may be defined as exposing the tradition's metonymic tendency to change the status of its gendered fictions from the effects of masculine fantasy to its causes. This displacement demonstrates the working of a general principle, *the principle of specular tautology*, which asserts that *the evil the mind constructs and represents is always displaced from [the mind] itself and blamed on the evil it constructs and represents.*[17] If, for example, Tasso's Armida is "identified as the concupiscible faculty of the soul, an emblem of libido," can this be anything other than a male soul or libido?[18] When Heale states that "Acrasia clearly represents more powerful and dangerous appetites" than Phaedria (69), whose appetites does she represent? And if "Acrasia represents a voluptuous revelling in sexual excitement," whose revelling does she represent?[19] Maleger and his "idle shades" expressly displace Phantastes's "idle phantasies" from within the temperate body to its perimeter.[20] Why shouldn't the same logic be extended to the Bower of Bliss?

To take specular tautology into account is to transform the transparent verbal window of speaking pictures to an opaque screen, a palimpsest, a text that evokes, interrogates, and overwrites its predecessors in the ghosts of poems past. "Perhaps no scene in *The Faerie Queene* is as intertextual as Acrasia's Bower of Bliss."[21] As the speaking picture modulates into a conspicuously textual history of embowerment, attention gets redirected from the agency of characters like Acrasia to that of multiple converging poetic sites. Thus a countertextual discourse of temperance demonizes Acrasia by activating the principle of specular tautology. The textual critique of temperance represents and undoes this process of displacement.

* * *

My current view of these palimpsestuous relations is chiefly indebted to the work of Theresa Krier and Lauren Silberman: to Krier's strong reading of the way the incompatible values of moralized epic and chivalric romance coexist in a single conflicted, and therefore anxiety-ridden, intertextual field; to Silberman's argument that in Book II the ideology of temperance promoted by moralized epic becomes a target of textual critique.[22] Krier's study clearly shows how, as one pre- or sub-textual allusion mutates into another, the process brings into view the contours of an enduring if shape-shifting cultural discourse; and how the story of the knight of temperance is deeply implicated in this discourse in a way that characterizes—that is, criticizes—both the knight and the discourse. But "characterizes" is too weak a term, for the argument is not simply the standard one about the epic poet's desire to overgo this or that poem or poet in order to produce "Things unattempted yet in Prose or Rhyme." The argument centers on critique rather than on mere emulation. Taken together, Silberman's and Krier's accounts suggest that the traditional contest between temperance and pleasure may itself be an illusion created to support the interests of a rectilinear, repressive, and violent discourse of temperance; a discourse that derives its authority from moralized epic but is complicit and tightly interwoven with the divagations of romance and the temptations of pleasure. Romance and pleasure are its creations, its scapegoats, its necessary others. Again and again, the poetry of Book II dramatizes the bad faith of that discourse in showing how the fear of being unmanned by one's own lust, the fear of becoming a "womanish weake knight," is transformed into the fear of being "in Ladies lap entombed" (II.v.36).

Krier's argument takes account of the often noted irony that Chaucer's *Sir Thopas* is (in Jonathan Goldberg's words) "a most unlikely and yet undeniable source for *The Faerie Queene*. . . . No doubt it is one of the wonders of *The Faerie Queene* that it can relocate—and dislocate—itself in this way." Spenser's poem "is so fully the rewriting of epic and romance . . . that it establishes a literary space that is located, in its play of text against text, on the deadpan side of parody."[23] The anamorphic shadow of tiny Sir Thopas's dream and pursuit of his "elf-queene" cast by the figure of "that most noble Briton Prince" in search of Tanaquill/Gloriana says it all. It cues the informed reader to recall how englished romance had already been reduced to the butt of Harry Bailly's displeasure; any poem intent on renovating the genre would have to acknowledge and live with that prior deflation. It may be that the values of romance are being conspicuously reinflated for a more congenial readership than fourteenth-century bourgeois innkeeper bullies. But it may also be that the reinflation is dogged by its Chaucerian shadow.[24] Does *The Faerie Queene* preemptively wear *Sir Thopas* as a deadpan parody of itself, a kind of cuirass or bullet-proof vest?[25]

The idea that Spenser's poetry is a critique of the poetic traditions it imitates goes back very far and was brilliantly articulated by C. S. Lewis. Writing in the thirties, he may not have been ideally situated to develop a gender-centered version of the idea, and I return to this problem below. But he surely did anticipate such a version. He found the Bower of Bliss sick because there is no sex going on, only the skeptophilia produced by "male prurience and female provocation."

He has been severely criticized for this emphasis, but I think he was on to something, though it took a paradigm shift to make that particular something plausible as an interpretive possibility.[26] Acrasia, he writes, "herself does nothing: she is merely 'discovered', posed on a sofa beside a sleeping young man." Why does he put the word "discovered" in scare quotes? And who "posed" her? And if, as he phrases it, "eyes, greedy eyes, are the tyrants of that whole region," whose eyes are they? The subversive reading all but articulated by Lewis is that Acrasia is not merely posed and discovered but *created* by those tyrannical greedy eyes, and that what is really sick about the Bower of Bliss—the sickness the poetry represents and invites us to recognize—is the displacement of responsibility and blame from male prurience to female provocation. The fantasmatic female provocateur materializes to justify both the prurient distemper and the reactive violence of the temperance congealed in the upright hero and his uptight guide.

Such a displacement is at once marked and demystified by the translatability of a name that designates disorder in the male ethos. As is so frequently the case, A. C. Hamilton's gloss makes all the relevant connections: "*Akrasia*" conflates two Greek words, one denoting humoral imbalance and the other impotence, and the second is reinforced by its links to Acrates and to Maleger's hags, Impatience and Impotence.[27] Book II represents temperance as fear of *akrasia*, a fear that creeps from the common noun toward the proper name, that is, from *a-krasia* toward *Acrasia*, from attributes of self toward the personification of the other, from incontinence and impotence toward their putative cause in Acrasia.

This logic of displacement leads me to conclude that Acrasia is the objectification of male hysteria, the seductive, lethal, and vampiric objectification of a narrative fantasy that shows itself at times dangerously seduced and vulnerable, that doesn't trust her to relent, or trust itself to be anything but relentless, in the violence with which it punishes her for its lapses. So, for example, it perversely fixes and feeds its "hungry eies" on hers (II.xii.78) even after it describes "her false eyes fast fixed in his sight" and "greedily depasturing delight" (II.xii.73). Acrasia is male in the double sense that she is placed in the position of dominance and that she is the product of male fantasy; a fantasy fascinated by the Venerean specter it creates as the effect, and installs as the cause, of its fear, its desire, its castration. In canto xii this fantasy expressly includes the positioning of our two furtive creepers (and peepers), Guyon and the Palmer, in the unenviable but self-justifying role of the injured party, the cuckold, the lame and jealous Vulcan. Remember that the poem also associates Vulcan with another figure of castration, that grimy loser, Mammon, whose gold fusts unused in—of all places—his lap (II.vii.4).

* * *

My argument, then, is that the misogynist and gynephobic representation of woman may be a target rather than a donnée of *The Faerie Queene*. This is hardly an inevitable conclusion. You are not likely to imagine the possibility that *The Faerie Queene* internally distances itself from its misogyny if you haven't first internally distanced yourself from the misogyny of academic culture. In 1966, it was still academic second nature for even younger critics like A. Bartlett Giamatti to describe the earthly paradise in Renaissance epic as the product of a line of male writers who seem to agree in identifying the enemy with the subject position of woman.[28] Giamatti is concerned with what Spenser inherited and adopted from his precursors, the fantasy of the earthly paradise that reflects "the vast extent of man's preoccupation with the place of bliss and delight." The "ambiguous nature of the gardens represents the conflicting forces at the center of . . . Renaissance poems, the conflicts between classical heritage and Christian culture, between Love and Duty, woman and God, illusion and reality" (5–6). The earthly paradise depicted "in the Renaissance epics" is "a place of reason overcome by passion, duty by pleasure, man by woman, spirit by sense" (289). Woman is not only the enemy of man and God but also the personification of passion, pleasure, sense, and illusion. Giamatti's Spenser goes along with this view, and so did mine, many years ago. You may well find the view offensively sexist; but if you accept it on Giamatti's terms, you'll want to say the same about the poem and its poet and its precursors and the western tradition.

Yet that isn't the only alternative. Giamatti himself twice mentions another. At one point he suggests that the garden is "an allegory for a self-deluding frame of mind, a false illusion or fantasy one creates, to one's detriment" (258). Who is "one" here? Later he suggests that by having Guyon and the Palmer pass through a gate of ivory, Spenser is introducing the Bower "as a false state of mind, a self-imposed illusion." In both these statements, the creative agency, the self that deludes itself, must be male, if for no other reason than that Giamatti's poets don't ascribe this sort of cognitive dissonance and conflicted agency to female subjects. But if the garden or bower is an allegory of self-delusion, doesn't its false state of mind consist in refusing to acknowledge this and displacing responsibility for it elsewhere? Doesn't the poetic mind maintain itself in bad faith by activating the principle of specular tautology? Can we show that the poem represents and undoes this process of displacement, that it demystifies and critiques the demonization of Acrasia?[29]

Giamatti broaches such a possibility only to refute it.[30] And although things have changed since then, the temptation to treat Spenserian misogyny as a given rather than as a target remains very strong. This is because much criticism in recent decades has been dominated by context-oriented interpretations that deny the poem anything but a participatory and submissive role in the tangle of cultural discourses flowing through and around it. That countertextualizing tendency was predictable in an older criticism guided, like Giamatti's, by the agendas of social, literary, political, and intellectual history. It persisted in Northrop Frye's claim (1976) that Spenser "kidnapped" erotic and chivalric formulas, and made them serve an Apocalyptic discourse expressing the religious and social ideals of the Reformation state.[31] This is a countertextual claim. In textual perspective, as I have tried to show elsewhere, Frye's kidnapped formulas have the effect of contaminating the integrity of the Protestant argument.[32] The tendency was less predictable but still evident in new historicist practice. It was thematized by Stephen Greenblatt, for example, when—after a brilliantly subversive set of textual readings—he chose to subordinate this level of analysis to the larger-scale exploration of Spenser's complicity in English colonialism and Protestant iconoclasm. Thus contained, the violent destruction of the Bower can easily be reinterpreted as a colonial and Reformation countertext, that is, a sign of Spenser's willing subordination of subversive textuality to colonialist and anti-papist ideology.[33] Finally, even in such an avowedly post-new-historicist historicism as Claire McEachern's valuable chapter on Spenser in *The Poetics of English Nationhood*, Book I is countertextually presented as following its religious and social leaders. McEachern tries to show that the doctrinal confusions and signifying practices affecting the continuum of Reformation discourses saturate and overdetermine Spenser's poem, so that it perforce reproduces the misogyny that operates along the whole continuum from radicals to conservatives.[34]

Such context-oriented approaches, like others currently in vogue in Spenser criticism (especially on the Irish front), are genuinely valuable as antidotes both to claustrophobic close analysis and to the broader, more diffuse, strains of allegorical and myth criticism. But they aren't likely to encourage readers to explore the possibility that

The Faerie Queene might internally distance itself from the sexist ideology and rhetoric by which the Reformation continuum is dominated. Nor are they likely to encourage exploration of this possibility in the poem's representation of its literary precursors, precursors notable for their instrumental deployment of the same misogynist and gynephobic constructions McEachern finds in the Reformation continuum. The poem's literary precursors and its Reformation contemporaries both rely more or less innocently on the principle of specular tautology, which transforms *akrasia* and its power over male subjects into Acrasia and her power over male subjects.

Specular tautology is a principle of self-evasion (or bad faith). Its dynamics of displacement is encapsulated in reflexive uses of the grammatical scheme of *correctio*. Puttenham more dramatically names this figure "metanoia or the Penitent" (compare *pentimento* in painting), but I prefer E.K.'s term, *epanorthosis*, because its etymological implications link it to the act of straightening oneself out, or up, and regaining one's rectitude.[35] Spenser uses epanorthosis not only to represent an act of self-correction but also to mark it as an act of self-exculpation.[36] In Books I and II, for example, epanorthosis is the vehicle of bad faith, that is, the rhetorical means by which the narrative and its male protagonists displace what they find intemperate or effeminizing in themselves to the alterity of the female. It is thus the founding trope of the virtues of perfect Holiness and Temperance, and it gives both rhetorical and narrative form to the proposition, articulated by Debora Shuger, that "the specter of female desire is also the structure of religious (and male) subjectivity."[37]

To take this principle into account is to convert Spenser's archive, his "everlasting scryne," from a backdrop, a fabric of influences, to the primary object of textual scrutiny. It is no longer enough to treat that archive as an intertextual ecology within which the poem metabolically exchanges material with other literary organisms. Literary ontogeny doesn't merely recapitulate phylogeny. It decapitates it. In this version of appropriative violence, the poem distorts the formulas it kidnaps in a manner calculated to impair the integrity of the Reformation argument. So, for example, in fusing the Christian quest for identity with the chivalric quest for manhood, Book I shows how the spiritual dangers connected with the loss of faith and joy are strategically displaced to—and misunderstood as—sexual dangers.

If it is true that through the seventeenth century a model of inwardness (male as well as female) persists in which, as Shuger beautifully puts it, "the voice of the soul is always soprano," it may well be that figures like Una and Alma (not to mention Prays-Desire and Shamefastnesse) conform to that model.[38] But this is represented as a source of anxiety for Spenser's male protagonists. And why not? What man would want to spend any time—any time at all—creeping about in a world so dominated by the various modalities of Big Sister—be they good, bad, or middling; gorgeous or grotesque; mother, matron, goddess, or queen; virgin or virago; wetnurse, witch, hag, or whore—so dominated that he cannot even call his body his own? Gloriana, Eliza, Una, Error, Duessa, Lucifera, Night, Celia, Fidelia, Speranza, Charissa, Medina, Belphoebe, Occasion, Phaedria, Philotime, Alma, Prays-Desire and Shamefastness, Impotence and Impatience, Acrasia—all those powerful, perfect, petulant, provocative, or appalling women, women wall to wall. Jeepers. Do you think it's any more fun to be scared in the woods by Belphoebe or led on a line by Una than to be decked by Occasion or Impotence or Acrasia? Especially when the familiar model of the tripartite soul featured in Book II, the soul divided into rational, irascible, and concupiscible faculties, is normatively and indeed resonantly male, so much so that one imagines its voice pitched more in the bass-baritone range than in that of the castrato.[39] But it is not true-blue masculine through and through, and therein lies its problem. Its subordinate and less worthy parts (concupiscence in the sensitive or animal soul, appetite in the nutritive or vegetable soul) may be marked as feminine, weaker, more antithetical to reason. Spenser hints at this during his description of the Castle of Temperance at II.ix.22 with the spelling, "fœminine," which, as Hamilton brilliantly observes, "suggests that the feminine is . . . opposed to the masculine."[40]

Given this gender imbalance, given, that is, the identification of the soul's *krasis* with masculinity, it is easy to understand the otherwise arbitrary distribution of internal and external agencies in the following passage: "Guyon is a man. Pyrochles and Cymochles are inward impulses or urges which he must fight. Acrasia, however, is external temptation, meaning that she must be an actual woman who ensnares many men . . . and whom Guyon successfully resists."[41] Nor is it hard to understand why threats against reason that imperil the soul's gender may be considered even more serious than excessive irascibility. In II.v.1 the narrator insists that the pursuit of temperance finds "no greater enimy" than the "stubborne perturbation" illustrated by Pyrochles's self-endangering enlargement of Furor. But after the subsequent account of Cymochles deliquescing in the Bower—a "womanish weake knight,/ . . . in Ladies lap entombed" (II. v.36)—and after the verse itself demonstrates Cymochlean desire by dallying for seven stanzas in a rhetorically lush fantasy of embowerment (II.v.28–34), the message changes:

A harder lesson, to learne Continence
In joyous pleasure, then in grievous paine:
For sweetnesse doth allure the weaker sence
So strongly, that uneathes it can refraine
From that, which feeble nature covets faine;
But griefe and wrath, that be *her* enemies,
And foes of life, *she* better can restraine;
Yet vertue vauntes in both their victories,
And *Guyon* in them all shewes goodly maisteries.
(II.vi.1, my italics for pronouns)[42]

"The weaker sense" of "feeble nature": the "fear of effeminization" that Stephen Orgel notes as "a central element in all [Renaissance] discussions of what constitutes a 'real man' " is fear of the woman within the man.[43] Book II dramatizes an ideology of temperance that interprets this fear as a good thing. To read the book as a critique of the ideology is to change the venue from a trial of sexuality to a trial of the fear of sexuality, a trial of the gynephobic fantasy that fear privileges.

* * *

> To write as a male reader, identifying unselfconsciously with Guyon's position, with Guyon's gaze, leads to a misrecognition of the gender-specific character of the self-fashioning process figured in Guyon's violent repression of his own sexual arousal. What is being fashioned here is . . . a male subject, whose self-defining violence is enacted against an objectified other who is specifically female . . . [and threatens] him with maternal engulfment.[44]

It is no wonder, then, that in Book II temperance is a "heroic" and "dynamic even frantic maintenance of order in the face of perpetual insurrection." These are Michael Schoenfeldt's words, and according to him they express Spenser's idea of the discipline necessary to protect the "fragile and unstable" self.[45] I agree with the description but not with the attribution. Although Schoenfeldt's account of the beleaguered temperate self applies as much to Alma and Medina as to Guyon, it's obvious that the generic self he is concerned with, the subject and agent of temperance, is more restrictively a male self than he allows—not the human self, not an androgyne self. He doesn't always make that clear, but he does register the complexity of the situation while describing the argument of canto ix: the castle's owner and tour guide is a woman who "leads the knights . . . through a body that is probably masculine . . . . The sexual ideology at work here is certainly masculinist, but in a conjunction of traits confusedly endowed with masculine and feminine meaning."[46]

Book II questions the unhappy, defensive, anxiety-driven structure Schoenfeldt eloquently depicts as temperance. Even as that virtue's classical and Christian antecedents are established, its cultural glamor and psychological efficacy are demystified.[47] The protagonist's behavior contributes to this effect. When Guyon first rides into view we see him initially through Archimago's eyes as a potential cat's paw, a muscular and domesticated but skittish terminator, "all armd in harnesse meete,/That from his head no place appeared to his feet." He travels with an old but "comely Palmer" who "with a staffe his feeble steps did stire" (steer and stir) and whose "slow pace" makes the knight temper "his trampling steed" (II.i.6–7), which suggests that the Palmer's job is to keep Guyon from pricking on the plain.

This is a comfortably familiar emblem of generational teamwork: wisdom tempers courage, prudence counsels self-restraint, *gravitas* commands *pietas*—comfortable, at any rate, to men; an exclusively male genealogy, a homosocial ideal of identity formation. The only trouble is that in Book II it is honored as much in the breach as in the observance. Several times Guyon rushes impetuously off to practice what the Palmer preaches—"the weake to strengthen, and the strong suppresse"—only to get misdirected by Archimago, lose his horse to Braggadocchio, take a beating from Furor and a boatride in the wrong direction with Phaedria, and end up half dead outside Mammon's cave.[48] Not an enviable record; less like the patron of temperance than a patient in need of it. At the conclusion of the first episode (the fiasco involving Archimago and Redcross), the Palmer reasserts his leadership with a competently ritualistic disengagement (II.i.31–33) and then guides his charge

> over dale and hill,
> And with his steedie staffe did point his way:
> His race with reason, and with words his will,
> From foul intemperance he oft did stay,
> And suffred not in wrath his hastie steps to stray. (II.i.34)

"Steedie"—a 1590 reading inadvisedly emended to "steadie" in 1609—picks out the locomotive function of the staff that "stires" the Palmer's feeble steps and is thus both the equivalent and the moderator of the hero's trampling steed. The colon ending the second line has the force of an *id est* leading to an allegorical interpretation of the visualized act. In its Faerie form, temperance is allegorical magic: rational and verbal restraint are no more difficult or problematic than the staff-pointing to which they are pastorally reduced. Nevertheless, the last two lines, especially "foul" and "oft" and "suffred," suggest that the allegory may be a whitewash. But at this early juncture in the poem, the moral force the staff represents is not seriously challenged, as it will be later (see p. 108 below).

One contextual allusion may frame the portrayal of the Palmer, his staff, and his moral leadership in a possibly wry set of associations. The portrayal is evocative of an important but problematic and often parodied figure in the cultural, moral, and sexual economy of Spenser's England: the humanist schoolmaster whose lessons are sometimes punctuated by the rattattoo of the palmer or the rod.[49] Recent studies of pedagogy and mimesis have isolated this figure as a significant factor contributing to the crises that beset the construction of masculine identity during the sixteenth century. Perhaps the Palmer is the personification of a punitive paddle.

Between Guyon's steed and the Palmer's staff there is an important difference in symbolic valency. The former derives ultimately from the embodied tripartite soul of Platonic tradition: whether it signifies irascibility or concupiscence, the steed connotes aspects of male virility associated with sexual difference and its bodily inscription. The staff, on the other hand, is a prosthesis dissociated from the body; a crafted object cunningly framed of "vertuous" wood and invested with an extra-organic genealogy. It represents phallic authority, and it comes into its own in canto xii, when Mosaic and Hermetic analogies affiliate it with the herald's staff, the divine magician's wand, the god's scepter. They give it an aura of antiquity that fixes attention on the continuity, the transmission, of traditional male authority from the gods to the Palmer.[50]

At the same time, this continuity is charged with negative meaning.[51] Through the analogy of the Palmer's staff to Mercury's caduceus in II.xii.41, our heroes' assault on the Bower of Bliss is compared to an invasion of the "Stygian realmes," and when, two stanzas later, they pass through an ivory gate, the assault is marked as a *katabasis*, a voyage down into an infernal region of false dreams.[52] From the Morpheus episode in Book I on, Spenserian *katabasis* is Virgilian rather than Christian in its mode and meaning, which is to say that it is represented not as a world-changing redemptive trip to the lower world but as a trope in which to journey "down" means to journey "back" through a syllabus of literary precursors to the region of the dead those precursors now inhabit. This is the region of the past, the *imperium* of *mos maiores*, the medium through which the all-male chorus of the dead poets' society perceive, understand, predict, and sing the future.[53]

All this suggests to me that as guide and teacher, the Palmer leaves something to be desired, and possibly something to be feared. That something, which is necessary to the success of his regimen, is *a-krasía*, or Acrasia. Greenblatt trenchantly articulates this relation in a comment that identifies Acrasia with "excess" and does so by appealing (in effect) to the principle of specular tautology:

> "Excess" is defined not by some inherent balance or impropriety, but by the mechanism of control, the exercise of restraining power. And if excess is virtually invented by this power, so too, paradoxically, power is invented by excess: this is why Acrasia [and what she is made to represent] cannot be destroyed. . . . For were she not to exist as a constant threat, the power Guyon embodies would also cease to exist.[54]

Thus, as Sprengnether and Silberman have demonstrated, temperance is not a defense against the self's instability. Temperance is its cause. The poem targets precisely the hyperactive conception of temperance Michael Schoenfeldt describes.[55] A paranoid ideal of security generates a nightmare of perpetual siege.

Consider, for example, the first stanza of canto xii. Why does the narrator describe the goodly frame of temperance in a figure that recalls Alma's castle/body and then rewrites it as a kind of dominatrix?

> Now gins this goodly frame of Temperance
> Fairely to rise, and her adorned hed
> To pricke of highest praise forth to advance,
> Formerly grounded, and fast setteled
> On firme foundation of true bountihed;
> And this brave knight, that for that vertue fights,
> Now comes to point of that same perilous sted,
> Where Pleasure dwelles in sensuall delights,

Mongst thousand dangers, and ten thousand magick mights.

Parataxis and three enjambments push the first and longer of the stanza's two clauses energetically forward through a summary of the work done by the preceding eleven cantos, and then maps it onto an image previously used to describe Alma's castle. By contrast, the second clause describing Guyon seems hobbled by hypotaxis. For just a moment, the castle is transformed into a threatening figure the seeds of which were planted in the ninth canto:

The frame thereof seemd partly circulare,
  And part triangulare, O worke divine;
  These two the first and last proportions are,
  The one imperfect, mortall, fœminine;
  Th'other immortall, perfect, masculine . . .

(II.ix.22)

Since lines 4 and 5 are reversible, the linear sequence seems to be arbitrarily scrambled: the circular part and the first proportion are prosodically linked to the imperfect feminine gender, so that the reader has to resist the word order in order to uphold the primacy of the masculine. The tension is increased, as I note above, by the spelling of "fœminine." It's as if a momentary challenge to the normative order materializes in the verse. This challenge revives in II.xii.1 in the looming figure whose "adorned hed" gestures complexly beyond Alma and toward more aggressive apparitions of female power—not only Gloriana and Elizabeth, but also Duessa, Lucifera, Mammon's Luciferan daughter, and, in the remote symbolic distances, the terrible Cybelean mother.

I have to confess that I find the figure engagingly sinister. The phallic *daunger* of Temperance is displaced to a feminized structure, and one that's still rising, still animated by her desire to advance toward a climactic fulfillment, which will be achieved when the knight "comes to point of that same perilous sted,/Where Pleasure dwelles." Even though "*that* perilous sted" is distinguished from "*this* goodly frame," its "point" converges with the "pricke of highest praise," and, in this moment, as the *a-krasía* of Maleger's shade gives way to that of Acrasia's, you may recall that Alma, like Pleasure, dwells "Mongst thousand dangers, and ten thousand magick mights." In fact, because "pricke" and "point" are also archery terms (Hamilton's gloss), they recall the several references in the preceding canto to the bowman, Maleger, and his archers. Commenting on the final stanza of canto xi in still another of his illuminating glosses, Hamilton notes that the description of Arthur wounded—"of his armes despoyled" and with Alma hovering about—"parallels that of Acrasia's victims." This prepares the way for the forces of Temperance to mutate into those of pleasure and Acrasia. Pleasure is the form Temperance takes in order to make its hero stand at the crossroads and "for that vertue fight." It may well turn out—to borrow a figure from Book I—that the castle of Temperance is built on the sands of the Bower of Bliss.

* * *

> Women are dangerous to men because sexual passion for women renders men effeminate: this is an age in which sexuality itself is misogynistic, as the love of women threatens the integrity of the perilously achieved male identity.[56]

The most significant pattern in canto xii's confrontation between Temperance and Pleasure is a transgendering of power in which accountability is gradually shifted from male to female agency. The Odysseyan voyagers first encounter shades of Charybdis and Scylla in the "Gulfe of Greedinesse" and "Rocke of Vile Reproch" (II.xii.2–9). But whereas Scylla and Charybdis are traditionally female, here they are rewritten as male monsters.[57] Like funhouse mirrors, they reflect in distorted form the calamities that befall men who succumb to the lure of "lustfull luxurie and thriftlesse wast" (II.xii.9). The message delivered by the allegory and the Palmer's moral is that this is strictly "a man thing." Victims of their own intemperance, these "miserable wights" have only themselves to blame.[58] Nevertheless, the discourse of temperance finds little comfort in this reflexive formulation, and steers away from it. During the remainder of the canto it gradually turns from male to female threats, and from the dangers of shipwreck to those of seduction.

This change is signalled in stanza 10, immediately after the Palmer's mini-sermon. As the Ferryman plied his oars, "the hoare waters from his frigot ran, / And the light bubbles daunced all along," and the "salt brine out of the billows sprong." At that moment the narrator brings the floating islands into view as if they too are bubbly effects of the temperate rowing that roils up the ocean; the trio of temperate travelers "espy" both the wandering islands and the giggling Phaedria alongside her "little skippet." The light dancing bubbles not only "anticipate Phaedria's appearance" (Hamilton, *FQ*, 283), they are its figurative origin. The islands and Phaedria, whose "boate withouten oare" propels itself, emerge here as a fantasy projected from the efforts of the stiff oars of temperance.[59] "Frigot" first appears in II.vi.7 as another name for Phaedria's "Gondelay." Martha Craig suggests an allusion to Italian "*frigotare*, 'to chuckle, to shrug or strut for overjoy,' " but the more obvious echo, "frigate," momentarily lights up a side-splitting image of Captain Phaedria.[60] In canto xii, the meaning of "frigot" is influenced by its introduction into the salty, "hoare," and frigorific context of the boat of temperance, and the identity of the two opposed forms of transport is thus suggested shortly before the perpetually "salt" Phaedria reappears in her "skippet."[61] When the boat of temperance finally approaches the "sacred soile, where all our perils grow," a strange thing happens. As Guyon prepares to disembark, "the nimble boate so well her sped/That with her crooked keele the land she strooke." Hero and guide sally forth while the boatman "by his boate behind did stay," and we hear no more about him (II.xii.37–38). But for some reason, the last reference to his boat all but turns it into a Phaedrian skippet.

Craig reads the representation of Phaedria as a critique of the effeminizing influence of Italianism, and particularly of Venetianism, on English morals.[62] Giving this interpretation another turn, I take Phaedria to be a light-hearted burlesque of that critique, that is, a jab at those who, like Ascham, warn against "the Siren songs of Italy" (among whose singers Ascham singles out Petrarch and Ariosto). Phaedria differs from similar Spenserian figures in that she and her little "gondelay" or "frigot" or "skippet" are both fun and funny, never more so than when she quotes Our Lord (via Tasso) as a way of lulling Cymochles to sleep (II.vi.15–17).[63] Outrageously but hilariously irreverent, she affords a familiar standpoint within the poem from which to smile at the principles of "Stoick" censorship Guyon and the Palmer are shown more or less hysterically, and not very effectively, to defend. Phaedria's is the standpoint of Richard Helgerson's Elizabethan prodigals.[64] Her antics, like theirs, send up the "rugged forehead" of the civic humanism represented by the Palmer and his staff, or rod. Phaedrian poetry temporarily disables the Palmer and laughs at the repressive discourse that invents it as a model of wicked woman's wiles only to castigate it as the "pleasing baite" "by which fraile youth is oft to follie led" (*FQ* IV.Pr.1). But "Phaedrian poetry" of course designates a mixed, indeed, a conflicted, form of expression in which the male narrator's ambivalence is as much the subject of representation as is Phaedria.

The Phaedrian experience first materializes as a mirage viewed through the eyes of the hapless Cymochles, who sees what appears to be a movable billboard—a "bush" in both senses of the term—that advertises the pleasures of embowerment:

he saw whereas did swim
A long the shore, as swift as glaunce of eye,
A little Gondelay, bedecked trim
With boughes and arbours woven cunningly,
That like a litle forrest seemed outwardly.

(II.vi.2)

Beginning with the devaluation implied by "glaunce of eye," "delay," and "cunningly," the terms of narratorial disapproval are threaded throughout the episode, but they seem to enable or justify rather than to suppress the delight in disorder sustained through eighteen stanzas of rapt attention to and quotation of the garrulous Phaedria. The narrator's Cymochlean excess is sublimely and pleasurably ridiculous because he gets carried away by his impersonation of Phaedria getting carried away. "A harder lesson, to learne Continence/ In joyous pleasure, then in grievous paine" (II.vi.1): by the time Guyon appears on the scene in 2.6.19 it has become clear that these plaintive words characterize not only the figures within the narrative but also the behavior of the narrative itself. Phaedria's refusal to let "the *Blacke Palmer*" board her "ferry" (vi.19) imitates and ratifies the absence of his restraining influence from stanzas that go on Phaedrian holiday before Guyon's arrival, stanzas that dwell perversely and pleasurably—and mischievously—on Phaedria's perverse and mischievous calls to pleasure.

The narrative's indulgence in "immodest Merth" reaches two climactic moments. The first is the cacophonous double allusion that intertextually complicates Phaedria's hedonistic sermon. The second occurs at the end of her fourth and longest utterance. In a skewed replay of Medina's impassioned plea (II.ii.29–31), she importunes Cymochles and Guyon to make love not war: "*Mars* is *Cupidoes* frend,/And is for *Venus* loves renowmed more,/Then all his wars and spoiles, the which he did of yore" (II.vi.35).[65] This is followed by one of the great moments in literary history: "Thereat she sweetly smiled." The narrator then celebrates her successful pacification of the two warriors with a pair of misapplied proverbs: "Such powre have pleasing words: such is the might/Of courteous clemencie in gentle hart" (II.vi.36). Yet throughout this performance, even as he dwells in delight on her gaucheries, he shows his moral and aesthetic sensibilities being persistently offended by her looseness and behavioral style.[66] The sum effect of so incontinent and unstable a performance is to make him sound as prudish as the Palmer, or as troubled and as ludicrously chivalrous as Guyon, who

> was wise, and warie of her will,
> And ever held his hand upon his hart:
> Yet would not seeme so rude, and thewed ill,
> As to despise so courteous seeming part,
> That gentle Ladie did to him impart,
> But fairely tempring fond desire subdewd,
> And ever her desired to depart
>
> (II.vi.26)

At the end, "She no lesse glad, then he desirous was / Of his departure thence" (II.vi.37), and in the remaining lines of the stanza, as Alpers notes, "Spenser keeps in touch with Phaedria's point of view . . . by making each line a separate accusation against Guyon" (317). But whether or not "the lines mean one thing to Phaedria and another to Guyon and us" (ibid.), the Phaedrian rhetoric and point of view that dominate the episode indelibly underscore the narrative's impatience with the rigid hero and his spoilsport guide. Phaedria finds them both a little slow on the uptake—a little "sluggish," perhaps, like "the dull billowes" through which "her flit barke" speeds with such legerity. But why did Guyon let her so easily whisk him away without even giving him "leave to bid that aged sire / Adieu" (II.vi.20)?

* * *

A major Phaedrian moment in Book II occurs in the little scene of frolic immortalized by C. S. Lewis:

> As *Guyon* hapned by the same to wend,
> Two naked Damzelles he therein espyde,
> Which therein bathing, seemed to contend,
> And wrestle wantonly, ne car'd to hyde,
> Their dainty parts from vew of any, which them eyde.

Sometimes the one would lift the other quight
Above the waters, and then downe againe
Her plong, as over maistered by might,
Where both awhile would covered remaine,
And each the other from to rise restraine;
The whiles their snowy limbes, as through a vele,
So through the Christall waves appeared plaine:
Then suddeinly both would themselves unhele,
And th'amarous sweet spoiles to greedy eyes revele.

As that faire Starre, the messenger of morne,
His deawy face out of the sea doth reare:
Or as the *Cyprian* goddesse, newly borne
Of th'Oceans fruitfull froth, did first appeare:
Such seemed they, and so their yellow heare
Christalline humour dropped downe apace.
Whom such when *Guyon* saw, he drew him neare,
And somewhat gan relent his earnest pace,
His stubborne brest gan secret pleasaunce to embrace.

(II.xii.63–65)

Lewis's cavalier reference to Cissie and Flossie, reducing Spenser's bathers to (what his colleagues might have called) "shopgirls" cavorting in a public pool, is misleading in part because these figures do more than duck and giggle and display themselves for the benefit of any male "which them eyde." They perform two of the major activities of the book of temperance. First, they wrestle, recalling Guyon the wrestler's fight with Furor, also Arthur's scrimmages not only with Pyrochles and Maleger but also with another pair of female brawlers, Impotence and that terminal dunker, Impatience. Second, they contribute to the spirit of intertextual pluralism that dominates canto xii by summoning up figures from an earlier text—the naked wrestling swimmers in Tasso's *Jerusalem Delivered* (XV. 58–66).[67] As to their wrestling, its target is not the chivalry of noble riders but the dirty and demeaning hand-to-hand struggle forced upon our unhorsed heroes by villeinous enemies in moments of humiliation, desperate frustration, and Pyrochlean fury. The bathers don't simply mock-wrestle; they wrestle "wantonly," advertising as an alternative to "dolefull . . . scarmoges" (II.vi.34) the more pleasurable contact sport in which predatory women reduce their disarmed heroes to "Love's warriors only" (*Ger. Lib* XV.63). In short, they enact the

Phaedrian program: "Another warre, and other weapons I/Doe love, where love does give his sweet alarmes,/Without bloudshed" (II.vi.34).

This is more than a come-on. The bathers play both men's and women's roles. They "seemed to contend" like men only to suggest that the wanton wrestling of two women is preferable to the angry brawling of two men. Their play glances at same-sex erotics while staging an aquatic strip-tease for men's "greedy eyes." The rhetoric of exuberant self-delight in play thus slides into the rhetoric of exuberant self-display, and the exuberance edges their energetic hide-and-seek with mockery. Under the pretext of careless abandon they watch themselves being watched, and with preemptive voyeurism stage a caricature of what it is "that men in women do require," the lineaments not of gratified desire but of men's pornographic fantasy. Theirs is a high-spirited travesty of the Acrasian nightmare that motivates and underwrites the ideology of self-restraint. But they flaunt it in a Phaedrian rather than Acrasian mode, an effect that sharpens when, after the double simile at stanza 65, the bathers notice Guyon and pull out all stops—but only after they "stood/Gazing a while at his unwonted guise" (II.xii.66).

The moment of pause, as if to allow them to take in their target and prepare their show, renders the Phaedrian reprise that follows more theatrical and comical. For over two stanzas they take turns frenetically alternating between coy and brazen poses, engaging in Elissan and Perissan capers, turning the roughly parallel contraries of Shamefastnesse vs. Prays-Desire and Impotence vs. Impatience into modes of flirtation, until Guyon's face begins to sparkle, at which point

> their wanton meriments they did encreace,
> And to him beckned, to approach more neare,
> And shewd him many sights, that courage cold could reare.
> (II.xii.68)

Finally, the translation and transgendering of power is repeated in the double simile at stanza 65. Spenser accurately if loosely translates the star figure from Tasso, departing from it in only one detail; he adds the masculine personification ("His deawy face") that confuses matters by altering the sex both of the bathers it's compared to and of the star itself, which is traditionally male in its hesperian manifestation but changes to Venus in the morning. The sex change is repeated when the rising of the morning star gives way to the birth of its eponymous goddess from the severed genitals of the father.

The androgynous structure of the house of Temperance, along with the hint of gender conflict registered in the spelling of "fœminine" (II.ix.22), has already been mentioned. Elsewhere, Spenser twice refers to the lability of Venus's gender: at *Faerie Queene* IV.x.41 ("Both male and female, both under one name") and at *Colin Clouts Come Home Againe,* ll. 800–801 (the God of Love was "Borne without Syre or couples of one kynd,/For Venus selfe doth soly couples seeme"). In the allegories of reproduction John Hankins collects from Spenser's sources, the foam-born Aphrodite is identified with "the masculine semen" and with "the desire caused in part by a superabundance of that fluid."[68] Thus although mythographers and others depict Venus as a goddess, they interpret her as an alienated figure of the masculine role in procreation.[69] Like the roiling sea-cradled sex of the castrated father from which she is born, Venus materializes—along with Phaedria and Acrasia—as a projection, an ejaculation, of male fantasy, constituted and empowered by the seminal spume of desire, and then, according to the logic of specular tautology, externalized as its object and its cause.[70]

As I suggest above, a comic version of this foamy genesis occurs when the wandering islands and Phaedria seem to materialize together like Aphrodite in a bubbly springtime fantasy stirred up by the "stiffe oares" that aggravate the ocean. For me, the double simile associates the journey of the "well-rigged . . . barke" of temperance (II.xi.4) with the birth of Venus and also of the Venerean/Circean intemperance named Acrasia. As products of a primal act of penile or literal castration, Venus and her avatars are abiding figures of the symbolic castration necessary (in David Miller's words) "to erect the . . . privilege of the phallus."[71] That privilege—which in Book II is called temperance—depends on, is supported by, the feminization and demonization of *akrasia.*

* * *

My treatment of Cissie and Flossie has been no different from Lewis's in one important respect. I have been describing them as if they are independent characters, autonomous agents, when obviously they are no such thing. They are what they signify, which is less *what* they imitate and allude to—the passage in *Jerusalem Delivered*—than *that* they imitate and allude to a topos within the Circean discourse: the temptation and unmanning of heroes by perfidious women. Thus all the intentions and effects I ascribed to the bathers in the preceding section must be reascribed to male discourse, and this includes the illusion that the bathers are autonomous—that deliberate female provocation (to replay Lewis's terms) is the cause of male prurience. Re-cognized as an effect of male discourse, the illusion flags the activity of specular tautology, the process by which the "sweetnesse [that] doth allure the weaker sence" (II.vi.1) is systematically alienated to, personified as, fantasmatic female provocateurs. To expose the process is to show how a traditional epico-romantic discourse provides the scapegoat that can be used to excuse and therefore to render more forgivable a hero's occasional lapse in the "whelming lap" (II.iv.17) of the temptress who flatters his manhood by displaying her desire.[72] Stephen Gosson, who noted in 1579 that "our wreastling at armes, is turned to wallowyng in Ladies laps," would have been sensitive to this exculpatory displacement: "the ornamentes" with which poets "beautifye their woorkes" are "the Cuppes of *Circes*, that turne reasonable creatures into brute Beastes.' "[73] Spenser defamiliarizes such clichés by taking them literally and treating them *as* displacements.

One of the strategies of textual critique is to represent the standpoint of the slandered scapegoat and have its agents talk back to temperance. Phaedria is the most loquacious of these agents, but I'm not sure "talk back" is the right expression for Cissie and Flossie, who are not major players and are not much with words, but who make a big splash in a deceptively small pool.[74] Inasmuch as they caricature not only heroic wrestling but also the pornographic fantasy they objectify, the bathers dramatize male self-mockery and self-despite. To see their contribution in this light is to see it as the acknowledgment both of self-disempowerment and of the slanderous reduction of woman to a spectral displacement that taunts its maker.

* * *

> The enforcement of temperance begins to demand forms of extreme violence that replicate the forces it intends to harness.[75]

The conventional focus on the quest formula encouraged by the titular emphasis, "The Legend of Sir Guyon, or Of Temperaunce," may divert attention from the scenario announced in the *Letter to Raleigh* and disclosed by Guyon to Medina at II.ii.43: the primary conflict in Book II is between the Palmer and Acrasia, with Guyon serving an instrumental function. Compared to Redcross's quest, Guyon's is, if anything, anti-erotic in the sense that he is less uncomfortable dealing with the dangers of irascibility than with those of concupiscence.[76] But his discomfort, which is comically featured in the Phaedria episode, is perforce thematized and amplified by the fact that his guide's major objective lies in the area of gender politics. And in this area the Palmer has problems of his own. Of the several flaws isolated by Anderson in her persuasive analysis of his early responses, the major ones concern his labored "Aesopic" aetiology of the stream that won't wash off the bloody-handed babe (II.ii.5–10) and his hilariously self-assured and misdirected insistence that heterosexual love is the filthy root of Phedon's problem (iv.34–35).[77] The former, as Anderson notes, "is basically a presentation of extreme opposites, of passionate lust and frigid purity" (162), with the Palmer praising the transformation of the nymph's "stony feare" into the "vertues" that make the water "chast and pure, as purest snow,/Ne lets her waves with any filth be dyde,/But ever like her selfe unstained hath beene tryde" (II.ii.8–9).[78]

It is generally agreed that the appearance of the angel and Arthur, along with the reappearance of the Palmer, around the stuprate Guyon in canto viii signal "a significant change [for the better] in the relationship of the Palmer to Guyon."[79] Guyon, at least, doesn't ramble off on his own, and for most of the next three cantos the reader gets a vacation from the Palmer. But after he returns in canto xii to take charge of the final leg of the quest, a significant change of another kind appears. When his staff was first described in II.i.7, emphasis fell on its allegorical potency as an ethical symbol: pointing the way was conflated with the restraining influence of words and reason. But in canto xii this potency is no longer adequate to the challenges that confront temperance. The "vertuous staffe" (II.xii.26, 86) becomes charged with thaumaturgical power; its "vertue" consists more in its magical than in its moral force. That force, and the objective it serves, are validated by assimilation to Biblical and classical precedents. Nevertheless, a review of its actual uses indicates that the very passages in which an august phallic genealogy is affirmed are the passages that most betray the phallic impotency of temperance as a defence against *akrasia*.

During canto xii, the Palmer delivers three strikes with his staff. First, after calming the terrified hero with the information that the sea monsters are illusions concocted by Acrasia to scare him off, he lifted "up his vertuous staffe on hye" and "smote the sea, which calmed was with speed" (II.xii.26).[80] This invests the action with the authority of multiple distinguished precedents covering all cultural bases: Moses in the Old Testament (Exodus 14–16), Christ in the New Testament (Matthew 8.26), and the classicized Hermit of Ascalon in *Gerusalemme Liberata* (XIV.73). To some extent, such allusionary overkill has a compensatory feel to it. Next, he quells the raging beasts outside the Bower with "His mighty staffe, that could all charmes defeat" and all "monsters . . . subdew to him, that did it beare," so that "In stead of fraying, they them selves did feare." The virtue of the staff is now identified with that of Mercury's caduceus (II.xii.40–41), and this association, together with the Palmer's subsequent actions, in turn identify the "vertue" of his staff with that of moly, Hermes's gift to Odysseus. Finally, when our heroes encounter Acrasia's beasts on their way out, Guyon asks what they "meant" and the Palmer tells him they are her "transformed" lovers, "turned into figures hideous,/According to their mindes like monstruous."[81] Guyon then asks that they be restored to human form, and with the third stroke of his "vertuous staffe" the Palmer obliges (II.xii.85–86).

Thus it is not until canto xii that we discover the Palmer is a magus with arcane powers, powers that match or duplicate those of Acrasia, the effects of whose spells he can reverse.[82] From early in Book II he had expressed predictably strong opinions about temperance, chastity, and love, and had also shown himself in possession of esoteric knowledge.[83] But in canto xii he does and says things that mark him as an Acrasian insider, an expert on Acrasian affairs. And by relegating the restoration of her lovers to the Palmer, the text conspicuously departs from its Homeric source, in which a domesticated Circe helps the hero and restores the men with her wand and medicine. Although this comparison with Circe further demonizes Acrasia, it places the Palmer in a strangely ambiguous position. To the extent that his role and action are partly affined to and defined by those of Circe, they must also be partly affined to—and defined by?—those of Acrasia. As a female figure of evil, an intemperate witch with a classical pedigree, Acrasia is the dark double of the good and temperate male magus whose name evokes a Christian institution. But the duplicity of mirroring powers casts unarticulated shadows that link the Palmer vaguely with his enemies—with Archimago as well as with Acrasia.[84]

I conclude not with an anecdote but with a parable, the parable of Pinocchio and his nose: the more he lies the bigger it gets. This logic is inverted in the parable of the phallus: the bigger it gets the more it lies. In short, this is the logic of castration, and it is founded on the alienability of the phallus, which can express masculine power "only symbolically (that is . . . not sexually)" and which—for the very reason that it is not a body part—can too easily be alienated.[85]

As I suggest above, the anxiety it produces is figured in the first stanza of II.xii. in the strange depiction of the "goodly frame of Temperance." Book II ends with a victory for Acrasia in that the imperfect restoration of her victims—"they did unmanly looke" and resisted or resented their liberation—signifies a last-minute breach of the powers previously integrated by the ambiguous epithet "vertuous": the Palmer's staff retains its magical potency but his resort to the violence of magic testifies to the failure of moral authority and to the alienation of *akrasia* to Acrasia.[86]

It is true that one stroke of his "vertuous staffe" can return her victims to their original form and show them for what they are:

> Streight way he with his vertuous staffe them strooke,
> And streight of beasts they comely men became;
> Yet being men they did unmanly looke,
> And stared ghastly, some for inward shame,
> And some for wrath, to see their captive Dame.
>
> (II.xii.86)

But this is only the mirror of Acrasian enchantment, whereas the aim of any Mulcasterian pedagogue prepared to use the "Palmer wyth a Rodde" whenever necessary is to work the more difficult magic of reformation of which this easy metamorphosis is a hyperbole. The Palmer's stroke restores their shapes but fails to improve minds and wills still subject to *akrasia*. Such a conclusion justifies and underscores the sense of futility conveyed by the "rigour pittilesse" with which Guyon destroys the bower. To imagine that the Bower is simply located in a particular place is an idyllic evasion because it leads to the mistaken impression that "man" can get rid of it, destroy it, be free of it, and move on. But since the Bower is a literary topos, a place in male discourse (and the "mind"), making it vanish as a mimetic topos only ensures its continuing power over the mind as a literary topos.

I note above (p. 84) that Elizabeth Heale offers two different explanations of the assignment of responsibility for suspending the instruments of Acrasia's victims: (1) "the delinquency is Acrasia's," and (2) it "is a sign of Spenser's realism" that "those who willingly seek out" the Bower will not be freed "from themselves" either by its destruction or by "the action of the Palmer's staff." My conclusion is that these judgments are incompatible, or to put it more tendentiously, that the first is a mystification and misrepresentation of the second.[87] The true genesis of Acrasia and her power is disclosed by the figure of Grill, who "chooseth, with vile difference,/To be a beast, and lacke intelligence" (II.xii.87). Although the Palmer characterizes this as "foule incontinence," a precise Aristotelian would note that what was just described is not incontinence but stubborn and dedicated intemperance: not *being* victimized but *getting* victimized; not lacking intelligence but choosing to lack it—disowning knowledge, "suspending" one's "instruments"—and thereby alienating the control of one's *akrasia* to its figural fullfillment in Acrasia. Grill represents what Guyon, his Palmer, and temperance fear to be, and what they blame on Acrasia. Or so it seems in 2002 as I continue to wonder what would have happened to Acrasia had the Palmer "with his vertuous staffe her strooke."

NOTES

1. I dedicate this essay to the Spenserians who, during this time, have been and remain my best critics and most sympathetic readers. It gives me great pleasure to express my gratitude to them for the enduring friendship and resistance that keeps me almost as honest (I hope) as they are.

Many thanks also to John Watkins for his careful and sensitive response to the original version of this essay. His suggestions for revision were extraordinarily helpful and led me to develop or modify my argument in a number of passages.

2. It's easy to make this sort of condescending remark so many decades later. But it would be both unfair and ungenerous to ignore the fact that the contributors to the *Variorum* edition made it possible for subsequent generations of readers to identify the traditional discursive landscape, the field of allusion, within which *The Faerie Queene* situates itself and from which it differentiates itself. The *Variorum* is much more than a storehouse of "sources and analogues" embellished with commentaries shaped by now obsolete categorical presuppositions. The citations and interpretations of such commentators as Upton, Kitchin, and Lemmi compose into a remarkable achievement. I often find myself reversing their opinions or putting them in scare quotes on the way to a more "ironic" reading. But the point about this is that my formulations remain parasitic on theirs. In some ways the most valuable replacement for and successor to the *Variorum* commentary is the Sidney-Spenser Discussion List.

3. John Webster, "Oral Form and Written Craft in Spenser's *Faerie Queene*," *Studies in English Literature* 16 (1976): 75–93.

4. Joel Fineman, *Shakespeare's Perjured Eye: The Invention of Poetic Subjectivity in the Sonnets* (Berkeley: University of California Press, 1986), 27.

5. Kenelm Digby, *A Discourse Concerning Edmund Spenser*, in *Spenser: The Critical Heritage*, ed. R. M. Cummings (New York: Barnes and Noble, 1971), 150. Thanks for this reference to William A. Oram, who cites it during a discussion of allegory

in his excellent chapter on the 1590 *Faerie Queene*: see Oram, *Edmund Spenser* (New York: Twayne Publishers, 1997), 77.

6. Mieke Bal, "De-disciplining the Eye," *Critical Inquiry* 16 (1990): 508, 506.

7. For more on this, see my "Archimago: Between Text and Countertext," *Studies in English Literature* 43, 1 (Winter, 2003): 20–32.

8. Gordon Teskey, *Allegory and Violence* (Ithaca: Cornell University Press, 1996), 23. See also Susanne Wofford, *The Choice of Achilles: The Ideology of Figure in the Epic* (Stanford: Stanford University Press, 1992), Chapters 4 and 5.

As Teskey observes elsewhere, when we adopt "the picture theory of language" that places "absolute meaning beyond words," the theory that underwrites the tradition of allegorical poetry, "we imagine that what is really true exists only in an empyrean of visual forms transcending language and cleansed of acoustic impurity" (Teskey, "Allegory," in *The Spenser Encyclopedia*, ed. A. C. Hamilton, et al. [1990; rpt. Toronto: University of Toronto Press, 1997], 21).

9. Countertextuality has a long history. We've been told that one picture is worth a thousand words since the early Middle Ages, when visual images were called the bible of the illiterate, who could look at them while they were hearing ritual and homiletic speech acts. In his famous vindication of images, Gregory the Great (c.540–604) writes that "the picture is for simple men what writing is for those who can read, because those who cannot read see and learn from the picture the model they should follow. Thus pictures are above all for the instruction of the people" (*Epistula ad Serenum*, trans. Wladislaw Tatarkiewicz, *History of Aesthetics*, vol. 2, *Medieval Aesthetics* [The Hague: Mouton, 1970], 104–105).

Some seven centuries later, around 1285, William Durand uses Gregory's dictum to introduce a discussion of church pictures: "what writing supplies to him who can read, a picture supplies to him who is unlearned and can only look. Because they who are uninstructed thus see what they ought to follow: and things are read, though letters be unknown." A little later he again cites Gregory on the value of pictures: "paintings appear to move the mind more than [written] descriptions: for deeds are placed before the eyes in paintings, and so appear to be actually going on. But in [written] descriptions, the deed is done as it were by hearsay: which affects the mind less when recalled to memory. Thus it is that in churches we pay less reverence to books than to images and pictures" (William Durandus, *Rationale of the Divine Offices*, trans. J.M. Neale and B. Webb, in *A Documentary History of Art*, vol. 1, *The Middle Ages and the Renaissance*, ed. Elizabeth Gilmore Holt [Princeton: Princeton University Press, 1981; orig. pub. 1957], 121, 123). Notice that this is more tendentious than the preceding statement, which only vindicates images as a kind of stopgap, a second-best if not a last resort. This one implies on the contrary that even if you can read words you'll get more out of "reading" pictures; the instruction will be more effective because more affecting; the indoctrination will be more thorough, will go deeper, because the medium of instruction is more vivid and immediate.

10. See Teskey, "Allegory," in *The Spenser Encyclopedia*, 21–22.

11. Elizabeth Heale, *The Faerie Queene*: A Reader's Guide (Cambridge: Cambridge University Press, 1987), 48.

12. See Sarah Greenleaf Whittier, *The Rhetoric of Embowerment: Evasive (In)action in the Lyric Poetry of Sidney, Spenser, Donne, and Marvell*, PhD. thesis, University of California-Santa Cruz, 1997.

13. Wofford, *The Choice of Achilles*, 306.

14. Heale, The Faerie Queene: *A Reader's Guide*, 48.

15. Colin Burrow, "Spenser and Classical Traditions," in *The Cambridge Companion to Spenser*, ed. Andrew Hadfield (Cambridge: Cambridge University Press, 2000), 224.

16. Mary Ellen Lamb, "Gloriana, Acrasia, and the House of Busirane: Gendered Fictions in *The Faerie Queene* as Fairy Tale," in *Worldmaking Spenser: Explorations in the Early Modern Age*, ed. Patrick Cheney and Lauren Silberman (Lexington: University Press of Kentucky, 2000), 95.

17. This is simply a way to convert a common idea about displacement into a structured practice of redistributing complicities—an idea compactly expressed in Judith Anderson's observation that Redcross "saw, or thought he saw, something wrong outside him when he was really seeing the result of something wrong within" (*The Growth of a Personal Voice: "Piers Plowman" and "The Faerie Queene"* [New Haven: Yale University Press, 1976], 52–53).

18. John E. Hankins, "Acrasia," in *The Spenser Encyclopedia*, 6. In both Heale's and Hankins's statements, "represents" carefully muffles any attribution of agency. Instead of "represents," Heale could have written "possesses" and Hankins "engages in."

19. Hankins, *Source and Meaning in Spenser's Allegory* (Oxford: Clarendon Press, 1971), 56.

20. See my "Narrative as Rhetoric in *The Faerie Queene*," *English Literary Renaissance* 21 (1991): 16–17, 34–35, for the argument that the castle's assailants are created and evacuated by repressive exorcism, "avoided quite, and throwne out privily" (II.ix.32), an argument first worked out by Silberman in "*The Faerie Queene*, Book II and the Limitations of Temperance," *Modern Language Studies*, 17. 4 (1987): 9–22. Maleger's troops are clearly stated to represent such internal properties as "lawlesse lustes" and "corrupt envies" (II.xi.8). "Foolish delights and fond abusions" are "by . . . ugly formes . . . pourtrayd" (II.xi.11). Hamilton's casual gloss on a line in II.xi.9 perfectly expresses the general logic of Malegerian displacement in these terms, but expresses it in reverse: "The attack from without is interpreted as an attack from within" (*FQ* 274).

21. Lamb, 93.

22. Theresa Krier, *Gazing on Secret Sights : Spenser, Classical Imitation, and the Decorums of Vision* (Ithaca: Cornell University Press, 1990); Silberman, "*The Faerie Queene*, Book II and the Limitations of Temperance," 9. The view that Spenser undermines his own allegory in Book II was put with great force by Madelon Sprengnether Gohlke in "Embattled Allegory: Book II of *The Faerie Queene*," *English Literary Renaissance*, 8 (1978): 123–40. My debt to this important essay is obvious. But I'm also deeply indebted to Krier's subtle elaboration of the idea that "a contest of genres" occurs in canto xii of Book II "as Guyon struggles to remain the hero of a moralized epic and to avoid the medieval romance and romance-epic elements of his book" (99). The action is divided "between a heavily traditional moral-allegorical journey over perilous seas and a heavily traditional romance garden devoted to pleasures 'not of the purest kind.' Both of these settings are indebted in part to the *Odyssey*," and the journey is also affiliated with the *Aeneid*, and before

we enter the bower and encroach on Tasso turf we briefly revisit the Phaedrian Idleness that indexes the *Romance of the Rose* (100–102; quoted passage on 100). David Quint's exploration of generic contestation in *Epic and Empire: Politics and Generic Form from Virgil to Milton* (Princeton: Princeton University Press, 1993) deals only incidentally with *The Faerie Queene.*

23. Jonathan Goldberg, *Endlesse Worke: Spenser and the Structures of Discourse* (Baltimore: Johns Hopkins University Press, 1981), 18–19. See the essays in the excellent collection edited by Krier, *Refiguring Chaucer in the Renaissance* (Gainesville: University Press of Florida, 1998), especially those by Craig Berry and Anderson.

24. Discussing the "English impatience with" and "demystification of courtly fictions," Michael McKeon calls Chaucer and the *Gawain* poet "the greatest proponents of . . . English romance as counterromance": McKeon, *The Origins of the English Novel, 1600–1740* (Baltimore: Johns Hopkins University Press, 1987), 146–47. Is *The Faerie Queene* then a countercounterromance?

25. Much of this paragraph repeats, in slightly varied form, comments that appear in my "Archimago: Between Text and Countertext" (see note 7 above), 29–30.

26. For a sympathetic and illuminating appreciation of Lewis, see Paul Alpers's entry on "The Bower of Bliss" in *The Spenser Encyclopedia,* 106.

27. A.C. Hamilton, ed., *Spenser: The Faerie Queene* (1977; rpt. New York: Longman, 1980), 294. Abbreviated to Hamilton, *FQ*, in subsequent references.

28. A. Bartlett Giamatti, *The Earthly Paradise and the Renaissance Epic* (Princeton: Princeton University Press, 1966).

29. Alpers deduces from the line, "The art, which all that wrought, appeared in no place" (II.xii.58), that Spenser "does not attribute his false paradise to the magic of its reigning sorceress." Rather, the phrase "directly invokes a topos of aesthetic praise; nor can he evade his own complicity in this paradise since 'the art which all that wrought' is in some sense his own" (Alpers, "The Bower of Bliss," 107). Yet nowhere does Spenser expressly distinguish the magic that produced Acrasia's illusions and metamorphoses from the magic that produced the Bower. Rather, he leaves the question of the source conspicuously open. If it is represented as "in some sense his own," the qualification makes room for the possibility that it is represented as in some sense not his own. As Alpers notes of the repeated hearsay formulas in the Gardens of Adonis passage, they "remind us that the myth is a creation of many men and has taken on a life of its own;" a life, he adds, that is "independent but still obviously capable of nourishing an individual poet" (*The Poetry of "The Faerie Queene"* [Princeton: Princeton University Press, 1967], 328).

30. In the course of insisting that Spenser attributes all evil agency to Acrasian art and magic, Giamatti takes exception to Robert Durling's gloss on the lines in stanza 42 that describe the Bower as "A place picked out by choice of best alive/That nature's work by art can imitate." Durling claims that Spenser distinguishes between art and magic, reserving the former term for the "artfulness of the human intellect." From this he deduces that Spenser presents the Bower as "an actual place which has been chosen, as it were, by a committee of experts, as most suited to their purposes" ("The Bower of Bliss and Armida's Palace," *Comparative Literature* 6 [1954]: 341). Giamatti dismisses out of hand the managerial fantasy in which Acrasia gets supplanted by this "anonymous committee" and by "sinister technological forces"

(256). This is precisely the fantasy I want to reinstate as the only one capable of taking into account the theme of self-delusion and the action of specular tautology. We don't need to retain the invidious managerial figure. Hamilton's simple gloss on the lines in question makes the point: "A place picked out by choice of best alive/ That nature's work by art can imitate." "For the poet," he writes, "art is the literary tradition of the locus amoenus which he picks out 'by choice of best alive', chiefly" the isles of Alcida and Armida (Hamilton, *FQ*, 288). Notice that Hamilton associates the sorceresses with their isles, not with their art; the art belongs partly to the ("committee" of) poetic experts who create them and partly to the corporate body of discourse, the collective expert, their work metonymically signifies.

Of course, Giamatti doesn't ignore this literary tradition. On the contrary, in both *The Earthly Paradise* and *Play of Double Senses: Spenser's "Faerie Queene"* (1975; rpt. New York: Norton, 1990), he treats literary emulation as a defining performative feature of Renaissance epic, for example, "Renaissance poets ennoble their matter by consciously surpassing previous literary images of nobility" (*Play of Double Senses*, 23). It is important, however, to distinguish emulation or overgoing from parody and critique, especially when the "matter" in question concerns attitudes toward misogyny.

31. Northrop Frye, *The Secular Scripture: A Study of the Structure of Romance* (Cambridge, Mass.: Harvard University Press, 1976), 28–30, 168.

32. See, generally, " 'Kidnapped Romance': Discourse in *The Faerie Queene*" in *Unfolded Tales: Essays on Renaissance Romance,* ed. George Logan and Gordon Teskey (Ithaca: Cornell University Press, 1989), 208–56. On the critique of Protestant ideology, see "Sexual and Religious Politics in Book I of Spenser's *Faerie Queene*," forthcoming in *English Literary Renaissance.*

33. Stephen Greenblatt, *Renaissance Self-Fashioning: From More to Shakespeare* (Chicago: The University of Chicago Press, 1980), 157–92. See especially the turn from close reading to "cultural poetics" and politics that begins on p.177 and continues to the end of the chapter.

34. Claire McEachern, *The Poetics of English Nationhood, 1590–1612* (Cambridge: Cambridge University Press, 1996). See further my "Sexual and Religious Politics in Book I of '*Spenser's Faerie Queene*' " (full reference, note 31 above).

35. See George Puttenham, *The Arte of English Poesie*, ed. Gladys Doidge Willcock and Alice Walker (1936; rpt. Cambridge: Cambridge University Press, 1970), 215–16.

36. See Carol Kaske's stimulating discussions of *correctio* in *Spenser and Biblical Poetics* (Ithaca: Cornell University Press, 1999), 65–97, 121–30, 180–81, and passim. See also my "Displacing Autophobia in *Faerie Queene* I: Ethics, Gender, and Oppositional Reading in the Spenserian Text," *English Literary Renaissance* 28 (1998): 163–82.

37. Debora Kuller Shuger, *The Renaissance Bible: Scholarship, Sacrifice, and Subjectivity* (Berkeley: University of California Press, 1994), 191.

38. Ibid.

39. The identification of the tripartite soul as masculine is clearly implied in Tasso's Allegory to *Gerusalemme liberata*. He flatly proposes Godfrey and Rinaldo as symbols of the rational and irascible faculties, but fails to do the same for the concupiscible

faculty, which therefore remains open to whatever invests, or attacks and occupies, it from the outside, and this power is of course feminized: "Armida is the temptation that sets snares for the appetitive faculty": Torquato Tasso, *Jerusalem Delivered*, trans. and ed. Ralph Nash (Detroit: Wayne State University Press, 1987), 474, 471.

40. Hamilton, *FQ*, 251.

41. Hankins, *Source and Meaning*, 128. Hankins is serious about this distinction. He argues that for Guyon, the dangers that "lurk in the environment about him . . . might" include such "corporal" temptations as "the proximity of a brothel or acquaintance with a 'free love' society. Yet these external hazards are dangerous only in so far as they find a response within the man himself and become a part of his internal warfare by moving his fantasy, perplexing his judgement, and stirring his emotions" (57). "They" are the initiators, and the momentary emphasis on *his* assent is overborne by the series of participles emphasizing *their* assault.

42. The final couplet has the hollow ring of obligatory applause, and virtue's vaunting will soon prove premature. When the narrative confronts Guyon with Phaedria eighteen stanzas later, it places him in an uncomfortable position and doesn't let him off the hook. On the contrary, it gives him enough play to make his temperate floundering both awkward and ridiculous. The situation doesn't improve in canto vii, when Guyon goes off on his own, replaces virtue as the vaunter, and, in a strangely scrambled appetitive figure, "himself with comfort feedes,/Of his owne vertues and prayse-worthy deedes" (II.vii.2).

43. Stephen Orgel, *Impersonations: The Performance of Gender in Shakespeare's England* (Cambridge: Cambridge University Press, 1996), 26.

44. Louis Adrian Montrose, "The Elizabethan Subject and the Spenserian Text," in *Literary Theory/Renaissance Texts*, ed. Patricia Parker and David Quint (Baltimore: Johns Hopkins University Press, 1986), 329. The phrase, "objectified other," is either redundant or else it alludes to a prior process of objectifying displacement in the mode of specular tautology, which is of course the way I choose to read it.

45. Michael C. Schoenfeldt, *Bodies and Selves in Early Modern England: Physiology and Inwardness in Spenser, Shakespeare, Herbert, and Milton* (Cambridge: Cambridge University Press, 1999), 73. See also the shorter version of this chapter, "The Construction of Inwardness in *The Faerie Queene*, Book II," in *Worldmaking Spenser*, 234–43. Time and again, Schoenfeldt brilliantly describes the anxiety and masculine insecurity he associates with the discipline of temperance.

46. Schoenfeldt, *Bodies and Selves in Early Modern England*, 57. It can't help that most of the real estate mentioned in Book II is owned by women (Medina, Phaedria, Alma, Acrasia).

47. It is worth noting that the conventional Greek term for "temperance" "self-control," "moderation," etc., is *sophrosyne*, and that this word, like its cognate, *sophron* (temperate, chaste, discreet, self-controlled), is etymologically connected to *sos* ("safe"). *Sophrosyne* may be translated as "safemindedness," a sense Plato often has Socrates feature in his ironic paraphrases of apprehensive interlocutors for whom to be temperate is primarily to protect oneself from the imagined *pleonexia* of one's fellow citizens. I suggest that the temperance represented in Book II and well described by Schoenfeldt is this form of safemindedness, or apprehensiveness, or fear of castration.

48. See the excellent comments by Oram, *Edmund Spenser*, 97–102. In attributing Guyon's limitations to those of "the kind of temperance he demonstrates" (98), Oram follows the line laid out by Hamilton in *The Structure of Allegory in "The Faerie Queene"* (London: Oxford University Press, 1961), 90–123, but his critique is more sharply and pungently attentive to the effects of the normative virtue on behavioral style.

49. "In his *Shorte Dictionarie for yonge begynners*, published in 1553, John Withals includes the following terms as among the essential vocabulary for 'The Schole with that belongeth therto'; 'a rod to doe correction with; to beate; to be beaten; A palmer to beate or strike scholers in the hande' . . . and, most alarmingly, 'the marke or prynte of a hurt in the body' "(Alan Stewart, *Close Readers: Humanism and Sodomy in Early Modern England* [Princeton: Princeton University Press, 1997], 93). The essay that most suggestively hints at the link between the representation of Acrasia and the aims and effects of humanist pedagogy is Lamb's "Gloriana, Acrasia, and the House of Busirane." See note 9 above.

The whole of Stewart's chapter on "the erotics of humanist education" (*Close Readers*, 84–121) is relevant and valuable as a background to Lamb's account because of its development of the thesis that "the value of the educational experience of a young man as a rite of passage or an act of institution—the making of the man—is fundamentally threatened by that experience itself" (102). See also Richard Halpern, *The Poetics of Primitive Accumulation: English Renaissance Culture and the Genealogy of Capital* (Ithaca: Cornell University Press, 1991), 21–60; Mary Thomas Crane, *Framing Authority: Sayings, Self, and Society in Sixteenth-Century England* (Princeton: Princeton University Press, 1993), 77–92 and passim. These references to and comments on humanist pedagogy are heavily indebted to Lynn Enterline's work in progress, "Imitating Schoolboys," and I am grateful to her for sharing it with me.

50. On the alienability of the phallus and its necessary dissociation from the organic body, see Mikkel Borch-Jacobsen, *Lacan: The Absolute Master*, trans. Douglas Brick (Stanford: Stanford University Press, 1991), 205–19.

51. "Like the staff of Mercury to which it is kin," Patricia Parker writes, the Palmer's staff "is able both to recall souls from the symbolic Hades of subjection to female power and also to 'rule the *Furyes*, when they most do rage' " (*Literary Fat Ladies: Rhetoric, Gender, Property* [London: Methuen, 1987], 59). The narrator, it is true, states that when Mercury "wonts the *Stygian* realmes invade," he uses his rod to rule the Furies, tame Orcus, and "asswage" the infernal fiends (xii.41). But he says nothing about recalling souls; the psycho-pomp function is a familiar enough aspect of this motif that many Spenserians (including Hamilton, *FQ* 288) mention it; therefore a closer look makes its exclusion here noteworthy. The staff of Temperance is impotent to recall souls from Acrasia's power. "Wonts . . . invade" indicates a practice that is habitual or recurrent, presumably because the temperance imposed by the rod is at best temporary; a practice that is both aggressive and relatively ineffective. In addition, it is a power that depends on, gets its energy and indeed its raison d'être from, the Acrasian power it opposes.

52. In the first of the two stanzas that describe this gate (II.xii.44–45) the sole reference to Medea picks out "Her mighty charmes, her furious loving fit." This is followed by four lines about Jason, the one mentioning his infidelity surrounded

(and minimized) by three that praise his heroic adventure. The second stanza intersperses within its admiration of the gate's artifice references to Medea's filicide and her murder of Creüsa. This shift of emphasis from Jason's heroics to Medea's crimes contributes to the general redistribution of complicity from male to female agencies that marks the narrative progress of canto xii. Perhaps that is the burden of the gate's false dream.

53. On Spenserian *katabasis*, see the excellent comments by John Watkins in *The Specter of Dido* (New Haven: Yale University Press, 1995), 103–108. See also my "Archimago: Between Text and Countertext" (full reference, note 7 above).

54. Greenblatt, *Renaissance Self-Fashioning,* 177. Excess is in fact personified in canto xii and associated with a transfer of power from male to female figures that takes place between stanzas 46 and 57. First we encounter Genius, the keeper of the ivory Medea gate, who is represented as the dark mirror of our true "Selfe" and who "of this Gardin had the governall," an office represented by the "staffe" he held "for more formalitee." After we read that he "With diverse flowres . . . daintily was deckt" (49) and that Guyon violently if easily broke his staff—no surprises here—we are given an account of the spacious plain "beautifide/With all the ornaments of Floraes pride,/Wherewith her mother Art . . . did decke her, and too lavishly adorne" (50). And after this the broken baton is handed on, so to speak, to the second gate-keeper, Dame Excess, where it becomes a gold cup, in which the plump inhabitants of a lascivious viticulture offer themselves to be "scruzd" by "All passers-by." That resonant word "scruzd" is memorable enough for us to recall and compare its previous occurrence at II.xi.46, when Arthur "scruzd" the life out of Maleger and threw him into a "standing lake."

55. See notes 20 and 22 above. Silberman argues, for example, that Maleger's assault is an effect rather than the cause of the strategies of defense embodied in and as the castle of temperance and that in the Bower of Bliss, "Spenser strips the veil from the sexual fear that motivates the elaborate sensual defenses of Book II" (19).

56. Orgel, *Impersonations*, 26.

57. See the repetitions of "he" and "his" in II.xii.3–6.

58. In a marvelous essay written long before colonialist critique came into fashion, Martha Craig suggestively comments on the way the episodes in canto xii's Odysseyan voyage allude to "the goals of the Elizabethan Merchant Adventurers" and "the ports they sought in ships like the 'Delight', the 'Desire,' and the 'Castle of Comfort' as they sailed for the expected sweet life of the West Indies." Craig cites references such as those to "thrift" and "credit" in support of the reading that "the journey to the Bower of Bliss reveals the financial disasters that resulted from adventuring in the hope of perfect pleasure." See Craig, "The Secret Wit of Spenser's Language," in *Elizabethan Poetry: Modern Essays in Criticism*, ed. Paul Alpers (New York: Oxford University Press, 1967), 465. The importance of her reading for my argument is that its focus is on a reference to male-identified ventures—commercial ventures—whose erotic charge may be more homosocial and romantic (as in "Westward ho!") than sexual, but whose romantic and mercantile trajectories may always be disrupted by the adventurers' vulnerability to *akrasia* in the form of "wanton joys and lusts intemperate" (II.xii.7).

More recently, the connection between romance and trade in the epic tradition from the *Odyssey* on was the subject of a perceptive analysis by David Quint in *Epic and Empire*, 248–67. Epic, he observes, "traditionally aligns itself with aristocratic, martial values; when, in the context of the voyages of discovery, it casts romance as its alternative 'other', it lends a mercantile, bourgeoise cast to the romance adventure" (248). Indeed, "The Rocke of Vile Reproch" is a conspicuously aristocratic epithet, associated with "fame for ever fowly blent" and with "shame and sad reproch" (II.xii.7, 9), as befits the moral education of "an Elfin borne of noble state" (II.i.6). But perhaps the process Quint finds Milton responding to is already at work during the sixteenth century: "the emergence of a merchant class" whose members "not only contested with the nobleman for power but also laid claim to the nobleman's very nobility" (265). For some evidence of this emergence see the data and interpretation provided by David Harris Sacks for Bristol in *The Widening Gate: Bristol and the Atlantic Community, 1450–1700* (1991; rpt. Berkeley: University of California Press, 1993), 85–127.

59. At II.i.51, Amavia refers to Acrasia's dwelling as situated "Within a wandring Island, that doth ronne/And stray in perilous gulfe." This would make it part of the same fantasy. However, the insularity of Acrasia's dwelling is not mentioned in canto xii.

60. Craig, ibid., 464. Thanks to Judith Anderson for reminding me of "frigate," which I had completely overlooked.

61. Phaedria reappears in stanza 14 as part of the topographia of the "Wandring Islands" and after they have been compared to the pre-Apollonian Delos in stanza 13. Once again, Craig's telling comment emphasizes the phantasmagoric character of this appearance: "the classical Delos, which Spenser etymologizes traditionally to *dêlos*, apparent because the islands simply appeared out of nowhere" (466).

62. "Secret Wit," 464, 466. See Roger Ascham, *The Schoolmaster*, ed. Lawrence V. Ryan (Ithaca: Cornell University Press, 1967), 62–63, 69, 73. See also the apposite comments by James Nohrnberg in *The Analogy of* The Faerie Queen (Princeton: Princeton University Press, 1976), 294n.14.

63. What could be cheekier than to lead off with a salutation more suitable to the Sermonizer on the Mount: "Behold, O man"! It's for this reason that I prefer the 1596 description of her performance, "with *a loud lay* she thus him sweetly charm'd" (my italics), to the 1590 "with a love-lay."

To be more specific about the work the allusion does, Christ's injunction to serve God rather than riches (Matthew 6:25–34) is mediated through and wickedly turned awry by the song of Armida's seductive bather (*Ger. Lib.* XIV. 62–64). Conspicuous allusion asks the reader not only to "consider the source" but also to consider the way it is characterized. In the ambages of epico-romantic discourse even Christ's words may be kidnapped, then contaminated, by the seducers of heroes.

This performance articulates the countermessage to Belphoebe's exhortation to honor (II.iii.50–52). In doing so it may remind us how ridiculously unworldly it was of Belphoebe to waste her pep talk on so inappropriate a recipient as Braggadocchio, the description of whom at II.iii.34–37 undermines the rhetorical purpose of her speech in advance.

64. Richard Helgerson, *The Elizabethan Prodigals* (Berkeley: University of California Press, 1976), chapter 2 and *passim*. In his subsequent study of the laureate system, Helgerson ingeniously shows how the poets of the next generation reversed the

prodigals' strategy and modeled the laureate role on "humanist ideals of sobriety, measure, and deliberation" (*Self-Crowned Laureates: Spenser, Jonson, Milton and the Literary System* [Berkeley: University of California Press, 1983], 33). But even though the laureate "presented himself as a poet, as a man who considered writing a duty rather than a distraction" (55), the "seductive, exuberant, self-regarding energy . . . [Spenser, Jonson, and Milton] condemn bears a troubling likeness to the energy of their own art. Surely Spenser owes as much to the sensual delight *of* Acrasia . . . as . . . to the counterforces of morally righteous judgment" (9–10, my italics). Is the italicized "of" an objective or subjective genitive? His delight in her or "her" delight? The claim that Guyon's destruction of the Bower represents the poet's overreaction to the Acrasian prodigality of his art (86–87) oddly diffuses the situation by psychologizing it: if the poet identifies himself with—reduces himself to—his protagonist, is his violence directed only at his own poetic energy or at his vulnerability to the seductiveness of the temptress he imagines or mentally "sees"? If *her* "sensual delight" is only the mirror and effect of *his*, such outwardly directed violence must be not merely futile but also self-deluding.

65. The replay is skewed in part because Phaedria, unlike Medina, is motivated not by an impartial desire to moderate extremes of behavior and restore the mean but by a desire to save Cymochles, who is in "deadly daunger," Guyon having just cleft "his head unto the bone" (II.vi.31–32).

66. For me, the most sensitive and nuanced reading of this episode remains that of Paul Alpers in *The Poetry of "The Faerie Queene"* (Princeton: Princeton University Press, 1967), 316–18.

67. For an excellent account of Spenser's departures from Tasso, see Durling, "The Bower of Bliss and Armida's Palace," 113–24 passim. Durling's amplification of C.S. Lewis's "skeptophilia" thesis is especially important: "the lust of the eyes is a technique of exquisite protraction of desire" in which the mind is "actively engaged in corrupting the appetite" (119). But whose mind? When Durling describes the self-corruption of the soul by intemperance, he clearly indicates the male soul, but when he refers to the narrative his emphasis is on "the lewdness of Spenser's bathers" and on Acrasia's seductive power (118–19).

68. Hankins, *Source and Meaning in Spenser's Allegory*, 242, 246. See my "Actaeon at the Hinder Gate: The Stag Party in Spenser's Gardens of Adonis," in *Desire in the Renaissance: Psychoanalysis and Renaissance Literature,* ed. Regina Schwartz and Valeria Finucci (Princeton: Princeton University Press, 1994), 91–119.

69. Conti's statement in *Mythologiae* (4.13) that "Venus is nothing but the symbol of the sexual impulse," prompts the same old rhetorical question: *whose* sexual impulse? Cited by C. W. Lemmi in *The Works of Edmund Spenser: A Variorum Edition,* ed. Edwin Greenlaw, C. G. Osgood, F. M. Padelford, et al., 11 vols. (Baltimore: Johns Hopkins University Press, 1932–57), 2:369. Hereafter cited as *Var.* 2.

70. From the Amavia episode on, Book II returns repeatedly to images of dysfunctional families or households. The various threats and seductions inscribed in the Odysseian allusions focus on the conflict between *andreia* and *nostos*—between heroic self-affirmation as a threat to Family Values and the desire of homecoming that will reaffirm them but jeopardize the hero's autonomy. Spenser's "Cyprian goddesse, newly borne / Of th'Oceans fruitfull froth" derives ultimately from Hesiod's account

of a primal dysfunctional family romance, the nightmare of terrible fathers hating, burying, swallowing their sons, of the son mutilating the father, of the paternal organ begetting the archetypal seductress who will enact his revenge by her ability to disempower and emasculate his sons.

71. David Lee Miller, *The Poem's Two Bodies: The Poetics of the 1590 "Faerie Queeene"* (Princeton University Press, 1988), 191.

72. As Anderson brilliantly observes, "the first immediate vision" of Acrasia "is specifically the narrator's, since Guyon and the Palmer" are still creeping about in the bushes, and the stanza describing the vision acknowledges not only "the narrative's implication in Acrasian pleasure" but also the phantasmatic entanglement of Acrasia and Verdant in each other's dreams and in each other's sight: "her sight beholding, his sight beheld, and his sight beholding" ("Narrative Reflections: Re-envisaging the Poet in *The Canterbury Tales* and *The Faerie Queene*," in Krier, *Refiguring Chaucer in the Renaissance*, 99).

After the two creepers show up, but before they destroy the vision, the narrative joins the lovers when it steals one more longing look, perversely fixing and feeding its "hungry eies" on Acrasia's even after it has described "her false eyes fast fixed in . . . [Verdant's] sight" and "greedily depasturing delight" (xii.73). Thus floating into view on the strains of a medley of Tassonian and Chaucerian airs, and then fixed, trapped, *dis-played*, in the crossed sight-lines of discursive longing and protagonistic fury, Acrasia, as I note above (p. 107), emerges as the objectification of male hysteria.

73. Stephen Gosson, *The schoole of abuse* (1579; rpt. New York: Garland Publishing, 1973), B8^{v}, A2^{r-v}. Gosson's telltale formulations were drawn to my attention by James Nohrnberg. See *The Analogy of "The Faerie Queene,"* 509.

74. "Infinit streames . . . continually" welling out of this fountain, fell into "an ample laver," "and shortly grew to so great quantitie, / That like a little lake it seemd to bee." Its "depth exceeded not three cubits hight," and it "seemd the fountaine in that sea did sayle upright" (II.xii.62). Notice how the description makes the laver appear both to swell and to shrink in size. The upright fountain has been called a phallic object, but it is also an after-image of the boat of temperance; a representation of temperance installed in the center of the garden; an icon of the power and desire associated with and now dissociated from the natural male organ and placed, so to speak, in Acrasia's hands.

75. Schoenfeldt, *Bodies and Selves in Early Modern England*, 44.

76. Mammon is an exception but it is also anomalous in that it concerns itself with "lust of the eyes" or *curiositas*. This is one opinion expressed in *The Allegorical Temper* that I still endorse.

77. Anderson, "The Knight and the Palmer in *The Faerie Queene*, Book II," *Modern Language Quarterly*, 31 (1970): 160–78. See also my "Narrative as Rhetoric in *The Faerie Queene*," 29–32.

78. The Palmer concludes that since this water will not cleanse the bloody hands, they might as well remain bloody so they can serve as a symbol "to minde revengement, / And be for all chast Dames an endlesse moniment" (ii.10). What could that mean? "Endlesse moniment" raises the same question here that it does in *Epithalamion*. The Palmer's sympathy is with Amavia, whose innocence he upholds,

but the phrase suggests that the bloody hands will be as much a warning to chaste dames as a memorial. They need to avoid Amavia's predicament, and perhaps the best way to do that is to follow the nymph's example and try to "dye a mayd" (ii.8). For a subtle intertextual analysis of the episode that brings out its darker implications, see Carol Kaske, "The Bacchus Who Wouldn't Wash: *Faerie Queene* II, ii," *Renaissance Quarterly* 29 (1976): 195–209. My reading differs from Kaske's in centering on the episode's darker gender implications.

79. Anderson, "The Knight and the Palmer," 177.

80. Of this moment Wofford notes that "the 'vertuous staffe' of allegory . . . here as elsewhere seems to define the kind of interpretation practiced by the Palmer as a specifically male skill" (*Choice*, 251).

81. This phrase expresses the speaker's impatience: Circe's victims are fools; their metamorphosis was essentially self-inflicted; they got what they deserved.

82. Durling's formulation brings out this specularity: "the enchantments of Acrasia, whereby the men become beasts, and the workings of the palmer's staff, whereby the beasts are first calmed (Stanza 40) and then returned to human shape, are the only magical events which occur in the Bower of Bliss" ("The Bower of Bliss and Armida's Palace," 120).

83. In this connection, Charles Ross cites literary examples that suggest palmers were "not just those who went to Jerusalem in the literary imagination, but [also] spoil-sports, particularly in matters of love," and he adds that such a figure would therefore be appropriate "to guard the knight of Temperance"—presumably because he knows enough about the sport he is appointed to spoil to do so effectively, as is indicated by his knowledge and capture of Acrasia (communication to the Sidney-Spenser List dated 2/12/02). That there are limits to his knowledge and power is indicated by the ease with which Phaedria whisks Guyon away from him.

84. Compare the initial descriptions of Archimago and the Palmer:

> An aged Sire, in long blacke weedes yclad,
> His feete all bare, his beard all hoarie gray,
> And by his belt his booke he hanging had:
> Sober he seemde, and very sagely sad . . .
>
> (I.i.29)

> A comely Palmer, clad in blacke attire,
>   Of ripest yeares, and haires all hoarie gray,
> That with a staffe his feeble steps did stire,
> ....
>
> And if by lookes one may the mind aread,
> He seemd to be a sage and sober sire . . . .
>
> (II.i.7)

Archimago had masqueraded as a pilgrim in Book I (vi.35–48). Most obviously, the similarity announces congruence of function—both act as guides, assistants, mages, and instructors—together with moral polarity. But the Palmer seems to me to be a veiled signifier, presented in a manner guaranteed to arouse perplexity or uncertainty in readers. A clue to this lurks in Amavia's report that before going in search of Mordant, "Weake wretch I wrapt my selfe in Palmers weed" (II.i.52). In a communication to the Sidney-Spenser List dated 2/14/02, Jacqueline Miller observes that since Amavia was pregnant, this may raise "some interesting questions . . . about what the Palmer's weed . . . can be used to hide." See also Todd's quotation from the 1605 *History of King Leir* at *Var* 2.192: "we will go disguisde in palmers weeds,/ That no man shall mistrust us what we are," which is, incidentally, an untrustworthy thing to do. Since he is given no proper name, "the Palmer" may seem to some readers to have the valency of a disguise, though precisely what it disguises isn't clear.

In Book II, Archimago's track record as a counter-Palmer is unimpressive: after his little charade with Duessa is foiled, he falls for Braggadocchio's bluster in canto iii and gleefully flies off to procure him Arthur's sword. His finest moment occurs in canto vi when he shows up with the sword and manages to heal the wounds Furor inflicted on Pyrochles. But in his last stand in canto viii he tries unsuccessfully to persuade Pyrochles that the sword can't be used against its rightful owner, and this failure contributes to Pyrochles's undoing. The Palmer doesn't avail himself of his magical power until well after Archimago has gone.

85. Mikkel Borch-Jacobsen, *Lacan: The Absolute Master*, trans. Douglas Brick (Stanford: Stanford University Press, 1991), 210, 213.

86. Roland Greene has ingeniously hypothesized a binary model of discourse, distinguishing an "ambassadorial" from an "immanentist" model, the first "a model of alterity" whose "worlds are multiple and independent . . . of each other," and the second a model "of envelopment" in which "worlds are situated within each other." Greene is interested in exploring the operation in Spenser's poem of a process of "narrative subduction" through which "a poetics of embassy is empowered and then disempowered, alterity and the differentiations of worlds continually offered and continually taken away." Applying this hypothesis to the Bower leads him to conclude that its "essential character . . . crosses the illusion of immanence with the reality of embassy, confronting its visitors with . . . alterity disguised as a version, albeit brought up from the depths of the interior, of the self" ("A Primer of Spenser's Worldmaking: Alterity in the Bower of Bliss," in *Worldmaking Spenser*, 11, 16, 25). This seems to me to be a precise but precisely inverted characterization of the thesis of the present essay, which is that the essential character of the Bower crosses the illusion of embassy with the reality of immanence, confronting its visitors with the self disguised as a version, albeit brought up from the depths of the interior, of Acrasian alterity.

87. Many thanks to Charles Butler, who took this argument seriously enough to resist it, and whose resistance forced me to rethink it.

GORDON BRADEN

Pride, Humility, and the Petrarchan Happy Ending

Pride and humility are among the paired opposites so important to Renaissance Petrarchism. They sometimes figure in an assessment of the moral state of the male lover, but their most common usage is in connection with the female beloved, and often not in a high-minded way: the woman's resistance to her would-be seducer's suit is frequently attacked as a sin of pride. Spenser's *Amoretti* is particularly full of discussions of the woman's pride, but as part of an unconventional pattern: from the start that pride is both attacked and praised. This alternation is part of the dynamics of courtship as it is dramatized in the sequence, and also closely linked to the lover's early (and accurate) confidence that his suit will be successful. Understanding the pattern here can help allay the confusion caused by the superscription to sonnet 58, and also lead to a fresh appreciation of the conceits of sonnets 45 and 75.

PETRARCHAN LOVE POETRY IN THE SIXTEENTH century is a site where fiercely contrasting qualities meet, often at close range; among these warring pairs is that of pride and humility. Lovers, Pietro Bembo writes in his *Asolani* as he runs through the symptomology, "are overcome by opposite afflictions, and pride and humility (*orgoglio e umiltà*), impatience and misgiving, war and peace all equally assail them at one time" (1.12).[1] Here as elsewhere Bembo, the great systematizer of Petrarchan imitation, is being somewhat more schematic than Petrarch himself, but he is responding to significant features in his revered model. The last poem in Petrarch's sequence prays to the Virgin Mary for help in untangling this particular oxymoron:

Vergine umana et nemica d'orgoglio:
del comune principio amor t'induca
miserere d'un cor contrito umile.

Canzoniere 366.118–20

(Kindly Virgin, enemy of pride, let love of our common origin move you, have mercy on a contrite and humble heart.)[2]

The greatest sin weighing on the speaker's conscience, more grievous than that of mere lust, is what Augustine identified as the central, primal human sin; its antidote is the most important and difficult of Christian virtues. In the self-arraignment that Petrarch dramatizes in his prose *Secretum*, the spirit of Augustine remorselessly analyzes "the reasons that you are puffed up with pride (*superbis flatibus elatum*), that prevent you from recognizing your low estate (*humilitatem conditionis tue*)," and is especially concerned with pride's capacity for dressing itself as its opposite: "there was one thing out of all you said a moment ago which you probably thought was most humble, but which seemed supremely arrogant to me."[3] A decisive victory of humility over pride within the speaker's soul is, in one of its dimensions, the moral goal of Petrarch's *Canzoniere*, but so intimate are those opposites with one another that victory is only to be imagined with the aid of a greater than human power, the resources of one "che per vera et altissima umiltate/salisti al ciel" (*Canzoniere* 366.41–42; who through true and highest humility mounted to Heaven).

Altissima umiltate intensifies praise already bestowed on the dead Laura ("alta umiltate"; *Canzoniere* 325.8); the adjective is not strictly speaking a contradiction of the noun, but the wording shimmers on the edge of being its own kind of oxymoron. We find such an oxymoron in one of Petrarch's late letters (*Seniles* 5.2), where he turns Augustine's accusation against Boccaccio—"I fear that this fine humility of yours is pride"—and draws attention to the boldness of putting it this way: "The epithet *proud* applied to humility (*ut superba dicatur humilitas*) is new to many and perhaps startling."[4] The epithet is here unambiguously critical, but this application has a different destiny within the general economy of Petrarchism, where its main reference is to the demeanor of women. Laura's own behavior during her life attracts an adjective very close to *alta* but more sharply paradoxical in its potential: "Qui tutta umile et qui la vidi altera" (*Canzoniere* 112.5; Here I saw her all humble and there haughty). Bembo distills this conflict into a double formulation: "piano orgoglio et umiltate altera" (*Rime* 34.4; quiet pride and haughty humility). Tradition will favor the second alternative, and versions of it can be traced to some far corners; in late seventeenth-century Mexico, Sor Juana Inés de la Cruz will write approvingly of *una altiva humildad*.[5] In English dress, the phrase will find its way into Edmund Spenser's celebration of his own marriage, and be honored with a particularly provocative placement:

> Now bring the Bryde into the brydall boures.
> Now night is come, now soone her disaray,
> And in her bed her lay;
> Lay her in lillies and in violets,
> And silken courteins over her display,
> And odourd sheetes, and Arras coverlets.
> Behold how goodly my faire love does ly
> In proud humility.
>
> *Epithalamion* 299–306[6]

The poem's most recent editor calls this "a daring oxymoron"; my intent here is to trace some of the ways in which the *Amoretti* prepares for it.[7]

Carol V. Kaske, in the most significant discussion of this topic so far, is I think close to the mark; the phrase in the *Epithalamion* "represents mutuality of desire, the bride humble in her surrender to her husband, but the groom also now a servant to her awakened desire."[8] Poised just before the physical consummation of this desire, it plays against the specific history of its component terms in post-Petrarchan Petrarchism, where explicit references to pride predominantly concern the woman's pride rather than the man's, and in a particular and reduced sense. Pride is the woman's capacity for resisting her would-be lover's persuasion:

> Still must I whet my younge desires abated,
> Uppon the Flint of such a hart rebelling;
> And all in vaine, her pride is so innated,
> She yeeldes no place at all for pitties dwelling.
>
> Samuel Daniel, *Delia* 17.9–12[9]

This diagnosis of what makes women hard to get achieves wide currency. A speaker in Marguerite de Navarre's *Heptaméron* offers the opinion that "where women are concerned, it's pride (*l'orgueil*) that ousts desire much more than fear, or love of God" (26).[10] In a seventeenth-century poem by Mary, Lady Chudleigh that theory is taken cheerfully for granted in urging other women never to marry; the man's pride here reenters the equation to important effect:

Wife and Servant are the same,
But only differ in the Name:
For when that fatal Knot is ty'd,
Which nothing, nothing can divide:
When she the word *obey* has said,
And Man by Law supreme has made,
Then all that's kind is laid aside,
And nothing left but State and Pride:
Fierce as an Eastern Prince he grows,
And all his innate Rigor shows . . .
Then shun, oh! shun that wretched State,
And all the fawning Flatt'rers hate:
Value your selves, and Men despise,
You must be proud, if you'll be wise.
"To the Ladies," ll. 1–10, 21–24[11]

It comes down to a question of your pride or his, a zero-sum game whose logic by the end seems to exclude not only marriage but any erotic yielding. Chudleigh is calmly indifferent to the outrageous courtship strategy implied by the convention: link the woman's resistance to the deadliest of Christian sins, and so place her submission, with or without the sanction of marriage, on the side of virtue. Any admiration of male cleverness in this regard needs to be tempered by remembering the almost universal premise of unsuccess that accompanies Petrarchan sonneteering. At least in lyric poetry, the ploy almost never seems to work. It is certainly more influential as diagnosis than as strategy. It is impressively elaborated by Petrarch himself, in a rare reproach against Laura, when he blames her for the time she spends before her mirror:

Il mio adversario in cui veder solete
gli occhi vostri ch' Amore e 'l Ciel onora
colle non sue bellezze v'innamora
piùgrave che 'n guisa mortal soavi et liete.
Per consiglio di lui, Donna, m'avete
scacciato del mio dolce albergo fora:
misero esilio! avegna ch' i' non fora

d'abitar degno ove voi sola siete.
Ma s'io v'era con saldi chiovi fisso,
non dovea specchio farvi per mio danno
a voi stessa piacendo aspra et superba.
Certo, se vi rimembra di Narcisso,
questo et quel corso ad un termino vanno—
ben che di sì bel fior sia indegna l'erba.

Canzoniere 45

(My adversary in whom you are wont to see your eyes, which Love and Heaven honor, enamors you with beauties not his but sweet and happy beyond mortal guise. By his counsel, Lady, you have driven me out of my sweet dwelling: miserable exile! even though I may not be worthy to dwell where you alone are. But if I had been nailed there firmly, a mirror should not have made you, because you pleased yourself, harsh and proud to my harm. Certainly, if you remember Narcissus, this and that course lead to one goal—although the grass is unworthy of so lovely a flower.)

The speaker understands how Laura could succumb to such a ravishing love object, but she risks the fate of Narcissus: a warning both against pride—mythologically the sin of Narcissus—and against narcissism in the modern sense. There is the seed here of a famous passage in Freud about female narcissism; Petrarch's imitators explore the complex of motifs with at times remarkable ingenuity:

Those whose kind harts sweet pittie did attaint,
With ruthfull teares bemond my miseries:
Those which had heard my never ceasing plaint,
Or read my woes ingraven on the trees,
At last did win my Ladie to consort them,
Unto the fountaine of my flowing anguish:
Where she unkind and they might boldly sport them,
Whilst I meanewhile in sorrows lappe did languish.
Their meaning was that she some teares should shed,
Into the well in pitty of my pining:
She gave consent and putting forth her head,
Did in the well perceave her beautie shining.

Which seeing she withdrew her head puft up with prid
And would not shed a teare should I have died.
The Tears of Fancy (1593) 32[12]

The lover's tears become a well of Narcissus where the woman beholds her own beauty and, having come to the brink of pity, withdraws into disdainful pride in the power she has over this poor man. Several generations of such poems prepare for the passage in *Paradise Lost* where the mother of the human race beholds herself in the water within moments of her creation and—"there I had fixt/Mine eyes till now, and pin'd with vain desire" (4.465–66)—threatens to become the mother of no one.

I know of no sonnet sequence that has more to say about female pride than the *Amoretti.* In places the atmosphere surrounding the topic is the usual one—reproachful, angry, hopeless:

But still the more she fervent sees my fit:
the more she frieseth in her wilfull pryde:
and harder growes the harder she is smit,
with all the playnts which to her be applyde.
What then remaines but I to ashes burne,
and she to stones at length all frosen turne?
Amoretti 32.9–14

In places the language seems to be reaching for new extremes:

But she more cruell and more salvage wylde,
then either Lyon or the Lyonesse:
shames not to be with guiltlesse bloud defylde,
but taketh glory in her cruelnesse.
Amoretti 20.9–12

Petrarch never has at Laura at anything like this pitch. The longterm history of the topic in Petrarchan imitation is one of escalating rage, and Spenser's sequence can be seen as a late chapter in that history. Veselin Kostić, tracing the stages of this history to Spenser through Petrarch and Tasso, locates its "logical conclusion" in lines by Suckling: "If of her self she will not love,/nothing can make her:/the divel take her."[13] For some, Spenser's handling of tradition here injects a sourness into the whole sequence, "the embittered Petrarchist psychic world with which the sequence opened" persisting as a shadow even behind the happier things to come: "The viper thoughts of the *Amoretti* anticipate the anxieties of the wedding poem, where much of the same labor of loving must be repeated."[14] There are moments when the *Amoretti* seems to be imagining something more pathological, a mutuality in which it is precisely the woman's cruelty, or at least the man's imagination of it, that satisfies his own deepest needs:

> The love which me so cruelly tormenteth,
> So pleasing is in my extreamest paine:
> that all the more my sorrow it augmenteth,
> the more I love and doe embrace my bane.
>
> *Amoretti* 42.1–4

No one to my knowledge reads the sequence quite that way, though seeing the whole story in terms of some kind of sadomasochistic bond—the title that Spenser gives his sequence does seem designed to make us think of Amoret and Busyrane—would be one solution to the problem of squaring our sense of the high level of anger with the fact that it is one of very few sequences of its kind that ends with the woman accepting the man's suit. If we are to find that outcome credible, we need to know why this time the argument from female pride has the desired effect, what it takes for a Petrarchan courtship to have a happy ending. The problem as such was brought into focus by J. W. Lever, who found a number of the sonnets (including 32 and 20, quoted above) so alien to what otherwise appeared to be the true theme of the sequence—"the condition of assured courtship awaiting its consecration in marriage"—that they had to be relics of more youthful and conventional sonneteering on Spenser's part, and were most appropriately disregarded in appreciating the current work: "There would seem to be only one way of doing justice to Spenser's sequence, and that is by setting apart those sonnets which evidently belong to an earlier phase and run counter to the general stream of thought and feeling."[15] Lever's solution has not found much favor, but the rift which he detected has stayed visible. A feeling that some of the poems do not fit right has occasioned later theories that in his angrier sonnets Spenser is in fact not thinking of the woman he was going to marry but of his monarch or her predecessor.[16] Even critics committed to the calendrical and numerological theories that posit a rigorously unified design to the sequence can find themselves struggling to save the phenomena. Kenneth J. Larsen takes some of the "more conventionally correct" sonnets to be artistic mistakes on Spenser's part, a failure to live up to his own program; 30 ends up being merely "a run-of-the-mill Petrarchist sonnet," and 22—the Ash Wednesday sonnet, critical to calendrical readings of the sequence—is worse, a clumsy mixing of disparate elements: "The final posturing and awkward hyperbole are false to the sonnet's opening spirit, because the intent of the Lenten fasting and praying is finally to appease a pagan goddess."[17] If later poems with the same components seem to fit better, that is because they are knowingly self-parodic; 47, for instance—a poem on Lever's list—"can only be read as travesty. . . . Spenser subtly laughs at the very convention he is employing."[18]

A more comprehensive thesis about self-parody is advanced in one of best known essays on the sequence. Many of Lever's "excommunicated sonnets," writes Louis L. Martz, "are done with such extravagant exaggeration of the conventional poses that they strike me as close to mock-heroic"[19]; and this exaggeration produces not so much a series of jokes at the expense of Petrarchism as a characterization of the man and woman in question and the kind of courtship being conducted:

> These are the conventions of love, the poet seems to say; these are the usual rituals of courtship; he will gladly pay these tributes, and even overpay them, since this is what his delightful damsel seems to expect, and she thoroughly deserves this state; at the same time a girl of her deep wit will know exactly how to take them, in the spirit offered. She can be expected to respond with a smile and a witty rejoinder, as she does in Sonnet 18, herself outdoing the Petrarchan poses.[20]

Martz's account sounds some false notes to present-day ears ("his delightful damsel"; a few pages earlier he is comparing the poet to Mr. Knightley), and alongside later, more aggressive theories his has tended to look softhearted. But it has also proved one of the most durable, and I think rightly so.

Finding parodic possibility in apparently serious contexts—and particularly in Petrarchan love poetry—is something at which literary critics are often too agile for their own good, but here it finds more than usual justification in the rhythms and strategies of courtship. A pair of sonnets which introduces the topic of female pride to the sequence sets up a major inconsistency in Spenser's management of that topic but also explains the purpose of such inconsistency:

Rudely thou wrongest my deare harts desire,
In finding fault with her too portly pride:
the thing which I doo most in her admire
is of the world unworthy most envide.

Amoretti 5.1–4

The speaker here replies to a presumably male friend who has lodged the conventional reproach against the woman, whose equally conventional Petrarchan demeanor has already been manifesting itself. The lover does not try to deny that his beloved is proud, but moves immediately to a strong affirmation that her pride is an important part of what makes her desirable; it is inseparable from the moral character that he would want her to have:

For in those lofty lookes is close implide,
scorn of base things, and sdeigne of foule dishonor:
thretning rash eies which gaze on her so wide,
that loosely they ne dare to looke upon her.
Such pride is praise, such portlinesse is honor,
that boldned innocence beares in hir eies:
and her faire countenance like a goodly banner,
spreds in defiaunce of all enemies. (ll. 5–12)

The following couplet offers a general proposition, with its own whiff of defiance: "Was never in this world ought worthy tride,/ without some spark of such self-pleasing pride" (13–14). Calling the woman's pride "self-pleasing" only strengthens its link to the primal sin of Christian theology; *sibi placere* figures centrally in Augustine's famous account of the fall (see *City of God* 14.14), and Petrarch echoes that usage in his condemnation of Laura's narcissism. There are two occurrences of "self-pleasing" in *The Faerie Queene*, both with strong Petrarchan overtones; one (VI.i.15.2) is unambiguously critical, the other (III.iv.6.1) at least partly sardonic. Taking account of this tradition, Larsen seeks to inflect the apparent praise of female pride in *Amoretti* 5 by ending the couplet with a question mark.[21] Other editors, however, follow the 1595 octavo in placing a simple period there, and emending it would be I think to deny Spenser the boldness of what he is saying in this particular context.

In the next sonnet he continues his line of thought into a more or less accurate anticipation of what the succeeding phase of this courtship is going to be like, including its eventual success.[22] He may still be talking to that friend, but he is also reassuring himself that the difficulties ahead will be worth it:

> Be nought dismayd that her unmoved mind
> doth still persist in her rebellious pride:
> such love, not lyke to lusts of baser kynd,
> the harder wonne, the firmer will abide.
> The durefull Oake, whose sap is not yet dride,
> is long ere it conceive the kindling fyre:
> but when it once doth burne, it doth divide
> great heat, and makes his flames to heaven aspire.
> So hard it is to kindle new desire
> in gentle brest that shall endure for ever:
> deepe is the wound, that dints the parts entire
> with chast affects, that naught but death can sever.
> Then thinke not long in taking litle paine,
> to knit the knot, that ever shall remaine.
>
> *Amoretti* 6

The lover in this sequence—unlike his fellows elsewhere in the tradition—has had the good luck to be smitten by a woman not already taken; he also knows with considerable clarity that marriage is his goal. What he affirms here is an important faith that the womanly pride that will make that goal difficult to attain is also what makes it possible to attain; the difficulties are essential to the tying of an enduring knot. The games of courtship, that is, not only have a goal but also have a point: the annoying paces they put people through are important in themselves, their importance directly linked the earnestness of the wooer's own intent. And seeing them in this perspective makes them easier to play as games: the playfulness that I think Martz accurately detects behind an apparent sadomasochistic extremity ("when I pleade, she bids me play my part"; 18.9) is not so much skepticism about the rules being followed as cheerfulness about their rationality in the long run, a cheer that more authentically desperate Petrarchists cannot share.

The year-long business of wooing will be a test on both sides: of the seriousness of the man's interest (the woman wants to know how much trouble he is willing to take on her behalf), and of the woman's potential faithfulness as a wife (the man does not *want* her to be easy to win). It also—and this is the point on which Spenser's sequence is explicit—will be the means by which the pride that makes the woman admirable is reconciled with the dependence that comes with accepting love. The seemingly straightforward solution to the problem posed by female pride would be the destruction of that pride—the woman's humiliation—but just putting it that way makes clear that that is not how it works. The best known Petrarchist sequence to enact such a possibility is that of Barnabe Barnes, which ends with the drug-induced rape of its still unwilling heroine: "Thine hard indurate hart, I must compell" (sonnet 105.14).[23] Within the larger context of the tradition it is a grim curiosity. Truly successful courtship cannot be simply a matter of pursuit and capture; the hunting metaphors prevalent in medieval and Renaissance love poetry have to break down at the end for a really satisfactory result. Spenser signals as much in *Amoretti* 67, his contribution to a Petrarchist subgenre that descends from *Canzoniere* 190 and has distinguished examples by Wyatt and Tasso.[24] In Spenser, the hunter captures the elusive deer, but only when he gives up and sits down and the deer returns to surrender on her own accord: an unrealistic development as far as the vehicle is concerned—there is no way to explain to real deer that you are interested in domestication rather than venison—but a wholly appropriate one for the tenor. She needed him to let up so she could consent rather than just get caught. The task is not to divest the woman of her pride, but to find a way for her to preserve it while finally saying Yes.

Along the way, the lover does not always talk as if that were the case; the more traditional attacks on female pride are also deployed, and at one point the woman's yielding is specifically imagined as her humiliation, to be achieved with love's coercive help:

> But her proud hart doe thou a little shake
> and that high look, with which she doth comptroll
> all this worlds pride bow to a baser make,
> and al her faults in thy black booke enroll.
> That I may laugh at her in equall sort,
> as she doth laugh at me and makes my pain her sport.
> *Amoretti* 10.9–14

Yet the lover also reminds himself at times of the teleology of sonnet 6–"Why then should I accoumpt of little paine / that endlesse pleasure shall unto me gaine" (26.13–14; similarly sonnet 51)—and tries on occasion to put the matter in more irenic terms:

In that proud port, which her so goodly graceth,
whiles her faire face she reares up to the skie:
and to the ground her eie lids low embaseth,
most goodly temperature ye may descry.

Amoretti 13.1–4

Proud humility, in other words—though the fullest articulation of the joint problem and promise of female pride is a mere juxtaposition, the paired sonnets 58 and 59. Roughly, pride is bad—

Weake is th'assurance that weake flesh reposeth
In her owne powre and scorneth others ayde:
that soonest fals when as she most supposeth
her selfe assurd, and is of nought affrayd . . . .
Why then doe ye proud fayre, misdeeme so farre,
that to your selfe ye most assured arre.

Amoretti 58.1–4, 13–14

and pride is good:

Thrise happie she, that is so well assured
Unto her selfe and setled so in hart:
that nether will for better be allured,
ne feard with worse to any chaunce to start . . .
Most happy she that most assured doth rest,
but he most happy who such one loves best.

Amoretti 59.1–4, 13–14

The two statements sit side by side, to uncertain effect.

Analyzing that effect has become entangled with an odd textual issue. Sonnet 58 comes with the superscription, "By her that is most assured to her selfe." No other poem in the sequence has any such label attached to it. The presence of the superscription would be adequately explained if we were meant to take the poem as, uniquely, spoken by the woman, though it is *prima facie* incongruous for such a title to introduce a poem attacking self-assurance. One theory detects here a printhouse mistake, and shifts the indication of female authorship to 59; Martz reports being inclined to this explanation, but thanks William Nelson and Leicester Bradner for converting him to the theory that "by" in this context means "concerning." The required sense is indeed there in the *OED* (26c) and still has a vestigial presence in modern usage ("he did well by her"); there are close analogues in George Gascoigne's *Hundreth Sundry Flowers*.[25] Glossing the superscription this way effectively does away with it as far as understanding the sequence is concerned: it becomes redundant, posing no problems aside from the question of why anyone took the trouble to include it.[26] A different course is advocated by Alexander Dunlop, that of both leaving the superscription where it is and of taking "by" to mean "just what we would normally take it to mean: that these are the words of the lady." If this is so, then the pride being attacked in sonnet 58 is the man's: the woman turns the tables on him and greets him with his own accusation against her. This shock finally makes him realize the error of his own ways and brings the story to its turning point: "The lover's response in the next sonnet, 59, conveys the recognition that her self-assurance, in contrast, has not been 'stubborn pride,' as he had insisted all along, but the wisdom of one who 'Keepes her course aright,' and ultimately the source of his own happiness."[27]

Dunlop's is the bolder move, and has found a certain amount of acceptance; it is indeed attractive and appropriate to have the male lover's pride, always implicitly at issue in a Petrarchan context, become a topic of open accounting. Sonnet 59 does not, however, mark a sudden break with a malign position on which the lover "has insisted all along"; rather, it reaffirms the perspective clearly established in sonnets 5 and 6. And making the male lover the specific subject of sonnet 58 grates in what I think are significant ways against its phrasing. The poem does intrigue with its gender references; in the octave it is "she" who is self-assured, and in the sestet it is "he." There are straightforward rationales for both usages—in the former case the antecedent is "flesh," imagined as a feminine noun; in the latter masculine is the default gender for a general statement about all human beings—and neither necessarily specifies the sex of the addressee in the last two lines. The formulaic "proud fayre," on the other hand, is very difficult to accept as specifically directed against the male speaker of the other 88 sonnets. The phrase clinches the sense that among possible manifestations of self-assured pride the one of central concern here is pride in one's physical beauty; and whatever other thought crimes may be detected in the male lover's behavior, excessive pride in his own physical appearance is not really in evidence.

In any case, not to see sonnets 58 and 59 as being about the same person is to avoid what is really challenging in their juxtaposition. Some leeway for rationalization is perhaps provided by the fact that

59 does not actually use the word "pride"; we might try to see the good self-assurance there described as conceptually distinguishable from anything going under that dangerous label. But the leverage thus gained is not great; "self-assurance" is very close to being a synonym for "pride" in the Augustinian sense, and what is praised in 59 presents little if any contrast to the laudatory attributes that have already been gathered under the rubric "pride." I think the absence of that word in 59 is at most a minor courtesy to the woman; the sonnets are supposed to contradict each other, with a clarity superior to the blending of opposites described in sonnet 13. That contradiction both defines what needs to happen in the courtship and dramatizes its difficulty. Yet difficult is not impossible: the logical paradox of both attacking and praising pride is not necessarily an experiential paradox—if it were, we would probably have no more marriages, or at least no happy ones. In context, this striking way of defining the task closely precedes the narrative turning point, and is somehow the gateway to the virtually unprecedented happy ending.

"Somehow" is a word that seems to want to push its way into the discussion here. By Kaske's reckoning, "there are several apparent resolutions of the debate over pride . . . each of which is somehow undercut"; 58–59 she considers "a stalemate."[28] In its wake arrows indeed continue to point in different directions. In 61 the lover renounces criticism of the woman's pride almost entirely:

> The glorious image of the makers beautie,
> My soverayne saynt, the Idoll of my thought,
> dare not henceforth above the bounds of dewtie
> t'accuse of pride, or rashly blame for ought. (ll. 1–4)

A decade later, though, her residual pride is a blemish which she is praised for dispersing—"fayre when that cloud of pryde, which oft doth dark/her goodly light with smiles she drives away" (81.7–8)—and in the *Epithalamion* she is mainly presented as a paragon of "humble reverence" (210)—

> Of her ye virgins learne obedience,
> When so ye come into those holy places,
> To humble your proud faces (ll. 212–14)

—until, of course, she greets her new husband in bed with proud humility. Yet if we look past the debate as such, I think we can detect a steadier sense of resolution. Some of what is going on is hinted at in sonnet 45, Spenser's revision of Petrarch's poem on Laura's narcissism:

Leave lady in your glasse of christall clene,
    Your goodly selfe for evermore to vew:
    and in my selfe, my inward selfe I meane,
    most lively lyke behold your semblant trew.
Within my hart, though hardly it can shew
    thing so divine to vew of earthly eye:
    the fayre Idea of your celestiall hew,
    and every part remaines immortally:
And were it not that through your cruelty,
    with sorrow dimmed and deformd it were:
    the goodly ymage of your visnomy,
    clearer then christall would therein appere.
But if your selfe in me ye playne will see,
    remove the cause by which your fayre beames darkned be.

Petrarch calls Laura's mirror his rival, but does not offer himself as its replacement in quite this way: let me be your mirror. Spenser's lady will find that arrangement entirely gratifying if she will make a small adjustment; her "cruelty" distorts the image which her lover's heart reflects back to her (it is left unclear whether the distortion is in the reflective power of his heart or in the image itself), but the removal of that impediment will allow her to experience the full joy of self-contemplation. The practical imperative into which the conceit develops has led some critics to see the poem as a seducer's disreputable ploy, the sort of thing the lover needs to learn to stop doing. According to Dunlop, "the poet here trivializes the concept of the lover's function as mirror" (since "the proper solution is not her submission, but his transcendence of the deforming passions");[29] William J. Kennedy calls the effort "a gesture of narcissistic self-promotion" on the lover's part, and thinks the poem "demonstrates how far the speaker really is from admitting his beloved's independence."[30] Eagerness to be stern, however, can keep us from registering the psychological resonance of what Spenser is proposing: accept my love and I can reflect back to you an image of your own best self. It seems to be fully in line with the goal of the sequence that the lady is being asked not to give up the pleasure of admiring herself in a mirror, but rather to relocate that pleasure in a way that makes the man an intimate collaborator.[31]

The service offered is theoretically within the capacity of any ardent lover, but it is easier if he is a poet; and in its search for a new home for the woman's pride, the *Amoretti* avails itself of the specifically Petrarchan braiding of the roles of lover and poet. The process is visible in the contrast of one earlier and one later sonnet; the first begins with an attack on the "fair proud" as austere as any Christian moralist's:

> Faire proud now tell me why should faire be proud,
> Sith all worlds glorie is but drosse uncleane:
> and in the shade of death it selfe shall shroud,
> how ever now thereof ye little weene.
> That goodly Idoll now so gay beseene,
> shall doffe her fleshes borowd fayre attyre:
> and be forgot as it had never beene,
> that many now much worship and admire.
>
> *Amoretti* 27.1–8

It turns out, though, that the speaker is trying to turn the woman's mind not so much to God as to himself:

> Ne any then shall after it inquire,
> ne any mention shall thereof remaine:
> but what this verse, that never shall expyre,
> shall to you purchas with her thankles paine.
> Faire be no lenger proud of that shall perish,
> but that which shal you make immortall, cherish. (ll. 9–14)

He is about to give her the laurel crown whose interpretation will occasion some tusseling in the next two poems; we are in the most overtly Petrarchan neighborhood in the sequence.

In sonnet 75 it is the same and different:

> One day I wrote her name upon the strand,
> but came the waves and washed it a way:
> agayne I wrote it with a second hand,
> but came the tyde, and made my paynes his pray.
> Vayne man, sayd she, that doest in vaine assay,
> a mortall thing so to immortalize.

for I my selve shall lyke to this decay,
and eek my name bee wyped out lykewise.
Not so, (quod I) let baser things devize
to dy in dust, but you shall live by fame:
my verse your vertues rare shall eternize,
and in the hevens wryte your glorious name,
Where whenas death shall all the world subdew,
our love shall live, and later life renew.

The arrangement proposed in sonnet 27 has, against almost all Petrarchan precedent, been accepted, but has also changed in the process. The poet is now immortalizing not the woman's physical beauty but her "virtues rare"—which I identify with "the fayre Idea of your celestiall hew" in sonnet 45–and the woman is now voicing on her own precisely the awareness of mortality that was being aggressively urged upon her earlier. She was not speaking for herself then, and now she is; we have no way of knowing who learned what in the interval, and it is possible the man simply got better at listening. Whatever the case, the static Petrarchan posture of worshipful frustration has relaxed into a transaction between the two of them, whereby her own soul is freed from the burden of pride by in effect entrusting that pride to him. Her profession of humility is cradled in his exaltation of the person he knows her to be.

NOTES

1. *Pietro Bembo's "Gli Asolani,"* trans. Rudolf B. Gottfried (1954; rpt. Freeport, New York: Books for Libraries, 1971), 29; with reference to the Italian text in Bembo, *Prose e rime*, ed. Carlo Dionisotti (Turin: UTET, 1966).

2. Text and translations for Petrarch's sequence are from *Petrarch's Lyric Poems*, ed. and trans. Robert M. Durling (Cambridge: Harvard University Press, 1976).

3. Davy A. Carozza and H. James Shey, *Petrarch's "Secretum" with Introduction, Notes, and Critical Anthology* (New York: Peter Lang, 1989), 69, 71.

4. Petrarch, *Letters of Old Age*, trans. Aldo S. Bernardo, Saul Levin, and Reta A. Bernardo, 2 vols. (Baltimore: Johns Hopkins University Press, 1992), 1:159.

5. *Obras completas de Sor Juana Inés de la Cruz,* ed. Alfonso Méndez Plancarte and Alberto G. Salceda, 4 vols. (Mexico City: Fondo de Cultura Económica, 1951–57), 50.25. Juana's usage is clearly inflected by Hispanic devotional literature that is often aggressively paradoxical in its language and sometimes closely parallels the language of Petrarchism; Teresa of Avila, for instance, urges upon worshippers "una humilde y santa presunción" (*Vida* 15.3; a humble and holy presumption). Juana, however,

is not writing about religious matters, but about a poem written in praise of her own poetry. See my *Petrarchan Love and the Continental Renaissance* (New Haven: Yale University Press, 1999), 150.

6. Quotations from this poem and the preceding sequence are from Alexander Dunlop's text in *The Yale Edition of the Shorter Poems of Edmund Spenser*, gen. ed. William A. Oram (New Haven: Yale University Press, 1989); I make some minor typographical adjustments.

7. Kenneth J. Larsen, ed., *Edmund Spenser's "Amoretti and Epithalamion": A Critical Edition* (Tempe, AZ: MRTS, 1997), 246.

8. Carol V. Kaske, "Spenser's *Amoretti and Epithalamion* of 1595: Structure, Genre, and Numerology," *English Literary Renaissance* 8 (1978): 282. See also Lisa M. Klein, " 'Let us love, deare love, lyke as we ought': Protestant Marriage and the Reason of Petrarchan Loving in Spenser's *Amoretti," Spenser Studies* 10 (1989): 131.

9. I quote from Daniel, *Poems and A Defence of Ryme*, ed. Arthur Colby Sprague (1930; rpt. Chicago: University of Chicago Press, 1965).

10. Marguerite de Navarre, *The Heptameron*, trans. P. A. Chilton (Harmondsworth: Penguin, 1984), 305. The speaker goes on to make clear that he is indeed talking about the genesis of the Petrarchan mistress, in a fairly self-conscious and calculating mode: "They impose on themselves the constraint of not daring to help themselves to pleasures they desire, and in the place of this vice they put another vice, one which they regard as more honorable: namely, cruel hardness of heart and vainglorious concern for reputation, by means of which they hope to acquire immortal renown."

11. I quote from *The Poems and Prose of Mary, Lady Chudleigh*, ed. Margaret J. M. Ezell (New York: Oxford University Press, 1993).

12. I quote, with some adjustments, from Thomas Watson, *Poems*, ed. Edward Arber (London: English Reprints, 1870). Watson's authorship of the sequence is denied by his latest editor; see *The Complete Works of Thomas Watson (1556–1592),* ed. Dana F. Sutton, 2 vols. (Lewiston, NY: Mellen, 1996), 2:380–81.

13. Kostić, *Spenser's Sources in Italian Poetry*, Filološki Fakultet Beogradskog Univerziteta Monografijei xxx (Belgrade: Novi, 1969), 70.

14. Joseph Loewenstein, "A Note on the Structure of Spenser's *Amoretti*: Viper Thoughts," *Spenser Studies* 8 (1987): 315–16–drawing on Loewenstein's fuller discussion in "Echo's Ring: Orpheus and Spenser's Career," *English Literary Renaissance* 16 (1986): 287–302.

15. Lever, *The Elizabethan Love Sonnet*, 2d ed. (London: Methuen, 1974), 100, 101.

16. See, respectively, James Fleming, "A *View* from the Bridge: Ireland and Violence in Spenser's *Amoretti*," *Spenser Studies* 15 (2001): 135–64; Charlotte Thompson, "Love in an Orderly Universe: A Unification of Spenser's *Amoretti*, 'Anacreontics,' and *Epithalamion*," *Viator* 16 (1985): 297–301. Fleming's argument is particularly adroit, and does bring out some uncanny parallels between the language of the sonnets and passages in *A View of the Present State of Ireland*.

17. Larsen, 23, 24–25.

18. Larsen, 38–39.

19. Martz, "The *Amoretti*: 'Most Goodly Temperature,' " in *Form and Convention in the Poetry of Edmund Spenser*, ed. William Nelson (New York: Columbia University

Press, 1961), 155–56. The essay is reprinted, in a modestly updated form, in Martz, *From Renaissance to Baroque: Essays on Literature and Art* (Columbia: University of Missouri Press, 1991).

20. Martz, 156.

21. Larsen, 70; on "self-pleasing," see 130.

22. Calendrical theorists have been arguing that the fictional time here is about three months, but whatever the case it will feel like a year: 23.11–12, 60. 5–6.

23. I quote from Barnes, *Parthenophil and Parthenophe: A Cricial Edition,* ed. Victor A. Doyno (Carbondale: Southern Illinois University Press, 1971).

24. For a particularly searching look at Spenser's relation to the tradition here, see Anne Lake Prescott, "The Thirsty Deer and the Lord of Life: Some Contexts for *Amoretti* 67–70," *Spenser Studies* 6 (1985): 33–76. Prescott isolates the key novelty of *Amoretti* 67 as far as Petrarchan sonneteering is concerned, and finds its possible inspiration in some unexpected places.

25. Martz, 162–63, 180. In addition to the headnotes to poems 10, 12, and 14 in Gascoigne's collection (cited by Martz), see *The Adventures of Master F. J.*, where any possibility that "by" might refer to physical proximity is precluded: "His Mistresse laughing right hartely, demaunded yit again, by whom the same was figured: by a niece to an Aunt of yours, Mistres (quod he)"; *A Hundreth Sundrie Flowres*, ed. G. W. Pigman III (Oxford: Clarendon Press, 2000), 166. Likewise *All's Well That Ends Well* 5.3.237: "By him and by this woman heere, what know you?"

26. The only theory I know to address the question on these terms is Larsen's suggestion (187) about "visual imaging": Spenser is deliberately imitating the fortuitous placement of a marginal note in the Geneva Bible concerning "assurance of thy salvation."

27. Alexander Dunlop, "The Drama of *Amoretti*," *Spenser Studies* 1 (1980): 113; so also, to similar effect, William C. Johnson, "Gender Fashioning and the Dynamics of Mutuality in Spenser's *Amoretti*," *English Studies* 74 (1993): 512–13. A desire to graph the arc of the male speaker's moral improvement has been strong in recent criticism, though a contrary disposition is voiced by Donna Gibbs: "arguments concerning the lover's gradual education in chastity do not provide adequate explanations for the developmental changes discernible in the sequence. The development is rather to be defined in terms of the increasing intimacy and confidence of the lover persona both in his address to, and his thoughts about, his mistress"; *Spenser's "Amoretti": A Critical Study* (Aldershot: Scolar Press, 1990), 27.

28. Kaske, 285, 284.

29. Dunlop, in the notes to his edition, 627.

30. William J. Kennedy, *Authorizing Petrarch* (Ithaca, NY: Cornell University Press, 1994), 239, 238.

31. Spenser's development of the conceit in *Amoretti* 45 appears to be original, but it moves through well travelled territory. A poem in Maurice Scève's *Délie* (229) distinguishes between the mirror in which the lady can behold her physical beauty and the lover's heart in which she can behold her *vertu*; a couple of verbal cues (*vive, diforme*) suggest that the poem may indeed have been on Spenser's mind. Catherine des Roches provides a female response at the end of her Charite-Sincero sequence, when the lady peers into her lover's open heart and indeed sees herself ("ha mon

Dieu! je me voy!"); Madeleine des Roches and Catherine des Roches, *Oeuvres*, ed. Anne R. Larsen (Geneva: Droz, 1993), 281. Bembo writes no poem on the topic, but in private correspondence to a mistress (which Spenser definitely would not have known) uses the trope to quite elegant effect; see my "Applied Petrarchism: The Loves of Pietro Bembo," *Modern Language Quarterly* 57 (1996): 418–20.

PATRICK CHENEY

Dido to Daphne: Early Modern Death in Spenser's Shorter Poems

Recent scholarship on early modern death provides a compelling context for viewing Spenser, especially his shorter poems. Such scholarship emphasizes a new philosophy of death emergent in late-sixteenth-century England: death is annihilation, desire is death, and so humans triumph only through willing the performance of death. Spenser's poetry can be situated along the historic divide between these secular notions and more Christian ones. In *November*, Spenser presents Dido's death within a Christian poetics: when Colin is consoled though his transcendent vision, Spenser advertises his ability to help the nation mourn. His *Complaints* and such elegies as *Astrophel* fulfill this advertisement. Yet one poem lies beyond the poetics of Christian redemption: in *Daphnaida*, the process of death does not lead to transcendence or consolation. In this poem, which shatters the intertextual line of mourning from Theocritus to Chaucer, Spenser enters the dark terrain of early modern fatality. Anticipating Renaissance tragedy, he tells how the "ghost" of Daphne haunts the early modern imagination, including his own. This haunting may animate *Fowre Hymnes* and *The Mutabilitie Cantos* to produce their final affirmation.

THE TOPIC OF DEATH IN SPENSER remains a largely undiscovered country, from whose bourn few travelers return.[1] The word *death* and its variants occur nearly 250 times in his poetry alone, and this count does not include such closely allied words as *dead*, *deadly*, *die*, or *dying*. Indeed, the terrain of death in Spenser is so vast and fertile that no essay—not even a group of essays or a book—can map or garden it. Spenser has a reputation for being a great Elizabethan poet of mourning and mutability, so his expansive representational land of death has witnessed heavy elegiac traffic.[2] Even so, *The Spenser Encyclopedia* contains no entry simply on "death," choosing rather to cross-reference the concept in articles on "Amavia," "elegy," "heaven," "Nature," and so forth.[3] The closest this monumental, folio-sized testament to Spenser's genius comes is a short article of less than a column, titled "Life and Death" (435–36), which turns out to pertain, not to the universals we might expect, but to two forgettable figures who show up in *The Mutabilitie Cantos* (1609). Nor has Spenser figured substantively in more recent books on the advent of early modern death itself: Robert Watson's *The Rest is Silence: Death as Annihilation in the English Renaissance*; Michael Neill's *Issues of Death: Mortality and Identity in English Renaissance Tragedy;* and Jonathan Dollimore's *Death, Desire and Loss in Western Culture.*[4] Perhaps this dearth of commentary arises from a widespread sense, provocatively articulated by Marshall Grossman, that Spenser "did not take death very seriously."[5] If Grossman is right, we might take his cue, and take the topic dead seriously. In this essay, let us first look briefly at what death is doing in the Spenser canon generally, and then let us fix on the shorter poems, cognizant that nowhere can death receive his due.

In contrast to English Renaissance tragedy, Spenser's typically comedic fictions tend only rarely to include memorable representations of a character's death. One thinks perhaps of Dido in the *November* eclogue of *The Shepheardes Calender* (1579), or Amavia and Mordant in Book II of *The Faerie Queene* (1590), or Old Melibee and his wife in Book VI (1596). Yet in its own harrowing way, death stalks the Spenserian text as surely as the unnamed fiend stalks Guyon in the Cave of Mammon: "And therefore still on hye/He over him did hold his cruell clawes,/Threatning with greedy gripe to do him dye" (II.vii.27).[6] As these lines indicate, Spenser represents death, sometimes through self-conscious verbal play, but always with grim awareness. Indebted to scriptural, classical, medieval, and early modern resources, his figure of Death boldly assumes fatal identity throughout his poetic corpus—and in a variety of contradictory roles: Death is at once a dancer (*Nov* 105) and a warrior (*Nov* 123); a judge *(VG* 447) and a thief (*Daph* 303); a gardener (*FQ* V.vii. 31) and a devouring eater (*RT* 52); a savior (*FQ* I.xi.48) and a theatrical performer (*FQ* I.viii. 40). Most intriguingly, Death appears as a fine-chiseling artist and writer—nowhere finer than when fashioning the beautifully laid out corpse of the eighteen-year-old Douglas Howard:

"those pallid cheekes and ashy hew,/In which sad death his pourtraicture had writ" (*Daph* 302–03). In Spenser, death assumes a face, acquires a physiology and an inwardness; this allegorical villain grimly inscribes his textualizing hand deeply on the bodies of those we love most.[7]

In his recurrent representations of death, Spenser approaches a historic divide: between "medieval" and "modern" notions. The three 1990s books mentioned above—by Watson, Neill, and Dollimore—are all profitably cut along this divide. By "medieval," we may designate a traditionally Christian understanding of death as primarily an event occurring sometime after creation and just before apocalypse. Here death is not a final problem in life but a necessary avenue for salvation. In the *November* eclogue, Spenser's authorial persona, Colin Clout, moves along this Christian track when Queen Dido dies. At first, her death leaves Colin and her other shepherds submerged in the deepest of griefs, for "She while she was, (that was, a woful word to sayne)/For beauties prayse and plesaunce had no pere" (93–94). Suddenly, however, as Colin gazes at Dido's beautiful body laid out on the funeral bier, he witnesses the apotheosis of her "unbodied" soul breaking free from its "burdenous corpse" (166). Colin's transcendent vision leads him to change his refrain from "O heavie herse . . . O carefull verse" (60, 62) to "O happye herse . . . O joyfull verse" (170, 172), because his visionary experience compels him to view death differently—not as an evil that produces fatal sadness but as a good that creates immeasurable joy. No longer does he fear death but now longs for it, and he discovers in the body's end the quickest route to the "Elisian fieldes" (179): "Dido is gone afore (whose turne shall be the next?)/There lives shee with the blessed Gods in blisse" (193–94). As E.K. indicates in his gloss, the origins of the idea of death as a divine good trace to Plato (283), but as Spenser's readers have probably always known, the classical origins are consonant with Christian thought. The elegy for Dido, the first of many elegies in the Spenser canon, reveals how the poet's representation of death is vital to the life of the nation: in his role as England's "new Poete" (E.K., *Dedicatory Epistle* 6), Spenser advertises his authority to help the nation move through mourning to meaning in times of grave communal loss.[8] Indeed, we might view Spenser's subsequent elegies in the course of his career not simply as occasional verse but in part as fulfillments of this national role.

According to Watson, Neill, and Dollimore, this medieval or Christian notion of death is subject to dissident contention in the early modern period, when "modern" notions of death firmly take root. While these critics share what appears to be a generational concern to chart a "new philosophy of death" (Neill, 35) that is lucidly secular in its imprint, each introduces a distinct model of early modern fatality: Watson, death as annihilation; Neill, death as performance; and Dollimore, desire as death.[9] Perhaps Spenser's representations of death have seemed uninteresting because our most powerful models efface his historical position within the early modern moment. Certainly we can be charmed by Camille Paglia's brilliant claim that Spenser's "wanton voice" from the dark side of paganism is historically more important than his "moral voice" from the bright side of Christianity,[10] as long as we acknowledge the poet's deep religious faith, which presumably undergirds his standing as one of the most significant Christian poets between Dante and Milton:

> But thence-forth all shall rest eternally
> With Him that is the God of Sabbaoth hight:
> O that great Sabbaoth God, graunt me that Sabaoths sight.
> (*Mutabilitie Cantos* VII.viii.2)

Yet even in this most passionate and moving testament to Christian faith, Spenser courageously opens his religious verse to the "crisis of death" articulated by Neill and the rest. Here England's national poet *prays* that the "great Sabbaoth God" will "graunt" him the "Sabaoths sight"—a sight he now lacks, has not yet envisioned, and therefore does not represent. We might speculate that Spenser fails to show up in the early modern register not simply because he *approaches* the faultline dividing medieval and modern issues of death but because he comes dangerously close to falling *inside*.[11]

Seeking to chart Spenser's precarious position, we might imagine his Christian voice, ingrained as it is with the dye of wanton paganism, as a late "medieval" complaint against the dying of the Christian light, a vigorous rear guard action designed to consolidate the sacred remnants of early modern faith. Thus, Death shows up as a happy dancer at the end of Dame Mutability's pageant, harmoniously linked with his companion for life:

> And after all came Life, and lastly Death;
> Death with most grim and griesly visage seene,
> Yet is he nought but parting of the breath;
> Ne ought to see, but like a shade to weene,
> Unbodied, unsoul'd, unheard, unseene.
> But Life was like a faire young lusty boy,

Such as they faine Dan Cupid to have beene.
(*Mutabilitie Cantos* VII.vii.46)

As Philippa M. Tristram observes in her article on "Life and Death" in *The Spenser Encyclopedia*, "although Death is said by the narrator to be the last in the procession (cf. III xii 25), Life is the last to be described . . . . The connection between Life and Death persists, but Life, like the *Eros funèbre* (the Cupid found on Renaissance tombs), is a power that frees the soul" (436). In Spenser's spectacular representation, Death has a body and a soul, a physiology and an interiority, but the allegory emphasizes Death's negating powers, his nihilism of nothingness ("nought . . . / Ne ought")—a grim parody of the mystery of the Incarnation and the Resurrection: "Unbodied, unsoul'd, unheard, unseene." Surely, these four words stand as the horsemen against whom Spenser's apocalyptic poetry arms itself: the body's annihilation; the evaporation of the soul; the voice's isolation; and the invisibility of Christian identity.[12]

Dollimore might well have cited this passage to show Spenser's participation in the "desire is death" cult of early modernism, the old man Death gleefully linked with the Cupidic "faire young lusty boy" in terms that did not make Spenser either blush or wince. Instead, Dollimore claims Spenser by citing another passage in *The Mutabilitie Cantos*: "thy decay thou seekst by thy desire" (VII.vii.59.3; Dollimore 69; also 78, 83, 101). While one could, then, colonize Spenser for this cult, we might register two cautionary points. First, Spenser does appear to fear that desire is death—but not so much for himself as for his second wife, Elizabeth Boyle, whom he married on June 11, 1594. So, toward the end of his great marriage ode to her, *Epithalamion*, he prays that "Cinthia" will his wife's "chast wombe informe with timely seed" (374, 386) and that Juno will bring "comfort" to "women in their smart" (394–95). Second, following from the first, Spenser most often imagines that desire is eternal life, a creative energy that gives birth to children destined to populate the New Jerusalem (*Epith.* 417–23).[13]

Accordingly, Spenser is rarely content to represent death as annihilation. Watson inadvertently concedes this point, although for the secular camp of paganism: "The most plausible and time-honored secular tactic in the human struggle against mortality is procreation. If tragedy insists we may not return to the Garden of Eden, comedy accepts its figuration in the Garden of Adonis, where (according to Spenser) creatures are 'eterne in mutabilitie,' and mortal transience is a necessary component of the machinery of life." "This is the alternative Hamlet overlooks," Watson continues, "in giving his father's deadly demands priority over his mother's hopes for his eventual marriage to Ophelia" (101). For Watson, *Hamlet*'s historical significance lies in its deep condemnation of "the illusions of afterlife it superficially encourages" (74). Spenser, it would seem, was under no such illusion, or more accurately, if he was, he combated it—and perhaps the secular "faith" Watson holds that Hamlet wields—through recurrently illuminating photographs from the afterlife in such poems as the *Hymne of Heavenly Love* and the *Hymne of Heavenly Beautie* (1596). In the latter, the erotic maternity of feminine wisdom, attired in regal dress as Sapience, rests powerfully in the heart of God:

> There in his bosome Sapience doth sit,
> The soveraine dearling of the Deity,
> Clad like a Queene in royall robes, most fit
> For so great powre and peerelesse majesty.
> (*Hymne of Heavenly Beautie* 183–86)

Unlike Shakespeare, who only approaches "heaven's gate" (Sonnet 29.12), Spenser takes us in, witnessing life as bliss in the absolute beyond.[14]

If for many in today's audience Spenser may lack modernist luster in his Christian representations of death as salvation, of death as eternal life, he is more shining in what he does with death as early modern performance. That final masquer bringing up the rear in Mutability's pageant may curiously serve as the presenter to Spenser's dramatization of such a well-suited issue of death. In Spenser, paradoxically, death lives; he is well. By contrast (according to Neill), early modern English tragedians—Shakespeare in *Hamlet*, for instance—typically show the hero dying precisely in order to stage his defiant victory over death. In a new post-Christian universe, lacking access to or certainty of salvation, the tragic hero confronts the real terror of death—its power to undifferentiate, to efface identity, treating king and clown without distinction—through the performance of defiance: "performance snatches distinction from the very jaws of oblivion . . . death paradoxically becomes a powerfully individuating experience, the supreme occasion for exhibitions of individual distinction" (34). By dying well, the tragic hero provides consolation for the grieving audience.

For his part, Spenser seems attracted to narratives in which characters miraculously survive death, but not through heroic performance, since they tend to fall into unconsciousness, as Redcrosse does in

Orgoglio's dungeon (*FQ* I.vii–viii), Guyon outside Mammon's cave (II.vii–viii), or Timias in the dark forest near Belphoebe's glade (III.v). Spenser does not confer distinction on such heroes, nor on the psychologically deep resources of individual subjectivity, but rather on external agents of divine grace sent directly by God, as represented through Arthur in the stories of Redcrosse and Guyon or Belphoebe in the story of Timias. Thus, Spenser confers distinction not on the dying but on the saving, not on interior but on exterior power, not on humankind but on the deity. In Book III, cantos xi and xii, it is as if the poet of epic romance is critiquing death by tragic performance, when Amoret appears in the Masque of Cupid bearing her heart in a basin (is she dead or alive?), a grim performance that the poet associates with the "tragicke Stage" of "some Theatre" (III. xii.12.3.9, 6).[15]

In contrast to his epic romance, Spenser's shorter poems often foreground the death of a heroic individual as a singular event. Indeed, we may wonder whether Spenser's fixation on death in this part of his corpus, in complaint and elegy alike, goes beyond fulfilling his role as national elegist from *November*; perhaps it speaks to a powerful need left unfulfilled by a fundamentally comedic poem that many think was to have ended with the marriage of Arthur and Gloriana. By contrast, in the shorter poems the mortality rate among figures we admire appears well above the national average. We have mentioned Dido in *November*, but we should not forget Colin Clout in *December*, where Spenser's persona stages the death of the author, turning not just an eclogue but an entire poem into a funeral elegy: "Winter is come, that blowes the balefull breath,/And after Winter commeth timely death" (149–50).[16] We have also mentioned Douglas Howard, whose funeral elegy Spenser sings in *Daphnaida* (1591), and with whom we shall soon find our Spenserian end. Before doing so, however, we might recall the elegies for Robert Dudley, earl of Leicester, in *The Ruines of Time* and *Virgils Gnat* (*Complaints*, 1591); of Sir Philip Sidney in *Astrophel* (1595); even of the butterfly Clarion in *Muiopotmos*, the city of Rome in *The Ruines of Rome,* and poetry itself in *The Teares of the Muses* (*Complaints*, 1591). With so much death around him, Spenser had good reason to be alert to changes in the fatal guard.

The closer we look, Spenser's shorter poems are not cut simply along the familiar axes of Eros and Thanatos (cf. Dollimore, 3–35), but more particularly along those of Marriage and Death. As the "ghost" of the bride tells her earthly husband in *Daphnaida*, "I, since the messenger is come for mee,/That summons soules unto the bridale feast/Of his great Lord, must needes depart from thee" (265,

267–69). Typically, the shorter poems extend their axes to a third term that we should expect from the author of this passage (and of the Book of Holiness or *Fowre Hymnes*): Resurrection. While *Amoretti* 6 captures something of the dyad Marriage and Death—"chast affects, that naught but death can sever" (12)—*Epithalamion* implies the triad that leads to Resurrection: "death, or love, or fortunes wreck did rayse" (8).

Death may stalk the Spenserian text, but it rarely occurs in isolation. Death is socialized and it is Christianized; almost always, it is eroticized and familialized. This is true, not simply of Amavia, Mordant, and their bloody-handed babe Ruddymane in the Legend of Temperance, but of Daphne, Alcyon, and their daughter Ambrosia in *Daphnaida*. The life of the family appears to be under siege in Spenser's poetry, but what the poet seems to be combating is the finality of family death itself, as if England's New Poet were uncannily prophesying his own family demise late in December 1598 and early January 1599, when Celtic forces sacked Kilcolman Castle. As Ben Jonson told William Drummond of Hawthornden, Irish rebels, "having robbed Spenser's goods and burnt his house and a little child new-born, he and his wife escaped, and after he died for lack of bread in King Street."[17] Alongside *November*, *Daphnaida*, and *Astrophel*, he pens such powerful marriage poems as *Amoretti*, *Epithalamion*, and *Prothalamion*. Marriage combats death for authority in Spenser's poetry, yet almost never are we left to wonder who will arise: in the funeral elegies, it is the soul of the departed person, whether uplifting to the Elysian Fields like Dido or enclosed eternally in a flower like Astrophel with his beloved *stella*; in the marriage poems, it is the spirit of the children born from the married couple.[18]

But one poem among Spenser's shorter poetry requires special care, since it so mysteriously resists the closure of transcendent consolation in *The Shepheardes Calender*, *Astrophel*, and especially *The Mutabilitie Cantos*, performing its resistance right within the dynamic of the early modern family. In *Daphnaida*, no transcendence, closure, or consolation intervenes in the process of death; in this poem alone, Spenser violates his elegiac pattern of national redemption. We might wish to brood over the historical moment of this striking anomaly more than we have done.[19]

We do not think Spenser actually knew Douglas Howard before she died in her late teens, but he certainly knew her husband, Sir Arthur Gorges, cousin to Sir Walter Ralegh, Spenser's friend and patron, and so he may have been especially saddened by the young woman's premature passing.[20] In the *Dedicatory Epistle* to "his Little Poeme," addressed to Gorges' aunt (by marriage), Helena, marchioness of Northampton, Spenser refers to "the great good fame" which he has "heard of her deceased," yet recalls "the particular goodwill" that he bears to her husband, "a lover of learning and vertue." There is evidence, however, that Spenser's extreme sadness in this elegy may also result from a death that we have not had occasion to mention, that of his first wife, Machabyas Childe. Thus he describes his narrator as "One, whome like wofulnesse impressed deepe/Hath made fit mate thy wretched case to heare,/And given like cause with thee to waile and weepe" (64–66).[21]

Instead of looking at *Daphnaida* as a register of the advent of early modern death, critics have attended primarily to the poem's formal, generic, intertextual, and characterological qualities in order to criticize what C.S. Lewis called "a great, flamboyant, garish thing of stucco disguised as marble."[22] More recently, the critic who has written most on the poem, William A. Oram, goes a step further: "It is a gloomy, tenacious, obsessive, long-winded poem."[23] In terms of its form, *Daphnaida* is "ragged and even shapeless," despite its inset complaint by Alcyon in seven groups of seven stanzas of seven lines each that has attracted the attention of numerologists: "the impression that the poem leaves is not one of intricate harmony."[24] In terms of genre, most critics agree in identifying the poem as a pastoral eclogue in the elegiac mode, but as most observe, in this poem Spenser stubbornly subverts the conventional consolation of the form.[25] As for the poem's intertextuality, critics have found a complex line of pretexts, from the death of Daphnis in Theocritus' first Idyll and Virgil's fifth Eclogue, to the myths of Apollo and Daphne and of Ceyx and Alcyone in Ovid's *Metamorphoses*, including Petrarch's accommodation of the Daphne myth in his *Rime Sparse*, and especially to Chaucer's *Book of the Duchess*, which itself retells the Ceyx-Alcyone myth and which Spenser so self-consciously reworks—with "immense inferiority," insists Lewis (370).[26] By far, however, it is Spenser's characterization of Alcyon that has drawn close to unanimous fire; in Oram's words, the allegorical figure for Gorges is "boorish," weak, self-absorbed, "narcissistic," and "histrionic."[27] To explain the oddity of Spenser's portrayal of a friend in such a damaging way, Oram argues that Spenser is offering Gorges "a warning against grieving too much" (141)—an argument that he has repeated in three subsequent essays and that has been cited by many.[28]

Among critics, however, Ellen N. Martin was first to champion the poem through condemnation of "such moralizing readings" as those inventoried above (84). Extending A. Leigh DeNeef's work on Spenser's representation of the poet in *Daphnaida*, Martin argues that "Spenser is portraying a *potential* poet and situating that *possibility* of poetry inside the experience of grief:" "To show how poetry arises from despair, Spenser arranges that Alcyon 'loses himself in the poetic recreation' " (90).[29] Instead of criticizing *Daphnaida* because it fails to bring consolation out of loss, Martin suggests that loss can also create useful poetry.

As such, Martin's argument suggests that prior to the production of most great English tragedy, Spenser was probing not so much "death as performance" but death as poetry—a secular version of the Christian transcendence the poem so curiously seems to evade. It is Alcyon himself who makes the connection with the dramatic form, when he criticizes "fond man" for reposing hope in the "worlds ficklenesse," when in fact the world "daylie doth her changefull counsels bend/To make new matter fit for Tragedies" (150–54).[30] Anticipating Shakespeare in *Hamlet*, Spenser in *Daphnaida does* represent death as poetry; he tells a story in which a tragic figure uses his art to out-duel death as consolation to the public, represented by the narrator. As critics emphasize, Spenser presents Alcyon as a type of poet and thus as a refraction of himself and his pastoral persona, Colin Clout: "the jollie Shepheard swaine,/That wont full merrilie to pipe and daunce,/And fill with pleasance every wood and plaine" (54–56; see 105).[31] By calling Alcyon's wife "Daphne," Spenser evokes Arthur Gorges in his role as Elizabethan poet, since Gorges used this name for Douglas Howard in his own verse.[32]

Finally, Alcyon sings a long pastoral complaint on the death of Daphne, during which he compares himself both to Orpheus (463–66) and to Philomela (474–76), classical (and Ovidian) types of the poet. The Orpheus allusion has long been identified as a crux because of its obvious mixing with the myth of Persephone:

> But as the mother of the Gods, that sought
> For faire Eurydice her daughter deere
> Throghout the world, with wofull heavie thought;
> So will I travell whilest I tarrie heere.
>
> (*Daphnaida* 463–66)

Rather than simply a crux, however, "Eurydice" may signal a poetics, a broken poetics marked by ellipsis, enigma, and fragmentation. The gender transfer, from Orpheus to Ceres, is in keeping with a male named Alcyon, cross-dressed from Ovid's and Chaucer's Alcyone, a wife grieving for her drowned husband.[33] Yet such cross-dressing is part of the Orphic myth, not simply when the great Bard of Rhodope turns in grief from the love of his lost wife to that of boys in Ovid's version, but when Virgil compares Orpheus to the nightingale "mourn[ing] the loss of her brood."[34] This cross-gender strategy recurs in Alcyon's use of the name "Philumene" a few lines later—a masculine version of Philomela that appears to have functioned as a code name for the male poet in Spenser and the Ralegh circle.[35]

Alcyon's complaint comes complete with a refrain at the end of all seven of the seven-stanza units: "Weepe Shepheard weepe to make my undersong" (245). For the shepherd-narrator addressed by this refrain, Alcyon's verse-command works, as the narrator's sympathy and indeed his larger, framing poem *make* the desired "undersong" of grief. Yet, since the song does not work for the singer himself, Spenser emphasizes the bifurcated effect of Alcyon's art: while his "cheekes wext pale, and sprights began to faint, / As if againe he would have fallen to ground," the narrator "Amooved him out of his stonie swound, / And gan him to recomfort" as he might (542–46). Everything about Alcyon suggests that in this figure Spenser is attempting to portray *a new type of poet*—one who shows more kinship with figures from Elizabethan tragedy than with those from pastoral elegy. Unlike Hamlet, however, Spenser's death-defying figure does not emerge in the least victorious.[36]

Accordingly, death as annihilation literally haunts the poem in the figure of Daphne's "ghost." It is perhaps characteristic of Spenser that his ghost would turn out to be, not of the father, but of the spouse. According to Oram, Alcyon "does not devote his penance to 'the heavens' but to Daphne's ghost; and it is she, rather than the God who created her, who continues to absorb his attention."[37] Spenser seems even to represent this very *aporia* when Alcyon laments, inexplicably, that Daphne is

> borne to heaven, for heaven a fitter pray:
> Much fitter than the Lyon, which with toyle
> Alcides slew, and fixt in firmament;
> Her now I seek throughout this earthlie soyle.
>
> (164–67)

The only explanation offered for why he would seek Daphne on earth, when he claims that she has gone to heaven, is a rather grim pun on the word "pray" and a literary allusion to a pagan principle of heroic constellation.[38] The *aporia* turns out to have geographical accuracy within the fiction, for Daphne herself tells Alcyon that she appears to him, not as an angel sent from heaven, but as a "ghost" (265) wandering in the liminal space between heaven and earth (260–66). Within this geography, Alcyon's "wandring pilgrimage" (372) refracts the early modern predicament: walking with "Jaakob staffe in hand devoutlie crost, / Like to some Pilgrim come from farre away" (41–42)—which even the narrator takes for a "disguize" (57)—Alcyon rails against divine injustice (197–99). Not even Marlowe in *Doctor Faustus* nor Shakespeare in *King Lear* would produce such an open icon of religious skepticism, as Alcyon furiously uses the staff of Jacob to cross the Christian deity.

Such evidence pinpoints parts of the text that Glenn Steinberg's very interesting recent argument does not touch. According to Steinberg, Spenser's "dark vision," represented both in Alcyon's inconsolable grief and the narrator's daunting failure, "arises specifically from Spenser's sense of himself . . . as an apocalyptic poet, embodying a prophetic, Calvinist theology that sees and mourns the cosmic struggle between good and evil in the world" (133). In this account, Spenser uses Alcyon and the narrator to "break the idols of beauty" (represented by Chaucer's *Duchess*) "in order to create a new, truer poetry" (140). This argument is compelling, but it forgets that the Protestant Reformation played a large role "in heightening the psychological burdens of mortality:" "Both the inscrutable determinism and the systematic iconoclasm of Calvinist theology created a blank wall between the living and the dead, encouraging the ominous inference that all might be blankness or darkness beyond it . . . . A challenge to traditional ideas of afterlife would have followed logically from . . . Reformation challenges to the manipulative institutions that had accreted around the original Word of God."[39] It is such a disturbing historical moment that Spenser in *Daphnaida* seems to capture, placing both Alcyon and the narrator in its dark fold—the very material way in which Calvinism led to annihilationism. Spenser's complex representation, we might speculate, is just the sort of thing that would have interested members of the Ralegh circle, infamous even in its own time for its religious skepticism, as the authorities at Cerne Abbas would insist. Indeed, one can imagine that the author of *Ocean to Cynthia* might well have been fascinated more by *Daphnaida* than by the poem for which he received a famous explanatory letter.

In an equally haunting way, then, for Alcyon desire is death. In his narrated allegory of Daphne's demise, the beautiful young Lyoness is killed by a "cruell Satyre with his murdrous dart,/Greedie of mischiefe ranging all about" (156–57), the satyr often being for Spenser a figure of desire, as it is in the story of Hellenore among the satyrs in Book III, canto x of *The Faerie Queene*.[40] But there might be even a more precise registration here of the Western genre of tragedy. If Spenser could publish E.K.'s coinage (mistaken, it turns out) in *The generall argument* to *The Shepheardes Calender* that the Greek word for "Aeglogai" means "Goteheards tales" (11–12), perhaps he knew that the Greek word for "tragedy" derives from *tragoidos*, meaning "goat-song," and therefore understood that the goatlike satyr was an emblem of tragedy, as recorded formally by the satyr play concluding the Dionysian festivals in the Athens of Aeschylus, Sophocles, and Euripides.[41] Whatever caused the death of Douglas Howard, the tragic brutality of masculine sexuality looks to be implicated.

Although in *Daphnaida* England's Virgil sets his tragic scene in the pastoral world of shepherds, and places his tragic action in the tradition of pastoral elegy, his title for the poem paradoxically evokes the tradition of classical epic, as Renwick's commentary suggests (174–75). We thus might come to think of *Daphnaida* not simply as a pastoral eclogue in the elegiac mode but also as an Elizabethan minor epic in the tragic mode—an anticipation of, say, Shakespeare's 1594 *Rape of Lucrece*, itself a "Black stage for tragedies" (766), including *Macbeth*.[42] Several formal features support this classification. As Richard A. McCabe observes, Spenser borrows Chaucer's harmonic rhyme royal stanza (rhyming *ababbcc*) but self-consciously "avoid[s] the resolution of the concluding couplet" in his un-harmonic rhyme of *ababcbc*.[43] Similarly, in this work Spenser addresses a new reader, he "whose heavie minde / With griefe of mournefull great mishap [is] opprest" (1–2), while the reader we might expect, typically coming to poetry for "pleasure" and "delight," is "banisht farre away from hence" (8–10). Even the heavily layered intertextual system evoking the elegiac line from Theocritus and Virgil to Petrarch and Chaucer seems less to work within the conventions of Renaissance "imitation" than to explode them. This is *overgoing* with a vengeance. Most surprisingly, Spenser's portrait of Alcyon does not receive authorial censure, the way Despayre does in Book I of the national epic or Timias in Book IV.[44] It is as if, in the wake of his own late wife's passing, encumbered by the recent deaths of Sidney, Leicester, and Francis Walsingham, Spenser stared at early modern death and did not efface it.[45]

Presumably such effacement was consonant with the pagan mindset of young Arthur Gorges after the death of his wife; if so, the allegorical figure of Alcyon functions as a device of audience accommodation quite different from the one usually cited. Rather than trying to warn the grieving husband about the dangers of excessive grief, Spenser creates a new kind of national poetry that seems willing to entertain the danger zone of early modern fatality. We must not forget: the husband whom Spenser imagines hearing the purified female voice of Christian redemption spoken by a spousal ghost wandering in purgatory will one day publish the first complete English translation of Lucan's superbly pagan, counter-Virgilian epic, the *Pharsalia*.[46] No wonder Alcyon uses the harmonic art of the poet so ferociously against the harmony of the poet, the likes of which we may not witness elsewhere in the Christian poetic tradition leading to Milton's *Lycidas*: his magnificently orchestrated sevenfold complaint calls into question the order of creation itself, a Spenserian version of Poor Tom's "nightmare and her nine-fold" (*King Lear* 3.4.121).

In Spenser's powerful elegy, the narrator does not invoke the "sacred Sisters" (11), nor even the Muse of Tragedy, the way Colin does in *November*. "In stead of them, and their sweete harmonie," he invokes "those three fatall Sisters, whose sad hands/Doo weave the direfull threds of destinie" (15–17), in hopes that "the dreadfull Queene/Of darkenes" and "grisly Ghosts" will come to "heare this dolefull teene" (19–21). If we can see this representation as a rather precise reversal of the pattern opening Seneca's *Thyestes* or Kyd's *Spanish Tragedy*, both of which stage the Furies' demonic agency in the unwitting lives of hapless mortals, we can measure the daring grimness of Spenser's invocation. Little does the narrator recognize what the consequences of it will be, and neither do we, until it is too late. He tells how, one day while out walking, devastated by his own grief, he comes upon his friend Alcyon, who initially refuses to talk about the death of his young wife. "Then be it so," the narrator replies, "that thou art bent/To die alone, unpitied, unplained" (78–79). In this firmly caring reply, we can hear one of Spenser's primary fears, as well as the consolation his art has to offer. *To die alone, unpitied, unplained*: to die in isolation, outside the community, without sympathy from others, unsung in ceremony or in poetry, sunk in oblivion: this is what finally haunts the Spenserian imagination. Hence, he devotes a good deal of his shorter poetry, as well as his epic romance, to its antithesis: a communal song of pity, raised in hopes of renown—and not simply his own, as Daphne poignantly testifies.

According to Alcyon, this young woman is worth dying for, as surely as Romeo believed Juliet to be—and nearly during the same historical moment:

> In pureness and in all celestiall grace,
> That men admire in goodlie womankinde,
> Shee did excell and seem'd of Angels race
> Living on earth like Angell new divinde,
> Adorn'd with wisedome and with chastitie:
> And all the dowries of a noble mind,
> Which did her beautie much more beautifie.
>
> (*Daphnaida* 211–17)

In Spenser's imagined recreation of Arthur Gorges's portrait of the young Douglas Howard, we may discern a spectacular predecessor to the young woman celebrated momentously a few years hence in *Amoretti*, *Epithalamion*, and elsewhere: a woman whose unmatched beauty purifies her mind with grace, nobility, and chastity—the female body functioning as "the sacred harbour of that hevenly spright" (*Amoretti* 76: 4), the very physiology of the Holy Ghost.

Hence, in *Daphnaida* the ongoing representational photography of death is refined in a breathtakingly soft register:

> Yet fell she not, as one enforst to dye,
> Ne dyde with dread and grudging discontent,
> But as one toyld with travaile downe doth lye,
> So lay she downe, as if to sleepe she went,
> And closde her eyes with carelesse quietnesse;
> The whiles soft death away her spirit hent,
> And soule assoyld from sinfull fleshlinesse.
>
> (*Daphnaida* 253–59)

It is hard to measure what is happening here. There is no overt performance, but rather the quiet slipping away of breath itself, the natural sequel to a life devoted to toil and travail. Yet there are agents on the scene, and the verse deftly implies their performance. The first is Daphne herself, who does not die terribly the way the imagination most fears—against the will, in a state of fearful disquiet. Freely, she lies down as if she is going to sleep, closing her eyes in elegant tranquility. The verse does not show the poet evading or transcending death but precisely pausing on it; the intense repetition in the superb chiasmic anadiplosis of "downe doth lye,/So lay she downe" works like instant replay, virtually stopping the action, only tragically to run it forward. Perhaps this is why "death" suddenly appears, sweeping Daphne's "spirit" away, freeing her "soule" from the "soyl" of corporeal corruption. Is it death who is "soft" or is it Daphne's spirit? The play of verse will not say. Is this the triumph of death's material annihilation or the transfiguration of death into messianic savior? The poem may hear our question, but it does not answer. The early modern boundary between annihilation and salvation disappears, leaving Alcyon inconsolable and the consoling poet powerless to enact one of the cardinal virtues of Spenserian art, the therapeutic use of speech and art to work through the grief of mourning: "Griefe findes some ease by him that like does beare" (*Daphnaida* 67). Alcyon strides forcefully beyond help, beyond the art of the poet; indeed, he toys with the beyond as the void itself:

> But he no waie recomforted would be,
> Nor suffer solace to approach him nie,
> . . .
> As one disposed wilfullie to die,
> That I sore griev'd to see his wretched case.
>
> (*Daphnaida* 547–53)

In his disposition to willful death, Alcyon forgets Daphne's charge to care for their child Ambrosia (288–94); but this is not the worst: even the poet writing the poem forgets the new orphan of grief. Like her mother, she slips quietly away, an unnerving premonition of young Ambrosia Gorges's death in 1600 at the age of twelve.

Failing to convince the grieving husband to turn aside to his "Cabinet" as the autumnal evening closes upon them (558), the poet is left with a haunting sight, the grief-stricken husband besieged by dark metaphysical agents, against which the Spenserian corpus powerfully militates:

> As if that death he in the face had seene,
> Or hellish hags had met upon the way:
> But what of him became I cannot weene.
> FINIS.
>
> (*Daphnaida* 565–67)

Who are these hags? what is their way? and what finally is finished? Spenser reports only that Alcyon walks quietly into the void of the poet's own opening invocation to three weird sisters, and that his own subjectivity follows after, each left to embrace oblivion—alone, unpitied, unplained. For this, and for the rest, Spenser is more than a great poet of mourning and mutability; on his way to *Fowre Hymnes* and *The Mutabilitie Cantos*, he is an important and eloquent registrar of the early modern struggle to resuscitate the body of death in the newly discovered bourn of oblivion.[47]

Notes

1. The present essay appears about the same time as *Imagining Death in Spenser and Milton*, ed. Elizabeth Jane Bellamy, Patrick Cheney, and Michael Schoenfeldt

(Basingstoke: Palgrave, 2003). This volume is the first extended treatment of its topic, and includes three essays on Spenser and three on Spenser and Milton, together with an introduction and an afterword. By editorial decision, the volume concentrates on *The Faerie Queene*, not Spenser's shorter poems (with the exception of one essay, which includes a section on *Epithalamion* and *Prothalamion*). The present essay grows out of work on this volume, even borrowing a few paragraphs from its introduction.

2. Most notably in several recent overviews of the elegiac genre: E.Z. Lambert, *Placing Sorrow: A Study of the Pastoral Convention from Theocritus to Milton* (Chapel Hill: University of North Carolina Press, 1978); Peter Sacks, *The English Elegy: Studies in the Genre from Spenser to Yeats* (Baltimore: Johns Hopkins University Press, 1985); G.W. Pigman III, *Grief and English Renaissance Elegy* (Cambridge: Cambridge University Press, 1985); Celeste Margurerite Schenck, *Mourning and Panegyric: The Poetics of Pastoral Ceremony* (University Park: Pennsylvania State University Press, 1988); and Dennis Kay, *Melodious Tears: The English Funeral Elegy from Spenser to Milton* (Oxford: Clarendon, 1990). See also Matthew Greenfield, "The Cultural Functions of English Renaissance Elegy," *English Literary Renaissance* 28 (1998): 75–94.

3. *The Spenser Encyclopedia*, Gen. ed. A.C. Hamilton (Toronto: University of Toronto Press, 1990).

4. Watson, *The Rest is Silence: Death as Annihilation in the English Renaissance* (Berkeley: University of California Press, 1994); Neill, *Issues of Death: Mortality and Identity in English Renaissance Tragedy* (Oxford: Clarendon, 1997); and Dollimore, *Death, Desire and Loss in Western Culture* (New York: Routledge, 1998). Neill's title explains why he does not examine Spenser; Watson observes that, even though he looks at both plays and poems, including Kyd's *Spanish Tragedy* and "Metaphysical poetry," he focuses on the Jacobean period (1–3); Dollimore also examines poems, including Shakespeare's Sonnets, but, as his title reveals, he opens his cultural lens wide enough to justify the neglect of many important writers. These studies continue to be so influential in Renaissance studies that it might be profitable to cast their fascinating shadows across the Spenserian corpus. As to be expected, all three studies emphasize English Renaissance tragedy, and especially Shakespeare and *Hamlet*.

5. Grossman, "Reading, Death and the Ethics of Enjoyment in Spenser and Milton," in *Imagining Death in Spenser and Milton*.

6. All quotations and citations from Spenser's poetry come from *The Poetical Works of Edmund Spenser*, ed. J.C. Smith and Ernest de Selincourt (Oxford: Clarendon, 1910). The *i-j* and *u-v* are modernized, as are other obsolete typographical conventions, such as the italicizing of names and places.

7. In *Bodies and Selves in Early Modern England: Physiology and Inwardness in Spenser, Shakespeare, Herbert, and Milton* (Cambridge: Cambridge University Press, 1999), Michael C. Schoenfeldt neglects the writerly dimension of his topic.

8. See Patrick Cheney, "Spenser's Pastorals: *The Shepheardes Calender* and *Colin Clouts Come Home Againe*," in *The Cambridge Companion to Edmund Spenser*, ed. Andrew Hadfield (Cambridge: Cambridge University Press, 2001), 79–105.

9. The three models naturally overlap, especially Watson's and Neill's. Indebted to both Lacan and Foucault (among other psychoanalysts and cultural historians),

Dollimore is intent to track his early modern model in antiquity, the Middle Ages, and beyond.

10. Paglia, "Spenser and Apollo: *The Faerie Queene*," in *Sexual Personae: Art and Decadence from Nefertiti to Emily Dickinson* (New Haven: Yale University Press, 1992), 170–93.

11. Thanks to John Watkins for provoking this line of thought.

12. For a complementary reading of this passage, foregrounding "Spenser as a poet who refuses to reify death," see David Lee Miller, "Death's Afterword," the afterword to *Imagining Death in Spenser and Milton*.

13. See Patrick Cheney, *Spenser's Famous Flight: A Renaissance Idea of a Literary Career* (Toronto: University of Toronto Press, 1993), 149–94.

14. Shakespeare, Sonnet 29, in *The Riverside Shakespeare*, ed. G. Blakemore Evans, et al. (Boston: Houghton Mifflin, 1997). Future quotations and citations from Shakespeare come from this edition. See Patrick Cheney, " 'O, let my books be . . . dumb presagers': Poetry and Theater in Shakespeare's Sonnets," *Shakespeare Quarterly* 52 (2001): 222–54 (esp. 245–47).

15. On Spenser's connection to the Elizabethan theater, see, most recently, Jeff Dolven, "Spenser and the Troubled Theaters," *English Literary Renaissance* 29 (1999): 179–200.

16. See David Lee Miller, "Spenser's Vocation, Spenser's Career," *ELH* 50 (1983): 197–231: "Colin turns into an icon of natural death" (204).

17. *Ben Jonson's Conversations with William Drummond of Hawthornden*, in *Ben Jonson: The Complete Poems*, ed. George Parfitt (London: Penguin, 1988), 465. In *The Life of Edmund Spenser* (Baltimore: Johns Hopkins University Press, 1945), vol. 11 in *The Works of Edmund Spenser: A Variorum Edition*, ed. Edwin Greenlaw, et al., 11 vols. (Baltimore: Johns Hopkins University Press, 1932–57), Alexander C. Judson may question whether the child referred to was Spenser's (198–99), but under the circumstances this seems indiscreet.

18. On Spenser's important contribution to children within the life of the family, see Ricardo J. Quinones, "Spenser," in *The Renaissance Discovery of Time* (Cambridge: Harvard University Press, 1972), 265–69.

19. As the following discussion suggests, commentary on this most maligned—and misunderstood—of Spenser's poems is slender in comparison with most of his other shorter works. For instance, in the recent *Cambridge Companion to Edmund Spenser*, it receives only two passing references (83, 151). Moreover, to my knowledge, it has never been anthologized, perhaps because it appears so unsettlingly outside the Spenserian pale.

20. For biographical details, see Helen Estabrook Sandison, "Arthur Gorges, Spenser's Alcyon and Ralegh's Friend," *PMLA* 43 (1928): 645–74.

21. On Spenser's first marriage, see Judson, 63, 175. On the narrator as still in mourning for this wife, see William A. Oram, "*Daphnaida* and Spenser's Later Poetry," *Spenser Studies: A Renaissance Poetry Annual* 2 (1981): 141–58, here at 154, 158n.21.

22. Lewis, *English Literature in the Sixteenth Century, Excluding Drama* (London: Oxford University Press, 1954), 370.

23. Oram, "*Daphnaida* and Spenser's Later Poetry," 141. See also his introduction to the poem in *The Yale Edition of the Shorter Poems of Edmund Spenser*, ed. William

A. Oram, et al. (New Haven: Yale University Press, 1989), 487–91; "*Daphnaida*," in *The Spenser Encyclopedia*, 208–09; and his unit in *Edmund Spenser* (New York: Twayne, 1997), 156–60.

24. See Maren-Sofie Rostvig, *The Hidden Sense* (Oslo: Universitetsforlager, 1963), 82–87; and S. Fukuda, "A Numerological Reading of Spenser's *Daphnaida*," *Kumamoto Studies in Language and Literature*, 29–30 (1987): 1–9.

25. On genre, see *Yale* ed., 488; Lambert, 220–21n11. On subversions of genre, see, e.g., Donald Cheney, "Spenser's Fortieth Birthday and Related Fictions," *Spenser Studies: A Renaissance Poetry Annual* 4 (1984): 3–31, here at 12.

26. On Chaucerian intertextuality, which by far has drawn the most attention and is discussed by most critics, see T.W. Nadal, "Spenser's *Daphnaida* and Chaucer's *Book of the Duchess*," *PMLA* 23 (1908): 863–81; Normand Berlin, "Chaucer's *The Book of the Duchess* and Spenser's *Daphnaida*: A Contrast," *Studia Neophilologica* 38 (1966): 282–89; Harris and Nancy L. Steffen, "The Other Side of the Garden: An Interpretative Comparison of Chaucer's *Book of the Duchess* and Spenser's *Daphnaida*," *Journal of Medieval and Renaissance Studies* 8 (1978): 17–36; Ellen Martin, "Spenser, Chaucer and the Rhetoric of Elegy," *Journal of Medieval and Renaissance Studies* 17 (1987): 83–109; and Glenn Steinberg, "Idolatrous Idylls: Protestant Iconoclasm, Spenser's *Daphnaida*, and Chaucer's *Book of the Duchess*," in *Refiguring Chaucer in the Renaissance*, ed. Theresa M. Krier (Gainsville: University Press of Florida, 1998), 128–43. On Theocritus, Virgil, Ovid, and Petrarch, see W.L. Renwick, ed., *Daphnaida and Other Poems* (London: Scolartis Press, 1929), 173–75, as well as his excellent annotation.

27. Oram, "*Daphnaida* and Spenser's Later Poetry," 143–44, 154.

28. See D. Cheney, 10; Kay, 80; Richard A. McCabe, headnote to *Daphnaida*, in *Edmund Spenser: The Shorter Poems* (London: Penguin, 1999), 643. In his 1997 version of the argument (*Edmund Spenser*), Oram does not respond to Martin's objections to his thesis; for a more recent rebuttal, see Steinberg.

29. Her inset quotation comes from DeNeef, *Spenser and the Motives of Metaphor* (Durham: Duke University Press, 1982), 45. DeNeef concludes that, even though Alcyon is a "failed Orpheus" (42), *Daphnaida* is a "poetic defense" (49): "The dramatization of how poetry can be abused is, at least in part, an attempt to ensure that this poem is used correctly. Against the false-speaking Alcyon, therefore, is the Right Poet Spenser" (49–50). This argument is important, but, as we shall see, it effaces the historical moment of Spenser's portrait of Alcyon. Although criticizing this portrait, DeNeef observes in passing that the shepherd may be "considerably more seductive than he initially appears, for despite his extreme point of view he still articulates a recognizably human perspective" (44). D. Cheney also finds *Daphnaida* a "curiously powerful poem" (10).

30. For Spenser's 1591 critique of the Elizabethan stage, both comedy and tragedy, see *The Teares of the Muses* 115–234. Cf. Oram, "*Daphnaida* and Spenser's Later Poetry": "Alcyon's language tends to hyperbole, associating him with the rhetorical overreachers of Elizabethan drama" (144).

31. See, e.g., Donald Cheney, "Spenser's Fortieth Birthday," 15.

32. Poems 94 and 98, in *The Poems of Sir Arthur Gorges*, ed. Helen Eastabrook Sandison (Oxford: Clarendon, 1953). See also poem 44 on the Daphne myth (D.

Cheney, 28n.19). For further detail on "eleven" poems "apparently addressed to Douglas or concerned with their relationship," see Steven W. May, *The Elizabethan Courtier Poets: The Poems and Their Contexts* (Columbia: University of Missouri Press, 1991), 107–09 (107).

33. Cf. Martin: "In the poem's allusion to Persephone, the name 'Eurydice' appears because of the greater situational similarity between Gorges's and Orpheus's losses: poets losing their romantic objects" (97).

34. Ovid, *Metamorphoses* X.78–85, in vol. 4 of *Ovid*, 2nd ed., trans Frank Justus Miller; rev. G.P. Goold, Loeb Classical Library, 6 vols. (Cambridge: Harvard University Press; London: Heinemann, 1984); and Virgil, *Georgics* IV.511, in vol. 1 of *Virgil*, trans. H. Rushton Fairclough, Loeb Classical Library, 2 vols. 1916–18; Cambridge: Harvard University Press; London: Heinemann, 1934–35).

35. See Ralegh, *Ocean to Cynthia* 26–28, in *The Poems of Sir Walter Ralegh*, ed. Agnes M.C. Latham (Cambridge: Harvard University Press, 1951); cf. Ralegh's *Commendatory Verse* to the 1590 *Faerie Queene*, line 2.

36. Regrettably, little has been written on Gorges as a poet; he is, for instance, overlooked in the *Dictionary of Literary Biography*, ed. David A. Richardson (Detroit: Gale, 1993–96), vols. 132, 136, 167, and 172. Not simply does Spenser take an interest in his career, granting him eight lines of praise and advice in *Colin Clouts Come Home Againe* (384–91), but Gorges left quite a bit of extant verse himself, spread across the late-Elizabethan and early-Jacobean periods; see Sandison's Oxford edition; and May, esp. 103–19, 321–23.

37. "*Daphnaida* and Spenser's Later Poetry," 147.

38. On Alcyon's exhibition of a "proto-pagan view of the world," see Oram, "*Daphnaida* and Spenser's Later Poetry," 159.

39. Watson, *The Rest is Silence*, 5.

40. See Richard D. Jordan, "satyrs," in *The Spenser Encyclopedia*, 628.

41. For this genealogy and etymology, see R.P. Winnington-Ingram, "The Origins of Tragedy," in *Greek Literature*, ed. P.E. Easterling and B.M. Knox, vol. 1 of *The Cambridge History of Classical Literature*, ed. P.E. Easterling and E.J. Kenney, 2 vols. (Cambridge: Cambridge University Press, 1982–85), 1–6, esp. 3–4. See, e.g., Horace, *Art of Poetry* 220–21, in *Horace's Satires and Epistles*, trans. Jacob Fuchs, intro. by William S. Anderson (New York: Norton, 1977): "A competitor in tragic song who sought to win the goat,/soon took away the forest satyr's clothes."

42. On the genre of minor epic, see Clark Hulse, *Metamorphic Verse: The Elizabethan Minor Epic* (Princeton: Princeton University Press, 1981). *The Rape of Lucrece* is typically understood to be "valuable as a precursor of Shakespeare's mature tragedies," especially *Macbeth* (Hallett Smith, intro. to the poem in the *Riverside Shakespeare*, 1815).

43. McCabe, *Edmund Spenser: The Shorter Poems,* 642.

44. See Pigman, *Grief and English Renaissance Elegy,* 75, 80.

45. See Oram on Alcyon as "a mode of behavior Spenser felt it necessary to suppress in himself," an embodiment of "at one level an impulse within the narrator" ("*Daphnaida* and Spenser's Later Poetry," 154).

46. On the "republican" implications of Gorges's 1614 translation, see David Norbrook, *Writing the English Republic: Poetry, Rhetoric and Politics, 1627–1660* (Cambridge: Cambridge University Press, 1999), 34, 41–42, 441. On the *Pharsalia* as a

counter-Virgilian epic, see Patrick Cheney, *Marlowe's Counterfeit Profession: Ovid, Spenser, Counter-Nationhood* (Toronto: University of Toronto Press, 1997), esp. 227–37. Gorges's translation of Lucan represents only one half of his biography; the other appears on his brass funeral monument in More Chapel, Chelsea Old Church, which represents him and his second family praying devoutly on their knees before another well-known book (Sandison, 667; for a reproduction, see the frontispiece to Sandison's edition of Gorges's poems). These biographical sides are not contradictory but speak to the full complexity of early modern identity, which Spenser eloquently renders in *Daphnaida.*

47. For different views of how *Daphnaida* fits into Spenser's literary career, see Oram, "*Daphnaida* and Spenser's Later Poetry," esp. 152–55; and D. Cheney, esp. 3–5 and 9–12.

GRAHAM L. HAMMILL

"The thing/Which never was": Republicanism and *The Ruines of Time*

This essay discusses Spenser's engagement with republican political thought in *The Ruines of Time*, parts of Book V of *The Faerie Queene*, and in Spenser's dedicatory sonnet to Lewkener's translation of Contarini's *De magistratibus et republica Venetorum* (*The Commonwealth and Government of Venice*). This essay proposes that in *The Ruines of Time* Spenser invents a republican principal of poetry, one that intensifies his readers' responsibility for political thought, and it then goes on to explore this readerly responsibility in the poem and in the engagement of *The Faerie Queene*, Book V, with the emergent Dutch republic. While Spenser's poetry stages the limits of its own political thought, through abstraction and negation, it also provokes and solicits readers who can overcome these limitations.

SPENSER'S POETRY IS OFTEN MOST INTERESTING when it struggles with political concepts, as opposed to expressing them straightforwardly. It is out of sensitivity to this aspect of the poetry that, in an exploratory essay to which this present essay is indebted, Andrew Hadfield asks what seems at first to be an audacious question: "Was Spenser a republican?" Even more surprisingly, he suggests that the proper response might be yes. Arguing against the vision of Spenser as a poet who in the 1590s became increasingly disgruntled and embittered by Elizabethan policy and subsequently retreated into pastoral privacy, Hadfield proposes that, as Spenser charts the increasing failures and problems of Elizabeth's reign, he also engages with republican political thought. "There are significant signs in Spenser's writings to suggest that he was certainly—at the very least—familiar with republican ideas, representing alternative possibilities of government in his works which challenged the system of hereditary monarchy currently operating in the territories ruled by the English monarch."[1] This interest in republicanism would not have been unusual for someone attached to the Essex circle, as Spenser was.[2] It is clear from the references to and influences of Machiavelli in the *View* that Spenser read the *Discourses* with some care. And it is easy to show that Spenser had some familiarity with other versions of republican thought, since he wrote a dedicatory sonnet to one of the first two republican treatises published in English, Lewkener's translation of Contarini's *De magistratibus et republica Venetorum* (*The Commonwealth and Government of Venice* [1599]), and since in that sonnet Spenser makes direct reference to material in Lewkener's translation.[3] Does this mean that Spenser was a republican? As Hadfield admits, none of these details cinches that proposition, and he concludes by noting that he cannot identify Spenser as a republican with "unequivocal decisiveness."[4]

I take the uncertainty of Hadfield's identification to indicate the particularly mediated quality of republican thought in Spenser's later poetry. In recent discussions of Spenser and republicanism, mediation is the missing category. In a recent critique of Hadfield's essay, David Scott Wilson-Okamura answers Hadfield's question with a resounding "no": Spenser was *not* a republican. So long as the issue of republicanism is cast in terms of identity, Wilson-Okamura will be right. But, as Hadfield notes in his response, *The Faerie Queene* resists easy interpretation of its author's motives.[5] More precise attention to the ways the poetry mediates political thought recasts the issue so that it is not longer Spenser's political position but now the poem's encoding of political thought and political history for particular kinds of readers. In this essay, I explore this mediation as it works in *The Ruines of Time*, which Spenser completed sometime between Walsingham's death in April, 1590, and December 30, 1590, when the *Complaints* was entered in the Stationers' Register, and which I take to be Spenser's first sustained engagement with continental republican thought. Doubtless any exploration of the *politics* of political thought must raise the question of rhetoric. Does Spenser's engagement with republican paradigms of thought support republicanism's antimonarchical program, or does his engagement instrumentalize republicanism in the service of monarchy? Answers to this question would lead to a discussion of Spenser's possible political positions. By mediation, I mean something slightly different. When Spenser engages with aspects of republican thought, his poetry also calls attention to the textual and literary strategies by which he represents that thought. While this aspect of mediation necessarily renders Spenser's position equivocal, it also shifts the focal point of political thought from that well known construct "Spenser the author" to the possible readerly positions that Spenser's poetry solicits and provokes. That is, the question is not just, how does Spenser construct and undermine a series of authorial poses, but more importantly, how does the mediation of republican paradigms in Spenser's later poetry posit a perspective, or multiple perspectives , from which those paradigms will be understood?

Spenser's struggle with political concepts is almost always a struggle enacted between rhetoric and mediation. The two terms can come into conflict: Spenser's attention to mediation can solicit skeptical responses that create some critical distance from the instrumentalization of republican thought. They can, however, also converge: Spenser's poetry can instrumentalize republicanism in the service of skepticism, or it can mobilize skepticism in order to sharpen a critique of certain kinds of republicanism. This last option is what happens in Spenser's dedicatory sonnet to Lewkener's translation of Contarini's *De magistratibus*. Although this essay focuses primarily on *The Ruines of Time*, I begin with a discussion of this dedicatory sonnet for two main reasons: first, because it is Spenser's most obvious engagement with republicanism, and second, because it demonstrates fairly tersely the way in which the poem's positioning of the reader becomes a determinate aspect of that engagement. One of the central distinguishing characteristics of republican thought, as J. G. A. Pocock has pointed out, is the thesis, contra theocracy, that government exists "in the dimension of contingency, without the intervention of timeless agencies."[6] This thesis leads to "the problem of explaining how a system of distributive justice, once defined as finite in space and time, could maintain its existence in a world where *fortuna* constantly presented threats which, because they were irrational, were always immediate rather than remote."[7] Spenser's dedicatory sonnet picks up on and is conceptually organized by this fundamental problem.

The antique *Babel*, Empresse of the East,
  Upreard her buildinges to the threatned skie:
  And Second *Babell* tyrant of the West,
  Her ayry Towers upraised much more high.
But with the weight of their own surquedry,
  They both are fallen, that all the earth did feare,
  And buried now in their own ashes ly,
  Yet shewing by their heapes how great they were.
But in their place doth now a third appeare,

Fayre *Venice*, flower of the last worlds delight,
And next to them in beauty draweth neare,
But farre exceedes in policie of right.
Yet not so fayre her buildinges to behold
As *Lewkenors* stile that hath her beautie told.[8]

Like Verlame, the main speaker in *The Ruines of Time*, who, as she puts it "nought at all but ruines now I bee,/ And lye in mine owne ashes, as ye see" (*RT* 39–40), here both Babylon and Rome, literally built from the ground up, are monuments in general to the finitude of the state and in particular to the ultimate failure of each to deal with the threat of contingency. At first, Venice seems more promising, only, whether or not this is so depends on the meaning of the phrase "policie of right." Although the phrase does not occur in Lewkener's translation of Contarini, read from the perspective of the Venetian buildings project, right and policy are more or less synonymous. As Contarini proposes, Venetian architecture is the outward manifestation of sound Venetian government, her "policie of right": "from the first building thereof, even until this time, being now a thousand and one hundred years, [Venice] hath preserved itself free and untouched from the violence of any enemy, though being most opulent and furnished, as well of gold as silver, as of all other things that might, yea even from the farthest parts of the world, allure the Barbars to so rich a booty and spoil."[9] Venice's policy of right is one that ensures "a happy and quiet life" through the bureaucratic administration of the commonwealth by an elite oligarchy.

But if we interpret the phrase from the perspective of Spenser's brief discussion of Venetian republicanism in the *View*, a more complex dynamic begins to emerge. Spenser concludes his argument that a governor of Ireland must not be constrained by English policy makers with a reference to Machiavelli. In the *Discourses*, Machiavelli proposes that when the state becomes corrupt, "good legislation is of no avail unless it be initiated by someone in so extremely strong a position [*una estrema forza*] that he can enforce obedience until such a time as the material has become good." The revivification of the corrupt state depends not on policy but on "the virtue [*virtù*] of some one person who is then living."[10] In the name of the public good, such a person must be willing to commit the most scandalous atrocities, "no small blood-letting [*dimolto sangue*]," in Machiavelli's phrase,[11] in order to reinstate the status quo of the state. Machiavelli solves the problem of ensuring the continuity of the state against the threats of contingency by sanctioning violence committed for the benefit of the greater good. As Gérald Sfez puts it, for Machiavelli "it is not a question of forbidding evil or finding a means to invalidate its effects, but of making a *leap* from evil committed in indecision to a decision upon evil. This leap is that from the apprehension of time as *chronos* to time as *kairos*: not two different times but time relinquished and time seized again."[12] Spenser has Irenius use this argument in the *View* to support his call for a strong colonial governor:

> For yt is not possible for the Councell here to dyrecte a gouernor there, who shalbe forced oftentymes to followe the necessitie of presente occasions to take the suddaine advantage of tyme, which being once lefte will not bee recouered whilst through expecting dyrections from hence, the delaies whereof are often tymes through greater affayres most yrkesome, the opportunities there in the meanetyme passe awaye and great danger often groweth, which by such tymelie prevencion might easelie be stopped, And this I remember is worthelie obserued by matchavell in his discourses vpon Livie, where he comendeth the manner of Romaines gouerment, in gyvinge absolute power to all theire Consulls and governors, which yf they abused they should afterwardes dearly Aunswere, And the contrarie thereof he reprehendeth in the states of Venice of Florence, and manye other principallities of Italie, who vsed to lymitte theire cheif offycers, so straightlie as that thereby oftentymes they haue lost such happye occasions, as they could neuer come vnto againe. (*View*, 217–18)

From this perspective, policy and right are nearly antithetical. Right means the duty a governor has to use extreme violence and terror in order to mend civic corruption, and policy must admit some room for the exercise of this right if a governor is to take full advantage of "presente occasions." Whether or not this latter is the meaning Spenser intended to give "policie of right," it's worth noting that once the possibility emerges, the poem shifts from praising Venice to praising the style of a piece of prose that translates another description of Venice. Though seemingly minor, this shift is important in that with it the sonnet gives a position from which to suspect its own seemingly straightforward praise of Venetian republicanism. To unpack the compacted line of reason the shift implies: if Lewkener's style is more beautiful than Venice, then perhaps there is something defective in Venetian republicanism that Lewkener excludes; and if the high praise of Venice over Babylon and Rome is due to Venice's "policie of right," then perhaps that policy is what Lewkener and Contarini are prettying up. If Venice has lasted so long, republicanism's legitimization of state violence is the reason, and you won't find this reason given in Lewkener's translation because Lewkener, following Contarini, has erased this republican insight by stylizing and beautifying it. The sonnet's implication of naive consciousness might stand as a general critique of Contarini's understanding of republicanism; but more than that, in a negative and characteristically Spenserian way, the implication of naive consciousness emphasizes the violence which that understanding leaves out, not to critique the use of violence but to critique shying away from the question of its legitimacy.

I am not suggesting that Spenser unequivocally says this. Rather, I am arguing that, regardless of Spenser's intentions, when his dedicatory sonnet calls attention to the mediated quality of Lewkener's translation, it provokes the possibility of skepticism from its readers and uses that possibility to consolidate a position from which Machiavellian violence can be read as the secret of republicanism that Lewkener's Contarini excludes. More generally, I propose that in the 1590s, as Spenser became increasingly frustrated with Elizabethan domestic and foreign policy, not only did he engage in alternative forms of political thought like republicanism, but also his poetry intensified its readers' responsibilities for political and historical thought. Spenser assumes a reader familiar with and engaged in republican political thought. By placing the burden of political thought on that reader, Spenser's poetry develops a strong counterforce to the moralizing, often conservative political thought of its own narrators, something like a republican principal of poetry.

As with the dedicatory sonnet to Lewkener's Contarini, *The Ruines of Time* also shows an interest in republican temporal paradigms of virtue and corruption. What is tricky about Spenser's application of these paradigms to late Elizabethan bureaucracy is that he points to political problems by abstracting from topical referents. In part, this abstraction is self-protecting. Whether or not *The Ruines of Time* was "cal'd in," as John Weever writes in his *Epigrammes*,[13] the poem charges Burghley with political corruption. Burghley, "that first was raisde for vertuous parts" (451), has rejected a Ciceronian model in which private virtue lays the foundation for public responsibility and, now that he "welds all things at his will" (447), simply protects his own political power, "broad spreading like an aged tree,/ Lets none shoot up, that nigh him planted bee" (452–53). Verlame claims that

Burghley's corruption is due to vanity, and, through the reference to *Ecclesiasticus* by which she introduces him, she elaborates that vanity as a disowning of responsibility. "There be two things that grieue mine heart, and the thirde maketh me angrie: a man of warre that suffreth pouertie: and men of vnderstanding that are not set by: & when one departeth from righteousnes vnto sinne: the Lord appointeth suche to thy sworde."[14] Burghley may like Solomon scorn the current condition, in which "learning lies unregarded,/ And men of armes doo wander unrewarded" (441), but Verlame also implies that he is like the third figure whom Solomon hates, the one headed for sin. The charge is implicit but extraordinarily forceful even so. Burghley's abuse of power is the cause of the very things he also grieves, and for this reason he deserves to be put to death. But more than indict Burghley, this passage also suggests that an administrator like Burghley threatens the freedom of the entire state. In both Harrison and Camden, Spenser's two sources for his poem's main speaker, Verlamium is a model of civic freedom, the city having attained the status of *municipium Romanorum* and thereby "the whole freedom of the Romans." As Harrison explains it, there is a great difference between *municipium Romanorum* and *colonia Romanorum*: "*municipium* is a city enfranchised and endued with Roman privileges, without alteration of her former inhabitants or privileges, whereas a colony is a company sent from Rome into any other region or province to possess either a city newly builded or to replenish the same, from whence her former citizens have been expelled and driven out."[15] While much of *The Ruines of Time* is Verlame's complaint about her own inability to maintain this status over time, when she proffers herself as an example for Burghley and those like him, "Let them behold the piteous fall of mee:/ And in my case their owne ensample see" (461–62), the poem insinuates that Burghley's self-serving politics threatens to corrupt English civic freedom.[16]

The poem opposes the threat of corruption through the figure of Sidney. Against Burghley's "[welding] all things at his will," the poem poses Sidney as a quasi-republican model for the connection of virtue and citizenship through the citizen soldier, "So life exchanging for his countries good" (301).[17] Spenser's representation of Sidney's death stands in subtle but distinct contrast to the various occasional poems written between 1586 and 1588. These poems portray Sidney's death in order to propose that loyalty to a Protestant God and to Elizabeth were so deeply analogous as to be the same thing. In *Vpon the life and death of the most worthy, and thrise renowmed knight, Sir Phillip Sidney*, Angel Day describes Sidney's "loue, seruice, and obedience, to *God*, his *Prince*, and his *Countrie*."[18] In *The Life and Death of Sir*

Phillip Sidney, John Phillips makes Sidney's Christianity and his loyalty analogous, so Sidney's obedience to God and loyalty to Elizabeth are both expressions of "the fruites of fayth."[19] Phillips then has Sidney describe how in Flanders he fought "the Spanish rout,/ That spit their spite against my God and Prince."[20] And George Whetstone, who emphasizes Sidney's service to Elizabeth less than do the other two, ends his poem, *Sir Phillip Sidney, his honorable life, his valiant death, and true vertues*, with Sidney telling his brother Robert to "Feare God, and liue: loue well my frendes: and knowe,/ That worldly hopes, from vanitie doe flowe."[21] Whetstone's Sidney continues to explain that, even though he was dying, how he desired to live "for publique good."[22] *The Ruines of Time* separates Sidney's death from monarchy and, like the citizen soldier in Machiavelli's *Art of War*, has Sidney prove his *virtù* by discipline and self-sacrifice in the service of a greater, national good.[23] To reinforce this *virtù* and to insist on a particularly Christian version of republicanism, Spenser portrays Sidney's sacrifice through christological figuration. Sidney's choice to fight at Zutphen, "that guiltie hands of enemies/ Should powre forth th'offring of his guiltles blood" (299–300), explicitly repeats Christ's "spotles sacrifise" (298). While christological figuration lets Verlame posit poetry as a monument more durable than "Pyramides . . . Or huge Colosses, built with costlie pain" (408–09), the implication for political thought is that Spenser uses Christian temporality to mythify the civic virtue of the citizen as the grounds for the continuation of the "countries good."

In an old historicist essay, William R. Orwen argues that *The Ruines of Time* responds to the increasingly serious problem of Elizabeth's succession: "The Queen's courtiers and councilors were eager to establish themselves with the next monarch, whoever he might be, for Elizabeth was growing old, and stood in constant danger of assassination. Moreover, James VI of Scotland, who held the presumptive title, threatened to combine with Spain, Catholic France, and Catholic England to depose Elizabeth."[24] This threat, Orwen continues, resulted in a general interest in civil war literature—the publication in 1590 of Lydgate's *Serpent of Division* in a volume with *Gorboduc*, the Countess of Pembroke's translation the same year of Garnier's *Marc Antoine* (published two years later), and the publication of Spenser's *Complaints*—that explores the "civil strife consequent upon an uncertain succession."[25] Orwen argues for the still pervasive picture of a nationalist Spenser whose primary political concern was Elizabeth and her succession.[26] But with its focus on Sidney's death at Zutphen, *The Ruines of Time* takes on a more trans-European historical content: England's failed intervention in the Low Countries. This was certainly a problem that concerned Spenser throughout the first half of the 1590s. In the 1590 *Faerie Queene*, chronological history concludes with Merlin's prophesy that Elizabeth's sovereignty will extend "ouer the *Belgicke* shore" (III.iii.49) as the English defeat the Spanish tyrants that reign there. It was a hope that in the mid-1580s might have seemed plausible. In 1585, after the assassination of William of Orange, the Dutch States General offered sovereignty over the Netherlands to Henri III, and, after he refused, the States General offered the same to Elizabeth. She also refused, but agreed to take the United Provinces under her protection and aid the Dutch in their war against the Spanish. While this agreement explicitly recognized the United Provinces as a sovereign state, it also implied strong incursions against Dutch state sovereignty. Elizabeth claimed the right to nominate the military and political head of the United Provinces, and she also demanded that England be given seats in the Dutch *Raad van State*.[27] Especially among more enthusiastic English Protestants, this agreement also tended to encourage the dream of a trans-European Protestant coalition headed by Elizabeth that could counter the extraordinarily powerful Hapsburg empire.[28] Merlin's prophesy that Elizabeth would "Stretch her white rod" over the Low Countries along with Spenser's strong affiliations with the Leicester circle both place him fairly firmly in this camp. Spenser envisages the possibility of a unified, Protestant northern Europe with Elizabeth at its head.

By 1590, however, the whole Dutch affair seemed to have become more trouble than it was worth. English forces had been outflanked by the prince of Parma, and, at least according to Burghley's spin, Leicester had irrevocably mishandled the ruling Dutch oligarchy, who were, in any case, entirely untrustworthy. Moreover, Leicester and Walsingham, the two main supporters of the Anglo-Dutch alliance, were dead. On December 30, 1590, Burghley wrote to Thomas Bodley, the senior English representative on the Dutch *Raad van State*, that he wished he were "rid of [the Dutch] . . . . In very truth her Majesty is herewith tempted greatly both to repent herself of aiding them and to attempt how to be quit of them."[29] Read from the perspective of Anglo-Dutch relations, Spenser's particular interest in republican strategies for dealing with the threats of contingency becomes more obvious. In *The Ruines of Time*, Spenser presents republican civic virtue in combination with Christian figuration in order to propose Sidney, exemplar of the virtuous citizen soldier, as a cultural solution to the historical problem of Protestant devolution that England's failure in the Low Countries was coming to represent.

Spenser can overcome Sidney's death and all it represents by making him emblematic of a Protestant *vita activa* and opposing that emblem to Burghley 's corrupt and self-serving politics. Spenser makes a similar gesture in Book V of *The Faerie Queene* when he opposes Arthur's decision to aid Belge to the "cowheard feare" (V.x.15) of the other members of court. "Cowheard" is a pun which links the members of the English court to the "cowheard" Eurytion (10), Geryon's cow herder who slays foreigners and feeds them to Geryon's carnivorous, purple cows. With the coward/cowherder pun, Spenser encourages his readers to reconstruct the cause of political inaction that the episode's undernarrative suggests: English failure in the Low Countries is due to the cowardice of members of the English court, who overvalued Spain's power out of fear, which also caused them to abate what should have been out-and-out enmity. In *The Ruines of Time*, Spenser uses a republican model of the *vita activa* to begin to work out a strategy that he will continue in Book V of *The Faerie Queene*, the use of a hermeneutic temporal form to emphasize and to correct that failure of history to do what it was supposed to do.[30] In Spenser's portrayal of it, the civic and Protestant eventfulness of Sidney's death allows it to transcend its own contingent occasion as well as contingency itself.

For a discussion of Spenser's political thought, it is not enough to recover the implied historical context of *The Ruines of Time*. We must also ask why it is that the poem abstracts from the historical content that it also implies. Why, that is, does *The Ruines of Time* obscure and render latent its concern with Anglo-Dutch relations? Spenser's use of republican thought is central to the question. If Spenser engages with republican thought because it offers a vocabulary for apprehending historical change in relation to ethical conduct, in *The Ruines of Time* Spenser's main focus is not on ethical conduct but on the corruption which that conduct opposes. Through the figure of Verlame, Spenser broadens the category of corruption so that what Nicholas Canny has called Spenser's "conviction that moral lapses and degeneration were little short of inevitable" also becomes the conviction that historical decay and ruin were little short of inevitable as well.[31] Verlame personifies a lack of memory and the destruction of monuments in an ex-nominated voice, "Name have I none (quoth she) nor anie being" (34), that bespeaks history as the relentlessly destructive force of decay and ruin. As an allegory of negation, Verlame abstracts all change into so many examples of relentless negativity. That is, she insists on the draining up of any significant event as the fundamental experience of time, as the "unstedfast state/ Of all that lives, on face of sinfull earth" (43–44), a shriveling of historical events into the landscape in such a way that the earth itself becomes simply a tribute to decay and ruin. In that republican paradigms stand here somewhat orthogonal to issues of political organization, this is a fairly conservative use of republican political thought, and it only intensifies the question I asked above: Spenser makes history into a general problem concerning the passage of time in order to avoid the particular historical problem that his poem addresses by implication. Why?

In order to answer this question, I need to make two points. First, in *The Ruines of Time* Spenser distances himself from his earlier modes of political rhetoric without giving a positive or particularly obvious alternative mode. Verlame begins her praise of Sidney by ventriloquizing the Spenser of *The Shepheardes Calender.* "I to future age doo sing," she begins (277), imitating the literary ambitions of "our new Poete" who "in time shall be hable to keepe wing with the best" (*SC*, Epistle 165–67). Although she charges Colin Clout with apathy and "guiltie blame" (*RT* 230) for not writing pastoral elegy at Leicester's death, through Verlame Spenser distances himself from his earlier assumptions about epidexis, revealing what Richard Rambuss calls Spenser's "developing ambivalence about the whole process of hiring himself out for patronage."[32] More generally, Spenser here distances himself from epidexis as a form of rhetoric that he had previously used to assert monarchical sovereignty. As Louis Montrose has argued, beginning with the *Aprill* eclogue (1579) and continuing through the 1590 *Faerie Queene* Spenser attempts to establish an equivocal relation between himself as professional poet and Elizabeth as sovereign power, a relation in which "ruler and ruled are mutually defining, reciprocally constituted."[33] And, as David Lee Miller has added, the historical allegory of the 1590 *Faerie Queene* supports that relation. The poem duplicates the legal fiction of the king's two bodies in such a way that an idealized body politic is sustained as the deferred telos of historical allegory.[34] When Verlame takes over this model, she opposes monumentalization with repression, abstracting ruin into a reified category of negativity much like the position she claims for herself: "the thing/Which never was" (346–47). Spenser uses Verlame to stage the limitations of his prior mode of political address.

Second, *The Ruines of Time* uses genre in order to mediate that limitation such that it becomes a problem of historical content for the readers that the poem solicits. While the complaint is a fairly conservative genre, identifying social, political, and economic changes only to cast them in a moral apparatus that prevents the complainer from fully engaging in social, political, or economic diagnosis, *The Ruines of Time* self-consciously foregrounds and even performs its own inadequacy to grasp the historical content to which it also gestures. Conservative as it is, the complaint is a particularly promising genre for provoking critical diagnosis, but only on the condition that it fairly explicitly solicit a readership that is skeptical of its didacticism and processes of abstraction. In his early translations, *The Ruines of Rome*, *The Visions of Bellay* and *The Visions of Petrarch*, and in his early *Visions of the Worlds Vanitie*, Spenser's narrator learns the lesson of the world's mutability by viewing emblems of ruin and destruction, but this narrator is unable to do anything about it. The narrator in Spenser's early complaints is simply left "with perplexitie" (*VP* 2.24), meditating on the "tickle trustles state/ Of vaine worlds glorie" (7.85–86). In *The Ruines of Time*, the poem's narrator becomes a conspicuous example of how *not* to read the complaint. The poem gives us a narrator who, as audience to Verlame's complaint, is by the end of the poem seduced into complaining himself, "[r]enewing her complaint with passion strong" even though her "meaning much I labored foorth to wreste,/ Being above my slender reasons reach" (*RT* 486–87). Much like the Redcross Knight listening to Duessa, "More busying his quicke eyes, her face to view,/ Then his dull eares, to heare what she did tell" (*FQ* 1.2.26.6–7), the narrator in *The Ruines of Time* conspicuously misses the referents in Verlame's complaint that undermine her credibility. For example, after comparing herself to ancient Assyria, Persia, Greece, and Rome, the four "cruel," "barbarous," and "insaciable" kingdoms who conquered the Israelites and the rest of the ancient world, as the Geneva Bible notes (gloss on Daniel 7:5), Verlame goes on to describe herself in terms that lead God to make Jerusalem "knowe her abominacions" (Ezekiel 16:2). The problem with Jerusalem is that she took her beauty, which God says "was perfite through my beautie which I had set vpon thee" (Ezekiel 16:14), and claimed it as her own. Verlame continues to do the same:

> To tell the beawtie of my buildings fayre,
> Adornd with purest golde, and precious stone;
> To tell my riches, and endowments rare
> That by my foes are now all spent and gone:
> To tell my forces matchable to none,
> Were but lost labour, that few would beleeve,
> And with rehearsing would me more agreeve.

High towers, faire temples, goodly theaters,
Strong walls, rich porches, princelie pallaces,
Large streets, brave houses, sacred sepulchers,
Sure gates, sweete gardens, stately galleries,
Wrought with faire pillours, and fine imageries,
All those (ô pitie) now are turnd to dust,
And overgrowen with blacke oblivions rust.

(*RT* 85–98)

The example of Jerusalem which Verlame recites serves as an implicit corrective to her blatant self-promotion, but more than that, it also serves as an indictment of the poem's narrator in that he does not catch the referent or its implication either. The situation is akin to the one that Harry Berger, Jr., explains in his rich discussion of narrative and rhetoric in *The Faerie Queene*. Berger argues that *The Faerie Queene* engages a textual, literary transaction between poet and readership and an oral, rhetorical transaction between storyteller and virtual audience, and he goes on to propose that in these transactions "the conventional discourses [of literary tradition] are marked as citational by the oral-formulaic style and thus occupy the inner framework of the rhetorical transaction where they supply the target rather than the substance of the literary transaction."[35] *The Ruines of Time* stages a rhetorical transaction between Verlame and the narrator and then has the narrator recite that transaction in order to make it the object of critical as opposed to sympathetic reading. However, a critical reading of this rhetorical transaction is not the poem's ultimate objective. While the narrator's sympathy for a wailing woman allows him not to see the very serious political question that poem raises, namely, what will happen to transnational Protestantism after the deaths of Leicester, Sidney, and Walsingham and the unchecked ascendancy of Burghley, the poem encourages the readership it solicits to understand that political problem historically. What Spenser's poem abstracts from and negates is an historical situation that he could not grasp. And when Spenser underlines the complaint as a genre that abstracts from its historical content, the poem also directs its readers towards it.

That is, the poem directs us towards an historical situation that neither Spenser nor the poem entirely comprehends. While for Spenser the political problem has to do with the failure of England and the Low Countries to sustain a transnational Protestant alliance against the Hapsburg empire, from another perspective, the problem is republicanism emergent in its concrete form. From the point of view of Dutch nationalism, England's intervention was paradoxically an ideological and political success. English efforts to assert monarchical versions of state sovereignty produced a backlash effect which allowed Johan van Oldenbarnevelt to wrest military and administrative power away from the *Raad van State*, more or less a mouthpiece for the English, to the States General, more or less a mouthpiece for the States of Holland.[36] Through Oldenbarnavelt's efforts, the States General became the executive branch of the nascent United Provinces. This shift in institutional power was accompanied by the first coherent, ideological articulation of Dutch republicanism. In March of 1587, Thomas Wilkes, an English member of the *Raad van State*, issued his *Remonstrance*, which attacked the States General and the States of Holland for undermining and usurping Leicester's authority. "Sovereignty [*Souverainiteit*]," Wilkes argues, belongs to a "legitimate prince," and in the absence of that, "belongs to the commonality" and not to the States General, "who are only servants, ministers, and deputies of the commonality and have commissions which are limited and restricted not only in time but also in subject matter. These are conditions as widely different from sovereignty as is the power of the subject from that of the prince or of the servant from that of the master, or, to express it more clearly, as heaven is from earth, for sovereignty is limited neither in power nor in time. Still less do you, gentlemen, represent sovereignty."[37] Later that year, in his *Short Exposition*, François Vranck replied to Wilkes that for eight hundred years Holland and Zeeland had been ruled by a system of mixed government in which representatives of these states "were lawfully charged and commissioned with the rule and sovereignty of these Countries," and that by treating the members of the States General as particular persons and not as fully invested representatives of the commonality, "*representerende de Staten*" as Vranck puts it, Wilkes misunderstands both "the virtue of their commission" and more generally the way in which the "common good" of the United Provinces has its foundation in the "authority of the States."[38] Vranck's argument became the foundation for the Batavian myth, which Grotius among others subsequently used to assert the antiquity of Holland's republicanism.[39] It would of course be wrong to hold Spenser responsible for not grasping the ideological implications of emergent Dutch state sovereignty in their fullest complexities; rather, the debate between Wilkes and Vranck demonstrates that what *The Ruines of Time* stages as the internal limit of Spenser's political thought is a limitation already imposed by national history. This limitation is in 1590 what is most historical about Spenser's relation to republicanism.

Does Spenser ever overcome this limitation? Yes, in that by the mid-1590s Spenser does not negate the Dutch republic in the same way. In Book V of *The Faerie Queene*, Spenser's poetry moves from an inevitable exclusion of emergent Dutch republicanism to a conspicuous blindness to it. In the Belge episode in Book V of *The Faerie Queene*, Spenser's narrator admits a general distinction between states and kingdoms that the poem nowhere else makes. "When those gainst states and kingdomes do coniure,/ Who then can thinke their hedlong ruine to recure?" (V.x.26.). This distinction between kingdom and state is one that began to emerge towards the end of the sixteenth century, and if an anonymous paper in the royal library of Charles I is to be trusted, it was a distinction that Elizabeth herself disdained. "At the latter end of Queen Elizabeth, it was a phrase to speak, yea for to pray for the Queen and the State. This word 'State' was learned by our neighborhood and commerce with the Low Countreys, as if we were, or affected to be governed by States. This the Queen saw and hated."[40] Instead of developing "state" into a political concept separate from and on par with monarchy, Spenser presents this distinction against the backdrop of its own erasure. As Arthur and Belge survey the damage Geryon has done to Antwerp, Spenser underscores the distinction he is about to make by attempting to ensure that at least in the present case it does not hold:

> That Castle was the strength of all that state,
> Vntill that state by strength was pulled downe,
> And that same citie, now so ruinate,
> Had bene the keye of all that kingdomes crowne.
>
> (26)

Moreover, at the end of this episode, after Belge "had settled in her raine" (V.xi.35), the kind of statehood by which Belge governs is something of an open question. As the widow of William of Orange, which is what Belge is according to the episode's topical allusions, will she continue the kind of monarchy that *The Faerie Queene* suggests William had? Or rather, given Arthur's refusal to accept the "guerdon" Belge says she wants to give him (V.xi.16), will she rule according to some kind of state sovereignty that the poem would just as soon not take up? Even by 1590, it was clear that the United Provinces constituted a sovereign nation and that it did not have a monarchical form of government. In July of that year, Thomas Wilkes writes that the Dutch "hated to be subject not only to a Spaniard but, tasting the sweetness of their liberty, to any kingly government."[41] By

1596, when Spenser has Belge settle in her reign, he makes Belge stand for a form of state sovereignty whose content remains notably unsettled. While this does not make Spenser a republican by a long shot, it does show a poem that acknowledges the limits of its writer's political thought, and it also shows a poem that makes its readers as much if not more responsible for these limits, then and now.

NOTES

1. Andrew Hadfield, "Was Spenser a Republican?" *English: The Journal of the English Association* 47 (Autumn 1998): 179.

2. For a discussion of Spenser's relation to the political thought of the Essex circle, see David Norbrook, *Poetry and Politics in the English Renaissance* (London: Routledge, 1984), 126–32. Norbrook traces the transition from a language of republicanism to republicanism as a political program in *Writing the English Republic: Poetry, Rhetoric, and Politics, 1627–1660* (Cambridge: Cambridge University Press, 1999; rprt. 2000). As Patrick Collinson has shown, in Elizabeth's later reign, the relation between queen and council was flexible enough to admit explicitly republican solutions to possible states of exception foregrounded by problems of succession. See Collinson, "The Monarchical Republic of Queen Elizabeth I," in *Elizabethan Essays* (London: The Hambledon Press, 1994), 31–56.

3. The other treatise was *The Counsellor*, published in 1598, which is a translation of Wawrynzyniec Grzymala Goslicki's *De optimo senatore libri duo*. For a discussion of both treatises, see Markku Peltonen, *Classical Humanism and Republicanism in English Political Thought, 1570–1640* (Cambridge: Cambridge University Press, 1985), 102–18.

4. Hadfield, "Was Spenser a Republican?" 179.

5. David Scott Wilson-Okamura, "Republicanism, Nostalgia, and the Crowd," *Spenser Studies* XVII (2003): 253–273; Andrew Hadfield, "Was Spenser Really a Republican After All?: A Response to David Scott Wilson-Okamura," *Spenser Studies* XVII (2003): 275–290.

6. J. G. A. Pocock, *The Machivaellian Moment: Florentine Political Thought and the Atlantic Republican Tradition* (Princeton: Princeton University Press, 1975), 190.

7. Ibid., 84.

8. *The Yale Edition of the Shorter Poems of Edmund Spenser*, eds. William A. Oram et al. (New Haven: Yale University Press, 1989). All quotations from Spenser's shorter poems are from this edition; references will be given parenthetically by line number in text as follows: *RT, Ruines of Time; SC, Shepheardes Calender*, and *VP, Visions of Petrarch*. Quotations from Spenser's *View* are from *A View of the Present State of Ireland*, ed. W.L. Renwick (London: Eric Partridge, 1934; rprt. St. Clair Shores, MI: Scholarly Press, 1971), and will be cited parenthetically by page number in text as *View*. Quotations from *The Faerie Queene* are from A.C. Hamilton's edition (London: Longman, 1977), and will be cited parenthetically in text as *FQ*.

9. Gaspare Contarini, *The Commonwealth and Government of Venice* (London, 1599), Sig. B3r.
10. Niccolò Machiavelli, *Tutte le Opere*, ed. Mario Martelli (Florence: Sansoni, 1989), 102; the translation is from *The Discourses*, ed. Bernard Crick, trans. Leslie J. Walker, S.J. (New York: Penguin, 1983), 159.
11. Machiavelli, *Tutte*, 102; *Discourses*, 160.
12. Gérald Sfez, "Deciding On Evil," in *Radical Evil*, ed. Joan Copjec (London: Verso, 1996), 129.
13. John Weever, *Epigrammes* (London, 1599), Sig. G3a.
14. *Ecclesiasticus* 26:29. All Biblical quotations are from *The Geneva Bible: A Facsimile of the 1560 Edition*, with an intro. by Lloyd E. Barry (Madison: University of Wisconsin Press, 1957). Subsequent reference will be given in text. When appropriate, I have changed *ſs* to *ss*.
15. William Harrison, *The Description of England*, ed. Georges Edelen (Ithaca: Cornell University Press, 1968, for the Folger Shakespeare Library), 211.
16. This interpretation is borne out by a passage in the *View* in which Irenius opposes the aristocracy in England and in Ireland. Irenius notes that rebellions in Ireland "are not begunn by the Common people but by the Lordes and Captaines of Countries vpon pride or wilfull obstynacie [againste the gouernment] which whensoeuer they will enter into they will drawe with them all theire people." By contrast, Irenius continues, there are fewer examples of this in England: "the Noble men how ever they should happen to be evill disposed haue noe commaund at all over the Commonaltye, though dwelling vnder them, because euerie man standeth vpon him selfe, and buildeth his fortunes vpon his owne faith and firme assurance" (*View*, 190). In *The Ruines of Time*, what Burghley threatens is precisely this freedom of the common people.
17. For discussions of Spenser's attempts to use Sidney as a literary model, see Margaret Ferguson, " 'The Afflatus of Rome': Meditations on Rome by Du Bellay, Spenser, and Stevens," in *Roman Images*, ed. Annabel Patterson (Baltimore: Johns Hopkins University Press, 1984), 37; and A. Leigh DeNeef, " 'The Ruines of Time': Spenser's Apology for Poetry," *Studies in Philology* 76 (1979): 262–71.
18. Angel Day, *Vpon the life and death of the most worthy, and thrise renowmed knight, Sir Philip Sidney* (London, 1586?), Sig. A2r. SCT 6409. The publication date of Day's volume is conjectured by the *Short Title Catalogue*.
19. John Phillips, *The Life and Death of Sir Phillip Sidney* (London, 1587/88), Sig. A3v. STC 19871.
20. Ibid., B2r.
21. George Whetstone, *Sir Phillip Sidney, his honorable life, his valiant death, and true vertues* (London, 1586/87), Sig. C1v. STC 25349.
22. Ibid., C2v.
23. Machiavelli characterizes the citizen soldier in opposition to the professional mercenary:

> Every well-governed commonwealth, therefore, should take care that this art of war should be practiced in time of peace only as an exercise, and in time of war, only out of necessity and for the acquisition of glory, and that

> it should be practiced, as in Rome, by the state alone [*e al publico solo lasciarla usare per arte, come fece Roma*]. For if any citizen has another end or design in following this profession, he is not a good man; if any commonwealth [*città*] acts otherwise, it is not well governed.

Machiavelli, *Tutte*, 307; English translation from *The Art of War*, trans. Ellis Farneworth, ed. and rev. by Neal Wood (New York: Da Capo Press, 1965), 19. An Italian edition of *The Art of War* was published in London in 1587.

24. William R. Orwen, "Spenser and the Serpent of Division," *Studies in Philology* 38 (1941): 206. Orwen relies on Conyers Read's *Mr. Secretary Walsingham and the Policy of Queen Elizabeth*, 3 vols. (Cambridge: Harvard University Press, 1925), esp. 3:337–44. Orwen probably overstates the threat that James posed, but his general point about the Elizabeth's worry over the threat of a general alliance among Scottish, English, French, and Spanish Catholics seems accurate. See also, R. B. Wernham, *After the Armada: Elizabethan England and the Struggle for Western Europe, 1588–1595* (Oxford: Clarendon Press, 1984), 464–60.

25. Orwen, "Spenser," 202.

26. For example, Richard Helgerson argues that the 1596 *Faerie Queene* "allows no place for the representation of a powerfully centralized and absolutist governmental order. It acknowledges and celebrates a sovereign lady, but it grants a high degree of autonomy to individual knights and their separate pursuits, represents power as relatively isolated and dispersed." See Helgerson, *Forms of Nationhood: The Elizabethan Writing of England* (Chicago: University of Chicago Press, 1992), 48.

27. See Jonathan Israel, *The Dutch Republic: Its Rise, Greatness, and Fall, 1477–1806* (Oxford: Clarendon Press, 1995), 219–20. R. C. Strong and J. A. van Dorsten, *Leicester's Triumph* (Leiden: University of Leiden Press, 1964), 22–23.

28. Charles Wilson, *Queen Elizabeth and the Revolt of the Netherlands* (Berkeley: University of California Press, 1970), 31–33.

29. B.M., Cotton MSS., Galba D vii, f.357; cited in Read, *Lord Burghley and Queen Elizabeth* (New York: Alfred A. Knopf, 1960), 463.

30. As Kenneth Borris discusses, Spenser's later political allegory seriously misrepresents English foreign policy and recasts recently past events within an apocalyptic temporality in such a way that translates topicality into anti-Spanish and anti-Catholic satire. See Kenneth Borris, *Spenser's Poetics of Prophesy in The Faerie Queene V, English Literary Studies Monograph Series*, no. 52, (Victoria, BC: University of Victoria Press, 1990), 36–61.

31. Nicholas Canny, "The Social and Political Thought of Spenser in His Maturity," in *Edmund Spenser: Essays on Culture and Allegory*, eds. Jennifer Klein Morrison and Matthew Greenfield (Aldershot: Ashagate, 2000), 116.

32. Richard Rambuss, *Spenser's Secret Career* (Cambridge: Cambridge University Press, 1993), 93.

33. Louis Adrian Montrose, "The Spenserian Subject and the Elizabethan Text," in *Literary Theory/ Renaissance Texts*, eds. Partricia Parker and David Quint (Baltimore: Johns Hopkins University Press, 1986), 320.

34. David Lee Miller, *The Poem's Two Bodies: The Poetics of the 1590 Faerie Queene* (Princeton: Princeton University Press, 1988), 71–82, 98–111.

35. Berger, "Narrative as Rhetoric in *The Faerie Queene*," *English Literary Renaissance* 21 (Winter 1991): 12, 25.
36. Israel, *Dutch Republic*, 238–39.
37. *Thomas Wilkes' Remonstrance to the States General and the States of Holland, 1587*, partially translated in *Texts Concerning the Revolt of the Netherlands*, eds. E.H. Kossman and A.F. Mellink (Cambridge: Cambridge University Press, 1974), 273. A full version of the *Remonstrance* can be found in Pieter Christiaansz Bor, *Oorsprongk, begin en vervolgh der Nederlantsche oorlogen, beroerten en borgerlijke oneenigheden*, 2 vols. (Amsterdam, 1679; originally published in 1595), 2:918–21.
38. François Vranck, *Short Exposition*, partially translated in *The Dutch Revolt*, ed. and trans. by Martin van Gelderen (Cambridge: Cambridge University Press, 1993), 230, 237, 238; Bor, *Oorsprongk*, 2:921. A fuller version of the *Short Exposition* can be found in Bor, *Oorsprongk*, 2:921–29.
39. For a discussion of the Wilkes-Vranck exchange, and for discussions of the significance of Vranck's reply for subsequent ideological assertions of Dutch republicanism, see Pieter Geyl, "An Interpretation of Vrancken's Deduction of 1587 on the Nature of the State's of Holland's Power," in *From The Renaissance to the Counter-Reformation*, ed. Charles H. Carter (London, 1966), 230–46; Martin van Gelderen, *The Political Thought of the Dutch Revolt, 1555–1590* (Cambridge: Cambridge University Press, 1992), 201–07, and van Gelderen, "The Machiavellian Moment and the Dutch Revolt: The Rise of Neostoicism and Dutch Republicanism," in *Machiavelli and Republicanism*, eds. Gisela Bock, Quentin Skinner, and Maurizio Viroli (Cambridge: Cambridge University Press, 1990), 213–16.
40. Cited in G.N. Clark, "The Birth of The Dutch Republic," *Proceedings of the British Academy* 1946 (32), 195; see also 213–17. See also Quentin Skinner, *The Foundations of Modern Political Thought*, 2 vols. (Cambridge: Cambridge University Press, 1978), 2:352–58. This understanding of the state stands in direct contrast to Helgerson's, who reads Elizabethan concepts of the state retroactively through Hobbes and Hooker in order to propose that "the state was almost indistinguishably identified with the crown." See *Forms of Nation*, 296.
41. R.B. Wernham, "The Mission on Thomas Wilkes to the United Provinces," in *Studies Presented to Sir Hilary Jenkinson*, ed. J. Conway Davies (Oxford: Oxford University Press, 1957), 452.

MARY ELLEN LAMB

The Red Crosse Knight, St. George, and the Appropriation of Popular Culture

This essay discusses early modern performances of St. George from pre-Reformation watches and ridings in urban centers such as Norwich and London, to the boisterous festivities of Wells in the early seventeenth century. This context restores a sense of Spenser's Red Cross Knight as a hybrid figure, existing in tension between the world of literate, even hyperliterate, readers, and a once common culture in the process of becoming increasingly, although by no means entirely, distinct. Through this creative tension, Book I forms a particularly productive site of contest as it engages the often complex and unstable cultural alliances of readers during a period of increasing social stratification in the late sixteenth century.

AS SPENSER SCHOLARSHIP AMPLY DEMONSTRATES, St. George was a hybrid figure composed of deep cultural contradictions. He was the patron saint of Protestant England and also a Catholic saint particularly despised by Calvin.[1] He was celebrated by the aristocratic Order of the Garter but also, according to Erasmus's *Praise of Folly*, appreciated primarily by the uneducated.[2] By the late sixteenth century, he had become a complex cultural sign, whose various and contradictory meanings circulated in written works that continue to inform most critical understandings of his appearance in Book I as the Red Cross Knight.[3] Without in any way detracting from Spenser's use of these written sources, it is the purpose of this essay to explore how Spenser complicated and deepened the contemporary meanings of Book I yet further by appropriating unwritten, and specifically performative, materials.

By the time Spenser was reading his Barclay, a very different St. George had made his appearance in midsummer watches and ridings; and he would continue to be part of the festivities of Wells and

Chester in the early seventeenth century. Some years ago, William Nelson acknowledged this tradition in his claim that because of the "buffoonery of village St. George plays . . . no Renaissance humanist could have thought the legendary life of St. George a respectable literary model."[4] Hugh MacLachlan, on the other hand, describes how, beginning as early as the fifteenth century, these widespread performances of St. George in "mummers' plays, pageants, and processions" engendered enough patriotic fervor by the early modern period to render him an appropriate figure to represent the English nation.[5] Whether assuming (or projecting) contemporary responses of contempt or enthusiasm, these opposite critical understandings reflect more upon attitudes towards the social milieu in which St. George was celebrated than on the figure himself. Underlying these very different perceptions is a primary principle informing my own approach: the meanings of this St. George were determined by the social circumstances in which he was performed.

This essay discusses how, rather than eliciting a single and stable contemporary response, performances of St. George became a highly sensitive barometer registering political and social ideologies that changed, sometimes gradually and sometimes quite abruptly, over the course of the sixteenth century. In Edward's reign, it was for his identity as Catholic saint that his ridings and other practices were suspended. In Elizabeth's reign, Puritan evangelicals denounced him, along with maypoles and hobbyhorses, as a figure of festivity. Underlying and working through these developments, performances of St. George from the fifteenth through the seventeenth century registered an ongoing process of social stratification in which elite and middling groups became increasingly alienated from a once-shared common culture. In response to economic, demographic, and religious factors of this period, more prosperous members of communities tended to distinguish themselves from less fortunate neighbors rapidly becoming, in the words of Keith Wrightson and David Levine, "not simply poor but culturally different."[6] In the mid-to-late sixteenth century, this social change registered linguistically in a language of "sorts" —the "common sort," the "better sort," the "ruder sort"—in a vocabulary of social dissociation reconstructing social identities at this time.[7]

As a period of transition, the sixteenth century provides a particularly useful time for the study of these cultural processes while they were still underway. Not yet self-evident, the meanings of these social changes were culturally produced and culturally contested through a variety of vehicles, including literary works such as Spenser's *Faerie Queene*. Through a discussion of performances of St. George, I seek to uncover some of the mechanisms through which this separation was eventually effected. In the process, I also hope to restore a sense of the complexity of the Red Cross Knight as a hybrid figure, negotiating the interests of literate, even hyperliterate, readers against the background of a once common culture which they had not, or had not yet, left entirely behind.[8]

I

What, then, can be inferred of the ideological significances of St. George within the sphere of public performance? Before the reformed Protestant England of Edward VI condemned his veneration as a Catholic saint, there is no indication that St. George was associated with a non-elite culture. On the contrary, St. George presented a primarily military and patriotic figure suited to reception by kings. St. George figured prominently in a ceremony at Bristol welcoming Edward IV after his defeat of Henry VI in 1461: "There was Seynt George on horsbakke uppon a tent fyghtyng with a dragon, and the kyng and the quene on hygh in a castell, and his doughter benethe with a lambe. And atte the sleyng of the dragon ther was a greet melody of aungellys."[9] St. George's victory resonates with Edward's recent triumph, as the "greet melody of aungellys" suggests heavenly partisanship of the Yorkist cause. A similar St. George pageant was also included with other displays to welcome Edward VI on his coronation in London. A small stage erected on a conduit presented "Seint George on Horsebacke in Compleat Harnes, with his Page in Harnes also, holding his Speare and Shield, and a faire Maiden holding a Lamb in a string."[10] By the time of Edward VI, this martial and illustrious St. George, together with the maiden and her lamb, had entered contemporary iconography. The church of St. Gregory in Norwich still exhibits, according to an observer, "a fine mid 15th century wall painting which shows St George killing the dragon, with the princess in the background holding a lamb."[11]

More festive are the royal Twelfth Night revels of 1494, in which a St. George entertainment interrupted (surely by plan) a "goodly Interlude" staged before King Henry VII and his court at Whitehall. Bursting into the hall were Saint George, played by William Cornish, later a Master of the Children of the Chapel Royal, with a "ffayer vyrgyn attyrid lyke unto a kyngys dowgthyr" who led a "Terryble & huge Rede dragun" who "as he passyd spytt ffyre at hys mowth."

After a short speech, Cornish began an anthem of St. George answered by the King's Chapel choir. As Cornish "avoydid" with the dragon, the entire hall joined in song.[12] Like the "greet melody of aungellys" in Bristol, the anthem sung by the chapel choir was to provide aesthetic pleasure. Breaking down the distinctions between performers and audience, the participation in song by the entire hall suggests a culturally cohesive group with a broad spectrum of taste, able to enjoy a fire-breathing dragon along with a program of devout music.[13]

Beyond the court, the figure of St. George was familiar in "ridings" on his feast day, April 23, in what Hutton has called "some of the most colorful rites of the early Tudor period."[14] As expressions of civic pride, these ridings could require considerable outlays of time and money. At Norwich, an active Guild of St. George created this procession as particularly elaborate, with money spent not only on St. George and his dragon, but on the Lady Margaret, on horses, on footmen, on shoes and gloves, on a linen cloth for the dragon.[15] In Newcastle, account books from 1510–11 reveal considerable care and expense, lavished especially on the dragon.[16] Hutton notes that "the popularity of St. George continued to grow up to the very beginning of the Reformation" with additional ridings also occurring in such cities as Leicester, Stratford-upon-Avon, Chester, Bristol, and Coventry.[17] Cressy observes that before the Reformation on St. George's day, when the knights of the Garter convened at Windsor, at least twenty-eight towns held fairs; and St. George also appeared in Chester to announce Whitsun plays with attention-getting "drume musicke and trumpetes."[18]

Throughout this period, an emphasis on St. George's armor identifies him as not only a saint, but as a soldier-knight, whose entourage and trappings demanded expense and considerable planning. While he maintained this aristocratic and martial role, the cheerful chaos of town watches may have detracted somewhat from his dignity. As described by Lodovico Spinelli, secretary to the Venetian ambassador, the London midsummer watch of 1521 appealed to a broad range of taste, with men in armor, a "very tall canvas giant," archers, musicians, "50 men and naked boys dyed black like devils," a serpent "vomiting very fetid sulphruic fire-balls," Turkish horsemen pursuing a castle float, choristers singing to the Virgin Mary, and St. George "in armour, choking a big dragon and delivering Saint Margaret."[19] This staging was followed and, in a sense, contextualized by a festive company dancing what Spinelli called the "morescha," a form of mimed combat, usually between Christians and non-Christians such as Moors or Turks in outlandish costumes.[20] These midsummer watches designed to promote social order during a time of revelry also contained within them the opposite potential for, according to Spinelli, the 2000 halberdiers who concluded the watch raised concern in the spectators that "as usual, these armed men should raise some tumult."[21] In 1585 John Montgomery noted that "in tyme past" watches drew together a "great rabble of the worst sort," so that they were "far better calculated to break the peace than to preserve it."[22]

These customs came to an abrupt halt, in any official sense, when the Reformation gathered force with Edward VI's accession to the throne in 1547. It was for St. George's significance as a Catholic saint that the lord protector Somerset banned his image and eliminated his feast from the 1552 prayerbook. Then, with the accession of Catholic Mary Tudor, the feast was restored, and her husband Philip himself led the customary procession of knights of the Garter on St. George's day in 1555.[23] Ridings were also restored to the villages. Financial records in York describe some form of a repeated "play" of St. George as part of his riding. In 1554, the City Chamberlains' Books detail a payment to the waites or singers for "rydyng & playing before St. George and the play," to the "king & Quene that playd," and to one John Stamper the not inconsiderable sum of 3 shillings 4 pence for "playng St. George." The agreement of the city fathers in 1558, the year of Elizabeth's accession, that "this yere St. George play shall be left & not playd," suggests an expectation based on performances in previous years.[24] While it is not clear if the term "play" refers to a scripted production or a pantomimed skirmish, the generous payment to the St. George actor suggests the development of a larger role.

During Elizabeth's reign, the signification of St. George became complicated by his identification with popular festivity; and it was as a festive as well as a Catholic figure that enthusiasts of the reformed religion exerted pressure against his appearances, along with maypoles, morris dancing, and church ales, all of which declined dramatically by the late sixteenth century.[25] It was probably because of his identity as a Catholic saint that, with the accession of the Protestant Elizabeth, the official ridings of St. George came to an end. While Queen Elizabeth continued to observe St. George's day by going in procession with her knights of the Garter to her chapel in state, records of his public appearances in watches are not in evidence. But she was not apparently offended by his appearance in a maygame. By June 24, 1559, in the first year of Elizabeth's reign, St. George had become a different kind of figure than in the ridings. Down from his stage, he mixed with morris dancers and Robin Hood; and he may have numbered among those giving speeches around London. The diary of Henry Machyn describes this Maygame: after the "gyant, and drumes and gunes," there was "then sant Gorge and the dragon, the mores dansse, and after Robyn Hode and lytyll John, and M[aid Marian] and frere Tuke, and thay had spechys rond a-bowt London." Not only was there no reference to offense or other trouble on that day, but on the next day, June 25, "the sam May-gam whent unto [the palace?] at Grenwyche, playng a-for the Quen and the consell."[26] Presumably this maygame would not have been allowed to play at Greenwich without the Queen's implicit approval, and Ronald Hutton gathers this with other evidence to suggest Elizabeth's favor for such festival performances. Yet such festivity declined steadily in her reign in large part, Hutton observes, through the forces of evangelical Protestantism.[27]

Whatever Elizabeth's own sympathies, the enthusiasts of the reformed religion curtailed or limited festive entertainments. As Cressy notes, the annual procession and play of St. George was suspended in York in 1558, while in Norwich, St. George and Lady Margaret were removed, although "for pastime" the mayor allowed the dragon Old Snap to continue his appearance.[28] The presence of this dragon memorialized St. George, as his conspicuous absence surely brought him forcefully to mind. St. George became an absent presence in other venues as well as, untainted with Catholic sainthood, George's dragon continued to make its appearance in Protestant England without him. As in the festivities of 1559, dragons mixed indecorously with other festival figures. A dragon cavorted and waged combat among the morris dancers and other figures in a procession described by Philip Stubbes as a repeated abuse in the realm of "Ailgna" or England. Along with their "Hobby-horses, dragons & other Antiques, togither with their baudie Pipers and thundering Drummers," the morris dancers "struck up the devils daunce withall," marching along towards the church, "their handkercheifs swinging about their heds like madmen, their hobbie horses and other monsters skirmishing amongst the route." According to Stubbes, these merrymakers set up a banqueting house in the churchyard, where they sold "certain papers" or badges, to "maintaine them in their hethenrie, . . . drunkenes, pride, and what not." Those who would not give them money were "mocked, & flouted at, not a little."[29]

Although Stubbes implies that funds benefited the participants themselves, in other respects this procession to the church and ensuing banquet suggests a church ale. Before the Reformation, the selling of food and drink outside churches had formed an established means of raising parish funds; and often these occasions also included morris dances and other crowd-drawing shows. Peaking in 1570, these church ales went into rapid decline by 1600.[30] Disapproval by Stubbes and his many fellow-thinkers invested these events with newly negative social and political meanings. Noting that "the Puritan voices against . . . morris dancing were strong by the 1590s," Forrest describes this process in this way: Morris dancers . . . became a vehicle for social protest against an ecclesiastical hierarchy that was insensitive to the needs of rural communities. So, although the dancers were at one point a force for social cohesion, having been branded as antisocial they became so—disturbing the peace and breaking the law (137, 214). The same may be said for the dragons, hobby horses, and other fellow travellers. Stubbes' representation of how those who would not contribute were "mocked, & flouted at" provides a local understanding of how social divisiveness might have escalated during such events. In the face of naysayers, what was once a communal activity assumed a disagreeable edge of defiance.

Especially with the loss of any established sponsor, these festive figures were liable to mingle together as common expressions of insubordination to those who would shut them down. In addition to common enemies such as disapproving villagers, they shared the activity of performed combat. A dragon skirmished, morris dancers mimed battle gestures, and Robin Hood invited trials of skill with friar Tuck and any other onlookers.[31] As Bruce Smith eloquently observes, there is no literary term to describe such performances. Lacking "verbal substance," they cross "generic boundaries: neither song nor dance nor drama, they are at once none of the above and yet all of the above." Dancing, fighting, drumming, "bodies move in rhythm with sound" to challenge the "authority of language" (136). In the process, they also challenge the authority of evangelical Protestants and respectable citizens of the middling sort. While St. George may not have appeared in person beside his dragon on official ridings, a quotation from Shakespeare's *King John* reveals that, far from forgotten, he also took on meanings associated with these events in this time period: "Saint George, that swing'd the dragon, and e'er since/ Sits on's horseback at mine hostess' door,/ Teach us some fence!" (II,i,288). Faulconbridge's St. George remained a martial figure able to teach fencing; but as he "swing'd" the dragon, to assume his place on the signs of taverns, he had also become, endearingly or reprehensibly, common.

Did St. George and his dragon gain an even more disreputable presence by joining morris dancers as they moved into more private venues? Such a mingling had already occurred with the figures from the Robin Hood group; and Forrest questions whether Maid Marian and Friar Tuck were "old morris characters that were grafted onto the Robin Hood legend, or vice versa."[32] By the 1590s, Puritan opposition to church ales and other festivities had left many morris dancers without any official sponsor. According to "The Auntient forme & payments of midsomer wach or show" in Chester in 1601, for example, the morris dancers who had once received ten shillings from the city would now have no fee but "the Curtesye after the show at eich house what they please."[33] As Forrest details, some troupes went into business for themselves, touring local villages and, by the time of the late Tudors, performing in private houses of rural gentry.[34] To attract an audience, morris dances absorbed new ideas and, more importantly, new participants in other similarly dislocated figures. Once an entertaining collector of contributions at church ales, the hobby horse became part of the morris in the early 1590s. The 1620 painting "Thames at Richmond" catches something of the sense of this unsponsored activity, with its representation of a somewhat bedraggled morris troupe with their Maid Marian, and a hobby horse turned outward to wheedle money from onlookers.[35]

As performers appealed to onlookers for contributions, did they join forces with St. George and his dragon, as well? Or did some St. George groups capitalize on a similarly unsponsored tour? Richard Hardin's recent observation of a striking parallel between an episode in Book I of the *Faerie Queene* and later mummers' plays of St. George provides material for speculation. After his defeat by Red Cross Knight, Spenser's Turkish knight Sansjoy is transported by Duessa to the underworld to be healed by Aesculapius. As Hardin notes, the plot of this episode resembles the hero-combat scripts recorded by E. K. Chambers as dating from 1788 and continuing into the twentieth century, in which a Turkish knight is similarly healed by a doctor after his defeat by St. George. Hardin concludes, "At the very least, Spenser's digression offers yet another tantalizing clue that, a century before the earliest known date, the Mummers' Play was well enough known to appear in a parody."[36] An early modern form of this tradition is supported by a transcription of a document written around 1685, according to its notation in the Thomas Croker MS.1206 in the Library of Trinity College in Dublin. This document describes a performance featuring St. George, a Turkish knight, a doctor, Beelzebub, and "a little Devil with a broom to gather up the money that was thrown to the Mummers for their sport." According to the author's statement that at the time of his childhood, it was already "an ancient pastime of the citizens," this custom apparently dated from the sixteenth century.[37] This assemblage matches to a striking extent the later performers recorded by Chambers, such as Beelzebub who dances with Big Head after the combat, and little Devil Doubt who appears with his broom to collect coins from the audience.[38]

While it would be naïve to assume that St. George plays recorded from the eighteenth and nineteenth century replicated an early modern custom in any pure form, it seems a reasonable conjecture that with the loss of official sponsors, various early modern performers, including St. George, morris dancers, hobbyhorses, and other unemployed performers, may well have pooled their resources to put on a show for compensation. The Turkish knight may have substituted for the dragon because the dragon's head was too costly to obtain and then to maintain. The modern performances of these St. George plays in the Christmas season may derive from the tradition by other mummers of inviting or extracting hospitality from wealthy landowners during that time. As early as the fifteenth century, English mummers disguised themselves by wearing masks or painting their faces to enter private residences to play dice or some other competitive game often during this season.[39] The practice apparently broadened to include other forms of often unspecified entertainment. As Thomas Pettit notes, " 'Mumming' seems to mean simply a seasonal (winter) house-to-house visit by a group of local people who put on some kind of show for the households on which they intrude."[40] On Twelfth Night of 1618, one Nicholas Assheton enters in his journal the following reference: "At night some companie from Reead came a Mumming: was kindly taken: but they were but Mummers."[41] If, as seems likely, Spenser was alluding to such a practice in the Aesculapius episode, then the prestige of the early modern St. George would not have been enhanced by performers such as those described by Assheton as "but Mummers."

Especially with the rise of the middling sort, a process of uneven but relentless social stratification invested some St. Georges with an edge not apparent in the fifteenth century. Efforts to discourage or to suppress popular festivities increasingly associated with the "ruder sort" invested them with an intensified power to offend. A spiral of prohibition and defiance lent them a renewed energy and potentially dangerous purpose. In this way, the social meaning of the performed St. George became produced not only by those who participated in festivities, but perhaps even more effectively, by those who did not. For those members of the gentry or middling sort distinguishing themselves from a less elite group, contempt for St. George served as a means of social self-definition. For members of these same groups caught up in the spirit of the event, however, social dissociation was not always simple or free from conflict. In a time of social transition near the end of the sixteenth century, the range of meanings possible for St. George, and their effect on Spenser's readers, were unusually multivalent.

On the accession of James I, the significances of the performed St. George became more complicated yet, as he reappeared with other festival figures to signify loyalty to the monarch against the rising power of evangelical Protestants.[42] He resumed his public appearances, accompanying his dragon again in the processions at Norwich. Yet even the support of the Stuarts could not dependably return St. George to his pre-Reformation dignity. According to a reference in John Fletcher's *The Woman's Prize* (1611), the St. George known for his battles with his dragon in Kingston had become a humorous figure, hen-pecked by a scolding female dragon: "Running foot-back from the furious Dragon,/ That with her angry tayle belabours him/ For being lazie."[43] His association with festival figures in the sixteenth century did not endear him to the "soberer sort" for whom, as Hutton notes, royal sponsorship of holiday customs rendered them only more political and more contentious.[44] He was increasingly falling out of favor with more educated members of the population, as well. Exploding St. George's combat with a dragon as mere myth, Peter Heylyn's scholarly attempts to separate fiction from the facts reveal his scorn for popular uses of this figure: "But now St. George must . . . poast away unto the Land of Faeries, and there remaine for ever, with other the chimeras of an idle head."[45]

A dramatic contrast in two performances of St. George in Wells and Chester reveals two very different productions of this figure as an ideological sign in the first decade of the seventeenth century. Reviving the custom of church ale with the approval of the Dean of Wells and the mayor, the citizens of Wells engaged eight weeks of what Smith has called "a veritable anthology of folk revelry."[46] In the traditional procession towards the church, St. George was joined by a melange of figures both popular and classical: a lord of the May, dancers, soldiers, Robin Hood and his men, a "sparked" or painted calf, drums, fifes and trumpets, two men in hair bearing between them an egg on crossed staves, "olde Grandam bunche that filthe slutte" carrying puddings in a wheelbarrow, Acteon converted into a hart, a coach with Diana and six nymphs in white, Noah's arch, a giant and giantess that "in loftly maner loked precise/ on after the other by degree," a naked feathered boy, an Egyptian king with his queen, and, finally, three hundred dishes to be consumed at the church.[47] When the citizens were about to return home after the first day of the church ale, the "fyrye Dragon" provoked a skirmish with St. George as he "laye in wayte/ for to devowre the princess streight."[48] But over the next weeks, the event disintegrated. In response to opposition by the constable and others, hostilities escalated in the form of demeaning parodies of its most respectable merchants (the haberdasher, pewterer, grocer, usurer, and scrivener), a charivari to the house of one Mrs. Yard, and a popular and sexually libelous "holing game" beneath the picture of this same Mrs. Yard. The Wells festivities became a Star Chamber matter.

As described in *Chester's Triumph in Honor of Her Prince* (1610), the stately St. George procession at Chester on the visit of Prince Henry could not have been more different in tone. Rather than Mother Bunch and Robin Hood, the Chester St. George rode on horseback accompanied by refined and highly abstract personages—Fame, Mercurie, Chester, Peace, Plenty, Envy, Love, and Joy—as well as presenters displaying three lavish prizes—a double gilt bell, a "massie Bell of Silver," and a "great piece of Plate, parcell Gilt, Bell fashion"—to be awarded to the three winners of the day's horserace. After the procession reached the mayor of Chester, various of these abstractions declaimed set orations in pentameter couplets on the prosperity and blessedness of the realm. Rumor mentioned St. George briefly, stressing his military might in placing "whole Hoasts of Heathens foes to flight" more than his defeat of "a hideous Dragon." The orations were followed by the horseraces, presentation of awards by Britain, Camber, and Rumor, and finally an invitation by a personified Chester to selected participants ("each noble worthy, and each worthy Knight") to share in a "small repast." This dignified civic event did not so much suppress popular taste as contain it, providing outlets in the excitement of the horse race and also in the hilarity of two acts designed to warm up the crowd at the beginning of the procession. The first was an acrobatic feat performed by a man throwing off fireworks while performing handstands on an iron bar on the church steeple. The second involved the only pageant of the procession: two "savages" dressed in ivy and bearing clubs fought with "an artificiall Dragon, very lively to behold," who demonstrated a particularly theatrical bent as he was slain "to the great pleasure of the spectators, bleeding, fainting, and staggering, as though hee endured a feeling paine, even at the last gaspe, and farewell."[49]

The ceremonies at Wells and Chester reveal contrasting strategies for managing social divisions in process but not yet entirely separate. The carnival performances at Wells at least initially received the endorsement of its highest civic authorities before disintegrating into hostilities directed at disapproving citizens. While allowing some latitude to the ordinary populace, the tightly controlled and scripted proceedings at Chester avoided the divisive conflict fostered by spontaneous celebration. In particular, the horserace, which undoubtedly represented the primary event to many onlookers, encouraged an inclusive collaboration of various groups: the wealthy horse-owners, the skilled horse-riders, and the heterogeneous watching crowd.[50] The differing strategies produced contrasting St. Georges, as well. The Wells St. George engaged with his dragon in a post-procession event designed to heighten the delight of the crowd. Lying in wait, the Wells dragon presumably pounced on a startled princess after the day's festivities were supposedly concluded. St. George's combat with this dragon represented an unexpected spectacle to the revellers, satiated and no doubt in some cases inebriated, after the church ale.

This sense of playing to a crowd clearly characterizes the prolonged and hilarious death-throes of the Chester dragon, as well; but the Chester St. George was much too dignified to mime combat with him. He was, instead, killed by "savages" with clubs. The dragon maintained distance not only from St. George, but from the abstractions—Peace, Plenty, Fame—whose elegant orations elicited very different responses: admiration and perhaps even boredom—but certainly not humor. Rather than the indiscriminate mixing allowing Diana metaphorically to rub elbows with Mother Bunch at Wells, the more deliberate Chester event sets up clear-cut artistic distinctions by placing the dragon with the firework-throwing acrobat at the beginning of the procession. The theories of Pierre Bourdieu provide a way of perceiving this separation of the dragon from St. George not only in space, but in aesthetics, as registering and justifying a relations of power:

> The denial of lower, coarse, vulgar, venal, servile—in a word, natural—enjoyment, which constitutes the sacred sphere of culture, implies an affirmation of the superiority of those who can be satisfied with the sublimated, refined, disinterested, gratuitous, distinguished pleasures forever closed to the profane. That is why art and cultural consumption are predisposed, consciously and deliberately or not, to fulfil a social function of legitimating social differences.[51]

The aesthetic discipline distinguishing this rehabilitated St. George marked a claim to elevated social status based on the awareness, and on the denial, of the more lively St. Georges who had earlier descended from horses to do battle with their dragons.

In the selection, and the deliberate forgetting, of his customary actions, the separation of the Chester St. George from his dragon engaged another process, as well, in this ongoing project of social distinction. In its purging of anything offensive or vulgar from his tradition, the Chester St. George participated in a "rhetoric of amnesia" representing the social counterpart of the deliberate forgetting of Catholic symbols described by Elizabeth Mazzola. Such forgetting entails, paradoxically, a heightened consciousness of what must be forgotten; and Mazzola's argument for the "afterlife for abandoned symbols" of the Catholic church applies as well to practices of a common culture, including the popular combats between St. George and the dragon.[52] In Chester, the defeat of the very thespian dragon by savages, instead of by St. George, foregrounded the extent to which this forgetting constituted a conscious act. Selecting from this long tradition, Chester's appropriation of the figure of St. George did not simply reject what did not fit, but used these differences to move towards social identifications not readily available in the reign of Henry VII.

II

What, then, are Spenser's uses of St. George in his construction of his Red Cross Knight in Book I of *The Faerie Queene*? In the performed St. George, Spenser inherited an involved and far-ranging tradition. Through histories, church iconography, and oral accounts, the cultural memories of his frequent appearances in civic ridings, watches, and court festivities in pre-Reformation England would not have yet faded by Spenser's day. From this tradition, St. George became an appropriate symbol of an "old" England during a period when a nation was searching for legends and heroes through which to represent itself. Through the processions of Queen Elizabeth and the knights of the garter on St. George's day, this nationalist significance remained alive even in the absence of a physical bearer of the saint. For Spenser's readers, the responses elicited by the popular associations of St. George and, in his absence, of his dragon in may-games, church ales, and mummings in Queen Elizabeth's reign, would have varied widely, depending on their age, geographical location, and religious sensibilities. As a figure of unsponsored and increasingly discredited festivity, St. George became a sign of a once shared common culture through which middling and elite groups were marking their social identity by establishing their differences. But since this process was still in transition, not only among but also within individuals, this aspect of St. George was capable of arousing various degrees of joy and hostility, nostalgia and disgust, sometimes at the same time. The St. Georges of the early seventeenth century suggest conceptual routes available to Spenser: to capitalize on his popular associations at the cost of alienating the soberer sort as at Wells, or to purify him of festivity in a deliberate forgetting as at Chester. Accomplishing both, and neither, of these alternatives, Spenser's Book I produces not only a narrative, but an aesthetic, capable of engaging readers at several levels simultaneously. As Spenser's uses of the performed St. George invest Book I with complex, and potentially profound, social meanings, it is a mark of his genius that the operations of this text provide opportunities for readers to fashion their individual identifications with a common culture through their own creative and unpredictable interpretations.

An awareness of St. George as the sign of a common culture enters *The Faerie Queene* as early as Spenser's letter to Raleigh, in which he describes the Red Cross Knight as "a tall clownishe younge man" who, after falling before Gloriana to request an adventure, "rested him on the floore, unfitte through his rusticity for a better place."[53] Spenser's use of this association is, however, open-ended. As the Red Cross Knight, the figure of St. George provides at least three possible identifications from which readers may choose. His initial appearance in Book I stresses his inexperience. Its "old dints" from previous encounters reveal that his armor was received second-hand, for "yet armes till that time did he never wield." He is disdained even by his horse, "angry" as he "did chide his foming bitt" (I.i.1). From such cues, Richard Hardin describes the text as "inviting us to consider that the clownish knight was . . . a product of the pageant and festival Saint George." And this inexperience is not confined to the first canto, for as Hardin notes, "until the last three cantos, in fact, the gullible rustic behaves more like a rude pageant actor than the authentic hero as imagined by chivalry."[54] In fostering an identification with the cruder St. George of unsponsored performances, the narrative of Book I also flows into a broader stream of folk tale plots. As an inexperienced rustic who succeeds in defeating the dragon and winning the heart of the princess, this St. George becomes indistinguishable from the tailors, the third sons, the Jacks in the beanstalks who also emerge from anonymity to accomplish great deeds. The function of such tales to provide wish-fulfillment to lives worn by labor and poverty creates the core narrative of Book I as a fantasy reflecting the conditions of the peasants of a common culture.[55] This identification is supported by his name, George, from *geos*, the earth, of the "heaped furrow" where a fairy had placed him, to be found and reared by a simple ploughman (I.x.66). This association with the soil is particularly evocative for a figure who participated in the tales, as well as the maygames and other practices, marking the seasonal cycles of the agrarian countryside. From this tradition, the overcoming of Una's initial resistance not only to accept but even to marry her rustic knight models a receptive response invited from readers.

With Contemplation's announcement of the Red Cross Knight's aristocratic lineage, born "from ancient race/ of Saxon kings" (I.x.65), a second and very different narrative mode comes into play in the tale of the remarkable personage whose extraordinary qualities derive from an aristocratic descent at odds with his or her apparently humble origin. From the legendary Arthur to Shakespeare's lovely Perdita of his *Winter's Tale,* variations of this narrative were particularly popular in early modern romances in prose and drama. The implied reification of the aristocratic class as innately superior to other groups appears in the implicit connection between the "bloudie battailes" fought by his royal ancestors and Contemplation's statement that "prickt with courage and thy forces pryde,/To Faery court thou cam'st to seeke for fame" (I.x.65, 66). From this perspective, rather than a common culture hero, the figure of the Red Cross Knight asserts the genetic superiority of the aristocratic group.

These contrasting narrative traditions complicate the relation to a common culture underlying the third and more metaphorical perspective on the Red Cross Knight as fallen man subject to flesh, as are all humans. This interpretation of St. George appeared prominently in Caxton's translation of Voragine's *Golden Legend:* "George is sayd of *geos* / whiche is as moche to saye as erthe and *orge*/that is tilyenge/so george is to saye as tilyenge the erthe/ that is his flesshe."[56] Summarizing other critics, MacLachlan notes that his discovery in a furrow of earth "ultimately becomes a sign of his inheritance from Adam (Hebrew: "adamah," "earth") and thus of his fallen nature."[57] Yet he may, like other Christians, become a saint through defeating the dragon Satan to become freed from sin. This rise from everyman's bondage to flesh is implicit in Una's acceptance of him as her knight only after he puts on the armor she provides, identified by Spenser as the "armour of a Christian man specified by Saint Paul v. Ephes." ("A Letter of the Authors," 738). As Kenneth Borris observes, it is only through Christian scripture, and God's grace, that the flesh may be subdued by the spirit, to attain a sanctification prefiguring "the spiritual or glorified body . . . of the general resurrection."[58]

From one perspective, this third version negates the other two. In his rusticity, the Red Cross Knight is no more or less unworthy than any other fallen human. Similarly, descent from Saxon kings or any other noble ancestry is of no value without the armor of God. But resonances remain, as do interpretive possibilities. The common culture may, if the reader wishes, become particularly implicated in the "*geos*" or earthly flesh that must be left behind, so abundantly present in the maygames, the drums and trumpets, the festivals, the spontaneous bodily delight of the "devils daunce withall" so offensive to Philip Stubbes. Similarly, the aristocratic birth of Red Cross Knight may, if the reader wishes, signal an inner form of nobility residing within any Christians chosen as God's elect. Both of these sets of choices provide opportunities for members of the middling sort to identify, or to distinguish, themselves from common and aristocratic groups alike.

The Red Cross Knight's associations with the performed St. George are most conspicuous in his encounters with the Saracens and with the dragon. As Hardin points out, the combat of Red Cross Knight with the Turkish knight Sansjoy in the house of Lucifera, the subsequent defeat of Sansjoy, Duessa's transportation of his wounded body to the doctor, here named Aesculapius, suggest a parody of an already established tradition of mummers' plays.[59] Perhaps the inclusion of Beelzebub and the little devil with a broom in the early modern tradition described in the Croker transcription informed Duessa's descent into hell, with its vivid descriptions of its inhabitants, including ancient Night herself, who rules over this realm. Unlike the cure expected for the mummer combatant, however, the success of Aesculapius's efforts is never determined. His placement in hell, where he vainly strives to restore his own health with salves to "slake the heavenly fire" (I.v.40) reveals his error in attempting to cure a spiritual disease through physical remedies. Whether or not Aesculapius can heal Sanjoy's wounds, he cannot relieve the spiritual ill Sansjoy represents.

Read as a parody of a mumming performance, the combat between the Red Cross Knight and Sansjoy, with the defeated Sansjoy's attempted cure, operates in various ways. Analogous to the contemporary use of ballad tunes for psalms, the vigor and free spirits of popular performance revitalizes the religious discourse of Spenser's allegory. The knight's spiritual battle seems more familiar, and more appealing, against this background of popular enactments. In this sense, this "Saint George of mery England" (I.x.61) accomplishes a drawing together of the Protestant Reformation with a common culture, demonstrating the open appeal of Protestant piety as it includes, rather than excludes, popular forms of pleasure. In this context, the figure of Sansjoy casts aspersions against the sobriety of ministers who disapproved so publicly of traditional pastimes. This reading represents Red Cross's fight against joylessness as a significant spiritual task within Protestant piety. The location of this combat within the House of Pride suggests a critique of the potentially prideful and self-serving alienation of the pious sort from their free-spirited neighbors. But the futility of the salves of Aesculapius to cure spiritual errors elicits a counter-identification with common culture, as well. With its drumming and stylized combat, the festive mirth of mumming performances was, by the standards of the reformation, a merely physical pleasure unredeemed by spiritual value. As Hardin argues, Sansjoy is the "old man" to be left behind (252). Made of "*geos*" or earth, this St. George battles in Sansjoy the joylessness of the fleshly desires so abundantly present in pastimes of a common culture.[60] From this angle, the figure of Sansjoy evokes not self-alienation from physical pleasures but the ultimate emptiness of such pleasures without spiritual grace. So which is it? In either reading, the struggle of Red Cross Knight with Sansjoy enacts a struggle within the self. Freely chosen, readers' interpretive choices mark or challenge their own forms of self-division.

Red Cross Knight's combat with Sansjoy evokes another interpretive choice as well. Throughout, the episode juxtaposes the associations with mumming and classical allusions. The doctor attending Sansjoy is Aesculapius, a physician of ancient Greece. The place to which Duessa carries Sansjoy resembles not only a Christian hell of "damned ghosts" (I.v.33), but an ancient Hades of the "trembling ghosts" (I.v.32) of classical figures as well. In the combat itself, the "darkesome clowd" (I.v.3) that hides Sansjoy from the deathstroke of Red Cross evokes a classical scene from Homer's *Iliad*, in which Venus's veil and then Phoebus' "sable clowd" hide Aeneas from a deathstroke until, protected by the "Sunne," he may recover from his wounds in a "goodly Temple."[61] Spenser's episode parodies this source through specific contrasts: the heroic Aeneas vs. the irascible Sansjoy, the loving Venus vs. duplicitous Duessa, and especially young manly Phoebus the Sun vs. the ancient female Night. By inviting an elite form of reading pleasure, this episode appeals to classically educated readers who may recognize these elements that both parallel and distinguish Spenser's work from Homer's. But the episode itself undoes the foundation of this textual kinship by casting doubts on the value of this knowledge. Rendered ineffective by his limitations as a pagan, Aesculapius cannot heal the soul. Confined to the domain of the body without the benefit of redeeming grace, the knowledges of Aesculapius and his fellow pagans fall as short as those of mummers. As the text presents this dramatic juxtaposition of two very different forms of identification—with common mumming combats and with Homer's *Iliad*—it also offers the opportunity to perceive in them a likeness as non-Christian traditions.

The allusions to mumming rituals in the Sansjoy episode reach further development in the final combat between Red Cross and the dragon that culminates Book I. Drawing together numerous themes and issues posed earlier in this book, Spenser's rendition of this struggle engages various interpretive modes simultaneously in a virtuoso display of his art. The multilevel significances of this narrative are by now well known within Spenser criticism. In defeating the dragon, the ordinary Christian finds salvation through God's grace; Christ Himself redeems mankind from the fall of man; Christ harrows hell; Christ overcomes Satan at the apocalypse; England puts down a papist Anti-Christ to become united with the true Church.[62] As an incarnation of evil, this truly terrifying dragon evokes few reminders of the much-loved dragon accompanying St. George. Yet the fall and the resuscitation of a combatant enacts a core event of a mumming ritual. In this battle, it is the St. George figure, not his opponent, who falls and rises again with outside assistance. Rather than a doctor to attend to his physical needs, the Red Cross Knight is revived in spirit by sacramental means: by the sacred fountain symbolizing baptism and the stream of balm from a tree symbolizing Christ's blood of the eucharist.

Distanced by the epic high-style describing this final conflict, evocations of popular mumming rituals resonate more strongly within the very different aesthetic written for the triumphant procession celebrating the dragon's defeat. As one of Spenser's few representations of a recognizably contemporary populace, this procession elicits popular associations in the "fry of children young" with their "wanton sports," the maidens singing with their timbrels, the crowning of the May queen with a garland, the "rude rablement" that gaze open-mouthed on Red Cross, and especially the overprotective mother who fears that the dead dragon's talons might yet "scratch" her son, or "rend his tender hand" (I.xii.6–11). Reflecting doubts as to whether the dragon is truly dead or liable to make a sudden move, this simultaneous experience of fear and delight undoubtedly parallels the crowd's responses to processional dragons like Norwich's Old Snap, named for his large clicking jaws, or the later Wells dragon, poised to pounce on the festival princess. By inviting a wide range of readers' identifications, from joyful participation in the crowd's delight, to nostalgia for the official entertainments of times past, to amused condescension at naïve responses to the dead dragon, this description provides another opportunity for readers to forge their own relationship to the rituals of a common culture.

The very different aesthetics written for Red Cross's soul-searing combat with the dragon and the popular celebration afterward pose a dilemma of interpretation reaching into the social sphere. Unlike the procession, the final conflict itself is intensely serious and literally apocalyptic in tone. Does the sacramental nature of the resuscitations of Red Cross discourage or even negate associations with mumming rituals? What is the effect of Spenser's divine parody of a debased secular practice? In short, does Spenser's use of the performed St. George place him on a conceptual path travelling closer towards Wells or Chester? Throughout *The Faerie Queene,* Spenser mixes common cultural associations with hyperliterate allusions from classical texts to create a stunningly rich and hybrid aesthetic. In this artistically bold maneuver, Spenser's process incorporates some of the productive mixture of Wells and, like the citizens of Wells, he risked the contempt of those who, like Gabriel Harvey, accused his "Hobgoblin" of running away "with the Garland from Apollo."[63]

But it is seldom clear whether *The Faerie Queene* fosters the acceptance or the reform of a common culture. Richard Hardin eloquently suggests, in another context, that "having seen folk plays with magical cures, Spenser transforms them from buffoonery to blessedness, while preserving their original meaning."[64] But Spenser's appropriation of mumming rituals, like most other appropriations, was almost inevitably double-edged. To interpret a mumming in terms of salvation and resurrection is to swerve from a recognition of the irremediable physicality of an experience aptly described by Smith as dying in O to "rise again in ha ha."[65] Inviting the joy and vigor of common practices into his text, Spenser also disciplined their meanings as he presented his reader not with a conflation, but a necessary interpretive choice. In his respect, his Red Cross Knight is closer to the Chester St. George as, purged of vulgarity, he enacts a deliberate forgetting even as the dragon's presence in his triumphal procession reminds his viewers of what must be forgotten.

Performances of St. George and his dragon represented one of a myriad of ways in which a common culture rose to public visibility. But what rose to visibility was not exactly the same culture that had been experienced in common by earlier generations. Through maygames, horseraces, and works such as *The Faerie Queene*, the figures and practices of a common culture came to generate new meanings they had never possessed before. As Garrett Sullivan and Linda

Woodbridge have discussed, what remains of popular culture has been largely mediated by the educated, whose appropriations operated according to their own interests and agendas. As they note, these distortions are still present today, for "once popular culture—the culture of the People, the Folk—had been created as a category, it was ever after available for ideological uses."[66] When *The Faerie Queene* was written, this category was in formation but not entirely in place. What is the relationship between appropriation and remembrance in this transitional time? While some points of identification within the Red Cross Knight episodes suggest social or religious agendas, others do not. The rich and even contradictory interpretive choices offered readers of *The Faerie Queene* reflect a range of identifications prevailing simultaneously not only within a single work, but within a single mind. In this, Spenser may be representative of other early moderns, whose relationships with a common culture were similarly entangled with conflicting allegiances. Their desires, whether to remember or to forget, were not always consistent with their individual projects of self-distinction, in which those memories could be put to some personal and practical use.

Notes

1. Hugh MacLachlan, "George, St.," *Spenser Encyclopedia,* ed. A. C. Hamilton (Toronto: University of Toronto Press, 1997), 329. John Calvin, *Institutes* III,xx, 27, discussed by H. L. Weatherby, "The True Saint George," *English Literary Renaissance* 17.2 (1987): 119.

2. Erasmus, *The Praise of Folly,* trans. Betty Radice (Harmondsworth: Penguin, 1971), 126. Appending a catalogue of all knights instituted in the Order of the Garter, Peter Heylyn, stresses St. George's aristocratic significance (*History of St. George* [London, 1633]).

3. Spenser's written sources, including relevant portions of the Latin *Legenda Aurea,* as well as works by Lydgate and Mantuan, are presented by Frederick Padelford in the Variorum, "Appendix IV: Sources of Book 1. The Legend of St. George," *The Works of Edmund Spenser. Volume 1: The Faerie Queene, Book One* (Baltimore: Johns Hopkins University Press, 1932), 379–88. Important discussions of written sources include Anne Lake Prescott, "Spenser's Chivalric Restoration: From Bateman's *Travayled Pilgrime* to the Red Crosse Knight," *Studies in Philology* 86.1 (1989): 166–97, and Paul Voss, "The *Faerie Queene* 1590–1596: The Case of Saint George," *Ben Jonson Journal* 3 (1996): 63. Voss acknowledges "a contradictory and confusing Saint George" as "an image capable of inspiring both reverence and hostility." The allegorization of St. George as a type of Christ was already a literary tradition. See MacLachlan's encyclopedia entry "George, St.," 329, and Patrick Grant, *Images and Ideas in Literature of the English Renaissance* (London: Macmillan, 1979), 42, 58–60.

4. William Nelson, *The Poetry of Edmund Spenser: A Study* (New York: Columbia University Press, 1995), 150; See also Weatherby, "The True St. George," 119; Padelford, 389–90.

5. MacLachlan, "George, St.," 329–30.

6. Keith Wrightson and David Levine, *Poverty and Piety in an English Village: Terling, 1525–1700* (New York: Academic Press, 1979), 2. Historians have discussed this social shift since Peter Burke's pronouncement that in 1500, "popular culture was everyone's culture; a second culture for the educated and the only culture for everyone else. By 1800 the clergy, the nobility, the merchants, the professional men—and their wives—had abandoned popular culture to the lower classes" (*Popular Culture in Early Modern Europe* [New York: New York University Press, 1978], 270). Among historians, Ronald Hutton has recently reminded us of the continued fluidity of social groups, and that it was only after 1800 that the "literate really did come to regard traditional popular pastimes as belonging to a different world from their own" (*The Rise and Fall of Merry England: The Ritual Year 1400–1700* [Oxford: Oxford University Press, 1994], 246). But knowledge that this separating process was not complete does not refute the fact that it was underway, and Burke's general concept—that the process of withdrawal had started by the late sixteenth century, and was already having an effect—still stands. For recent work demonstrating intricate interdependencies that still eroded any clear binary between popular and elite, high and low, or even literate and oral subgroups during this period, see Adam Fox, *Oral and Literate Culture in England 1500–1700* (Oxford: Clarendon Press, 2000); Roger Chartier, "The *Bibliotheque bleue* and Popular Reading," in *Cultural Uses of Print in Early Modern France,* trans. Lydia Cochrane (Princeton: Princeton University Press, 1987), 240–64; Marina Warner, *From the Beast to the Blonde: On Fairy Stories and Their Tellers* (New York: Farrer, Straus and Giroux, 1994), 24. For a parallel discussion of the giant, another figure that signaled social changes at this time, see Benjamin Griffin, "The Breaking of the Giants: Historical Drama in Coventry and London," *English Literary Renaissance* 29.1 (1999): 3–21.

7. Wrightson, " 'Sorts of People' in Tudor and Stuart England," *in The Middling Sort of People: Culture, Society, and Politics in England 1550–1800,* ed. Jonathan Barry and Christopher Brooks (New York: St. Martin's Press, 1994), 31.

8. For the argument that for some readers, this common culture was part of childhood memories, see my essay, "Gloriana, Acrasia, and the House of Busirane: Gendered Fictions in *The Faerie Queene* as Fairy Tale," in *Worldmaking Spenser: Explorations in the Early Modern Age,* ed. Patrick Cheney and Lauren Silberman (Lexington: University Press of Kentucky, 2000), 81–100.

9. *Three Fifteenth-Century Chronicles,* ed. James Gairdner. Camden Society. NS 28 (1880; New York: Johnson Reprint Corp., 1968), 85–86. Printed from Lambeth MS 306, the handwriting was "apparently contemporary with the events related," 81.

10. John Leland, *Collectanea* (London, 1770), 4.319, as cited in Padelford, *Variorum,* 390.

11. David Galloway, *Records of Early English Drama: Norwich 1540–1642* (Toronto: University of Toronto Press, 1984), xxvi.

12. From Robert Fabian's manuscript chronicle of London, published as *The Great Chronicle of London*, ed. A. H. Thomas and I. D. Thornley (London, 1938). Cited

in Sydney Anglo, "William Cornish in a Play, Pageants, Prison, and Politics," *Review of English Studies*, n.s. 10 (1959), 348–49.

13. Hutton describes a similar episode occurring on a Twelfth Night eight years earlier, when the court of Henry VII traveled to Westminster Hall to see a pageant of St. George and the dragon, along with a play and "disguisings" by courtiers. See *Rise and Fall,* 16.

14. Ronald Hutton, *The Stations of the Sun: A History of the Ritual Year in Britain* (Oxford: Oxford University Press, 1996), 214.

15. *Records of Early English Drama: Norwich 1540–1642*, 4, 10–17; see also xxvi.

16. Chamberlains' Account Books for Newcastle (1510–1511), *Records of Early English Drama: Newcastle upon Tyne,* ed. J. J. Anderson (Toronto: University of Toronto Press, 1982), 13–16.

17. Hutton, *Stations,* 214–15.

18. David Cressy, *Bonfires and Bells: National Memory and the Protestant Calendar in Elizabethan and Stuart England* (London: Weidenfeld and Nicolson, 1989), 20–21; *Records of Early English Drama: Chester,* ed. Lawrence Clopper (Toronto: University of Toronto Press, 1979), 1:324.

19. Letter from Lodovico Spinelli, Secretary of the Venetian Ambassador in England, to his brother Gasparo, Secretary of the Venetian Ambassador in France," *Calendar of State Papers and Manuscripts Existing in the Archives and Collections of Venice. Vol. 3: 1520–1526,* ed. and trans. Rawdon Brown (1869; Nendeln, Liechtenstein: Kraus Reprint, 1970), 136–37; also see John Forrest, *The History of Morris Dancing: 1458–1750.* Studies in Early English Drama, 5 (Toronto: University of Toronto Press, 1999), 98.

20. Forrest notes the translation of this term into "morris dance" as a similar form of mimed combat often against "others" of the nation (*History of Morris Dancing,* 89).

21. Spinelli, letter in *Calendar of State Papers,* 137.

22. John Mountgomery, "A Booke conteyning the Manner and Order of a Watche to be used in the Cittie of London," Harleian MS 3741, in *Harleian Miscellany . . . being the first supplemental volume*, ed. Thomas Park (London: 1812), 9:389. See also Forrest 95.

23. Hutton, *Stations,* 216.

24. *Records of Early English Drama: York,* ed. Alexandra F. Johnston and Margaret Rogerson (Toronto: University of Toronto Press, 1979), 318–19, 327.

25. Hutton, *Rise and Fall,* 111–52.

26. Henry Machyn, *Diary of a Resident in London, 1550–1563* (London: Camden Society, 1848), 201.

27. Hutton, *Rise and Fall,* 124,143.

28. Cressy, *Bonfires and Bells,* 20–21, 96.

29. Philip Stubbes, *Anatomie of Abuses* (London, 1583), M2v, M3r.

30. Forrest, *History of Morris Dancing,* 172.

31. These trials of combat especially related to Robin Hood are discussed by Bruce Smith, *The Acoustic World of Early Modern England: Attending to the O-Factor* (Chicago: University of Chicago Press, 1999), 149–50.

32. Forrest, *History of Morris Dancing,* 153, 163.

33. BL Harley 2150, f 201, in *Records of Early English Drama: Chester,* 478.

34. Forrest, *History of Morris Dancing,* 259, 270, 327.
35. Forrest, 231, 259; this painting is reproduced on Forrest's book jacket.
36. Richard Hardin, "Spenser's Aesculapius Episode and the English Mummers' Play," *Spenser Studies* 15 (2001): 251.
37. In the absence of an original, Hutton discounts this transcription as unreliable noting that, "for example, a slip when copying the date, of '1685' for '1785' would make a crucial difference" (*Stations of the Sun,* 75). But in lieu of any actual evidence for a slip of the pen, this document may be taken, not as absolute proof, but as a serious piece of evidence to be placed beside others.
38. E. K. Chambers, *The Medieval Stage* (Oxford: Oxford University Press, 1903), 1:214–17; Chambers, *The English Folk-Play* (New York: Haskell House, 1966), 6–9. Hutton has sensibly dismissed groundless claims of pagan origins for these performances, claimed by Chambers and others as an ancient solstice rite (*Stations of the Sun*, 70–73). Hardin, "Spenser's Aesculapius Play," has rejected another proposed origin for these mummings in Richard Johnson's *Seven Champions of Christendom* because of significant dissimilarities in plot as well as presentation (252).
39. Ample evidence of this custom is presented in Meg Twycross and Sarah Carpenter, *Masks and Masquing in Medieval and Early Tudor England* (Burlington: Ashgate, 2002), 82–92, 97–100. This custom seems to inform Cornish's sudden interruption of the interlude before Henry VII described above, and also Father Christmas's sudden intrusion with his company in Jonson's *Masque of Christmas* (1616).
40. Thomas Pettit, "Early English Traditional Drama: Approaches and Perspectives," *Research Opportunities in Renaissance Drama* 25 (1982): 8.
41. *The Journal of Nicholas Assheton of Downham*, ed. F. R. Raines (Manchester: Cheltham Society, 1848), 74–75.
42. See, for example, Leah Marcus, *The Politics of Mirth: Jonson, Herrick, Milton, Marvell, and the Defense of Old Holiday Pastimes* (Chicago: University of Chicago Press, 1986) and Peter Stallybrass, " 'Wee feaste in our Defence:' Patrician Carnival in Early Modern England and Robert Herrick's 'Hesperides,' " *English Literary Renaissance* 16 (1986): 234–51.
43. John Fletcher, *The Womans' Prize in The Dramatic Works in the Beaumont and Fletcher Canon: Vol.4,* ed. Fredson Bowers (Cambridge: Cambridge University Press, 1979), I, iii, 16–21.
44. Hutton, *Rise and Fall,* 261.
45. Peter Heylyn, *The Historie of that most famous Saint and Soldier of Christ Jesus; St. George of Cappadocia; Asserted from the Fictions, of the middle ages of the church, and opposition of the present* (London, 1633), D7v, FF3.
46. Smith, *Acoustic World,* 135.
47. This pageant is described in Gamage's verse reprinted by C. J. Sisson, *Lost Plays of Shakespeare's Age* (Cambridge: Cambridge University Press, 1936),178–83 and in *The Records of Early Modern Drama: Somerset, including Bath*, ed. James Stokes (Toronto: University of Toronto Press, 1996), 1:267–69 and *passim* 260–367. The verse, along with the other records, is preserved as evidence in court trials.
48. *The Records of Early Modern Drama: Somerset, including Bath,* 268.
49. Robert Amerie, *Chester's Triumph in Honor of Her Prince* (London, 1610), A4r–v, A3v, C1v, D1r.

50. This form of cross-group collaboration confirming rather than diminishing social classifications is well described by Barry Reay, "Introduction: Popular Culture in Early Modern England," *Popular Culture in Seventeenth-Century England*, ed. Reay (Beckenham: Croom Helm, 1985), 15–16.

51. Pierre Bourdieu, *Distinction: A Social Critique of the Judgement of Taste,* trans. Richard Nice (Cambridge, Mass.: Harvard University Press, 1984), 7.

52. Elizabeth Mazzola, *The Pathology of the English Renaissance: Sacred Remains and Holy Ghosts* (Leiden: Brill, 1998), 1.

53. "A Letter of the Authors," *Spenser: The Faerie Queene*, ed. A.C.Hamilton, 2nd ed. (New York and London: Longman, 2001), 738. All quotations are from this edition.

54. Hardin, "Spenser's Aesculapius Play," 252.

55. The understanding of folktales has become widespread. See for example Jack Zipes, *Breaking the Magic Spell: Radical Theories of Folk and Folk Tales* (Austin: University of Texas Press, 1979), 27.

56. Quoted by MacLachlan, "George, St.," 212.

57. Ibid.

58. Kenneth Borris, "Flesh, Spirit, and the Glorified Body: Spenser's Anthropomorphic Houses of Pride, Holiness, and Temperance," *Spenser Studies* 15 (2001): 17–52. Press.19.

59. Hardin, "Spenser's Aesculapius Play," 251.

60. Borris's interpretation of Lucifera's house as signifying corrupted flesh, rather than the sanctified body of the house of Holiness, supports this reading (19).

61. *Chapman's Homer. Vol. I: The Iliad,* ed. Allardyce Nicoll. Bollingen Series 41 (Princeton: Princeton University Press, 1967), 5.328–432; Padelford, *Variorum* 228, also lists other episodes from the *Aeneid* and the *Gerusalemme Liberata.*

62. Some of these, with their criticism, are summarized in Belinda Humphrey, "Dragons," *Spenser Encyclopedia*, 223–24.

63. Gabriel Harvey, "Three Proper and Wittie Familiar Letters," *Spenser: Poetical Works*, ed. J. C. Smith and E. de Selincourt (1912; Oxford: Oxford University Press, 1991), 628.

64. Hardin, "Spenser's Aesculapius Play," 253.

65. Smith, *Acoustic World,* 163.

66. Garrett Sullivan and Linda Woodbridge, "Popular Culture in Print," *The Cambridge Companion to English Literature 1500–1600,* ed. Arthur Kinney (Cambridge: Cambridge University Press, 2000), 289.

BART VAN ES

"The Streame and Currant of Time": Land, Myth, and History in the Works of Spenser

From his "most kyndly nurse" London "on *Themmes* brode aged backe" to his Irish home on "the *Mullaes* shore," Spenser recurrently situated himself in relation to rivers. In so doing the poet drew upon an established tradition of chorographic verse and prose. That tradition (which centered on Camden's *Britannia*) characteristically combined the description of land, myth, and history. This article approaches "The Place of Edmund Spenser" in relation to this mode of what George Wither called "topo-chrono-graphical" writing. In particular, it looks at the Marriage of Thames and Medway in Book IV of *The Faerie Queene* and at *Colin Clouts Come Home Againe*. Both, it suggests, are concerned with chorography, and in particular with the historical and mythic differences between Irish and English rivers when described by way of this form. Looking in detail at the *Britannia* and Spenser's river verses, the article sets out their complex engagement with what Camden himself termed "the stream and current of time."

WHEN, IN *THE RUINES OF TIME*, SPENSER paid tribute to William Camden as "the nourice of antiquitie," he did so with the best possible form.[1] By taking ruins and a river as the starting point for a story about the past, he replicated the essential features of the narrative mode that Camden adopted for his great project. In the preface to the *Britannia,* Camden had complained that to engage with misconceptions about the island's past was to "strive with the streame and currant of *Time*."[2] The river metaphor through which the antiquarian expressed his impotence, however, also gestured towards the form that allowed his empowerment. Established historical genres—bound up with custom, providence, or high politics—proved unwieldy when attempting to formulate a new description of the land's earliest days.[3] There was an aspect of the *Britannia*, however, that made its encounter with the past significantly different: it was a chorography.

The form of the *Britannia* meant that the "currant of *Time*" could be diverted. Other modes, such as the chronicle, began with the earliest times and progressed gradually towards the most recent. Partly as a result of this structural characteristic, their authors found it difficult to avoid the established outline of British history.[4] Chorography, by moving spatially across the nation, allowed a different picture to emerge. Etymologically based upon the Greek word for "earth," chorography used *land* as the organizational template governing its narrative. Proceeding landmark by landmark, region by region, Camden's description delivered its account of the past in response to individual concrete objects. One of its defining attributes was a tendency to work from the basis of the physical and temporal *present*, the "here" of specific architectural remains and the "now" of the moment of narration. It was the present, in both senses of that word, that became a springboard to the past.

Recent criticism has done much to show the ways in which chorography, as part of a wider project of "mapping," allowed early modern England to develop a new sense of itself as a physical entity.[5] Yet, as *The Ruines of Time* shows, the impact of the form was as much historical as geographic.[6] Whilst the word "chorography" did not intrinsically require a concern with the past, the texts to which it was attached routinely combined these two kinds of description.[7] Spenser's poem is characteristic in giving voice to a localised sense of myth and history: in one sense obscured by "ruines," but in another inherent in their very substance.[8] The poet's address to Camden thus neatly encapsulates the characteristics of the antiquarian's text. For the *Britannia,* too, recurrently combines land and myth with an emergent archaeological history. As the centrepiece of a broader chorographic and antiquarian tradition, it allowed a new picture of the nation's past to develop. That picture was constructed from both poetic and physical fragments. Covering all of England, Wales, Scotland, Ireland, and even the smaller British islands, Camden's work offered an unprecedented survey of a cultural, ethnographic, and architectural heritage. At once comprehensive and localised, his text presented a landscape in which the imagined and actual past existed alongside one another. Just as Camden found myth and history suspended in the "streame and currant of *Time,*" so Spenser encounters them on the banks of the "Silver streaming *Thamesis.*"[9]

It is my argument here that "The Place of Spenser" may usefully be examined in relation to this mingled historical terrain. Recent work on historicism, nationalism, and cultural geography has found hidden depths in even the most orthodox of Renaissance compositions, and the Spenserian rivers are one such territory now meriting renewed exploration. Camden and his fellow chorographers popularised both a new vision of the past and a new narrative mode. In light of the work of past decades on Spenser's politics (in particular in relation to Ireland), the impact of this approach to land, myth, and history is worthy of reassessment. Most significantly, in *Colin Clouts Come Home Againe* and *The Faerie Queene*'s Marriage of Thames and Medway, we find Spenser comparing English and Irish landscapes. The context of sixteenth-century chorography foregrounds the historiographical and political sophistication of this comparison.

* * *

Spenser explicitly celebrates Camden's *Britannia* in *The Ruines of Time,* but it is in the Marriage of Thames and Medway that the scope of the Renaissance chorographic project finds its fullest expression. The Marriage has long been recognised as a product of this broad generic impulse. Bringing together all the rivers of the world, and prefaced by an appeal to Clio, "noursling of Dame *Memorie*," the episode in some ways provides the same exemplary and synecdochic locus for chorography that Alma's castle provides for chronicle.[10] Certainly, its place in a tradition of English and European river poetry is well-established. Osgood described Spenser's river verses as "specimens of a type not uncommon in their time," and pointed in particular to parallels with Leland's *Cygnea Cantio,* Camden's *De Connubio Tamis*, and Vallan's *Tale of Two Swans.*[11] These observations have been confirmed and expanded over the decades, culminating in Wyman Herendeen's extensive work on the river in history.[12] These studies confirm the linkage between myth and place established through this mode of landscape poetry. Repeatedly, Spenser's pageant moves from rivers "present" at the marriage to old and new histories. All the rivers have their stories, from the Thames which anciently wore "famous Troynouant" (IV.xi.28.8) on its back and the Tyne "along whose stony bancke/That Romaine Monarch built a brasen wall" (IV.xi.36.1–2) to the Granta beside which Spenser himself was once a Cambridge student (IV.xi.34.5–9).[13]

The rivers who mingle at the marriage banquet that Marinell attends thus provide us with a very different perspective on national histories from that presented in the earlier chronicle sections of the poem. As Spenser's introduction to the canto makes clear, they are the source of "endlesse" narratives.[14] Running from famous exploits of the past to the very latest discoveries, these are very much the kind of stories that would be brought together at a wedding party. In many respects this union of diverse voices typifies Renaissance river poetry. The accounts of English rivers (drawn largely from Harrison's "Description" in Holinshed's *Chronicles*) are familiar, and so too is the tone of celebratory union that characterises Spenser's treatment of them. If anything, the poet's verse here seems more laudatory and idealising than that of his contemporaries. Roche calls it "orderly in the extreme" and even Helgerson, who is otherwise quick to point to tensions in the work of the poet, contrasts the subservience of Spenser's "courtly" rivers with the politics of Drayton's later depiction.[15] Characteristically, critics conclude that the episode subsumes history in what Herendeen calls "perceptual myths" —imaginative constructs which organize the meaning of landscape.[16] Even where such myths are seen to explore the disorder of origin, Spenser's work is considered largely untroubled by temporal disjunctions.[17] Though uncomfortable allusions have been spotted, there seems nothing fundamentally dangerous about the historical mode that Spenser has adopted in the canto.[18]

There is, of course, good evidence on which to base this critical consensus: as a centrepiece of the Legend of Friendship, Spenser's pageant thematizes harmonious union. The joining of the Thames and Medway contributes to a prevailing theme of concord that finds its ultimate expression in the union of Marinell and Florimell, whose anticipated marriage echoes that of the rivers. To pair this event with the celebration of a new form of national description is highly appropriate, and to some extent the pageant shares the enthusiasm of the very first chorographers. It is likely that the origins of Spenser's English descriptions run back before the 1580s, roughly contemporary with Harrison's 1577 "Description" and Leland's earlier *Cygnea Cantio*.[19] From the beginning, this new kind of description was regarded as a great achievement, and Spenser's composition reflects this fact. With the arrival of the *Britannia* in 1586, however, the more critical capacity of chorography became increasingly apparent. Old assumptions were more difficult to maintain, and the distinction between myth and history became decidedly more pronounced. In this respect the chorographic project could also have disruptive effects on the national self-image. That development, too, would make its mark on the works of Spenser.

It was from the *Britannia*, as well as his own experience, that the poet derived his knowledge of the Irish rivers, and it is here that the ramifications of the new mode of historical perception are most acute. The meeting of Irish and English rivers was a feature absent from Spenser's poetic predecessors; certainly neither Camden nor Vallans had seen fit to invite them to their river marriages. To a degree this reflects a broader, more ambitious, geographic vision: even the unmapped Orinoco finds a place in Spenser's pageant (IV.xi.21.7). In terms of myth and history, however, these rivers are not so easy to accommodate. As Andrew Hadfield has observed, they circulate some uncomfortable tales amongst the wedding guests.[20] And from the way in which he presents them it is clear that Spenser is not entirely comfortable with their presence:

> Ne thence the Irishe Riuers absent were,
> Sith no lesse famous then the rest they bee,
> And ioyne in neighbourhood of kingdome nere,
> Why should they not likewise in loue agree,
> And ioy likewise this solemne day to see?
> They saw it all, and present were in place;
> Though I them all according their degree,
> Cannot recount, nor tell their hidden race,
> Nor read the saluage cuntreis, thorough which they pace.
> (IV.xi.40)

Spenser's question—"Why should they not likewise in loue agree,/And ioy likewise this solemne day to see?"—appears at first glance merely rhetorical, as if it prompted a rejoinder cheerfully affirming the love and joy of the Irish rivers. The lines which follow, however, by merely insisting again on a presence of which we were already aware, leave room for a different reading. Potentially, they shift the rivers from the past to the political present, making Spenser's question no longer rhetorical but genuine. For, asked why the Irish rivers should "not likewise in loue agree" the more knowing Elizabethan reader would surely pause to question why these streams had, in reality, proved so reluctant to pay tribute to the Thames. Significantly, one answer to such a question was to be found in the kind of chorography that Spenser himself was reading.

Describing the English rivers, Spenser had encountered a physical, historical, and ethnographic landscape that was reassuringly familiar. The Tyne, for example, marked a point of conflict between the

Romans, Britons, and Picts (IV.xi.36). In contrast, the history encoded within the Irish landscape proves neither easy nor comforting to read. Spenser is at once forthcoming and strangely reticent about the stories that these rivers have to tell: all were present, yet he "Cannot recount, nor tell their hidden race,/Nor read the saluage cuntreis, thorough which they pace" (IV.xi.40.8). The double meaning of the word "race"—offering at the same time a geographic and ethnographic reading—highlights precisely the double vision of chorography.[21]

Why is it that Spenser "Cannot recount"? Is it because this is a wild country for which we can find no geography or history? Or is there also a suggestion that he is not allowed to tell, that the tales these rivers hold within them will be ill-received among the coterie so flatteringly in attendance on the Thames? Certainly, the possibility of this reading is strengthened when we come to the last of the rivers mentioned in Spenser's report. Here, despite the assurances to the contrary, the unwelcome message about the "saluage cuntreis" and their "hidden race" begins to leak out. At first the stanza suggests that all is well with the rivers of Ireland:

There also was the wide embayed Mayre,
The pleasaunt Bandon crownd with many a wood,
The spreading Lee, that like an Island fayre
Encloseth Corke with his deuided flood;
And balefull Oure, late staind with English blood:
With many more, whose names no tongue can tell.
All which that day in order seemly good
Did on the Thamis attend, and waited well
To doe their duefull seruice, as to them befell.

(IV.xi.44)

The river that runs through the middle of this stanza cuts a fissure that ultimately threatens the triumphal conclusion to the pageant. The description of the bloodstained Oure not only shocks us with a sudden dramatic change of scene; with typical chorographic prolepsis, it also punningly wrenches the reader away from the mythological past to face the harsh reality of our present "hour." The "balefull Oure" alludes to Glenmalure, the valley into which Lord Grey had sent half his men at the beginning of his Irish campaign, only for them to be routed. This is an event at which Spenser may well have been present, and of which he would certainly have had intimate knowledge.[22] It is also exactly the kind of recent political detail to be found in the otherwise featureless Irish section of the *Britannia*. As with the earlier pun on "race," the poet's wording here plays astutely on the form and content of chorography. For the way in which the "balefull Oure" is both a location and a moment in time opens the stanza to a very different reading. The "many more, whose names no tongue can tell" can now also be read to refer to the other bloodstained Irish rivers, or to the other English soldiers who have died. Those "which that day in order seemly good/Did on the Thamis attend" may be either men or rivers; either way, their service has come at a terrible cost. The shock of this secondary meaning is extraordinary: it alters not only the stanza but the entire mood of the canto. Ending as it does with another suggestive pun in "befell," it potentially transforms our reading of the Irish landscape: exposing a savage geography and a savage history as well. In this double capacity for rendering both place and action, we find a key feature of the chorographic mode.

Much more than a way of putting local myth and history in perspective, chorography provided Spenser with a tool for exploring his nation's geographical and historical integrity. Yet, writing and reading in an Irish context, the results of that exploration would have been increasingly disquieting. In *The Ruines of Time* the poet had responded with fascination to the *Britannia*: mimicking its chorographic structure to explore the ways in which history and myth mark the English landscape. So too, for example, in the 1590 *Faerie Queene*'s depiction of Merlin he had offered a physical setting for the mythology of Wales. But in 1596, to an English resident of Ireland, the *Britannia* would have been a less comfortable read, not least because a form that by nature expressed geographical and historical *connection* could also draw attention to a genuine divide. This aspect of the *Britannia* was to become graphically evident in the frontispiece to the 1607 edition, which, of course, appeared after Spenser's death (see page 00). The map at its centre displayed both a physically marginalised Ireland, pushed beyond the edge of the frame, and also a historically denuded one that lacked the kind of ethnographic specificity inscribed upon the landscape of Britain. Ireland's rivers did not have the names of ancient tribes engraved alongside them, and instead of reaching to the heart of the nation, they stopped short just a little way in from the coast.

Even in 1586, the neat one-word title of the *Britannia* obscured not only a multiplicity of local histories, but also a geographical and historical divide between Great Britain and Ireland. Camden had

Fig. 1. Frontispiece to Camden's *Britannia* (1607). By permission of the Bodleian Library, Oxford

determined to write his book on England, Wales, Scotland, and Ireland. Yet Ireland had never formed part of the Roman "Britannia" that had given Camden's book its name and structure. Because of this, the section on Ireland was conspicuously thin, and had an entirely different aspect from that on England and Wales. Instead of an ordered Roman framework interlaced with native legends, which was the pattern elsewhere, the section on Ireland alternated between foreign myth and more recent political history. Local conflict like that at Spenser's "Balefull Oure" featured prominently in this portion of the text. Here, for Camden, there was no ancient civil infrastructure and no patchwork of local literary myth. The sea dividing Britain and Ireland was thus both geographically and historically dominant. As if anticipating the later frontispiece, the 1586 edition of the *Britannia* even physically divided the sections on Britain and Ireland by placing between them a separate essay devoted to the sea (p. 489). On the page, as in reality, a stretch of water divides two lands and histories.

The uncomfortable tales and doubtful unions of Spenser's Marriage of Thames and Medway owe much to the form in which the episode is cast. Reading Camden's text, the poet would have found a description of Ireland that explicitly acknowledged its strangeness to an English audience. Unlike the native British tribes, its ancient inhabitants had not been successfully mapped or civilised by Roman invaders. In the 1610 edition Camden was himself to voice what was implicit in the version that Spenser knew, declaring what a "blessed and happy turne had it beene for Ireland, if it had at any time been under [Roman] subjection" (66). In that edition, too, Camden was to commend the extraordinary cruelty of Spenser's employer Lord Grey in his treatment of Irish rebels (75)—thus adding still further to the litany of recent violence that already marked this portion of his text. The way in which the Irish rivers are strangers at Spenser's marriage banquet—their unrecorded peoples, obscure legends, unknown landscapes, and unmentionable recent troubles—all find expression in the chorography that he used as a source. Having shifted from an English to an Irish perspective, the poet came to experience Camden's *Britannia* in a significantly different way.

* * *

Of all Spenser's works, the one whose treatment of Ireland bears the most obvious parallels to the Marriage of the Thames and Medway is *Colin Clouts Come Home Againe.* Indeed, in the Marriage, which appeared a year after *Colin Clout*, Spenser refers back explicitly to his earlier creation and its role in setting Irish rivers on the literary map (IV.xi.41.9). Unlike the Marriage, *Colin Clout* is not usually placed in the tradition of chorographic poetry; ranging from pastoral singing contest to neoplatonic complaint, its generic makeup is famously difficult to determine. At its centre, however, the poem is about a transition from Irish to English land. As the conclusion of Spenser's marriage pageant testifies, that transition had been complicated by the advent of national chorography. From the perspective of Camden, Ireland could be seen as alien not just in terms of its political condition, but also in terms of the legends and history attached to its physical terrain. In a poem that is deeply concerned with a sense of place and displacement, this tradition of local historical description could not fail to make an impact. Although more marginal, the presence of chorography in *Colin Clout* is therefore also worthy of examination.

Like its successor, *Colin Clout* begins by attaching stories to rivers. Following its pastoral preamble, the opening narrative also bears comparison with the chorographic starting points of *The Ruines of Time* and *Prothalamion.* For Colin, the poem's principal speaker, here immediately establishes for himself a position beside the Mulla (or Awbeg) that flowed through Spenser's Irish estate:

> One day (quoth he) I sat, (as was my trade)
> Under the foote of *Mole* that mountaine hore,
> Keeping my sheepe amongst the cooly shade,
> Of the green alders by the *Mullaes* shore:
> There a straunge shepheard chaunst to find me out.
> (*Colin Clout*, ll. 56–60)

That shepherd—a figure for Ralegh—turns out to be "the shepheard of the Ocean by name" (l. 66), and it is across the ocean (or least the sea) that he is soon to draw the river-loving Colin. Once he has arrived at his destination, moreover, Colin is to pay tribute to Cynthia. Like the Marriage, therefore, the poem also concerns a point of contact between a river and a monarch described as ruler of the sea.

The entire first section of the poem, dealing with the meeting of the two "shepheardes" and their journey to see the Queen has a strong chorographic element, the tone of which is already established at the beginning of Colin's story. Colin's song is not merely sung beside a river, it also tells of rivers and is itself structured like one. It is no surprise that the first of several interjectors should himself be borne along by this pervasive metaphor:

> There interrupting him, a bonie swaine,
> That *Cuddy* hight, him thus atweene bespake:
> And should it not thy readie course restraine,
> I would request thee *Colin*, for my sake,
> To tell what thou didst sing, when he did plaie.
>
> (*Colin Clout*, ll. 80–84)

The "readie course" of Colin's tale, it soon becomes clear, *is* restrained by the diversion which Cuddy puts upon it. The shepherd proceeds to tell a long story concerning the river Bregog and its illicit underground journey "into the *Mullaes* water" (l. 144). In a nice twist on the tradition, these rivers were attempting to *avoid* an arranged river marriage. Thus, when Mulla's father, the mountain "old *Mole*" (l. 104), discovered their subterfuge he punished the Bregog by sending "downe from his hill/Huge mightie stones" (l. 149–50). As a result, the Bregog was "lost emong those rocks into him rold" and "Did lose his name: so deare his love he bought" (ll. 154–155).

The story of the Bregog's love brilliantly exploits the generic diversity of *Colin Clouts Come Home Againe*. In part it is a political allegory in the pastoral tradition, representing Ralegh's recent fall from Queen Elizabeth's favour.[23] But it is also a river legend in the chorographic mode: the regret about the Bregog's loss of name, for example, echoes the same complaint by Verlame in *The Ruines of Time*.[24] Despite its up-to-date political content, Colin insists the tale is "No leasing new, nor Grandams fable stale,/But auncient truth confirm'd with credence old" (ll. 102–3). That "credence" is very firmly linked to a specific physical location:

> Old father *Mole,* (*Mole* hight that mountain gray
> That walls the Northside of *Armulla* dale)
> He had a daughter fresh as floure of May,
> Which gave that name unto that pleasant vale;
> *Mulla* the daughter of old *Mole*, so hight
> The Nimph, which of that water course has charge,
> That springing out of *Mole,* doth run downe right

To *Buttevant,* where spreading forth at large,
It giveth name unto that auncient Cittie,
Which *Kilnemullah* cleped is of old:
Whose ragged ruines breed great ruth and pittie,
To travailers, which it from far behold.
(*Colin Clout*, ll. 104–15)

The combination of myth and geographic detail, the rendition of etymological fables, the reference to the old name for an ancient city, the description of ruins, the mention of present day travelers—all are features of chorography. The subsequent unrecorded song of "the Shepheard of the Ocean," moreover, appears to continue this strain of myth and history, being "all a lamentable lay,/Of great unkindnesse, and of usage hard,/Of *Cynthia* the Ladie of the sea" (ll. 164–66).

This claim on localised legend provides a cover for Spenser's allegorical complaints about the Queen's injustice. Yet this is not to say that such geographical exactitude is itself without political purpose. By telling stories and describing ruins the poet is also making more personal claims on the land. In the absence of, or in opposition to, existing local legends, Spenser and his companion are seen to render their own mythology and history of space. The *Britannia* had described a land denuded of literary fiction: unsung by English poets and marked instead by a series of bloody skirmishes. By describing the land as he does Spenser implicitly makes a bid for its inclusion in the "civilised" landscape that is the proper subject of chorography.[25] If, as the *Britannia* itself wishfully anticipates, Ireland were subjected to a "civilising" re-conquest, the tale of the Mulla and Bregog would surely become a suitable object for the attention of a future chorographer.

The action which follows, like that of the Marriage of Thames and Medway, brings the Irish world of stories into contact with one located on the other side of the sea. After Colin and the Shepherd of the Ocean have exchanged tales, the latter persuades the former through "hope of good, and hate of ill" (l. 192) to leave the "waste" where he is "quite forgot" (l. 183) and travel to see the now apparently bountiful Cynthia. The two cross "A world of waters heaped up on hie,/Rolling like mountaines in wide wildernesse" (ll. 196–7). As the pair approach the British Isles the distinctive perspective of the chorographic muse comes once again to the fore:

We *Lunday* passe; by that same name is ment

An Island, which the first to west was showne.
From thence another world of land we kend,
Floting amid the sea in jeopardie,
And round about with mightie white rocks hemd,
Against the seas encroching crueltie.

(ll. 270–75)

Spenser's move here from the eye-level perspective of the Shepherd Colin to the overview of the shape of Cornwall is strongly reminiscent of Camden, who at several points describes the difficult travels of his "ship of Antiquity" and who at this point makes great play of the "course" which he is to take across the ocean.[26] Even the antiquarian's analysis of the etymology of the name of the peninsula is repeated:

The first to which we nigh approached, was
An high headland thrust far into the sea,
Like to an horne, whereof the name it has,
Yet seemed to be a goodly pleasant lea:
There did a loftie mount at first us greet,
Which did a stately heape of stones upreare,
That seemd amid the surges for to fleet,
Much greater then that frame, which us did beare:
There did our ship her fruitfull wombe unlade,
And put us all ashore on *Cynthias* land.

(*Colin Clout,* ll. 280–89)

Chorographic meeting points, it is already apparent, have the capacity to become a locus for the expression of elements beyond the geographic. Thus, in the first place, the move from Ireland to Cornwall involves a transition from Spenser's to Ralegh's land: the poem's dedication prominently advertised the knight's position as "Lord Wardein of the Stanneries, and Lieutenant of the Countie of Cornwall." It is an exchange that, like the earlier exchange of songs, allows Spenser to compliment his friend and patron. By landing in Cornwall, however, Colin also takes the first step of that great journey set out in Camden's *Britannia*—a point of contact that again hints at aspects of the tradition in which he is writing. As Camden tells us, Cornwall is "the first of all Britaine": the inevitable starting point for a chorographic survey—constituting both the geographical and historical beginning of the nation.[27] It is in the treatment of Cornwall that the chorographic topoi of geography, myth, and antiquarian enquiry fall most easily together. The western-most part of the island of Britain, Cornwall was the natural entry-point for a geographical reading of the nation. It was both the supposed landing place of the Trojans—a myth which, in the 1610 *Britannia,* Camden presents in the form of a quotation from "a late-borne Poet—and the repository of the earliest remains of the land's ancient inhabitants.[28] In several ways Cornwall may be figured as the birthplace of the nation. It is appropriate in more than one way, then, that Colin's ship should unload its "fruitfull wombe" in precisely this location (l. 288).

The landing of Spenser's shepherd replicates the moment of Britain's first settlement—Colin, like the first Briton colonists, travels over the sea to a land of "fruitfull corne, faire trees, fresh herbage" and "all things else that living creatures need," including rivers "No whit inferiour" to those of the home country, Ireland (ll. 298–300). Here, however, the geography of homecoming becomes complicated: as Colin moves away from his supposed land of origin (Ireland) the poet moves *towards* his (England). Home is a place of both beginnings and returns, but the question of which home we are considering remains problematic throughout the poem.[29] The "again" of the work's title draws attention to this problem. Are there two homecomings, or even more? Colin, in his role as narrator, has come home to Ireland after his trip to visit Cynthia, but the poet who is shadowed in him (Edmund Spenser) would initially have returned home to England, only to find himself returning home "again" to Ireland—a location which has earlier been described as a "waste" and place of banishment. The tale of what is obviously the shepherd's first sea passage, full of naïve terror, is irresistibly evocative of how we might imagine the poet's first voyage from his native land (to Ireland). Like the return journey, it seems to move simultaneously towards and away from home.

In common with the Marriage of Thames and Medway, *Colin Clout* exploits the uncertainties that surround the division between England and Ireland. The landscape of Ireland should be as familiar as that of England, but it is not; we ought not to be surprised at the presence of the Irish rivers at the wedding, but we are. Colin's arrival in Cynthia's land—in other words, England—brings to a head the pervading sense of misplacement that must have characterised the opening of the poem for the English reader. Once more, this quality has a historical and mythic aspect as well as a geographical one. From the beginning, the apparent familiarity that Spenser bestowed upon an indecipherable Irish landscape must have been disorientating. As Jack Oruch has observed, Spenser's personal names for the Irish rivers complicate what, for a London audience, would already be very obscure details.[30] It is on arrival in England, however, that this effect would have been felt most strongly. In a striking reversal of the *Britannia*'s sense of Irish alienation, Spenser treats Cynthia's land as a foreign country. That conspicuous oddity is made still more so by the interventions of Colin's audience:

> What land is that thou meanst (then *Cuddy* sayd)
> And is there other, then whereon we stand?
> Ah *Cuddy* (then quoth *Colin*) thous a fon,
> That hast not seen least part of natures worke:
> Much more there is unkend, then thou doest kon,
> And much more that does from mens knowledge lurke.
> For that same land much larger is then this,
> And other men and beasts and birds doth feed:
> There fruitfull corne, faire trees, fresh herbage is
> And all things else that living creatures need.
> Besides most goodly rivers there appeare,
> No whit inferiour to thy *Funchins* praise,
> Or unto *Allo* or to *Mulla* cleare:
> Nought hast thou foolish boy seene in thy daies.
> (*Colin Clout*, ll. 290–303)

The return to the Irish rivers of poem's opening highlights the reversal still more strongly: instead of familiar English rivers being used as a measure against which to judge alien ones, it is unknown Irish rivers which are described as familiar where the English rivers are strange. The reversal raises troubling questions strikingly similar to those which precede the description of the Irish rivers in Book IV of *The Faerie Queene*. Why is it that the Shepherd knows nothing of Cynthia and her dominion? Why is the Queen absent from Ireland? Cuddy, like a parody of the audience greeting the New World explorer, declares himself amazed that there should be a land other than that he stands on. Colin's response takes on the tone of one patronising an unknowing yokel; his praise for Cynthia's land, however, gradually becomes a more and more open assault on the shortcomings of Ireland:

> Both heaven and heavenly graces do much more
> (Quoth he) abound in that same land, then this.

For there all happie peace and plenteous store
Conspire in one to make contented blisse:
No wayling there nor wretchednesse is heard,
No bloodie issues nor no leprosies,
No griesly famine, nor no raging sweard,
No nightly bodrags, nor no hue and cries;
The shepheards there abroad may safely lie,
On hills and downes, withouten dread or daunger.
(ll. 308–17)

As our reading progresses, the hints about what kind of Ireland this is become gradually stronger. The famine, raging sword, night raids and "hue and cries" finally bring us unmistakably to the Ireland of Spenser's day. In a sense, Spenser's presentational strategy here is the reverse of that which he was to employ for the Marriage. If in *The Faerie Queene* the Irish rivers are too little-known for the poet to "tell their hidden race," here they are all too familiar. The effect, however, is the same: in both cases an encomiastic account of English landscape is given a critical edge by means of implied contrast with Ireland. Undeniably there is a strong element of union. In the Marriage and *Colin Clout* alike, rivers are conjoined in relation to a ruler of the seas, since Proteus and Cynthia share the same sphere of government. As well as a medium for unification, however, the ocean is something that divides. When at the end of *Colin Clouts Come Home Againe,* its protagonist is once more in Ireland under "glooming skies," that sense of division remains all too apparent (l. 954).

* * *

Neither *Colin Clout* nor the Marriage of Thames and Medway is consistently chorographic. They do, however, illustrate the effectiveness with which Spenser manipulated traditions of local historical description. Chorography, in this sense, is a mode that surfaces recurrently in Spenser's prose and poetry. Much more than just a source, it is a way of writing that facilitates a nuanced interchange between the physical present and the past, whether imagined or actual. Works as far apart as *A View of the Present State of Ireland* and *Prothalamion* make use of that productive double vision. But in the Marriage of Thames and Medway and *Colin Clouts Come Home Againe* it is especially prominent. Here Spenser not only combines land, myth, and history, he also negotiates the transition between English and Irish landscape. For Spenser, as well as for antiquarian chorographers like Camden, that transition proved especially troubling. As a result, it reveals with unusual clarity the unique vision of the chorographic mode.

Spenser's Irish river verses each reveal anxiety about the historical and mythic difference between two landscapes—a difference that showed up all the more strongly in the light of achievements in English chorography. Through narratives that progress in opposite directions (from English to Irish, or from Irish to English rivers) the poems confront a division that is more than simply geographical. This uneven cultural topography is one that Spenser both exposes and attempts to reverse. The historical content of his poetry draws attention to the failures of recent governance, yet it also endorses an imperialist programme that he hopes will bring a successful transformation. In a more diffuse manner, the poet's mythmaking may be said to have the same twin objective: on the one hand confronting an English readership with awkwardly foreign tales, on the other familiarising it with a new—perhaps newly invented—local mythology. The fact that Spenser's river verse came to be anthologised alongside the *View* in Sir James Ware's antiquarian *History of Ireland* reflects at least the momentary triumph of this strategy.[31] In combination, these texts mark the island with Spenser's vision in terms of both history and myth. Above all, they reflect the impact of the *Britannia*, a work that allowed the poet and his contemporaries to perceive and imagine the past in a new way. When Spenser first considered the achievements of "*Cambden* the nourice of antiquitie" (*Ruines*, l. 169) even he is unlikely to have envisaged how far he would be carried by "the streame and currant of time."

NOTES

1. See *The Ruines of Time*, l. 169, in *The Yale Edition of the Shorter Poems of Edmund Spenser*, ed. William A. Oram et al. (New Haven: Yale University Press, 1989). Subsequent references to this poem, and also to *Colin Clouts Come Home Againe*, are to this edition and appear in the text.

2. William Camden, *Britain*, trans. Philemon Holland (London, 1610), 6. These exact words did not appear in the 1586 edition that Spenser knew, but as a geographical feature and as a metaphor for knowledge, the river already featured prominently in Camden's first preface. All subsequent quotations in the text are to 1610 translation. In order to facilitate examination of the Latin text to which Spenser had access footnotes (where necessary) also give page numbers for *Britannia* (London, 1586).

3. On the Renaissance distinctions between "historians" (whose principal concern was with high politics, and who tended to use a chronological approach) and "antiquarians" (who concentrated on culture, law, or architectural remains, and might produce chorographies) see D. R. Woolf, *The Idea of History in Early Stuart England: Erudition, Ideology, and "The Light of Truth" from the Accession of James I to the Civil War* (Toronto: University of Toronto Press, 1990), 21–22. It was, of course, possible for individual authors to adopt more than one historical mode, something that Camden himself demonstrated when he went on to write the *Annales Rerum Anglicarum, et Hibernicarum Regnante Elizabetha* (Leyden, 1615–25).

4. This outline, beginning with the island's supposed first conqueror, Brutus of Troy, and reaching its zenith in the empire of King Arthur, had its roots in Geoffrey of Monmouth's *Historia Regum Britanniae.* Although widely questioned, it appeared in all national chronicles. Even "progressive" scholars like the compilers of the 1587 edition of Holinshed's *Chronicles* could do little more than express doubts about these old stories while continuing to give them pride of place at the beginning of their collections.

5. A seminal work here is Richard Helgerson's chapter "The Land Speaks" in *Forms of Nationhood* (Chicago: University of Chicago Press, 1992), 103–47. Other important surveys include David Ian Galbraith, *Architectonics of Imitation in Spenser, Daniel, and Drayton* (Toronto: University of Toronto Press, 2000), 113–21 and Andrew Hadfield, "Spenser, Drayton, and the Question of Britain," *Review of English Studies* 51 (2000): 582–99.

6. The historical function of chorography has long been recognised, and predates Helgerson's focus on national identity. On the form's historiographical capacities see, for example, William Keith Hall, "A Topography of Time: Historical Narration in John Stow's *Survey of London,*" *Studies in Philology* 88 (1991): 1–15 and Anthony Grafton, *Bring Out Your Dead: The Past as Revelation* (Cambridge, Mass: Harvard University Press, 2001), 31–61.

7. *OED,* "Chorography," n. 1–3, refers to the description of a particular region or district without specifying the presence of an historical element. The sixteenth- and seventeenth-century texts which the *OED* mentions, however, almost all combine geographic and historical material. The work of Greek and Roman writers (including Strabo, Varro, and Seneca) to which the term was applied shares these qualities, as does that of the great Italian antiquarian Flavio Biondo.

8. On this double quality of the *Ruines* see Millar MacLure, "Spenser and the Ruins of Time," in *A Theatre for Spenserians,* ed. Judith M. Kennedy and James A. Reither (Manchester: Manchester University Press, 1973), 3–18 (here 4); Wyman H. Herendeen, "Wanton Discourse and the Engines of Time: William Camden—Historian among Poets-Historical," in *Renaissance Rereadings: Intertext and Context,* ed. Maryanne Cline Horowitz et al. (Urbana: University of Illinois Press, 1988), 142–58.

9. *Ruines,* l. 2. On Spenser's treatment of the Thames as the river of "tempus" or time, see R. A. McCabe's discussion of another of the poet's chorographic works, *Prothalamion* in *Edmund Spenser: The Shorter Poems,* ed. McCabe (London: Penguin, 1999), 729.

10. See *The Faerie Queene,* ed. by A. C. Hamilton, 2nd ed. (London: Longman, 2001), IV.xi.10.2. All subsequent references are to this edition and appear in the

text. Spenser's Briton and Fairy chronicles have, of course, been the subject of extensive commentary focusing on their treatment of providence and moral instruction.

11. Charles G. Osgood, "Spenser's English Rivers," *Transactions of the Connecticut Academy of Arts and Sciences,* 23 (1920): 65–108 (here, 101). The last two, he pointed out, may themselves have been inspired by Spenser's lost or projected work *Epithalamion Thamesis,* but Leland's Latin work clearly provided the earliest English example. For Leland's *Cygnea Cantio* and Vallan's *A Tale of Two Swannes,* see Thomas Hearne, ed., *The Itinerary of John Leland the Antiquary,* 3rd ed., 9 vols. (Oxford: James Fletcher and Joseph Pote, 1770), 9:1–106, 5: v-xx. Fragments of Camden's *De Connubio Tamae* appear in their most complete form in the 1610 translation of *Britannia.* For an attempt to reconstruct the poem in its entirety, see Jack B. Oruch, "Spenser, Camden, and the Poetic Marriages of Rivers," *Studies in Philology* 64 (1967): 606–24.

12. Oruch, "Spenser, Camden," collects and corrects a number of observations on the Marriage, including those of Osgood. In addition, see Gordon Braden, "riverrun: An Epic Catalogue in *The Faerie Queene,*" *English Literary Renaissance* 5 (1975): 25–48; David Quint, *Origin and Originality in Renaissance Literature: Versions of the Source* (New Haven: Yale University Press, 1983), 133–66. Wyman H. Herendeen treats Spenser as part of an extensive chronological survey. See *From Landscape to Literature: The River and the Myth of Geography* (Pittsburgh: Duquesne University Press, 1986). See also Herendeen, "The Rhetoric of Rivers: The River and the Pursuit of Knowledge," *Studies in Philology* 78 (1981): 107–27.

13. Parallels with other chorographic writing are strong, as William Keith Hall says of the *Britannia*'s treatment of the Thames: "in a manner of speaking, the river *moves* into and out of history, winding through the ruins of antiquity into the narrator's present" ("From Chronicle to Chorography: Truth, Narrative, and the Antiquarian Enterprise in Renaissance England" [Ph. D. thesis, University of North Carolina, 1996], 21).

14. *Faerie Queene,* IV.xi.9.8; Spenser repeats the word "endlesse" to refer to the "seas abundant progeny" at the beginning of the next canto (IV.xii.1.1–2).

15. Thomas P. Roche, Jr, *The Kindly Flame: A Study of the Third and Fourth Books of Spenser's "Faerie Queene"* (Princeton: Princeton University Press, 1964), 178; Helgerson, *Forms of Nationhood,* 141–42.

16. Herendeen, *Landscape,* 251.

17. Braden, for example, notes that the Thames and Medway never actually meet on land, and goes on to make a number of convincing observations about the passage's exploration of the disorder of origin. He does not, however, focus on tensions between the kinds of history to be found in the pageant. Berger reaches a similar conclusion in his essay "Two Spenserian Retrospects: The Antique Temple of Venus and the Primitive Marriage of Rivers," *Revisionary Play: Studies in the Spenserian Dynamics* (Berkeley: University of California Press, 1988), 195–214.

18. Notably, Andrew Hadfield has pointed to the secret history attached to Irish rivers. See *Edmund Spenser's Irish Experience: Wilde Fruit and Salvage Soyl* (Oxford: Clarendon Press, 1997), 142–45, 158–59. None of the above studies, however, discuss the historical vision of the *Britannia* or its political implications.

19. Spenser mentions his "*Epithalamion Thamesis*" in the first of the *Three Proper and Wittie, Familiar Letters* (1580), in *Spenser: Poetical Works,* ed. J. C. Smith and E.

De Selincourt (1912; rpt. Oxford: Oxford University Press, 1970), 612. For a discussion of the evidence that the Marriage of the Thames and Medway may in some way be an adaptation of this lost or projected poem, see Oruch, 613–22; Josephine Waters Bennett, *The Evolution of "The Faerie Queene"* (Chicago: University of Chicago Press, 1942), 155, 174–75, and 276; Osgood.

20. As noted above, Hadfield draws attention to these stories. See Hadfield, *Irish Experience*, 142–45,158–59; Hadfield, "Spenser, Drayton," 588. A number of the points made below about the Irish references in the pageant are already to be found in this analysis.

21. A "race" can be a rush of water or an ethnic group (*Faerie Queene,* 516, n.). This combination appears repeatedly in Camden's *Britannia,* which tends to work by associating pre-Roman tribes with specific rivers.

22. See Alexander C. Judson, *The Life of Edmund Spenser* (Baltimore: Johns Hopkins Press, 1945), 88. The incident is also related in Hooker's continuation of the History of Ireland contained in Raphael Holinshed's *Chronicles,* 3 vols. (London, 1587), 2:169–70. For Grey's complaints about the lack of support for his mission, see Judson, 87 and 94.

23. It is not quite clear whether the poem initially referred to Ralegh's secret marriage with Elizabeth Thockmorton, or to an earlier more minor indiscretion. Certainly it would be hard to imagine anyone reading the episode, when published in 1595, as referring to anything other than the 1592 marriage. See Carmel Gaffney, "*Colin Clouts Come Home Againe*" (Ph. D. thesis, University of Edinburgh, 1982), 13.

24. *Ruines,* l. 34. The idea that a name may be lost under a mass of stones is a major concern of this earlier part-chorographic composition.

25. For a brilliant reading of *Colin Clouts'* assertion of material possession see Louis Adrian Montrose, "Spenser's Domestic Domain: Poetry, Property, and the Early Modern Subject," in *Subject and Object in Renaissance Culture*, ed. Margreta De Grazia et al., Cambridge Studies in Renaissance Literature and Culture, 8 (Cambridge: Cambridge University Press, 1996), 83–130 (here, 105).

26. *Britain* (London, 1610), "Scotland, Ireland, and the British Ilands," 201 (sig. 4R5[a]); *Britannia* (London, 1586), 525. The navigational metaphor is also deployed at the close of Camden's work. See *Britain* (1610), 233 (sig. 4V3[a]); *Britannia* (1586), 556. Camden's journey, of course, is in the opposite direction.

27. *Britain* (1610), 183; *Britannia* (1586), 67.

28. For Camden, Cornwall is a repository of ancient humans as well as artefacts, because it is "inhabited by that remnant of Britans, which Marianus Scotus calleth *Occidentales Britones,* that is Britans of the west parts, who in the British tongue (for as yet they have not lost their ancient language) name it *Kernaw*" (*Britain* [1610], 183; *Britannia* [1586], 67). Yet it is also a fecund mythological source, a place of strength and fertility the roots of which lie both in geography and early history. Drayton, building on the material Camden had collected, called it "A Husband furthering fruite; a Midwife helping birth" (*Poly-Olbion,* in *The Works of Michael Drayton,* ed. by J. William Hebel, 5 vols. [1933; rpt. Oxford: Basil Blackwell, 1961], 4.1. 252–12 [here, 7–8]).

29. On Spenser's position in Ireland, and in particular its depiction within *Colin Clouts Come Home Againe,* see McCabe, "Edmund Spenser, Poet of Exile," *Proceedings of the British Academy,* 80 (1991): 73–103 (especially 89–94); Montrose, "Domestic Domain."

30. Oruch, "Spenser, Camden," 622–23.
31. *The Historie of Ireland, Collected by Three Learned Authors,* ed. Sir James Ware (Dublin: Society of Stationers, 1633) is made up of the *View,* a set of Spenserian verses, Edmund Campion's *History of Ireland,* and Meredith Hanmer's *Chronicle.* On the nature of this volume, see Bart van Es, "Discourses of Conquest: *The Faerie Queene,* the Society of Antiquairies, and *A View of the Present State of Ireland,*" *English Literary Renaissance* 32 (2002): 118–151.

GRANT WILLIAMS

Phantastes's Flies: The Trauma of Amnesic Enjoyment in Spenser's Memory Palace

The problem of Guyon's inauthentic subjectivity may be approached effectively by understanding his quest within the context of the discourses and practices of remembering rather than by detecting traces of a repressed libido. In Book II, the House of Alma constitutes a fantasy that takes the symbolic form of the memory palace, a phenomenological space regularly advocated by the art of memory. This memory palace, along with forays into zones of forgetting, impresses upon Guyon the injunction to know thyself common to the depiction of interiority in natural history discourse. The fantasy of remembering and forgetting ultimately shapes Guyon's desire to remember, constructing as the object of that desire the mnemonic image. However, when extracted from the fantasy field of Alma's house, mnemonic images are seen to be what they actually are: Phantastes's flies, buzzing and swarming with a life of their own. Surpassing the imaginary limits of identity formation in early modern mnemonic activity, Book II exposes the underside of amnesic *jouissance* to be found in the corporeal memory palace.

AN OLD PROBLEM IN SPENSER CRITICISM still has relevance for reading Book II of *The Faerie Queene* today. As a hero, Guyon appears passive and puppet-like, too ludicrously virtuous to sustain readerly interest. He does not slay a single foe but performs, for the purposes of didactic moral allegory, tiresome Aristotelian gymnastics of balancing the golden mean.[1] Consequently, he seems bereft of any desire that would enable readers to identify with him. In order to overcome the problem of his inauthentic subjectivity, critics have sought out conflicted motivation for his asceticism: at times, Guyon not only betrays un-Christian weakness, such as self-sufficiency, but also represses libidinous urges, whose infrequent eruptions in the narrative humanize him.[2] Unfortunately, the latter solution to Book II leaves more than a residue of the original problem. Despite experiencing a few bouts of fallibility, Guyon still disaffects and annoys readers by resisting so effortlessly the lures of concupiscence. I want to argue, instead, that Book II does indeed flesh out Guyon's subjectivity with desire, but a desire more representative of early modern mnemonic culture than of modernity's preoccupation with repressed libidinal energy: Guyon embodies the desire to remember. The fullness of his desire reveals itself most compellingly in the House of Alma, a fantasy fabricated from the symbolic architecture of the memory palace. The memory palace permits Guyon to know himself by mastering corporeal interiority; conversely, his quest involves defeating the forces of oblivion that threaten to invade his well-managed interiority. Book II elucidates at length early modernity's profound imaginary investment in the discourses and practices of remembering and, through the vicissitudes of Guyon's desire, surpasses the insights of these discourses and practices by inadvertently exposing the trauma underlying the early modern memory palace. As a result of recognizing Guyon's desire, the stakes of his quest are raised from the honor of having passed a test set by rarefied codes of morality to the preservation of a fantasy that cuts to the quick of identity formation in mnemonic culture.

Book II's narrative disappoints readers expecting conventional heroic action, primarily because Guyon conducts an introspective odyssey. Characterizing Book II as the most heavily landscaped part of the poem, James Nohrnberg guides the reader down a rewarding path, when discussing the implications that the House of Alma has for interiority: "Guyon's exploration of the Castle doubtless fulfills the Socratic precept of self-knowledge. This self-knowledge includes the stories of past selves in history, or the collective memory, and Guyon and Arthur settle down to read about their progenitors, in a tribute to their intellectual appetites."[3] The classical pursuit of *nosce teipsum*—the philosophical injunction made famous by the inscription on the Apollonian temple at Delphi—wonderfully enhances our understanding of temperance in Book II. To "know thyself" suggests the self-reflective effort required to earn the virtue, for Erasmus comments that this adage "recommends moderation and the middle state" and "bids us not to pursue objects either too great for us or beneath us."[4] However, there is another, in my view, richer dimension to knowing oneself that illuminates Guyon's tour of the House of Alma. In the anatomical handbook *Mikrokosmographia*, Helkiah Crooke interprets the Apollonian inscription rather differently than Erasmus and Norhnberg do. *Knowing thyself* is neither a genealogical exercise, as it may appear to be in Eumnestes's chronicles, nor a Socratic attitude of reflecting upon one's moral blindness. Because Socrates, in Crooke's view, deems it mad to chase "high matters" while remaining ignorant of the matters "that bee in our selves," knowledge of man's self may be obtained "by the dissection of the body."[5] Only through turning inward, that is, studying the frame and composition of the body, can one come to knowledge of the soul. Crooke materializes and interiorizes the self, not simply in terms of the spiritual, but in terms of corporeality.

Crooke's reading of *nosce teipsum* is not inconsistent with early modern surveys of the body's interior. Sixteenth- and seventeenth-century treatises on ethical and natural philosophy quite regularly appeal to the wisdom of *know thyself*, before systematically surveying the body's souls, members, organs, passions, and processes. Inviting psychoanalytic inquiry, "knowing thyself" constitutes for early modernity a veritable imaginary act tantamount to the Lacanian mirror stage, whereby the subject constructs the self through a bodily imago.[7] Knowing one's self, simply put, means knowing the corporeal other. Before surveying the body's members, Pierre Charron's *Of wisdome* articulates the debt identity formation owes to corporeal reflection: "we have no cleerer looking glasse, no better booke than our selves, if as we ought we doe studie our selves, alwayes keeping our eyes open over us, and prying more narrowly into our selves."[8]

This early modern imaginary act, however, varies slightly from Lacan's modern account insofar as it entails not only capturing the body's surfaces and actions but also "prying" into its cavities, recesses, and folds.

The imaginary act of prying into the body's interior could not explain more precisely the peculiar activity of *knowing thyself* that engrosses Guyon's energies in the House of Alma. Just like the reader of natural historical treatises, Guyon explores corporeal interiors and structures, whose workmanship elicits from both knights wonder, praise, and delight.[9] Consonant with the admiration that these treatises express for the microcosm, Guyon's reactions verbalize the *Eureka* pleasure—the mirror-stage experience—of (mis)recognizing the self.[10] The tour taken by Guyon reveals to him a corporeal self coordinated in its functions and coherent in its form. The tour generally accords with the descriptive order found in natural history treatises. As Walter R. Davis says of the House, "the descriptive procedure is by function rather than by simple toe-to-top anatomy," moving up through the three powers or parts of the soul (the vegetable, the sensitive, and the intellectual);[11] despite its odd numbering of the soul's powers, De Mornay's *The true knowledge of a mans owne selfe* proceeds similarly from the vegetative, through the sensitive, the appetitive and the motive, to the intellectual.[12] *Knowing thyself* entails spanning the major regions of interiority, the seats of the stomach, the heart, and the brain. In the House of Alma, this order not only represents a corporeal hierarchy, but also epitomizes the cooperation among the interior regions, for it traces the route that food takes to be converted into the three spirits, the last of which, the animal spirit, allows the brain to function. In other words, the three orders best demonstrate the body's carefully coordinated operations.

But there is more to this coordinated and coherent corporeal imago than meets the eye. In the practice of *knowing thyself* championed by natural history discourse, interiority assumes a symbolic layout characteristic of early modern mnemonic culture. The subject knows himself by penetrating into the body as though he were entering a building: Charron states, "Now if we will know man we must take more than ordinary paines in this first booke, taking him in all senses, beholding him with all visages, feeling his poulse, sounding him to the quicke, entring into him with a candle and snuffer, searching and creeping into every hole, corner, turning, closet, and secret place, and not without cause."[13] Emptied of its viscera, the body becomes an architectural space with chambers capable of being imaginatively entered and explored. In a survey of the body, Samuel Purchas's *Purchas his pilgrim* expresses wonderment at the "manifold inclosures of this Building," explicitly maintaining the space of the palace with its courts, rooms, and offices.[14] *Knowing thyself* very much involves for natural history discourse the conversion of the body into a memory palace in order to master its impenetrable depths.

What exactly is a memory palace? Committed to enhancing one's ability to remember, the art of memory has taught since classical times the importance of domesticating and managing interiority. The practitioner associates the things to be remembered with images and then locates these images in an orderly architectural setting, so that later he can revisit the setting and systematically retrieve the various deposits from their guardians.[15] The imagined building, by no means restricted to a palace blueprint, is the overall layout that the practitioner designs for arranging images and places. It is my contention, however, that the memory palace's significance to early modern subjectivity extends well beyond the perfunctory and pragmatic implementation of mnemonic techniques suggested by classical treatises. The memory palace is a fascinating phenomenological space, a fantasy of interiority for mastering the self. In constructing the palace, the subject removes the densely clotted viscera of doubt and imaginatively makes visible and knowable inner regions that otherwise deny accessibility.

The House of Alma is a spectacular instantiation of the memory palace practiced in natural history discourse and described in memory treatises. It masters corporeal interiority by creating differentiated space in which the self can pass freely without obstruction and without threat of disorientation. The *Ad Herennium*, the first extant treatise with an explanation of the *ars memoriae*, advises the practitioner to differ the places in "form and nature," because "if a person has adopted many intercolumnar spaces," their similarity will confuse him as to what image belongs to each place.[16] Spenser complies conscientiously with this advice, avoiding confusing doubles by making each place a distinct room. The integrity of each room is further fortified by the room's correspondence to a physiological function. In total, the correspondences to the body create a conspicuous arrangement, fulfilling another important precept: the places should be arranged in a series "so that we may never by confusion in their order be prevented from following the images."[17] When proceeding backward or forward from any spot, the practitioner must be able to arrive at each of the places within the edifice. In following the route of food through its many material transformations, Guyon's memory sequence could not be more memorable. The superimposition of the three powers of the soul over the building establishes a syntax, whereby one room, naturally leading to the next, permits the reader to locate images easily. Moreover, each room, befitting a house of temperance, seems to be well proportioned and well lit, separated by moderate intervals from its neighbors.[18] The memory palace converts interiority into a traversable, hospitable, and familiar space, while still preserving the architectural awe worthy of the microcosm.

As a fantasy space, the House of Alma intensifies the imaginary encounter with the corporeal other found in natural history discourse. Where it parts company with this discourse is in its unusual emphasis on the mnemonic image. Consistent with the art of memory, mnemonic images do not roam about Alma's house. They know their allocated places, the exception being Alma—the ideal ego, who, functioning as the exemplary mnemonic practitioner, moves freely through the house with the knights. The mnemonic images that they encounter in the well-defined interior space actually enact their roles as mnemonic images; that is, the memory palace reflects upon itself as memory palace. Although critical discussions of memory in Alma's house usually confine themselves to Eumnestes's library with its chronicles, most of the rooms figuratively stage the body's involvement in remembering.[19] The language of memory predominates so much so that the house may be taken as a fantasy of the body whose motions and functions have been reduced to the single overriding imperative to remember.

Embodied by the castle's kitchen, the stomach recalls an admonitory trope used by early modern mnemonic treatises to warn readers against overfeeding the memory with indigestible learning.[20] Under the supervision of the master cook and kitchen clerk, Alma's stomach presumably does not succumb to such gluttony. The clerk, who "Did order all th'Achates in seemely wise,/And set them forth, as well he could deuise" (II.ix.31.4–5), performs a duty cognate with a figure of speech explicated by Thomas Wilson: "digestion is an orderly placing of things, parting every matter severally."[21] The clerk literally puts into practice the chief rhetorical activity of the art of memory by ordering the food as one would dispose images in a sequence of places. Continuing the same process, the marshal and the steward seat the guests and distribute the meat in the dining area (II.ix.28.3–6).

The heart, corresponding to the parlor, has long been a trope for memory too.[22] The Old Testament, for example, enjoins the son to write the father's wisdom upon "the table" of his "heart" (Prov. 3:1–3), attesting to the importance of memory for ensuring patriarchal continuity. Retrieving wisdom from this internal tablet, Arthur and Guyon locate versions of themselves in the parlor: Prays-Desire and Shamefastnesse. Yet Spenser's heart, the seat of sensation, exhibits a peculiar absence that David Lee Miller calls "one of the more baffling features of Alma's castle."[23] The parlor is richly arrayed with royal tapestries "In which was nothing pourtrahed, nor wrought,/Not wrought, nor pourtrahed, but easie to be thought" (II.ix.33.8–9). The absence of portraiture may find a satisfactory explanation in the heart's association with erotic love, since, as every sleepless sonneteer knows, the heart is the secret locus for a specific kind of portrait, the image of the beloved.[24] Medical discourse, however, regards the persisting imprint of the beloved's image as a symptom of love melancholy.[25] And, therefore, when a lover has been cured of the malady he effectively "forgotten" his beloved as "if he had taken a dramme of oblivion."[26] The absence of a beloved's image in Alma's heart seems to bear out the statement that she "had not yet felt *Cupides* wanton rage" (II.ix.18.2). The presence of thoughts to the exclusion of portraiture may indicate less the privileging of Spenser's own allegorical mode over idolatrous imagery than the triumph of chaste inscriptions over the beloved's form, that is, the triumph of biblical memory over its pathologization in love melancholy.[27]

The two other turret chambers have also been designed with a view to remembering. The cell of imagination appears to be, in the words of one mnemonic treatise, "the servant of memory" or, even more forcefully in those of a natural history treatise, "memoria imperfectior," since the idle fantasies adorning the walls illustrate the rules for composing images in the art of memory.[28] The *Ad Herennium* encourages the mnemonist to compose active images (*imagines agentes*) as striking as possible so that they will leave a lasting impression.[29] Phantastes's cell appropriately emphasizes sundry colors (II.ix.50.2) and the grotesque (hags, centaurs, fiends), the bestial (apes, lions, eagles), and the beautiful (lovers, children, dames) (II.ix.50.8–9). Out of all the rooms in the house, however, the middle chamber, often identified as belonging to Reason, falls squarely into the discourse of the *ars memoriae*—even more neatly than Eumnestes's chamber does. The room's walls, "painted faire with memorable gestes" (II.ix.53.3), and representing "All artes, all science, all Philosophy" (II.ix.53.8), invoke two famous mnemonic chambers in the Renaissance: Camillo's memory theater with its mystical images spanning all of knowledge or, less ambitiously, Lady Drury's Oratory whose walls displayed fifteen vertical rows of emblematic pictures in columns of four.[30] The upper turret's middle chamber may be covered in emblems too; simple pictures could not communicate laws, arts, science, and philosophy. Because the unnamed sage meditates on the pictures "all his life long" (II.ix.54.3) observing the mnemonic art's frequent injunction to practice continually,[31] he could very well be the proper personification of memory in the turret. He literally converts artificial memory—the images on the walls—into natural memory—his own wisdom. Furthermore, he is of the "ripe and perfect age" (II.ix.54.2). For what? For possessing a proper memory. Aristotle says that the young and the old do not retain images as well as the middle-aged, the unnamed sage thus occupying the seat of the golden mean between two extreme forms of himself.[32]

In the fantasy represented by Alma's house, the overall body relies on memory for its growth and health, since its primary activities (digestion, sensation, imagination, meditation, and recollection) have been each transformed into a function of remembering. In effect, the memory palace reflects upon itself as a memory palace insofar as its coordination of image and place enacts, even as it figures forth, the miracles of memory. This elaborate fantasy imagines the body to be simultaneously remembered and remembering and reflexively imagines memory to be both incorporated and incorporating. But fantasy does not stage desire fulfilled or terminated. Since it is "through fantasy," that, according to Slavoj Zizek, "we learn how to desire," the house's staging of the self-reflexive image teaches Guyon an important lesson.[33] From top to bottom, the body's overriding desire is to remember and the object of that desire is none other than the mnemonic image.

At the level of the vegetable soul, the activities in the stately hall and the labors at the cauldron circle tirelessly around the meat, the ostensible reason for the festivity. Here, the mnemonic image occupies the place of lovingly prepared viands, which serve to whet the body's appetite and nourish its parts. At the level of the sensitive soul, female personifications vouch for the desirability of the mnemonic image. In Proverbs, the heart's tablet mixes memory with desire, since its impressions take the feminine form, either the harlot's image or the female personification of wisdom. Alma's memory tablet, by no means austere either, provides Arthur and Guyon with the opportunity to encounter Prays-Desire and Shamefastnesse. These two images stimulate deep feelings in the heroes: the prince is stirred up by the speech of Prays-Desire whose fair beauty embodies the "great desire of glory and of fame" (II.ix.38.7), while Guyon's blushing prompted by Alma's comments on Shamefastnesse indicates a similarly impassioned response. At the intellectual level, each of the three sages spends his life devoted to the mnemonic image: Phantastes generates the striking imagery of the art of memory; the middle sage sits transfixed by the pictures that he voraciously converts into his own wisdom; and finally Eumnestes tosses and turns books without end—a flurry which captures the interminable exercise of mnemonic desire (II.ix.58.2). His chamber also promises to culminate in a scene of arriving at the truth of the mnemonic image, which only prolongs their desire. There the knights find two ancient volumes that enkindle in them a "feruent fire" to recover their ancestral past (II.ix.60.6). For each level, the mnemonic image is the object of desire that captivates Guyon, impelling him to know himself as he journeys through the interior.

The desire to remember explains rather cogently the way in which Book II conceives of heroic subjectivity. Book II's intersection with, as well as divergence from, the *Odyssey* proves particularly instructive in this regard. Guyon's kinship with Odysseus is often based on narrative parallels: the perilous sea voyage Guyon makes at the beginning of Book II and his much anticipated meeting with the Circe-like Acrasia. Aside from specific episodes, the entire book shares with the *Odyssey* the quest to *know thyself.* Yet their quests do not simply intersect at the existential search for self-knowing, an archetypal template which may be superimposed on every epic hero.[34] Odysseus is the remarkable hero who knows himself through the passionate persistence of memory. The poet encodes his desire to remember who he is most significantly in his quest to return home—to arrive at his stable place in an unstable world. W. B. Stanford observes, not surprisingly, that the Stoics and the early Church Fathers employed the homeward bound Ulysses as an "emblem for nostalgia or for spiritual aspiration."[35] Opposed to Odyssean desire are emissaries of oblivion, namely, seductresses, monsters, and even entire cultures, such as the lotus-eaters, who were people that, eating of the lotus tree, forgot their friends and families and losing any desire to return to their native country, abandoned themselves to luxurious lethargy in Lotus land.[36] Alexander Ross's *Mystagogus Poeticus*, a seventeenth-century English mythological handbook, underscores the menace that this land holds for early modern readers, when praising Ulysses for a wisdom that subdues "all delightful pleasures, which make us (as the Lotos did Ulysses his fellowes) forget to return home into the way of righteousness out of which we have wandered, and have refused to return."[37]

Emissaries of oblivion plague Guyon too. Phaedria strives to do to him what she did to Cymochles: she soothes his fiery mind bent on knightly revenge, lulling him to sleep with song and then drugging him with a nepenthe-like liquor (II.vi.18.3).[38] Mammon tempts Guyon to retire from his quest with underworld riches, then with love of recognition, and finally with false knowledge, the last temptation involving a bizarre invitation to sit on a silver stool. Nohrnberg identifies this seat with the "chair of forgetfulness," which held fast Theseus in Hades.[39] And, had she had the chance, Acrasia would have done to Guyon what she did to Verdant: "his braue shield, full of old moniments,/Was fowly ra'st, that none the signes might see" (II.xii.80.3–4). Sensual pleasure has erased from the warrior's memory tablet the traces of battle.

Guyon's divergence from the *Odyssey* is equally illuminating. His quest, while maintaining a heroic loyalty to memory, significantly turns the goal of Odyssean travels inside out. Whereas Odysseus circumvents waylayer after waylayer on his journey to Ithaca, Guyon drives toward the waylayer, so that every emissary of oblivion is not an interruption of the journey but the journey itself. The former avoids the entrapments of forgetting in order to return home; the latter seeks to confront forgetting in order to vanquish it. It is as though remembering and forgetting were symmetrically related. Not only is forgetting the negation of remembering, but remembering, according to Guyon's quest, is also the negation of forgetting.

This divergence from the *Odyssey* draws out the early modern form of forgetting at work in Book II. Remembering may come into being through direct opposition to forgetting, because both struggle to gain control over the corporeal other. In natural history discourse, *forgetting thyself* is, therefore, the dialectical counterpart of *knowing thyself.* Thomas Rogers's *A philosophicall discourse, entituled, The anatomie of the minde* explicates fully the motion of this dialectic:

> Knowe thy selfe, and thou shalt not offend: forget thy self, and what wilt thou not do? Neither reason from wickednesse, nor religion from ungratiousnesse hold thee backe. Art thou an *Aristides* for uprightnes? forget thy selfe, and what art thou but an *Acteon* for covetousnesse? A *Lucretia* for chastetie? forget thy selfe, and thou shalt be a *Messalina* for incontinencie . . . .forget thy and what art thou but a beast? And such a beast, as surpasseth all beasts in beastlinesse.[40]

If knowing one's self means mastering the corporeal other, then forgetting one's self entails relinquishing control of the self to the corporeal other. The body overwhelms the self with its alien, horrific corporeality. Degeneracy of the body and degeneracy of identity are accordingly indistinguishable.

In early modernity, the degeneracy induced by forgetting may assume several distinct corporeal forms, the chief of which, as Rogers says, is the bestial. Grill best illustrates the bestial in the Bower, where many knights who have disregarded the injunction to know themselves have fallen prey to Acrasia. After having been restored to his human shape, he laments the loss of hoggish form, prompting Guyon to moralize: "See the mind of beastly man,/That hath so soone forgot the excellence/Of his creation" (II.xii.87.1–3). Verdant incarnates degenerate forgetting too. His nobility, "so foule deface" (II.xii.79.4), and the "old moniments" on his shield, so "fowly ra'st," signify the body of the aristocratic warrior who has lost his masculinity because he has abandoned himself to "lewd loues, and wastfull luxuree" (II.xii.80.7).[41] Besides the exemplum of Mark Antony's seduction by Cleopatra, a potential locus classicus for the aristocratic warrior slipping into effeminacy through forgetting is Sardanapalus, the king of the Assyrians, who, renouncing the company of men, consorted only with harlots. Consequently, he was "so much addicted unto voluptuousnes & pleasure" that "forgetting all humanitie" he spent his time wearing women's clothes and speaking with a female voice.[42] A third form of degeneracy induced by forgetting is the racial. In Richard A. McCabe's examination of the Irish influence on Spenser, the Bower poses the same threat that Ireland poses to English colonizers. According to Spenser's *A View of the Present State of Ireland*, which McCabe reads alongside *The Faerie Queene*, the English have fallen into "a dangerous lethargy," for they "have grown to be as very patchhocks as the wild Irish."[43] Grill and his compatriots dramatize the tale of Englishmen who have vitiated their stock through cultural assimilation.[44]

In Spenser, all three forms of forgetting thyself attribute to female kind the power to corrupt the interiority of male corporeality. As well, the fact that two out of the three primary emissaries of oblivion are feminine draws attention to the considerable gender implications of Guyon's quest, not pursued here. In this volume of essays, Berger's feminist reading of Acrasia's demonization teases out the nuances of gender in male fantasy. Although my argument is centered on the dialectic between remembering and forgetting, Berger's conceptualization of specular tautology—that is, the displacement of responsibility and blame onto a female provocateur—reminds us that male fantasy in Book II frequently inflicts violence on women. *Knowing thyself* often entails removing from the male interior traces of the *femme fatale*, which are really projections of what male identity formation cannot accept within itself: its susceptibility to and dependence on the imaginary other.

Although Guyon's dismissive response to Grill, who regrets having been changed back into human form, may seem more befitting a moral automaton than a compassionate rescuer, Guyon does speak from the experience of having investigated firsthand the interiority of the degenerate body. If Book II conforms to the discourse of natural history in exploring the corporeal other as one would enter a memory palace, then it startlingly surpasses the imaginative achievement of this discourse: Guyon also enters the body that does not know itself. He explores interiorities similar to those of Grill and Verdant. Nohrnberg's formulation of "the principal of allegorical chiasmus"—whereby "a man in an enviornment here often stands for the environment in the man"—brilliantly accounts for the ease with which Guyon moves from the inside to the outside and back again.[45]

I want to argue that Phaedria's Lake, the Cave of Mammon, and Bower warp the phenomenological space of Alma's Castle. To a certain extent, my argument is not new. Commentators have long noticed the fertile correspondences between Alma's house and Book II's threatening zones.[46] Each zone grotesquely fragments the castle's tripartite order (vegetable, sensitive, and intellectual), magnifying one of the powers of the soul into a malignantly intemperate bodily desire, as if it were perverting natural history discourse. Phaedria's idle lake, an expansion of Phantastes's cell, is the seascape of the imagination cut off from, yet unrestricted by, the higher mental faculties. The imagination was said to be at its greatest freedom during sleep, when reason could no longer control it. It is no wonder, then, that Guyon, leaving the Palmer behind and entering the bark navigated by Phaedria's desire, finds himself captive to her "fantasticke wit" (II.vi.7.2). She is borne aloft on sluggish waters engrossed with mud, a lucid reference to the melancholy-saturated faculty: "euen as slime and durt in a standing puddle," says Thomas Nashe, "engender toads and frogs and many other unsightly creatures, so this slimie melancholy humor still thickning as it stands still, engendreth many mishapen obiects in our imaginations."[47] Mammon's cavern distorts the powers of the nutritive and digestive system in Alma's house.[48] First encountering Mammon in a pile of gold near a "hole full wide" (II.vii.6.4), Guyon follows him into an excremental netherworld, entering from the anal not the oral end, thereby reversing the direction that he took in touring the House of Alma. The subterranean bowels lead eventually to a place of consumption, but the immoderate production of the stomach dominates the complex. The fundament chamber retentively hordes along with carcasses and bones an exceeding store of Gold produced by the monstrous kitchen with its hundred furnaces. And Acrasia's bower intemperately heightens, of course, the powers of the senses as though Alma's house no longer had impenetrable walls. Rather appropriately, the bower's thinly wrought gate shows the self to be on the verge of becoming indistinguishable from the outer world. But Guyon steels himself from capitulating to sensual pleasure. He duly rejects overtures to his five senses: "the sweet spirit and holesome smell" (II.xii.51.9), the "sappy liquor" in Excesse's cup (II.xii.56.3), the strip tease of the two naked damsels, the quire of birds and the lovely lay (II.xii.76.1–2), and the touch of Acrasia attired in magical lingerie. Guyon and the Palmer handle her with the mediation of a net.

But what is the symbolic architecture of these phenomenological spaces? They are obviously not memory palaces. Again, natural history discourse orients us to Book II's topography, this time providing a fleeting yet discerning glimpse of unknowable interiority. There are moments when microcosmic buildings give way to nightmarish spaces: Crooke and Purchas both detect the labyrinthine in corporeal parts such as the brain, but also recognize "man" as a labyrinth too.[49] Whereas the temple, storehouse, and palace order the body by establishing spatial propriety, familiarity, and sanctuary, the labyrinth is an anti-domicile, incapable of vouchsafing subjectivity permanence and protection. It houses the forbiddingly monstrous body. In their respective projects, Crooke and Purchas momentarily register the possibility of the self becoming lost in unknowable interiority.[50] Charron insinuates further the impossibility of establishing a corporeal memory palace. Before progressing systematically through its divisions and offices, he describes the intellectual part of the soul as "a depth of obscuritie, full of creeks and hidden corners, a confused and involved labyrinth, and bottomless pit."[51] In his depiction of corporeality, the labyrinth constitutes not a cultural construction, but a natural space outside domestication and impervious to epistemological mastery.

The Faerie Queene envisions and enters into at length what early modern natural history discourse only tentatively gestures toward. Unlike memory palaces, which are designed to retrieve oneself, labyrinths are designed to lose the self. The zones of forgetting by the same token engulf Guyon in their labyrinthine expanses.[52] Like Charon's depiction of the intellectual soul, their arboreal landscapes, subterranean caverns, and strange watercourses thwart the purpose of *knowing thyself*—culture's capacity to stabilize subjectivity through remembering recedes as nature encroaches into the memory palace. The zones release unruly bodily desire by breaking down the symbolic structure of the art of memory: the images and the places are not coordinated by the subject's desire to remember. Conforming to neither a suitable proportion nor order, the places within these palaces resist the subject's masterful gaze. Phaedria's isle, antithetical to the fixed mnemonic place, floats in a sea whose margins are not visually defined, and her wandering ferry, like the isle, is equally disconnected to other reference points. Similarly, Acrasia's bower has, according to Paul Alpers, perplexed readers with its nebulous boundaries, and it is only when Guyon gives himself up to iconoclastic frenzy in what may be a garden maze that the reader hears of a palace, banquet houses, and other buildings.[53] Mammon's cave also breaks the rules of the art of memory—by not bathing the places in enough illumination (II.vii.29) and by populating a single place with too many images. In the plain before Pluto's gate, the consort of figures (II.vii.22–23) are grouped together confusingly with clouds of flying creatures overhead.[54]

As malevolent as they may appear, these zones, however, are integral to Guyon's quest. Because he achieves heroic remembering through confronting and negating forgetting, the zones actually extend the fantasy topography of Alma's house; as dialectical counterparts, they make possible its symbolic structure. In effect accomplishing on a large scale what Maleger's army does on a small scale, they separate memory from forgetting, as though forgetting befalls the body from the outside. Book II urges us to accept unquestioningly the purity of the desire within the memory palace, the body that knows itself. We should, therefore, not be duped into taking the zones as the actual threat to Guyon's heroic subjectivity, since, in Slavoj Žižek's words, fantasy "enables us to mask the real of our desire," to conceal "some traumatic, real kernel."[55] Instead, we should try to traverse Guyon's fantasy in order to break the imaginary grip that the memory palace has on early modern subjectivity. When we traverse a fantasy according to Lacanian psychoanalysis, Žižek explains, "we break the constraints of the fantasy and enter the terrifying, violent domain of pre-synthetic imagination, the domain in which *disjecta membra* float around, not yet unified and 'domesticated' by the intervention of a homogenizing fantasmatic frame."[56] By moving outside the fantasmatic frame that reverently holds in place the object of desire, we can anamorphoically see the real trauma or rather the trauma of the real menacing Guyon's quest to know himself.

Guyon assists us in traversing the fantasy since he himself disturbs the fantasmatic frame when he gets too close to his object of desire, the mnemonic image. Because desire in Lacanian psychoanalysis is a function of a lack not an actual object, the danger to subjectivity does not arise from losing the object but grasping that object's inherent emptiness. Consequently, when the subject gets too close to the object cause of desire, he or she experiences anxiety triggered by the disappearance of desire.[57] And so, at the point in the tour where the mnemonic image promises ideal attributes described by the art of memory, Guyon encounters more than he is looking for. He walks into a plague. Phantastes's images at once exemplify the *agentes imagines* of the *ars memoriae* and deviate perversely from that art. The most compelling this evidence for this deviation is found in Spenser's recasting of a popular mnemonic topos. The bee commonplace, whose rich genealogy in the classical and medieval tradition is partly sketched by Mary Carruthers, "likens the placement of memory-images in a trained memory . . . to the honey-making of bees."[58] Spenser converts the bee commonplace into the following analogy:

> And all the chamber filled was with flyes,
> Which buzzed all about, and made such sound,
> That they encombred all mens eares and eyes,
> Like many swarmes of Bees assembled round,
> After their hiues with honny do abound.

(II.ix.51.1–5)

Spenser's analogical figure replicates this commonplace straightforwardly, the bees standing for mnemonic images and the cells for mnemonic places. In contrast, his ground for the analogy gives the reader pause. The comparison of flies to bees is strikingly curious. The analogy, functioning according to inverted logic, posits differences through similar objects of comparison.[59] Early modern flies are honey-less, cell-less, and anti-social insects.[60] In other words, the flies, which are said to represent idle thoughts and lies, have no proper homes to return to. The bee analogy highlights in Phantastes's chamber a tumult radically antithetical to the art of memory. In explaining the origin of the art, Cicero recounts how Simonides, after the collapse of a building on banqueters, was able to identify their mutilated corpses through recollecting the seat in which each of them had been sitting; Simonides subsequently discovered that "the best aid to clearness of memory consists in orderly arrangement."[61] Bees emblematize ideal mnemonic arrangement through making, as Pliny says, "their own habitations & storehouses," while a fly, an image without a place, conversely, foils the purposes of mnemonic architecture.[62]

Phantastes's flies are only comparable to bees by virtue of their tendency to plague people.[63] Their buzzing and swarming generate such confusion that the eyes and ears of all men are "encumbered" —etymologically meaning "to block up." This blockage of sight and sound flies directly in the face of the art of memory, which enhances vision.[64] Because the memory palace must render every phenomenon visible, no place can be said to be "confounded or troubled wyth the multytude of the fygures or Images."[65] Phantastes's cell shows the disquieting truth of memory: the mnemonic image is, indeed, chaotic, unplaced, and encumbering. It has a horrific, agitated life of its own. What appears as the object of desire in the remembering body is seen outside the fantasy frame to be the *objet petit a* with all its disgusting and futile attraction:

> The Lacanian formula for this object is of course *objet petit a*, this point of Real the very heart of the subject which cannot be symbolized, which is produced as a residue, a remnant, a leftover of every signifying operation, a hard core horrifying *jouissance*, enjoyment, and as such an object which simultaneously attracts us and repels us—which *divides* our desire and thus provokes shame.[66]

The real resides at the very place where we expect memory to occur. And so Alma cannot dispense with Phantastes's imagery, hoping that the nightmare will go away. The early modern mnemonic image is not an easily cast off rhetorical substitute for some other process that occurs inside corporeality. No, this could not be further from the case. Rather than an artificial supplement to an authentic phenomenological space, the memory palace is a supplement in the Derridean sense of the term.[67] Artificial memory is always already natural memory for early modern psychology: just as the materials of the memory palace consist of images and places, the brain functions by circulating images among the three inner senses—commonsense, imagination, and memory, each located in its own ventricle.[68] The faculty system with its division of the brain into separate cells is a memory palace *avant la lettre*. In Elizabethan mental schemes, architectural language frequently organizes the brain, and the functions of the inner senses are often personified.[69]

The disorienting zones of forgetting also shadow forth the real of desire that precedes and necessitates the fantasy of remembering. The three zones flicker in a murky twilight. When situated within the delusional certainty of corporeal mastery, they defiantly mock the integrity of Alma's house and warn all subjects to know themselves. But, as the light wanes, they too reveal Phantastes's flies, buzzing and swarming with a life of their own. The mnemonic image materializes anamorphoically as an oneiric image, an excremental image, and a carnal image, all of which do not remember. Embracing both *verba* and *res*, Phaedria's images invoke the memory palace's capacity to stockpile, for she possesses a "store-house" (II.vi.6.5) of merry tales and her floating island boasts a "great store" (II.vi.11.9) of pleasant flora and fauna. Yet the imagination has taken over the memory palace to such a degree that the mnemonic image, no longer tied to mnemonic content, operates as an oneiric image with its own agenda. Both Phaedria's vain toys and the island's flora and fauna seem to conspire "to allure fraile mind to carelesse ease" (II.vi.13.6), inducing soporific effects in the hapless Cymochles. The mnemonic image is the bearer of unconscious forces beyond the control of the knight. With Acrasia's bower, the memory palace has been overrun by the senses so much so that the image operates not as a sign, but as a seductive idol. Linda Gregerson's analysis of the wider interpretive phenomenon of idolatry applies to the bower: "the conjunction between lust, or uxoriousness, and the carnal misreading of signs, or idolatry, is one to which the Old Testament and the Apocypha give repeated testimony."[70] The mnemonic image loses its memory content asserting only its carnal dimension. And so Grill's beastly mind, which has been captivated by this mnemonic image, "hath so soone forgot the excellence/Of his creation" (II.xii.87.2). With Mammon's cave, the memory palace has been flooded by an insane overproduction, an anally obsessive and retentive, or better yet an autistic, desire to stockpile a single image at the expense of diversification and differentiation. Even though Maurice Evans claims the Cave of Mammon to be a traditional representation of the art of memory, Nohrnberg rightly points out that the traditional notion of memory as a treasury starkly contrasts Mammon's excessive storehouses.[71] The mnemonic image operates as excrement, a disgusting surplus of the same: gold coins, smelted gold, gold roof, gold floor, golden pillars, the great gold chain, and golden apples. Midas's infantile reduction of his world to one metal has resulted in useless, excremental memory architecture.

Taking one step further Phantastes's suggestion that the mental space houses alien, turbulent sense impressions—strange foreign bodies—the zones of forgetting specify the real of desire inherent in the mnemonic image: its oneiric, excremental, and carnal attraction. The images are, therefore, not amnesic blanks, duds that can no longer perform the offices required of them by artificial or natural memory. In the zones of forgetting, Guyon draws near to an alienating *jouissance* that both disgusts and fascinates him. The mnemonic image with its striking impression entices him to lose himself in amnesic *jouissance*, whether it be the vertiginous whirlpool of decay where "full many had with haplesse doole,/Beene suncke, of whom no memorie did stay" (II.xii.20.3–4) or the mermaids whose siren-like singing lures travelers to their deaths. Outside fantasy, the mnemonic image, the object cause of desire, which promises to yield a memory that will fill in corporeal interiority and enable Guyon to know himself, only immerses him in the real of his desire—his desire to give himself up to the pleasures of the dream, his desire to lose himself in infantile obsession, and his desire to abandon himself to hedonistic senses. It besets him on all sides with the temptation to forgo the symbolic order for the preimaginary realm that precedes the subject's entry into the differential field of identity.

Guyon's desire allows readers to flesh out his subjectivity, animating his quest with a purpose that would have deeply moved a culture devoted to remembering. In the dedicatory epistle to *The Castel of Memorie*, a translation of Gulielmus Gratarolus's mnemonic treatise, William Fullwood justifies his enterprise of aiding the memory by explaining what ultimately is at stake: "Therfore I briefly thus conclude,/take Memorye away: What is a man? What can he doe?/or els what can he say?"[72] Fullwood's effort to shore up memory from a forgetting that threatens to undo the self epitomizes Guyon's imaginary quest. Informed by natural history discourse and the art of memory, Guyon plays out the early modern fantasy of defending the memory palace of interiority against the emissaries of oblivion.

Although I would not argue that Spenser is critiquing interiority outright, his deployment of romance narrative to probe the recesses of bodies that know themselves and bodies that do not know themselves uncovers more than he might have been willing to find. On one hand, he implements the art of memory and natural history discourse to colonize and masculinize interiority, activities which negate the imaginary other, the incarnated threat of forgetting. But on the other hand, Guyon's descents into managed and horrific interiority change the terms of that descent. For Spenser, Guyon's quest does not merely reflect the imaginary boundaries of the discourse and practice of remembering; it traverses those boundaries, shedding further light on the precarious stability of the early modern subject who remembers. Just as Guyon gets too close to the object of desire in the House of Alma, he pries too deeply into the body that does not know itself. The questionable outcome of his quest forcefully drives this point home. Though he makes Acrasia his prisoner, Guyon cannot be said to secure a victory on behalf of memory. Not content with capturing the emissary of oblivion, Guyon seeks to raze the zone of forgetting with what Hamilton calls a "Dionysian act."[73] Guyon totally abandons himself to a radically psychotic forgetting. He slips into amnesic *jouissance* at the moment he believes himself to be advancing the cause of remembering. In a world where emissaries of oblivion surround the subject from all sides, the real trauma opened up by Book II is not forgetting per se, but the unthinkable possibility that memory itself could be a menacing yet beguiling enjoyment capable of losing the subject in unknowable interiority. To his credit, Spenser, the poet of interiority, does not hinder Guyon from encountering the real of subjectivity.

Notes

I want to thank Theresa Krier for her insightful and thoughtful guidance through the revision process of earlier drafts.

1. For Guyon's passivity, see Kathleen Mary Williams, *Spenser's World of Glass: A Reading of "The Faerie Queene"* (Berkeley: University of California Press, 1966), 68. Harry Berger Jr., *The Allegorical Temper: Vision and Reality in Book II of Spenser's "Faerie Queene"* (New Haven: Yale University Press, 1957), 13, sums up Guyon's

dullness well: he appears to be a mouthpiece for allegorical propaganda. Of course, this note is not meant to hypostatize Berger, whose ongoing oppositional readings of *The Faerie Queene* have been a model for Spenser studies in process, that is, the criticism of renewal.

2. Berger redeems Guyon from inauthentic subjectivity by detecting his susceptibility to original sin. Madelon S. Gohlke, "Embattled Allegory: Book II of *The Faerie Queene*," *English Literary Renaissance* 8, 2 (1978): 123–40, rehabilitates him by drawing attention to the demonic energies raging beneath the book's placid rhetorical surface. David Lee Miller, *The Poem's Two Bodies: The Poetics of the 1590 "Faerie Queene"* (Princeton: Princeton University Press, 1988), 190, reads Book II's image of the temperate body as sublimating and displacing desire continually. Michael C. Schoenfeldt, *Bodies and Selves in Early Modern England: Physiology and Inwardness in Spenser, Shakespeare, Herbert, and Milton* (Cambridge: Cambridge University Press, 1999), provides an innovative interpretation of Book II that takes issue with the repression model favored by Miller and Stephen Greenblatt, *Renaissance Self-Fashioning: From More to Shakespeare* (University of Chicago Press, 1980), 157–92. Contextualizing Alma's house within the discourses of moral health, Schoenfeldt argues, "Self-control is for Spenser a means of legitimating, not negating, desire" (53).

3. See James Nohrnberg, *The Analogy of "The Faerie Queene"* (Princeton: Princeton University Press, 1976), 326, 347.

4. Desiderius Erasmus, *Adages Ivi1 to Ix100*, trans. R. A. B. Mynors, *Collected Works of Erasmus* 32 (Toronto: University of Toronto Press, 1989), 62.

5. Helkiah Crooke, *Mikrokosmographia: a description of the body of man* (London, William Iaggard, 1615), 12.

6. Thomas Rogers, *A philosophicall discourse, entituled, The anatomie of the minde* (London, I[ohn] C[harlewood], 1576), preface. Pierre La Primaudaye, *The French academie*, trans. T. B. (London, Edmund Bollifant, 1586), 11. Philippe de Mornay, *The true knowledge of a mans owne selfe*, trans. A. M. (London, I. R[oberts], 1602), 1–2. Pierre Charron, *Of wisdome three bookes*, trans. Samson Lennard (London, Eliot's Court Press, 1608), 1. Samuel Purchas, *Purchas his pilgrim. Microcosmus, or the historie of man* (London, W[illiam] S[tansby], 1619), 6–7.

7. See Jacques Lacan, "The mirror stage as formative of the function of the *I* as revealed in psychoanalytic experience," in *Écrits: A Selection*, trans. Alan Sheridan (New York: Norton, 1977), 2.

8. Charron, *Of wisdome,* 4.

9. Besides the narrator's general exclamations, the knights admire Port Esquiline (II.ix.33.1–4), the middle sage's goodly reason (II.ix.54.6–9) and Eumnestes's endless exercise (II.ix.59.1–2).

10. See Purchas, 25–32, who expresses wonder for the microcosm that begins his survey of the body.

11. Walter R. Davis, *Spenser Studies* 2 (1981): 122–23.

12. The soul—signifying all the body's motions not a spiritual essence—was usually conceived in terms of three powers. See J. B. Bamborough, *The Little World of Man* (London: Longmans, 1952), 31–32.

13. Charron, *Of wisdome,* 6.

14. Purchas, 32. For another wondrous palace, see Robert Burton, *The Anatomy of Melancholy*, ed. Thomas C. Faulkner, Nicolas K. Kiessling, and Rhonda L. Blair, 3 vols. (Oxford: Clarendon, 1989–1994), 1:144.

15. See [Cicero], *Rhetorica Ad Herennium*, trans. Harry Caplan (Cambridge, Mass.: Heinemann, 1954), 209.
16. *Rhetorica Ad Herennium*, 211–13.
17. *Rhetorica Ad Herennium*, 209.
18. *Rhetorica Ad Herennium*, 213.
19. Judith Anderson, " 'Myn Auctour': Spenser's Enabling Fiction and Eumnestes' 'immortal scrine'," in *Unfolded Tales: Essays on Renaissance Romance*, ed. George M. Logan and Gordon Teskey (Ithaca: Cornell University Press, 1989), 16–31, explores Eumnestes's implications for recorded memory as though his presence were the only meaningful representation of memory in Alma's house. Elizabeth Mazzola, "Apocryphal Texts and Epic Amnesia: The Ends of History in *The Faerie Queene*," *Soundings* 78, 1 (1995): 134, recognizes only Eumnestes's chamber as the seat of memory in the House of Alma. Going a little further, Lynette C. Black, "Prudence in Book II of *The Faerie Queene*," *Spenser Studies* 13 (1999): 65–88, observes that the process of memory is "not confined to Eumnestes' chamber alone" but is "embodied by the three sages" (74–75). However, her analysis stops short, neglecting to consider the entire house in terms of the art of memory.
20. Gulielmus Gratarolus, *The Castel of Memorie* [1562], trans. William Fullwood, The English Experience 382 (Amsterdam and New York: Da Capo Press, 1971), G2v. John Willis, *The Art of Memory As It Dependeth Upon Places and Ideas* [1621], The English Experience 634 (Amsterdam and New York: Da Capo Press, 1973), 56–57. For a further discussion of the stomach and memory, see Schoenfeldt, 63.
21. Citations and quotations are taken from *The Faerie Queene: Book Two*, ed. Edwin Greenlaw, *The Works of Edmund Spenser: A Variorum Edition*, ed. Edwin Greenlaw, Charles Grosvenor Osgood, and Frederick Morgan Padelford, vol. 2 (Baltimore: Johns Hopkins University Press, 1933). Thomas Wilson, *The Art of Rhetoric (1560)*, ed. Peter E. Medine (University Park: Pennsylvania State University Press, 1994), 223.
22. Robert A. Erickson, *The Language of the Heart, 1600–1750* (Philadelphia: University of Pennsylvania Press, 1997), 15, states that the heart "gave rise to a multitude of 'house' images," such as "a store-house of secrets, memories, or lived experience" and "the dwelling place of Christ."
23. Miller, *Poem's Two Bodies,* 174.
24. See sonnet 45 of the *Amoretti* in *Minor Poems: Part Two*, ed. Edwin Greenlaw, in the *Variorum*, vol. 8.
25. See Jacques Ferrand, *A Treatise on Lovesickness*, trans. and ed. Donald A. Beecher and Massimo Ciavolella (Syracuse: Syracuse University Press, 1990), 257.
26. Burton, *Anatomy of Melancholy*, 3:215.
27. Miller, *Poem's Two Bodies,* 175, regards the presence of thoughts as privileging the allegorical mode.
28. Willis, A4v-A5r. Nicholas Mosley, *Psychosophia: or, Natural & divine contemplations of the passions & faculties of the soul of man* (London, Humphrey Mosley, 1653), 77.
29. *Rhetorica Ad Herennium*, 221.
30. Frances A. Yates, *The Art of Memory* (Chicago: University of Chicago Press, 1984), 129–59, provides a full description of Camillo's theatre. For a detailed discussion of Lady Drury's Oratory, see Norman K. Farmer, Jr., *Poets and the Visual Arts in Renaissance England* (Austin: University of Texas Press, 1984), 77–105.

31. *Rhetorica Ad Herennium*, 225.

32. Aristotle, "De Memoria et Reminiscentia," in *The Basic Works of Aristotle*, ed. Richard McKeon (New York: Random House, 1941), 609.

33. Slavoj Žižek, *Looking Awry: An Introduction to Jacques Lacan through Popular Culture* (Cambridge, Mass.: MIT Press, 1991), 6.

34. For the traditional view of the quest of self-knowing, see Thomas E. Maresca, *Three English Epics: Studies of "Troilus and Criseyde," "The Faerie Queene," and "Paradise Lost"* (Lincoln: University of Nebraska Press, 1979), 12.

35. William Bedell Stanford, *The Ulysses Theme: A Study in the Adaptability of a Traditional Hero* (Oxford: Blackwell, 1954), 175.

36. Homer, *The Odyssey*, trans. A. T. Murray, vol. 1 (Cambridge, Mass.: Harvard University Press, 1919), 309.

37. Alexander Ross, *A Critical Edition of Alexander Ross's 1647 Mystagogus Poeticus, or The Muses Interpreter*, ed. John R. Glenn (New York: Garland, 1987), 560.

38. Her liquor sounds like Helen's drug for inducing forgetfulness of pain. See Homer, 123.

39. Nohrnberg, *Analogy of "The Faerie Queene,"* 342–43.

40. Rogers, preface. Charron, 5, uses the same expression of forgetting oneself.

41. Mordant too knows not himself because of the "chaines of lust and lewd desires" (II.i.54.3).

42. Richard Barckley, *A Discourse of the Felicitie of Man* (London: William Ponsonby, 1598), 11.

43. Edmund Spenser, *A View of the Present State of Ireland*, ed. W. L. Renwick (Oxford: Clarendon, 1970), 64.

44. Richard A. McCabe, "Edmund Spenser, Poet of Exile," *Proceedings of the British Academy*, 80 (Oxford: Oxford University Press, 1993), 85–86.

45. Nohrnberg, 327. Isabel G. MacCaffrey, *Spenser's Allegory: The Anatomy of Imagination* (Princeton: Princeton University Press, 1976), 213, similarly sees Book II in terms of threatening interiority: "the devices that Spenser employs are designed to take us into the dark world of somatic experience at the roots of our nature."

46. I am indebted to the work of Berger and Nohrnberg, whose tracings of the interconnections between the House of Alma and Book II's other spaces suggest a clash of interiorities.

47. Thomas Nashe, "The Terrors of the Night," in *The Works of Thomas Nashe*, ed. Ronald B. McKerrow, 5 vols. (Oxford: Basil Blackwell, 1958), 1:354.

48. For an extended comparison between Mammon's cave and the House of Alma, see Nohrnberg, 343–51.

49. On the brain, see Crooke, 431, and Purchas, 83. On the entire person, see Crooke, 493, and Purchas, 302.

50. For Crooke, 493, anatomical research enables us to negotiate labyrinthine corporeality; for Purchas, 302, the "clew of Scripture" brings us through it.

51. Charron, *Of wisdome,* 54.

52. Theresa M. Krier, *Gazing on Secret Sights: Spenser, Classical Imitation, and the Decorums of Vision* (Ithaca: Cornell University Press, 1990), 101, observes that both land and sea in Book II lead to oblivion, whereas the land in the *Odyssey* and the *Aeneid* offer stability after "the chaos and homelessness of the sea."

53. Paul Alpers, "Bower of Bliss," *Spenser Encyclopedia*, 105.

54. Spenser inserts his places into spaces whose dimensions thwart visual mastery: when Guyon uneventfully enters the Garden of Prosperina through a path, he finds out later that the main tree's broad branches overhang the river Cocytus which, surrounding the garden, contains "many damned wights" (II.vii.57.2).

55. Slavoj Žižek, *The Sublime Object of Ideology* (London: Verso, 1989), 45.

56. Slavoj Žižek, "The Fantasy in Cyberspace" in *The Zizek Reader*, ed. Elizabeth Wright and Edmond Wright (Oxford: Blackwell, 1999), 122.

57. *Looking Awry*, 8.

58. Carruthers, *The Book of Memory: A Study of Memory in Medieval Culture* (Cambridge: Cambridge University Press, 1990), 35–36.

59. For an explanation of how analogy works, see Edward P. J. Corbett, *Classical Rhetoric for the Modern Student* (Oxford: Oxford University Press, 1990), 104.

60. Whereas bees regularly signify the symbolic system's uninterrupted operation, early modern flies signal the threat of the system's disintegration. In Pliny, the Elder, *The Historie of the World*, trans. Philemon Holland, 3 vols. (London, Adam Isli Press, 1635), 1:312, bees belong to a commonwealth ruled by a king and possessing admirable civil fashions and customs; in William Shakespeare, *3 Henry VI*, ed. Andrew S. Cairncross (London: Methuen, 1964), 2.6.8–17, the traitorous commoners swarm like summer flies, when the king gives ground to his enemies.

61. Cicero, *De Oratore: Books I-II*, trans. E. W. Sutton and H. Rackham (Cambridge, Mass.: Heinemann, 1942), 467.

62. Pliny, *Historie,* 1:312.

63. The noisome quality of the flies recalls the fourth plague in Exodus, where the swarms are said to "corrupt" the earth, as though the flies were capable of destroying the terra firma of place (8:21–24).

64. The mnemonist is synecdochically reduced to "the eyes of the mind," a popular phrase used by Fullwood (Gratarolus, H3v) and Willis (8, 21). For the power of vision in the art of memory, see *De Oratore*, 469.

65. Gratarolus, *Castel of Memorie,* H1v.

66. *The Sublime Object*, 180.

67. See Jacques Derrida, *Of Grammatology*, trans. Gayatri Chakravorty Spivak (Baltimore: Johns Hopkins University Press, 1974), 269–316.

68. In natural philosophy there is some disagreement as to the number of inner senses. See Ruth Leila Anderson, *Elizabethan Psychology and Shakespeare's Plays* (Iowa City, IA: The University, 1927), 14–16.

69. Du Laurens, *A Discourse of the Preservation of Sight; of the Melancholike Diseases; of Rheums, and Old Age*, 1599, trans. Richard Surphlet (London: Oxford University Press, 1938), 73–74, calls the intellective soul a royal palace where the Queen, Reason, holds court between her handmaids: Imagination and Memory.

70. Linda Gregerson, "Protestant Erotics: Idolatry and Interpretation in Spenser's *Faerie Queene*," *English Literary History* 58, 1 (1991):8.

71. Maurice Evans, *Spenser's Anatomy of Heroism: A Commentary on "The Faerie Queene"* (Cambridge: Cambridge University Press, 1970), 81, and Nohrnberg, *Analogy,* 348.

72. Gratarolus, *Castel of Memorie,* A5v.

73. A. C. Hamilton, *The Structure of Allegory in "The Faerie Queene"* (Oxford: Clarendon Press, 1961), 131.

GALINA I. YERMOLENKO

"That troublous dreame": Allegory, Narrative, and Subjectivity in *The Faerie Queene*

Inspired by the studies of medieval dream vision allegories, this article explores the relationship between allegory and subjectivity in two "troublous" (i.e., insomniac and false) dream passages from *The Faerie Queene*: Redcrosse's sleep at Archimago's Hermitage (I.i.36–ii.6) and Scudamour's sleep at Care's Cottage (IV.v.33–46). The exploration focuses on the distinction between what is external and what is internal to the subject of the "vision," because the heroes' ability to understand their selfhood and the readers' ability to understand allegory's moral claims largely hinges on this distinction. The study relates the inner/outer dynamics within these passages to the workings of the narrative, namely, to the interaction between the main story (first-degree narrative, diegesis) and additional, or parallel stories (second-degree narratives, *metadiegeses*). The author argues that the shifting and collapsing of the boundaries between these narratives correlate with the blurring of the boundaries between the internal and external worlds, precluding both the heroes and the readers from recuperating the meanings of these "visions" satisfactorily.

AS READERS OF *THE FAERIE QUEENE* know, the deficiencies of Redcrosse's moral and spiritual vision, which were only suggested in the opening lines of Book I and in his battle with the monster Errour, become evident during his restless night at Archimago's hermitage. While intermittently falling asleep and waking up, the knight is constantly torn between conflicting emotions and impulses—"wanton blis and wicked ioy" (I.i.47), "great passion of vnwonted lust" and "wonted feare" of doing something "amis" (I.i.49), dismay and half-rage (I.i.50).[1] He has a hard time distinguishing dream from reality, inner from outer, and subjective from objective. Redcrosse, of course, misinterprets the passing events. The employment of two figurative devices, both of which call for an act of interpretation, and hence, for an interpreting subject—the allegorical theater and the dream—strongly suggests that this passage is about the woe that's in interpretation. The distinction between what is internal and what is external to the subject constitutes the major challenge that allegorical dream narratives present to both the protagonists and the readers, since allegory does not differentiate clearly between the representations of consciousness and those of the external world, both "identically materialized and objectified."[2] Yet on this distinction often hinges the heroes' ability to understand their selfhood and the readers' ability to understand allegory's moral claims. As we know, Spenser's poem constantly thwarts the external/internal dichotomy, which *is* why the phrase "frustrating interpretations" has become part of Spenser criticism.

The present essay explores the external and internal dynamics in two "troublous dreame" passages from *The Faerie Queene*: Redcrosse's sleep at Archimago's Hermitage (I.i.36–ii.6) and Scudamour's sleep at Care's Cottage (IV.v.33–46).[3] Although the inner/outer differential equivocates throughout the entire poem, the "troublous dreame" passages more sharply problematize the relations between reality and subjectivity, exteriority and interiority. Here we see the self in a very close relation to allegory, because the allegorical spectacle, presented for the dreamer's contemplation and interpretation, is played out in his consciousness.[4] Viewing the Archimago Hermitage episode and the Care Cottage episode as allegorical dream narratives allows us to probe deeply into the relations between subjectivity, allegory, and narrative in *The Faerie Queene*. This essay looks closely at the ways in which the external/internal dynamic manifests itself through the unfolding narrative. My approach rests on the belief that the dreamer's self is inextricably tied to the production of narrative, because the act of narration constructs and presents the subject to the reader. Specifically, I would like to argue that the confusion between the inner and outer planes in the two dream episodes occurs due to the shifts between the first-degree narratives and second-degree narratives, as I explain below. At the moments when the boundaries between these narrative levels collapse, the heroes and the readers experience interpretive ambiguity. In other words, I locate the source of interpretive ambiguity within the text's narrative strategies.[5]

Only a handful of isolated episodes in *The Faerie Queene* render the characters' dreaming. In some cases, such as Arthur's dream of Gloriana (I.ix.13–15) or Britomart's dream in the Temple of Isis (V.vii.12–16), dreaming becomes a way of obtaining meaning and truth, a source of important personal revelations or prophetic truths—what Macrobius's classic hierarchy of dreams terms *somnium*, *visio*, or *oraculum*. Far more problematic are such "troublous," insomniac, and false dream visions, as Redcrosse's sleep at Archimago's Hermitage or Scudamour's sleep at Care's Cottage, which unfold in dense allegorical settings, present the heroes with a kind of allegorical theater, and deal with their interiority in figurative terms. While the Care Cottage episode occupies only a dozen stanzas and plays a minor role in the overall development of Book IV, the Archimago Hermitage passage, by contrast, gives us one of the most extended and complex allegorical representations of the self in the poem, and the closest analogue of the allegorical theater coming into play in the hero's consciousness. The passage takes central place in Book I, in that it highlights Redcrosse's succumbing to a grand illusion which will determine his actions and the course of the entire book.

Obviously, the relationship between allegory and subjectivity in such a generically eclectic work as *The Faerie Queene* must needs be different from that of traditional dream poetry. Spenser's poem is neither a dream vision, nor a consistent narrative allegory. As a Protestant epic chiefly concerned with the Neoplatonic search for transcendental truths about God and human nature and with an imperialist, nationalist agenda, *The Faerie Queene* lacks the explicitly personal touch of medieval lyric poetry or dream vision narratives (e.g., *Le Roman de la Rose*). The poem's readers have no direct access to the heroes' psyche or consciousness, as they would in traditional first-person allegorical dream visions. Spenser's narrator makes occasional direct, personal comments, but his personality and his ability to portray the characters' inner life adequately are highly questionable. His predictably conventional, formulaic, and didactic responses to the events do not produce accounts of interiority, but rather reflect his largely Everyman, emblem-book view of the world. He functions more as an allegorist, a personification, and a rhetorical construct than a consistent dramatic persona.[6] Nor do the protagonists of *The Faerie Queene* act, strictly speaking, as consistent psychological entities; they are human beings but also emblems of knightly virtues.

However, one can trace a number of dream-vision conventions in the two "troublous dreame" passages: for example, the description of the hero's falling asleep and the start of the dream (I.i.36, 55; IV.v.39); the alternation of the hero's dreaming and waking states;

and the resulting hesitancy concerning the borderline between the two states (at least in the Archimago Hermitage passage; see I.i.47–49, 53; ii.4–6, etc.).[7] But what particularly marks these two passages as complex dream narratives is the text's tremendous interest in the heroes' perception of the events, namely in the subject's ethical preoccupations and states of consciousness, as well as in their attitude towards the allegorical representations and spectacles. The interplay between various narrative perspectives within these dream passages reveals them as products of perception and writing and as texts imbued with subjectivity.[8]

The constant oscillation between the external and internal worlds in these dream passages erodes any certainty about what "reality" is.[9] As the dream narratives involve a series of alternating and mutually equivocating dreaming and waking states, the heroes become progressively incapable of separating dream from waking life, subjective from objective, and falsity from truth. I see these states as moments of interpretive hesitation for both characters and readers: both hesitate between what belongs to the vision and what to the waking state, what to "reality" and what to imagination, what is literal and what is figurative, or what is inner and what outer. Such moments highlight the interpretive dilemmas that lie at the core of the heroes' ability to understand their inner selves. The heroes must separate the two worlds—dreaming from waking; reality from allegory—in order to distinguish Truth from multiple illusions, or they must integrate the two worlds in order to obtain an authentic allegorical vision.

Readers experience similar interpretive uncertainty as the frequent reversals and interweaving of internal and external worlds thwart their expectations of allegorical dream vision conventions. At the basis of readers' ambiguous perception of the allegorically treated events lies a conflict between the "norm," that is the standard conventions that the readers come to expect in a narrative allegory, as well as the standard attitudes that readers adopt with regard to the dream vision genre, on the one hand, and deviation from the norm, that is, the stylistic violation of these conventions which consequently thwarts readers' expectations, on the other. In the latter case, the strictly figurative reading of the episode and the successful recuperation of the allegory's meanings, are momentarily precluded. Thus, the text's writing strategies become a major object of scrutiny for readers.[10]

The continuous interpenetration of the boundaries between external and internal worlds, through which the self is constructed in allegorical dream visions, has its temporal and spatial manifestations in gaps and shifts between the narrative levels. In narratological terms (in the tradition of Gerard Genette), these involve gaps between the first-degree narrative (main story, or *diegesis*), on the one hand, and the second-degree narratives (additional or parallel stories, or *metadiegeses*), on the other.[11] Genette lists at least three main types of relationships between *diegesis* and *metadiegesis*: (1) direct causality, when the second narrative performs an *explanatory* function; (2) a purely *thematic* relationship, involving contrast or analogy, but no spatio-temporal continuity; and (3) no explicit relationship, except that the very act of narrating a metadiegetic story fulfils the function of distraction or obstruction within the diegesis.[12] Such complex narrative relations manifest not only thematic, but also structural types of subjectivity.

The interplay between first-degree and second-degree narratives, as well as between various temporal registers within the narrative (narrated time and narration time),[13] parallels the interplay between external and internal worlds in the two dream passages. The difference between narrated time and narration time often substitutes for the expression of time, which serves as a conventional revealer of subjectivity in medieval first-person narratives.[14] The shifting or collapse of the boundaries between these two narrative levels blurs the boundaries between external and internal worlds. The resulting breaks in narrative coherence preclude both the heroes and the readers from recuperating the meanings of these visions satisfactorily.

The House of Care episode (IV.v.33–46) vividly demonstrates the reciprocity and blurring of the internal and external worlds in Scudamour's psyche, through the blurring of the diegetic and metadiegetic narrative levels. The scene presents a classic example of the allegorical treatment of the psychological state of worry. Scudamour enters Care's cottage agonized by jealousy, kindled in him earlier by the false Duessa and the hellish "mother of Debate," Ate, who had told him that his beloved Amoret loosely and wantonly "sleepes, and sports, and playes" (IV.i.47) with another knight. The fourteen-stanza-long allegorical tableau of Care's ceaseless working at his forge parallels and mirrors Scudamour's suffering from the grip of anxiety ("care") and insomnia. The agonizing mind's restlessness (the "vnquiet thoughts, that carefull minds inuade," IV.v.35) is literalized through a series of conventional iconographic images and details—a rather complex blacksmith machinery, with Care being a walking emblem of a worried man, uncaring about his state and never ceasing in his work (IV.v.34–35); his six assistants symbolizing various degrees of discord;[15] and blacksmith tools (hammers, bellows, coals, anvils, and pincers) enacting the ardent work of the jealous mind.[16]

Yet, despite its seemingly simple emblematic message, the dramatization of the hero's interiority generates considerable interpretive ambiguity. To some extent, this ambiguity originates in the images' possessing both literal and metaphorical meanings, that is, the images' resembling both the blacksmith's forging and the mind's "forging." But interpretive uncertainty also arises from the constant oscillation between two types of action in progress here—the story of Scudamour's lodging, on the one hand, and the dramatized allegorical tableau, Care's forging, unfolding parallel to the main story, on the other. Initially, the events in these two stories exist, as it were, in two separate orders or worlds (real/natural vs. symbolic/allegorical) and two separate registers of narrative time: the allegorical description of Care's dwelling, his portrait, and his work (IV.v.33–37) is followed by the more direct account of Scudamour's restlessness (IV.v.38–45). At some points, however, the main/diegetic story and the parallel/metadiegetic story start competing with each other and then converging. Stanza 40 gives the direct account of Scudamour's ceaseless restlessness:

> And oft in wrath he thence againe vprose;
> And oft in wrath he layd him downe againe.
> But wheresoeuer he did himselfe dispose,
> He by no meanes could wished ease obtaine:
> So euery place seem'd painefull, and ech changing vaine.

The following two stanzas describe the same action allegorically:

> And euermore, when he to sleepe did thinke,
> The hammers sound his senses did molest;
> And euermore, when he began to winke,
> The bellowes noyse disturb'd his quiet rest,
> Ne suffred sleepe to settle in his brest.
> And all the night the dogs did barke and howle
> About the house, at sent of stranger guest:
> And now the crowing Cocke, and now the Owle
> Lowde shriking him afflicted to the very sowle.
>
> And if by fortune any litle nap
> Vpon his heauie eye-lids chaunst to fall,
> Eftsoones one of those villeins him did rap
> Vpon his headpeece with his yron mall;
> That he was soone awaked therewithall,

And lightly started vp as one affrayd;
Or as if one him suddenly did call.
So oftentimes he out of sleepe abrayd,
And then lay musing long, on that him ill apayd.

(IV.v.41–42)

The text continuously oscillates between the mimetic portrayal of Scudamour's insomnia—for example, his long musing and fleshly weakness, until sleep at last "his wearie sprite opprest" and "all his senses did full soone arrest" (IV.v.43)—and the figurative presentation of his state: With that, the wicked carle the maister Smith

A paire of redwhot yron tongs did take
Out of the burning cinders, and therewith
Vnder his side him nipt, that forst to wake,
He felt his hart for very paine to quake.

(IV.v.44)

The allegorical host and his guest never really communicate throughout the entire episode. The two parties exist, as it were, on two separate planes, without interacting dramatically or verbally, the way, for instance, Redcrosse and Despair interact in I.xi. Although Scudamour at first much admires the work of the blacksmiths, and even attempts to inquire of their purpose, "they for nought would from their worke refraine,/ Ne let his speeches come vnto their eare" (IV.v.38). Likewise, when Scudamour is leaving Care's cottage the next morning, the host is nowhere to be seen (IV.v.45). The text never resolves the interplay between the two orders—narratively, between the *diegesis* and *metadiegesis*—in a definitive way, which becomes a source of ambiguity for both the hero and the readers. Scudamour is very confused by this strange spectacle. Naturally, he considers the external events in the cottage to be the cause of his insomnia: when he feels the red hot iron tongs in his side or the hammers on his headpiece, he attributes them to the provocations of Care and his servants. He even starts up "auenged for to be/ On him, the which his quiet slomber brake," but "round about him none could see" (IV.v.44), and the dark atmosphere of the night does not ease his doubts.

The readers also share in the hero's ambiguous perception of the events, as the blurring of the cause-effect relations makes it unclear to what extent Scudamour's misery comes from inside, and to what extent, from outside. It seemed quite plausible that the noises in the smithy ("The hammers sound his senses did molest"; "The bellowes noyse disturb'd his quiet rest," IV.v.41), the outside noises (dog's barking, cock's crowing, and owl's shrieking), or the hideous poking by Care and his "villeins" cause his insomnia. But then it looks as if Scudamour cannot sleep because of his wrath (IV.v.40) and jealousy (IV.v.43) concerning Amoret. Even when emblem-book-savvy readers figure out that Care is a projection of Scudamour's mind, a lot remains unclear. For instance, we find the relation between the end of stanza 43 and the beginning of stanza 44 quite confusing as we move from "His ydle braine gan busily molest,/ And made him dreame those two disloyall were" at the end of 43, to "With that, the wicked carle the maister Smith/ A paire of redwhot yron tongs did take/ Out of the burning cinders, and therewith/ Under his side him nipt" at the start of 44. Does Care's poking the hero with red-hot tongs represent an internal or an external event in relation to Scudamour's dream of Amoret's infidelity? Is Scudamour dreaming of both Amoret and Care? Does his dream of Amoret represent his consciousness, while Care's actions represent his psychological state? Does his dream of Amoret represent his worry mimetically, while Care's actions render other modalities of his psychology allegorically?

While on the surface of the narrative, Care's actions appear to be external to Scudamour's dreaming, at this moment, inner and outer, and subjectivity and allegory become totally indistinguishable. Readers' interpretive uncertainty is further provoked by the ambiguous "smart" remaining in Scudamour's side (IV.v.44): is it a physical wound or an internal pain, or both? And what do the lines, "Yet looking round about him none could see;/ Yet did the smart remaine, though he himselfe did flee," actually mean? Is the first line literal and diegetic, and the following line metaphorical and metadiegetic? Does Scudamour "flee" literally or metaphorically, that is, does he move to another corner of the cottage, or does he wake up from his nightmare? Should we view the cottage as an external space or an internal space? Which events are we to take literally and which metaphorically? Why does this rather conventional emblematic spectacle problematize its own representation in such a complex way? With readers' constant hesitation between literal and metaphorical meanings of these events, the allegorical interpretation of this passage becomes indefinitely suspended. Having grappled with such questions, readers start questioning not only the nature of the events narrated, but also the nature of the text which narrates them.

In the Archimago Hermitage episode (I.i.36–ii.6), Redcrosse's sleep and insomnia also equivocate between two different worlds (real and symbolic) and two narrative levels (diegetic and metadiegetic). The passage shows how fine the boundary is between Truth and Falsehood, and how easily it can be transgressed, if one does not possess clear moral or spiritual eyesight. Doubleness here serves as both a controlling metaphor for the duplicity of meaning and a textual, narrative strategy designed to show how duplicity is taking a firm hold of Redcrosse's psyche.[17] The duplication of persons and events, as well as the lexical, syntactic, and structural doubling and redoubling reflect the deficiency of Redcrosse's inner perception. Yet divisions between the doubles are never clear-cut, but blurred. Redcrosse becomes increasingly unable to distinguish dream from reality, subjective from objective, and internal from external. The knight's interpretive hesitation manifests itself mostly through his inability to recognize appearances and false figurations, whether created by Archimago or by his own imagination.

The inner/outer and subjective/objective dichotomies are directly tied to the workings of the narrative. We see Redcrosse as not only the central human subject, but also the focus of tremendous figurative and narrative activity in this episode. His self is constantly put in relation to other "actants" of the narrative, to use Greimas's term (even if these are the projections of his mind) and to various narrative dynamics within this passage. The complex relations between Redcrosse and other "selves" are reflected in the entanglement of the diegetic and metadiegetic stories. Rhetorical and figurative digressions, such as the description of Morpheus's dwelling (I.i.39–44) or Venus's wedding pageant (I.i.48), which serve as the second degree narratives, are so smoothly knit into the main story that it is not clear where they originate—in Archimago's witchcraft or in Redcrosse's fantasy. The blending of the figurative and literal elements of narration—for example, in stanzas 47–49, where Redcrosse's state is rendered in part literally (I.i.47.4–6 and I.i.49) and in part metaphorically (the rhetorical figures of "that false winged boy" and "Dame" Venus in I.i.47; the personifications of Venus and her train in I.i.48)—erodes the distinctions between appearance and reality, perception and sight, or lie and truth.

The elaborate and extensive poetic description of the god of Sleep, Morpheus, and his dwelling (I.i.39–44), against which Redcrosse's sleep unfolds, presents an inner space, a moralized landscape of self-forgetting and self-oblivion that simultaneously reflects the sleeping mind in general and the knight's state of mind at the moment of his falling asleep. This metadiegetic digression establishes a metaphoric connection between the hero's sleep and Sleep as a generally dangerous condition for a Christian soul, a state in which judgment and reason are suspended.[18] The diegetic and metadiegetic stories—and through them, the self and allegory, the inner and outer—overlap through the abundant verbal echoes and parallels between Morpheus and Redcrosse: for example, the similar water images that lull them into "swowne" (I.i.36, 41); the drowning-like nature of their sleep (I.i.40–42, 44; I.i.36, 53); their troubled minds (I.i.42; I.i.55; ii.4); and their rude awakening (I.i.42–43; ii.4).[19]

The entanglement of the diegetic story and the metadiegetic story obscures important claims that the allegory is trying to make about Redcrosse's self in this passage. Allegorically, the dreaming Knight looks like a victim of Archimago's evil spells and Morpheus' power: at Archimago's request, Morpheus's conjures up a "fit false dreame . . . out of his prison darke" (I.i.43–44), while Archimago, through his "hidden artes," creates a semblance of Una out of the spright supplied by Morpheus. Redcrosse's fantasy, originally "void of euill thoughts," is then abused with these "false showes" (I.i.46), and he is made to dream "of loues and lustful play" (I.i.47).

Yet the reciprocity between the diegesis and metadiegesis subverts this clearcut cause-and-consequence relation. Morpheus's sleep precedes Redcrosse's sleep in terms of the narration time, but in terms of the narrated time, it parallels the Knight's sleep, unfolding *while* Redcrosse is sleeping "soundly void of euill thought" (I.i.46) and *within* Redcrosse's dream. The relation between the two sleeps, then, involves both causality and simultaneity. The Morpheus story performs multiple functions in this episode: a cause of Redcrosse's troublesome dream; an allegorical analysis of Redcrosse's sleeping state; and an allegorical tableau of Sleep. The Morpheus description is thus simultaneously diegetic and metadiegetic,[20] and it serves as both the cause and consequence of the Knight's sleep, and a general emblematic tableau of Sleep, which can stand on its own outside the main story. In other words, Morpheus represents both the inside and outside causes of the hero's troublesome vision (that is the internal and external registers of his subjectivity), and the general workings of the sleepy mind devoid of particular individuality. Such multiple functions of the Morpheus description within the narrative create a rather complex interweaving of interiority and exteriority, subjectivity and allegory in this passage.

The interplay of heterogeneous narrative processes prevents the audience from reading every event in this passage as internal. Spenser's allegory artfully interweaves both internal and external allegories, and such blending puts the subjects in relation to the world, rather than confining them within their solipsistic minds. Critics have treated Morpheus as solely a projection of Redcrosse's mind.[21] But if events in Archimago's House project Redcrosse's mental state, then we have to interpret everything in it metaphorically, which means that we must discard the main story line as irrelevant, and consider all the pitfalls of falsity the text so carefully attempts to portray as insignificant, in view of the later events of the book. Do all the events in this episode (or in Book I, in general) carry only inner significance, or can they stand for nonpsychic reality?

As a literalization of a sleeping state, Morpheus does duplicate Redcrosse's state to some extent, but he is not only in Redcrosse's mind.[22] He "exists" in Redcrosse's mind only spatially—as a rhetorical expansion on the main story and a parallel narrative retelling the story of the Knight's sleep in a different way. But as an independent second-degree narrative, the Morpheus passage develops the image of the mind imprisoned by sleep. The depiction of Morpheus's dwelling as "prison darke," out of which he creates a "diuerse dreame" for Redcrosse, as located somewhere very low and down, "Amid the bowels of the earth full steepe,/ And low, where dawning day doth neuer peepe" (I.i.39), suggests the imprisonment of Redcrosse's mind.[23] In addition, the Morpheus description literalizes the physical effects of sleep on the mind—the reader's as much as Redcrosse's: ironically, the god of sleep, powerful enough to induce sleep in others, becomes himself an emblem of a sleeping state. Morpheus is thus both a figure for Sleep and a literalization of sleep. The presentation of Morpheus as both a personification of dreams and, figuratively, a dreaming man exemplifies the collapse of the inner and outer planes onto one another within one narrative level (i.e., the second-degree narrative).[24]

After the Morpheus description, the main story (that is, Redcrosse's sleep) turns into a dream vision narrative, with a characteristic fusion of the inner and outer allegories, except that the device of the allegorical dream is reversed here in its function as a revelation of truth. The irony is that Redcrosse perceives his sleep as a prophetic vision. To readers, however, the appearance of the mythological figures traditionally associated with self-oblivion (Morpheus) or erotic love/lust (the bawdy Venus and her train mocking a wedding procession) in this passage calls into question the veracity of the knight's vision. Redcrosse's nocturnal experience emerges not as a prophetic vision (*somnium/visio*, in Macrobius's terms), which indirectly makes the meaning apparent to the hero, but rather as a disturbing, unprophetic nightmare or apparition (*insomnium/visum*), which designates the disturbing, agitated, or erotic dreams caused by mental or physical distress (*insomnium*) or the indistinct images appearing in the intermediate state between waking and slumber (*visum*).[25] Unlike *somnium* or *visio*, *insomnium* and *visum* carry no important meaning and allow no interpretation.[26] The falsity of Redcrosse's vision shows through the consistent use of the "false" imagery in this passage: for example, the "fit false dreame" conjured up by Archimago "to trouble sleepy mindes" (I.i.36) and the "false shewes" (I.i.46) abusing Redcrosse's fantasy; the "falsest two" sprites "fittest for to forge true-seeming lies" (I.i.38), the false Una created out of "liquid ayre" (I.i.45), and a Squire created out of "subtile aire" (I.ii.3), that is, out of nothing; Redcrosse's "troublous dreame" that "gan freshly tosse his braine" (I.i.55) after the false Una's visitation. Later, when Redcrosse almost manages to get "more sound repast" after the "troublous sights/ And dreames," he is awakened by Archimago to yet another disturbing vision (I.ii.4).

The continuing sequence of false dreams does not reveal Truth to Redcrosse, but rather "saddles him with a fiction."[27] Redcrosse's dream embraces the meanings of *phantasia* as imagination, in the sense of false visions and hallucinations, on the one hand, and as a bad, unreliable dream (Lat. *visum*, Gr. *phantasma*), in Macrobius's system, on the other. *Phantasia* designates what is visible or made visible.[28] Redcrosse is thus the maker of his own fictions, the "victim of self-generated illusions,"[29] because he equates truth with what he sees. Figuration here points to Redcrosse's own imagination as the source of his illusion. This becomes particularly evident in the scene where the goddess Venus herself enters Redcrosse's dream, accompanying Una to his bed:

> Then seemed him his Lady by him lay,
> And to him playnd, how that false winged boy
> Her chast hart had subdewd, to learne Dame pleasures toy.
>
> And she her selfe of beautie soueraigne Queene,
> Faire *Venus* seemde vnto his bed to bring
> Her, whom he waking euermore did weene
> To be the chastest flowre, that ay did spring
> On earthly braunch, the daughter of a king,
> Now a loose Leman to vile seruice bound:
> And eke the *Graces* seemed all to sing,
> *Hymen* to *Hymen*, dauncing all around,
> Whilst freshest *Flora* her with Yuie girlond crownd.

(I.i.47–48)

Although Archimago's sprite makes Redcrosse dream "of loues and lustful play" (I.i.47), the figures of "that false winged boy" Cupid and of Dame Venus in his dream are not exactly conjured up by Archimago, the way Morpheus, the two sprites, and other mythological figures are brought into this story (cf. I.i.37–39; 43). These conventional emblems of erotic love literalize Redcrosse's own sexual fantasies concerning Una. The mention of Venus, clearly a *Venus vulgaris*, in this context and later, in the scene where the false Una and false squire "knit themselves in *Venus* shameful chaine" (I.ii.4–5), indirectly manifests what the allegory does not say directly, and it characterizes Redcrosse's inner state more than it does Archimago's witchcraft. *Venus vulgaris* projects Redcrosse's own erotic *phantasia* which is hypocritically concealed here and presented as an outer phenomenon, as the allegorical Other.[30]

Redcrosse is totally unable to distinguish between appearance and essence, outer and inner at this stage. He abhors the lasciviousness of the "Una" he had considered to be "the chastest flowre" and treats the apparition as an enemy, as "some secret ill, or hidden foe of his" (I.i.49). He perceives the false Una—a mere imitation of the real Una's outfit by Archimago (I.i.45)—as the real Una, even though he cannot see the apparition's face behind the black "vele." He equates the false Una's outer looks, i.e., the veil and black stole (I.i.4), with the real Una's inner substance—Truth.

Redcrosse's inner confusion at this point shows through the intense narrative, syntactic, and verbal psychomachy. The syntax and pronoun reference totally blur in stanzas 49 and 50. In stanza 50, "secret" and "hidden" point inward, while "foe of his" points outward. "Seeming to mistrust" suggests that Redcrosse attempts to mistrust the outward appearance, but in fact he does trust it. He attempts to "proue his sense" (I.i.50), yet he trusts not common sense, but rather his senses—what he sees on the outside, the appearances, the visibilia. "Seeming to mistrust/ Some secret ill, or hidden foe of his" implies his hesitation about the source of this vision. His inner struggle expresses itself in the interplay of the inner/outer forces in a series of unresolved equivocations:

All cleane dismayd to see so vncouth sight,
    And halfe enraged at her shamelesse guise,
    He thought haue slaine her in his fierce despight :
    But hasty heat tempring with sufferance wise,

He stayde his hand, and gan himselfe aduise
To proue his sense, and tempt her faigned truth.
(I.i.50)

He means to test Una (to "tempt her faigned truth," I.i.50), yet is himself being tempted with "her faigned truth." His doubting makes him as duplicitous a figure as the false Una (Duessa): when she offers him a kiss "halfe blushing" (I.i.49), he is "halfe enraged at her shamelesse guise" (I.i.50). If the false Una's "halfe blushing" suggests her pretense, what does Redcrosse's being "halfe enraged" imply? Does it mean that he and the Truth (the real Una) have already begun to split in "halfe"?

The pronoun reference to Redcrosse and Archimago and the syntactic distinctions become totally indistinguishable in I.i.55. Is Redcrosse's fear created out of nothing, just like Archimago's apparitions? We cannot distinguish syntactically Redcrosse's troubled spiritual state, his "irksome spright" (I.i.55), from Archimago's "misformed spright."[31] The knight's setting the vision apart from himself, his anger at Una, and his readiness to fight ("He thought haue slaine her in his fierce despight," I.i.50) signal his inability to see the true origin of this false vision and to act upon it correctly. While allegory shows the dreaming mind as beset by the devil, and the contrast between wakefulness and dreaming as that between Truth and Falsehood, the blurring of literal/metaphorical and inner/outer oppositions calls such divisions into question. The collapse of the inner/outer distinction in Redcrosse's mind shows through the blurring of the boundary between the mimetic presentation of the knight's dreaming and waking states (the first-degree narrative) and the figurative presentations of his state (the second-degree narratives), which quickly succeed one another. For instance, Redcrosse's dream of Venus and her train (I.i.47–48) is immediately followed by the false Una's appearance at his bed (I.i.49–54), after which he is "yrockt" to sleep again (I.i.55) only to wake up to the "lewd embracement" of "Una" and the squire (I.ii.4–5). The quick alternation of the knight's dreaming and waking states, as well as the quick alternation of the competing narrative lines create the psychological and narrative discontinuity in this passage, thereby rendering the effect of the discontinuous, decentered, and lost self.

At this point, Redcrosse loses any touch with reality, and his mind is entirely in the grip of illusion. As Judith Anderson puts it, Redcrosse now "wakens" to an inner world and inner landscape: the external and internal landscapes have blurred into one; everything now reflects and embodies the Knight's own passions.[32] This becomes evident in the blurring of the narrator's and Redcrosse's vision, when the readers see the false Una and squire's copulation (I.ii.4) through Redcrosse's eyes:

All in amaze he suddenly vp start
With sword in hand, and with the old man went;
Who soone him brought into a secret part,
Where that false couple were full closely ment
In wanton lust and lewd embracement:
Which when he saw, he burnt with gealous fire,
The eye of reason was with rage yblent,
And would haue slaine them in his furious ire,
But hardly was restreined of that aged sire.

(I.ii.5)

The "secret part" points to a number of "chambers"—the anatomical chamber (genitalia); the secluded chamber where the coupling is taking place; and the "chamber" of Redcrosse's mind—all of which become indistinguishable. The language of these stanzas betrays Redcrosse's inner confusion, as the references to his heart, "guiltie sight," and "inward gall" suggest in I.ii.6. When Redcrosse flees from the sight of Una's infidelity, he flees from himself, "from his thoughts and gealous feare" (I.ii.12).[33] He is now "diuorced" (I.iii.2) from Una (Truth) and enters the path of Falsehood which leads to his despair and near self-destruction practically until the end of Book I—until his healing in the House of Holiness (I.x) and the final battle with the dragon (I.xi).

This discussion of the two "troublous dreame" passages shows how closely the subjective/objective and inner/outer registers of allegory are tied to the workings of the narrative. The nonlinear, entangled narrative structure in the dream episodes reflects the complex nature of the self and the complex structure of relations between subjects, and it allows for a degree of uncertainty in representing human interiority. Readers are once again reminded of the instability of allegorical representation, as their experience of the text is brought into direct relation with the unfolding of events and the meaning of the narrative.

NOTES

1. All quotations from *The Faerie Queene* in this essay are taken from the 1977 Longman edition by A. C. Hamilton.

2. Michel Zink, *The Invention of Literary Subjectivity* (Baltimore: Johns Hopkins University Press, 1999), 146.

3. The encounter between the subject and the narrative, and the link between subjectivity and narrativity, was one of the major developments in medieval dream visions and allegorical narratives. The first-person dream narratives always represented the subject in relation to the act of narration. On the idea that the subject was first fully displayed in medieval narrative literature see Evelyn Vitz, *Medieval Narrative and Modern Narratology: Subjects and Objects of Desire* (New York: New York University Press, 1989) and Zink, *The Invention of Literary Subjectivity*. Cf. also Bakhtin's idea that a reflective attitude toward language came out of romance, which is another kind of narrative.

4. The intimate connection between the self and allegory was first established in medieval allegorical dream visions. Macrobius, in his *Commentary on the Dream of Scipio* (trans. William Harris Stahl; N.Y.: Columbia University Press, 1990), also related these two concepts by stressing the dreamer's participation in his/her dreams and his/her interpretation of them. By exteriorizing the dreamer's inner concerns through the figures and images of another world, the dream vision revealed the dreamer's self. Through contemplating a dream vision or acting in it as a fictional hero, the dreamer (the hero, the narrator, or the poet) received consolation for his real life predicament or achieved some sort of self-understanding upon waking up. See Zink's book, *The Invention of Literary Subjectivity*, 130 ff., and his article (coauthored with Margaret Miner and Kevin Brownlee), "Allegorical Poem as Interior Memoir," in *Images of Power: Medieval History/ Discourse/ Literature* (*Yale French Studies* 70 [1986]): 100–26, here at 107, 110.

5. My approach thus rests on the assumption that interpretive ambiguity is represented within the text itself, as well as on the widely accepted premise that the poem's modes of writing are mixed. For discussion of the heterogeneous narrative and rhetorical strategies, styles, and modes of writing in Spenser's poem, see, for instance, Paul Alpers, "Narration in *The Faerie Queene*," *English Literary History* 44 (1977): 19–39 and "Narrative and Rhetoric in *The Faerie Queene*," *Studies in English Literature* 2 (1962): 27–46; Harry Berger, "The Discarding of Malbecco: Conspicuous Allusion and Cultural Exhaustion in *The Faerie Queene* III.ix–x," in *Revisionary Play: Studies in the Spenserian Dynamics* (Berkeley: University of California Press, 1988), 154–71 and "Narrative as Rhetoric in *The Faerie Queene*," *English Literary Renaissance* 21 (1991): 3–48; John Webster, " 'The Methode of a Poete': An Inquiry Into Tudor Conceptions of Poetic Sequence," *English Literary Renaissance* 11 (1981): 22–43 and "Oral Form and Written Craft in Spenser's *Faerie Queene*," *Studies in English Literature* 16 (1976): 75–93; and Susanne Wofford, *The Choice of Achilles: The Ideology of Figure in the Epic* (Stanford: Stanford University Press, 1992).

6. On this interpretation of Spenser's narrator in *The Faerie Queene*, see John Bender, "Narrative," in *The Spenser Encyclopedia* (Toronto: University of Toronto Press, 1990), 497–98; Harry Berger, "Kidnapped Romance," in *Unfolded Tales:*

Essays on Renaissance Romance, ed. George M. Logan and Gordon Teskey (Ithaca: Cornell University Press, 1989), 208–56, 250; and Susanne Wofford, *The Choice of Achilles*.

7. For discussion of typical elements and motifs of medieval dream-poetry, see Francis X. Newman, "Somnium: Medieval Theories of Dreaming and the Form of Vision Poetry" (Ph.D. diss. Princeton, 1963) and A.C. Spearing, *Medieval Dream Poetry* (Cambridge: Cambridge University Press, 1976). For an additional bibliography, see J. Stephen Russell, *The English Dream Vision: Anatomy of a Form* (Columbus: Ohio State University Press, 1988).

8. On various meanings of literary subjectivity, see Zink, *The Invention of Literary Subjectivity*. Cf. also Benveniste's argument, in *Problems in General Linguistics*, trans. Mary Elizabeth Meek, Coral Gables, FL: University of Miami Press, 1971), that subjectivity in language is constituted by the relations between linguistic statements rather than by the statements themselves (223–30). Such "relations" include the interplay between the text's narrative perspectives and levels.

9. Besides the narrator's general exclamations, the knights admire Port Esquiline (II.ix.33.1–4), the middle sage's goodly reason (II.ix.54.6–9), and Eumnestes's endless exercise (II.ix.59.1–2).

10. Here, I am drawing an analogy with Tzvetan Todorov's definition of the *fantastique* as a moment when both the characters and the readers hesitate between the natural and supernatural explanations of the fantastic events. In *The Fantastic: A Structural Approach to a Literary Genre*, trans. Richard Howard; Cleveland: The Press of Case Western Reserve University, 1973), Todorov closely studies a number of stories and novels in which the events begin to exist in two orders simultaneously—natural and supernatural—precluding both the heroes and the readers from certainty. Todorov analyzes the *fantastique* as a phenomenon situated on the borderline between the more definitive genres, but not a genre of its own, and involving specific linguistic and structural characteristics.

11. Cf. Genette's typology of narrative layers: *extradiegesis* (the narration of the events); *diegesis* (the events); *metadiegesis* (second-degree narratives, or stories told by the characters of the diegetic layer); *meta-metadiegesis* (additional stories within the metadiegetic layer). See his *Figures III* (Paris: Éditions du Seuil, 1972); *Narrative Discourse: An Essay in Method*, trans. Jane E. Lewin (Ithaca: Cornell University Press, 1980); and *Narrative Discourse Revisited*, trans. Jane E. Lewin (Ithaca: Cornell University Press, 1988). Although Genette's *metadiegesis* also includes embedded stories, for the purpose of my analysis, I apply this term to narratives that parallel, add, or do both to the main story line. Here I view the main story, or first-degree narrative, as an account of events advancing the hero's progress towards his destination. Additional, or second-degree, narratives are usually action-filled rhetorical and figurative amplifications on the events depicted in the main narrative; they differ from extended epic similes in that they more actively interact with the events of the main story.

12. Genette, *Narrative Discourse*, 232–33.

13. These are standard narratological terms. On the distinction between *erzählte Zeit* (narrated time) and *Erzählzeit* (narrative time, or narration time, or time of narration), see Gunther Müller, "Erzählzeit und erzahlte Zeit," in *Morphologische Poetik* (Tübingen: M. Niemeyer, 1968). For the significance of the relations between

narrated time and narration time for literary analysis, see Genette, *Narrative Discourse*, 35.

14. Zink, *Invention*, 120ff. On narrative markers of the dreamer's desire and interiority in *Roman de la Rose*, see Vitz, *Medieval Narrative and Modern Narratology*, chapters 2 and 3.

15. Steadman, "Care," in *The Spenser Encyclopedia*, ed. A.C. Hamilton et al. (Toronto: University of Toronto Press, 1990), 135–36.

16. See Steadman, "Spenser's House of Care: A Reinterpretation," in *Studies in the Renaissance* 7 (1960): 207–224.

17. As Gareth Roberts put it, in *"The Faerie Queene"* (Philadelphia: Open University Press, 1992), "there appear to be two of everything" in this episode (36). For the discussion of the images of doubleness in this passage, see Roberts, 35–37; and Stephen Barney, *Allegories of History, Allegories of Love* (Hamden: Archon Books, 1979), 118.

18. On sleep as a type of spiritual death for a Christian soul, see Douglas Brooks-Davis, *Spenser's "Faerie Queene": A Critical Commentary on Books I and II* (Manchester University Press, 1977), 24.

19. On the similarities between Morpheus and Redcrosse, see Judith Anderson, "Redcrosse and the Descent into Hell," *English Literary History* 36 (1969): 470–92, here at 473–75; Barney, 117; and Donald Cheney, *Spenser's Image of Nature: Wild Man and Shepherd in "The Faerie Queene"* (New Haven: Yale University Press, 1966), 29.

20. In terms of Genette's three types of relationships between *diegesis* and *metadiegesis* (see pp. 256–57 above), the relations between the Morpheus passage and the description of Redcrosse's sleep involve both a causal and a thematic spatio-temporal continuity. However, we can also view this story as the third-type relationship in the sense that the very act of describing both literalizes the distraction of Redcrosse's sleepy mind and itself performs the function of a rhetorical distraction for the reader.

21. For the argument that Morpheus represents an aspect of Redcrosse's nature, and that "in a figurative and spiritual sense" he is dreaming progressively from the time he abandons Una and accepts Duessa, see Anderson, 473; 482. See also James Nohrnberg, *The Analogy of "The Faerie Queene"* (Princeton: Princeton University Press, 1976), 122, for a similar interpretation. For the opposite position, see Isabel MacCaffrey, *Spenser's Allegory: The Anatomy of Imagination* (Princeton: Princeton University Press, 1976), who argues that Redcrosse's disturbed sleep "is a metaphorical statement of the fact that he is, at that point in the narrative, a 'sleepy mind' " (179). I drew my reading of the connection beween Morpheus and Redcrosse from McCaffrey's position (see 179 ff.).

22. See MacCaffrey, 185.

23. Cf. Lars-Håkan Svensson's observation that the image of Sleep as a form of mental imprisonment occurs later in Book I, in the pun on Morpheus's "arresting" the courtly company with his leaden mace (iv.44). See "Morpheus," in *The Spenser Encyclopedia*, 480.

24. As Roberts writes, this moment "is an instance where the fiction of the poem's narrative and its figurative language begin to collapse into each other," and thus the distinction that enables this metaphor to operate disappears (36–37). Cf. also Cheney's remark that Morpheus's "walled towne" (I.i.41) implies that "the disturbance

is as likely to be within the walls as without, and hence . . . there is no clear boundary between dreamer and dream" (31).

25. Macrobius, *Commentary*, 88–89. Among examples of *insomnium*, Macrobius mentions "the lover who dreams of possessing his sweetheart or of losing her, or the man who fears the plots or might of an enemy and is confronted with him in his dream or seems to be fleeing him" (88). *Insomnium* and *visum* often cause people to flee when they awake (89).

26. Macrobius, *Commentary*, 89–90. See also Zink, "Allegorical Poem," 106–07.

27. Nohrnberg, 132.

28. Cf. the synonyms "phantasy," "fancy," "feigning," and "image." For a recent discussion of the meanings of *phantasia* as false visions and as weakened sensations in Plato's *Republic* and Aristotle's *De anima*, see Theresa M. Kelley, *Reinventing Allegory* (Cambridge: Cambridge University Press, 1997). For the classical sources on this topic, see Murray W. Bundy, *The Theory of Imagination in Classical and Medieval Thought* (Urbana: University of Illinois Press, 1927) and Isabel MacCaffrey, *Spenser's Allegory*, 14–23.

29. MacCaffrey, 180.

30. I am drawing here on the ideas of my mentor, Michael McCanles, concerning the hypocrisy of the allegory in Books I and II of *The Faerie Queene*, which he expressed in his courses and our conversations, as well as in his unpublished manuscript, "Toward a Deconstructive Reading of *The Faerie Queene*." McCanles claims that metaphors in *The Faerie Queene* serve as both the modes of vision and of delusion, which often makes the recuperation of the text's meaning impossible. The problem is that Spenser's metaphors are almost always literalized, or rather "unmetaphorized," which happens when a metaphor becomes so clichéd that it loses its metaphoricity and is perceived literally. (On the theory of "unmetaphorizing," see Rosalie L. Colie, *"My Ecchoing Song": Andrew Marvell's Poetry of Criticism*. Princeton: Princeton University Press, 1970.) McCanles sees a twofold literalization of metaphor in *The Faerie Queene*: (1) every sign within an allegory requires translation into a "literal" text; and (2) every sign within an allegory is already the literalizing of what is "metaphorical" outside it. The perception of second literalization calls into question the first. In this process, the origins of the projections in the hero's psyche become concealed behind the illusion of their literalness. In projecting "onto others the secret sins of the self," allegory emerges as an essentially hypocritical mode. Hypocrisy, maintains McCanles, is the central problem of interpretation in Books I and II.

31. See A.C. Hamilton's comment on line 5 in I.i.55 in his edition of *The Faerie Queene*, 43.

32. Anderson, 475.

33. Anderson, 475.

Part III
Spenser Opening to the Future

A. C. HAMILTON

Reminiscences of the Study of Spenser in Cambridge in the Late 1940s

Editor and critic A. C. Hamilton recalls his study of Spenser at Jesus College, Cambridge in the late 1940s and early 1950s, a post-World War II England that now seems more remote than only half a century ago, more like fairyland than the ordinary world. It is also remote from contemporary English sudies and literary criticism, and particularly from the contemporary understanding of Spenser's *Faerie Queene*.

WHEN ROLAND GREENE TOLD ME THAT HE WANTED to open this conference [in Cambridge, July 2001—eds.] by having some relics of the antique age reminisce about what things were like "away back then," I agreed to participate. If ever I am going to reminisce about Spenser, what better time than now when I am almost 80, what better place than Cambridge, where I began writing a doctoral dissertation on Spenser's *Faerie Queene* over fifty years ago, and before what better audience than Spenser critics so many of whom I have come to know through editing *The Spenser Encyclopedia* and *The Faerie Queene*? The opportunity to speak here brings the wheel full circle. To this end, I shall vacate the first room in the stately turret of Alma's castle, that of Phantastes where most critics spend most of their time, for the third room, that of Eumnestes. Here I must depend entirely on Anamnestes for what I remember of those early years.

I recall that time and place as a golden age even though I know it was, in fact, far otherwise. In England in the aftermath of the war, mere living remained difficult. Food was severely rationed: there was very little fruit, and nothing as exotic as a banana or an orange; and the best that the University Library could offer for lunch was beans on toast. Gas for heating was so restricted that one's rooms could be heated for only one or two hours a day, and we gathered in the Library chiefly to get warm. Post-war housing was inadequate. For a while my wife and I lived in Oyster House on Garlic Row in Stourbridge Common, which was as primitive as it sounds: after several centuries, the ground dirt floor was still strewn with oyster shells. Out of nostalgia, I returned there several years ago only to find in its place a modern housing development. I am sure I would prefer living in Oyster House even with the bats.

Since my fellowship was inadequate, I became a supervisor in English for a number of colleges, some ten to fifteen hours a week. I needed the fees, I must admit, in order to build a library. The bombing of London had led to a flood of second-hand books, which David's marketed in his stall every Saturday morning at 8.30. It was not a time to be missed; books were grabbed as soon they were placed on the table. I am sorry that Anamnestes has reminded me that one Saturday morning after I had taken my wife by ambulance to the Mill Road Maternity Hospital and she had just given birth to our first son, instead of remaining with her, I dashed to David's stall and picked up a considerable number of Jacobean dramatists in the "Library of Old Authors" series. Guilt still bothers me whenever I pick up one of those volumes. One memorable Saturday morning, Mr. David brought out from one of his tea-cases a volume in wretched shape that I knew instinctively was sixteenth-century; I grabbed it before he could put it down. It cost all of two shillings sixpence. It proved to be Conrad Gesner's *Bibliotheca universalis*, a catalogue of Latin, Greek, and Hebrew writers that was edited, I believe, in 1574–the title page was missing. When I brought it home, I discovered that it had been annotated very extensively, and signed at the end by John Dee, with the date that I can't recall but it may have been 1574. Presumably it was a volume in his library at Mortlake when Elizabeth came to visit it in 1575, and disappeared when his library was ransacked in 1583. It remained on my shelves for many years until Julian Roberts edited two volumes of Dee's annotated books. I wrote to him, telling him of my volume, and it proved to be the most extensively annotated of all Dee's books. I sold it to the Bodleian and with the money built a cabin, named the John Dee Cabin, on our lake property north of Kingston.

To help build our library, my wife worked at *The News of the World*. Since that newspaper was then, and perhaps still is, a notorious sexual scandal paper, I should add that the editor had established a John Hilton Bureau in Cambridge. Readers were invited to send their requests for information about the newly-established National Health program, Pensions, or whatever, and Mary with others directed their questions—there were many hundreds every day—to a group of experts: lawyers, doctors, dentists, civil servants. Curiosity got me involved, and I replied to one question: "Dear Mr. Hilton, how does one pickle a human heart?" by asking in effect, "Just why do you want to know?", but I never got an answer.

In retrospect, however—in myth, then, but all the more powerful for that—I look back on those years as a golden age. "Golden" if only because the end of the war heralded a "brave new world" for those who survived, a time when I had been discharged from the navy, when I was still young, when the world seemed young and I was newly and happily married to a woman who proved to me over fifty years now that no greater joy can come to a man than the love of a good woman. Like Wordsworth in 1804, "Bliss was it in that dawn to be alive,/But to be young was very heaven." It really was, and the older I get the more I realize that youth has everything, age has only reminiscences such as I am offering now.

I am not concerned now with larger issues at the university at that time except to mention one in passing, the proposal by the Senate to admit women to degrees. As a Canadian who had experienced only co-education, I was shocked by the protests, especially by students. For many, it seemed to be the beginning of the end of Cambridge as a male preserve, as proved true when, years later, women were admitted to the male colleges. Of course, of course, of course, we all agree, especially in Canada and the United States, that women should not be excluded. Years later I happened to be a Fellow at St John's College when women were to be admitted for the first time, and I felt sorry for some of the resident bachelors who were deeply disturbed. Throughout all their years in school and at college, they had never encountered women except as servants, and now they must. To their credit, most submitted graciously.

For the present occasion, I note it as a time, at least in Cambridge, before graduate studies had become bureaucratized, and before Spenser studies had become industrialized. At that time as a D.Phil. candidate, I was required only to complete a publishable thesis after three or four years. No courses were required, and therefore no examinations. An oral defence of the thesis was required but need not be formal. For some reason my external examiner, Rosemary Freeman, did not come up. I was sorry not to have met her, for she remains in my mind not only because of her valuable book on the emblem and another on *The Faerie Queene* but because with the intolerance of youth I had been very indignant about something she had written. I complained about her to my supervisor, E. M. W. Tillyard, and he told me that she was very ill at the time. That taught me that scholars and critics are human beings, and finally led me to endorse Wilde's remark to the effect that all criticism is autobiographical. My internal examiner was Enid Welsford, who came to our flat because I was busy preparing to leave for my first academic appointment at the University of Washington. She became so enchanted with our two-week-old son that she spent most of the time holding him. From our brief encounter, I recall her as a diminutive woman, not in any way formidable in appearance but formidable in her keen mind, as she had revealed in her excellent book on the English masque and would later reveal in her more important book on the fool.

Research students were not discouraged from attending an occasional lecture if it seemed of interest, but at that time no lecturer was interested in sixteenth-century literature except Tillyard, and he was interested only in Spenser's *Faerie Queene* as an English epic. Nor was there much interest in Spenser elsewhere in England, except for C. S. Lewis at Oxford and Janet Spens at London. That excellent critic W. L. Renwick was much earlier, and he was a Scot. With the intolerance of youth, I recall being disappointed by the English faculty as it was then, sensing what it could have been. The ghost of I. A. Richards still hovered around the school of English though he had long left for the other Cambridge, and I didn't get to know him until over twenty years later after he had returned. I admired him greatly for his physical and intellectual vigour, as one might expect of a mountain climber. One year when we were staying in Merton House, a seventeenth-century house owned by the College, he took enormous pleasure in showing me the third-floor bedroom. An eighteenth-century wit had installed a sliding wall to make two bedrooms, and would invite a well-known bachelor to sleep in the one and a well-known spinster to sleep in the other. During the night, the wall would slide back. In the morning and to their great discomfort, he would ask them if they slept well. William Empson's *Seven Types of Ambiguity* published in 1930 must remain the most brilliant book ever written by an undergraduate, and if he had stayed at Cambridge, he might have brought New Criticism to the English Faculty. That's a very big "if," I admit, because New Criticism is indigenous to the New England states, as indigenous as New Historicism is to California. Elsewhere it is an import that doesn't travel well. What reigned in the English Faculty at this time was a genteel classical-based learning by men of letters, which I associated, and I don't think unfairly, with F. L. Lucas and L. J. Potts, both of whom I respected, but grudgingly. There must be some reason, though I don't know what it is, why scholarly interest in Spenser is overwhelmingly American, as indicated both by the *Variorum Spenser* centred at Johns Hopkins University and the University of Washington, and, a generation later, by the Spenser sessions at Kalamazoo. In contrast, say, to Milton: in the immediate postwar era, Tillyard was writing on Milton in England, Douglas Bush in the United States, and A. S. P. Woodhouse in Canada.

The one exception among the lecturers was the renegade, F. R. Leavis, whose lectures I attended though not for what he would say about Spenser. For him, Spenser belonged to the proscribed Milton-Tennyson poetic tradition that was invoked only to highlight the virtues of the Shakespeare-Donne-Hopkins tradition. In the twenty volumes of the very influential journal, *Scrutiny*, which he edited and dominated, only one article considers Spenser: writing on Langland, Derek Traversi says in passing of Spenser and Milton: "No two men have done more, by their very genius, to crush the true poetic tradition of England." Leavis was very popular with students. The room would be engulfed in laughter at his critical evaluations: when he would say, for example, "Let us now consider Wordsworth's mind," and then add, *sotto voce*, "if we may say that he had a mind." Perhaps we shouldn't have laughed, for it is true that one may profitably consider Milton's mind, say, in ways that would only distract us from Wordsworth's poetic power, or Spenser's. What was centrally important to me at that time was that Leavis made the reading of poetry matter to his students and to society at large, and for that I was ready to honour him, and still do.

Apart from being required to be in Cambridge during term, a research student's only obligation was to meet with a supervisor. Fellow students told me that their supervisors were available only once or possibly twice a term, if they were lucky. Except when Tillyard was lecturing in the United States and Canada, we would meet every several weeks. In the biweekly essays that I wrote for him, he seemed to be interested not in what I said but in how I said it. For him, style included punctuation. I hear him now: "How would it be, Hamilton, if we took out that comma there and put it here?" Since for me punctuation was something to be scattered throughout an essay like salt on food I was entirely nonplussed even paralyzed by such a question. (In memory of him, I have just taken out six commas from that sentence though I think one should be put back in after "food.") As a consequence, I learned much from him, and now think he was right: take care of the rhythm of a sentence, and the sense will follow, and only then may one judge if it is worth saying. The next step was to profit from what Frye taught me, that a thought does not exist until it is expressed in its proper words. Later as a lecturer, I tried to impress on students that only when they know how to write will they be able to think and say something worth reading. When I started lecturing at the University of Washington in 1952, English was a service department, and teaching composition was our bread-and-butter. Every university student was required to take three classes in composition. In the first quarter, they were taught to write a sentence; in the second quarter to write a paragraph; and in the third quarter to write an essay. For instructors who yearned to teach literature, the program was boring; for students, it couldn't have been a better preparation for studies in any subject.

Tillyard was very fond of one paper on the English Tripos that was intended to supplement the paper on "Life, Literature, and Thought," an early version of cultural criticism. It was called "Passages of English Prose and Verse for Critical Comment" that he helped design. The candidate was asked to date unidentified passages of prose and verse, giving reasons why. That exercise taught me how minor poetry belongs to its age, and how major poetry transcends it. It taught me the difference between poetry that spoke to readers in its own age and that which speaks now. One lasting consequence is that I have never been able to understand the New Historicist's claim that *all* poetry is inextricably embedded in its age.

Tillyard believed that, in addition to informal meetings, a supervisor served a candidate in two ways: to answer any bibliographical questions about the thesis, and to tell a candidate when, in his judgement, the thesis was ready to be submitted to the examining committee. For over three years, then, I was left entirely on my own. If one ignores actual living conditions, I was free with the Duke in *As You Like It*, to "fleet the time carelessly as they did in the golden world." Only later did I understand why: the university and college systems were set up for undergraduates, and graduate students (apart from those in the sciences) were admitted in order to cash in on the American demand for the doctoral degree. Once graduate students were admitted, though, the administration didn't know what to do with them, except let them be.

After my first academic appointment, I became acutely aware of how graduate studies are bureaucratized in North America: how completely graduate students are controlled, and how little leisure they are allowed. It is an inheritance, I believe, of our Puritan origins: if they are not tested continuously, sloth will lead them into sin. After two or three years of seminars, each requiring a class report, a term essay, discussion, and a final examination, students at Queen's were allowed a year of freedom, but that was given to allow them to prepare for the comprehensive written and oral examinations. When we thought that they needed more seminars, the comprehensives became less and less comprehensive, and the time to prepare for them reduced to a summer. At every stage of their graduate career, they are closely monitored; no Calvinist ever suffered more under the continual threat of a higher judgement. They are hurried through the system to complete the degree and get on the market as quickly as possible in order to increase their chances of an academic appointment. The best may be well-rounded scholars, but never scholars in that word's etymological sense, for they enjoy very little leisure, and even less when they get an academic appointment (if they are lucky) and begin their arduous ascent up Philotime's ladder.

In contrast, I enjoyed more than three years at Cambridge, doing what I wanted to do, which was to read Spenser's *Faerie Queene*. I had become aware of Spenser through Northrop Frye, and I had come to know him through my wife who worked with his wife, Helen, on the literary section of a newspaper, *The Toronto Star*. Since that sounds more "literary" than it was, I'll add that they were in charge of the photo library. If the Saturday edition included a short story in which, say, the heroine was a blonde who was courted on a river-bank and all they had was a photo of a redhead with a man in a canoe, they included that photo and then revised the manuscript accordingly. It may have been this non-academic connection that prompted the always reticent Frye to give me proofs of his *Fearful Symmetry*. From this book I inferred that his intention to write on Spenser would be displaced by his interest in critical theory, and that would leave Spenser for me.

At that time, it was generally assumed that somehow poetry could be better understood by going to the country where it was written, visiting the places to which it referred, and living where the poet lived. Perhaps it is still assumed, as the site of the present conference would suggest. Leavis, for example, believed strongly that one needed to be English in order to write on English poets. In response to this mysterious connection between blood and soil, I went to England, and to Cambridge, and my first act was to visit Pembroke College to see Spenser's portrait. It is true that the portrait is uninspiring, if not positively off-putting, but it does give a face, a person, and therefore a personal presence to his poetry, especially as it hangs on the wall of his college. At that time, it meant much to me, though I don't recall exactly what—Anamnestes isn't being helpful here—to be in the hall where Spenser served, in the library where he read books, in the college where, somewhere, he had his "digs," and in the town where he may have lived for almost a decade. Cambridge has the great advantage of being largely unchanged over centuries, at least in comparison to elsewhere: one can see so many buildings, structures, and places that Spenser saw, not only in the town itself but its surroundings. A walk along the Cam to Ely Cathedral may be much the same as in his time, and since my student days, remains for me the best introduction to Cambridge. It ought to be required of every visitor.

I had been sufficiently influenced by the prevailing historical criticism to assume that the key to *The Faerie Queene* would be found through study of some background. Since the poem's literary background, rather than its religious or socio-political context interested me, I spent a year in the Rare Book room of the University Library using the Short Title Catalogue to read every work in the Middle Ages and Renaissance that had ever been regarded as an allegory. That proved to be a wasted year: I did not find any key that would unlock the poem's allegory, and I have never returned to my notes. All I learned is that no other allegory, and very little written on allegory, helps me understand *The Faerie Queene*. The poem remains unique to itself. In desperation, I resorted to a tactic heretical at that time, and perhaps still heretical: I tried to understand the poem by reading it. Soon I realized that the poem interprets itself: the meaning of any episode is to be found in the canto of which it is part, the meaning of that canto is to be found in the book of which it is part, the meaning of the book is to be found in the other books, the meaning of all the books is to be found in what Sidney calls the poem's "idea or fore-conceit" and—this I know remains heretical—that "idea" is Spenser's intention in writing the poem, namely to fashion the moral virtues. At least for me, the more I read *The Faerie Queene*, the more I understood it. I read it then—I read it today—as a Reformer ideally reads the Bible: as a work that is self-contained, self-validating, self-authorizing, and self-referential with nothing, absolutely nothing, prior to it or beyond it.

In those early post-*Variorum* years I did find a key that allowed me to enter Spenser's poem and stay there. It was not a key hidden in the past but one directly in front of me: Sidney's *Defence of Poetry*. Reading that work persuaded me that, however it came about, Spenser shared Sidney's poetic, specifically, that the poet presents images of the virtues, vices, and passions "so in their natural seats laid to the view, that we seem not to hear of them, but clearly to see through them," that his images, therefore, are meant to "be worn in the tablet of the memory," and that readers looking only for fiction in *The Faerie Queene* "use the narration but as an imaginative ground-plot of a profitable invention." I concluded that Spenser intended his poem less to be understood than to be lived with. His purpose was Sidney's in the *Arcadia*, as described by Fulke Greville: "to limn out such exact pictures of every posture in the mind, that any man being forced, in the strains of this life, to pass through any straits or latitudes of good or ill fortune might (as in a glass) see how to set a good countenance upon all the discountenances of adversity, and a stay upon the exorbitant smilings of chance."

In writing a thesis on Spenser, I was helped because traditional historical scholarship had been fully and finally embalmed in the *Variorum Spenser*. It seemed that nothing more need be done unless one wished to bring back such oldie-goldies as "Was Spenser a Puritan?" At that time of critical innocence, its successor, the New Criticism, was unknown to me. In Cambridge at least there prevailed a genial humanism, scholarly but benign. As an example, I cite the concluding page of Tillyard's chapter on *The Faerie Queene* as an epic:

> Finally, has the *Faerie Queene* a choric character, does it speak for a large body of people? In its own day it did. The Elizabethans had no doubt that it was their great poem. Its amplitude, its blend of medievalism, Protestantism, and Plotinian idealism hit off their taste perfectly. From the Augustan age on it has never lacked readers, and a high class of readers, but it has never got home to the big heart of the reading public (and I do not intend this phrase in a pejorative sense). Spenser in fact has been something of an oddity. It is not that people cannot understand the things Spenser saw. The gap between the best man can imagine and the actual world is something of which we are all aware in some degree and whose vigorous exploitation in poetry we can enjoy. People can easily recognise and enjoy Spenser's excursions into the actual world. What they find odd is the way round he sees things. Ordinary people will put up with and admire large measures of the extraordinary if it is reached from an ordinary beginning.

So Tillyard goes on. "Bland?" I suppose so in the absence of the incomprehensibility that distinguishes much later criticism. But it is a personal voice engaged in a civilized, though admittedly donnish, conversation with educated readers. This is by and large how he spoke, and that is one test of criticism: not what one writes, or reads as I am doing now, but how one speaks. He hardly needed to tell me that he wrote his books in long-hand and submitted them to the publisher to be printed unrevised—they read as though they were. Since my ancestors on both sides are from central London, I may wonder if in the 1590s they did regard *The Faerie Queene* as "their great poem." I hope they did, but perhaps they couldn't even read. Also I wonder how Tillyard can be so sure that "Plotinian idealism," however that term may be understood, hit off their taste "perfectly," for there was no Gallup poll to which they had responded: "Would you say that Spenser's Plotinian idealism hit off your taste perfectly, less than perfectly, or not perfectly at all?" Yet I am not prepared to challenge him because in our industrial age of criticism, it is hard now even to imagine critics writing so openly and directly, or caring how "ordinary people" respond to Spenser's poem. Or if critics did, having their work published.

In my graduate years I had the leisure simply to read Spenser's poem, neither to read out of it into something else nor read something else into it. There was no massive critical barrier, as there is now, between myself and the poem. I need only read it with sufficient care to possess it and be possessed by it, to see it (from my own perspective, admittedly) in its totality and thereby become imaginatively identified with it. I came to realize the profound truth of Wallace Stevens's claim that "Anyone who has read a long poem day after day as, for example, *The Faerie Queene*, knows how the poem comes to possess the reader and how it naturalizes him in its own imagination and liberates him there." That opportunity to respond to the poem without any distraction and be liberated by it, leaves me now, of course, like a beached whale. I may understand why other readers condemn him for his misogyny, his elitism, his Eurocentrism, his racism, and his imperialism, but I only pardon him as a product of his age. Where others see contradictions, fissures, discord, repressions, aporias, or whatever, I see unity, harmony, and wholeness. I simply cannot sit in judgement on him, or even find fault in him. Where others cut Spenser down to their size, I still remain in awe of him, or rather not him but his poem, caught up in a vision of it I gained during those years. What I had anticipated to be an obscure allegory that could be understood only by an extended scholarly study of its background became more clear the more I read it until I had the sense of standing at the centre of a whirling universe of words each in its proper order and related to all the others, its meanings constantly unfolding from within until the poem is seen to contain all literature, and all knowledge needed to guide one's personal and social life.

My experience of reading the poem intensely resulted in my meeting him, though only once, and, of course, in a dream. (I am embarrassed now to recall this meeting but it is a youthful reminiscence that Anamnestes brought to mind, and I am not going to permit old age to censor him.) Two men dressed in long gowns asked me if I would like to meet Spenser, and when I said that I would, they conducted me, one on each side, down a long and gradually sloping valley at a time of day that was neither light nor dark but rather dusk. Suddenly we turned to the left and there sheltered under a large rock I saw him, a short, quiet figure, restrained and formal in manner. We talked for some time but alas, not even Eumnestes, that "man of infinite remembrance," recalls one word of what he said before I was escorted back by my two guardians.

Early in my career, and therefore formative of it, I was impressed by a music-hall story. The Master of Ceremonies announced: "And now Miss Fanny 'all will sing, 'Faithful and True.' " A voice came from the audience: "Fanny 'all is a 'ore." With scarcely a pause, the Master of Ceremonies continued: "Never-the-less, Miss Fanny 'all will sing, 'Faithful and True.' " I feel for Fanny, and ever afterwards began any lecture on an announced topic with a silent "Nevertheless." In part, the sense of unworthiness has excluded me from engaging in critical controversy, telling others what I think about what they think the poem means. Early in my career, I learned from Frye that critical interpretation is a matter of arguing a thesis that provokes an antithesis and then another thesis, and so it goes on without end. Tillyard told me that after he read any interpretation of a poem he would reread the poem to see if made any difference, and if it didn't, he would throw it out. It may be a consequence of what my mentors told me that I have eschewed interpretation for annotation. In teaching an adult-education course at the University of Washington in the mid-1950s, I was surprised at the singular lack of any annotated text of Spenser's poetry to help students with the meanings of Spenser's words. To fill that gap I edited a selection in the Signet Classic series, and that led to the Longman Annotated edition of *The Faerie Queene* in 1977, and to its 2001 revision.

Of course, I do not deny the need for continual interpretation. Sir John Harington is correct to say that one may pick out "infinite Allegories" from "poetical fictions" because *The Faerie Queene*, being such a poetical fiction, is inexhaustible. That makes it a classic even though Spenser is not a popular poet, not even among our academic colleagues. Fastidious readers have been known simply to give up after the bawdy opening line, "A gentle knight was pricking on the plaine." The poem is kept alive for each generation of readers by critics who fashion and refashion it in their own image, or, more fairly, into images that reflect their primary concerns and those of the age. As a consequence, Spenser criticism thrives. In my knowledge of it over the past fifty and more years, it has never been better than it is now, never more lively, perceptive, more informed, and more intelligent. I hope, and fully expect, that in another fifty or more years, someone here today, by then a relic of the antique age, will say much the same. As it changes, Spenser criticism may even revert to the impressionistic criticism from which in the beginning English studies fled in fear that it would be labelled "a soft option," and tell common readers how and why they may enjoy reading *The Faerie Queene*.

THOMAS P. ROCHE, JR.

Spenser, Pembroke, and the Fifties

An anecdotal reminiscence about the year that Roche spent in Pembroke College, Cambridge, at the point when he became a Spenserian, owing to the influence of Harold Bloom and the arrival of C. S. Lewis at Cambridge. Concludes with the influence of Rosemond Tuve on his work and that of Alastair Fowler.

IN SEPTEMBER 1954 I ARRIVED AT THE GATE OF PEMBROKE College to begin my year as a Henry Fellow with the princely stipend of £750 and a project to redefine Senecan influence on Elizabethan drama. I was duly enrolled as "student not at present enrolled for degree" and was sent off by Matthew Hodgart, the tutor for graduate students, to see if F. L. Lucas, who had written the authoritative book on the subject many years before, might be interested in my project. I found Lucas in his rooms at King's, sitting crosslegged on a small round table, from which vantage he declared himself categorically unwilling to return to the study of Seneca. Thank you. I attended lectures on the drama by Muriel Bradbrook and Enid Welsford where, very often the only other attendee was a Woodrow Wilson scholar from Bryn Mawr, Bobbie Ann Roesen, who has since become Ann Barton. She accepted my invitation to the Pembroke May Ball, and in the wee hours of a balmy May night I found myself punting Ann up to Grantchester for breakfast in the least happy experience of my academic career.

Academic life was pretty dim too. Fortunately for me, I lived directly above a young man who was completing his dissertation on Shelley for Frederick Pottle at Yale. I had seen him shambling around the Library in New Haven but had made no attempt to get to know him. Proximity prevailed, and that is how I got to know Harold Bloom, whose daily miseries and jeremiads galvanized the life of the whole college. In honor of Christopher Smart, one of the then five Pembroke poets, Bloom organized The Smart Set, which met for a formal dinner twice a term in memory of Kit Smart's total lack of concern for sartorial proprieties; the only requirements of The Smart Set were the ability to hold one's liquor fairly well and old clothes, much to the consternation of the college servants. I think that Bloom got the whole idea to inaugurate his Cornish fisherman's outfit, heavy knitted sweater and baggy trousers, an outfit that caused him grief soon after the dinner. One of the members of The Smart Set was a young poet named Ted Hughes, who thought it might be a lark to get Harold out on the river in a punt because, like Marc Anthony, Harold was and is a land person. With our captive Falstaff seated firmly in the center of the punt, Ted shoved off, but Harold demanded to be let out at the landing of Trinity College where he forgot his principles of physics. As he stepped toward the landing, the punt was pushed back, and we saw Bloom, hanging onto his glasses, subside beneath the placid surface of the Cam. Clambering out and cursing us, he dripped his way back to Pembroke.

Shortly after I arrived at Pembroke, it was announced that C. S. Lewis had accepted the Professorship of Medieval and Renaissance Literature, and Bloom decided that I must read Spenser with him because we were both Christian. I suspect some revenge here since Bloom loathed Lewis for his bad theology. Nonetheless, even though I assured Bloom that I had read only Book I of *The Faerie Queene*, he insisted, and I wrote Lewis to ask to read with him. The next day I got the following reply: "Dear Roche, I have left Oxford to avoid students, in particular American students, Yrs, csl." Prompted by Bloom, I went to Matthew Hodgart, who must have told Lewis that I was a New Critic from Yale, for the next day I got the following note from Lewis: "Dear Roche, come to my rooms at 4 on Thursday, having read SC." I did, but I must admit that I had to ask Bloom what SC was, and that was the beginning of my career as a Spenserian, and it all began at Pembroke.

In the 1950s Spenser was neither easy nor fashionable. The New Critics could not cope with him. The old critics had done him in and embalmed him in that *Variorum* with its tedious source studies and modern punctuation, but it was readable—if you could get a copy if you could afford it. There was the R. E. Neil Dodge Cambridge edition, with scant notes, which I used as an undergraduate. There was the one-volume Oxford in print so small that it induced instant blindness. There was the three-volume Everyman, readable but no notes, but why should there be notes since the *Variorum* supplied all that one could possibly ask? It was not easy to read him; I am very glad that Bloom insisted that I buy the three-volume Oxford.

But then something happened in the mid-fifties: some of us found Spenser and realized that the older generation of critics who had so painstakingly created the Spenser *Variorum* had not asked all the questions that might be asked about Spenser and most certainly had not given satisfactory answers. They were interested in sources, but their early training in those beginning stages of ENG LIT made them almost xenophobic toward the Italian poets from whom their sage and serious poet had stolen his laundered text. But there were no texts in those days; we called those things poems. A poem has a life beyond what I want to say about it; a text is about to submit to the scalpel, to deconstruct, to theorize, and even to intertextualize, which is a little too close to necrophilia for my taste. But back to the fifties! In 1957 Harry Berger brought out his *The Allegorical Temper.* It was an astonishing breakthrough in reading Spenser. I had read it in its doctoral dissertation form at the Yale Library, in a copy that had been annotated by W. K. Wimsatt, whose handwriting I knew because Wimsatt was the director of my undergraduate thesis at Yale, and his handwriting had seared itself into my soul, or at least the drafts of my thesis. I must admit that there were few examples of his script because Wimsatt had declared himself incapable of reading undergraduate prose without the perpetrator's sitting before him as he read it. You have not known fear or sweat unless you have sat in front of six feet, seven inches, of grimace and grunt, to be exceeded only by a direct gaze of mute condemnation of your offending sentence. Harry, I hope you escaped this.

One of the things that impressed me about *The Allegorical Temper* was Harry's invention of that remarkable phrase "conspicuous irrelevance." It had a Jamesian flair. Brilliant, but one did not know where to have it. And nowhere was it more brilliantly displayed than in Harry's analysis of the description of Belphoebe's unpappy paps, in which "did she or didn't she?" is the very least of the questions to be asked. Wimsatt's comment on this sticky wicket was: Why do girls wear sweaters? The world fell away beneath me at this concatenation of typescript and pencil. That comment could not—or would not—be written today. There was Wimsatt with his World War II Betty Grable pin-up reading and Harry with his (well, you have all read what he has written) . . . . Is this generational reading or evolution?

The Allegorical Temper did much more than invent "conspicuous irrelevance"; it was the first critical book to deal with a single book of the poem, and it started with a three-word title followed by a colon and a lot of fussy words to tell folk what the book was about. I am sorry, Harry, that I followed your lead because at the MLA following the publication of *The Kindly Flame*, some gushy soul came up to me and asked if I had heard of the new book on Spenser, *Lead, Kindly Light*.

This sudden emergence of a book on Spenser while I was in the clutches of anxiety of influence (although that anxiety had not been invented then) was even more complicated when Bert Hamilton's *Structure of Allegory in the Faerie Queene* came out in 1961. Bert was not into the three-word title but was one of the first to do "the structure and meaning" trick, which was meant to supply all the connectives that the *Variorum* lacked. Bert, I did not cop the "structure and meaning" topos from you. It is there in my 1958 dissertation.

Whatever we accomplished in those three books, we have remained true to Spenser. Bert went on to mastermind the *Spenser Encyclopedia*, in which he was particularly vigilant that Lewis's "Cissie and Flossie" should never make an appearance. I remember well at Kalamazoo "the Four Hims" (Hamilton, Cheney, Blissett, Richardson) leaving sessions early to convene their coven. Patrick Cullen and I began *Spenser Studies*, and I have now lured Anne Prescott and Bill Oram into the Complaints line. Harry has been more subtle. Like Archimago he has manipulated his minions to get out for him that long series of brilliant articles, on which he has been working through the years.

Bert and I have something else in common: we both did editions of *The Faerie Queene*. Let me say at once that you need both. Bert's Longman's has secondary materials in his notes, which I was denied in my Penguin. My text is better than his because he was forced to use the older Oxford text, happily changed in the revised edition. I used as copy text the Huntington Library copy on microfilm so that anyone could check up on the accuracy of the text, but unfortunately the page-turning photographer was a little careless in that every once in a while a page does not appear in the microfilm. I supplemented these lapses from one of the five copies of the 1590–1596 in the Firestone Library, duly noted in my note on the text. I had been told that the Penguin typesetters could easily differentiate long *s* from *f*, sent off the manuscript films and received them back almost immediately because the long *s* man had retired or demurred. I think that my wife and I are probably the only readers of *The Faerie Queene* who have read it only to identify the long s—with a red marker. This was in the days when there were no scanners, or at least they were not known to me. If there is anything worse than getting up in the morning to the realization that you have 35,000 more lines to go, it is the "red-eye mark the s" gambit. At the moment when hysteria was about to set in, I thought of a justification for all this pain—write an article on the occurrence of s in Spenser. You will be happy to learn that I have no intention of writing such a piece, which even *Spenser Studies* would turn down, because I can tell you in five seconds. By overwhelming odds Spenser uses s more often in battle scenes.

But enough of these three guys on the panel. There was also another event happening in the late fifties, and her name was Rosemond Tuve. She decided in the early fifties that she needed to impart her immense learning to graduate students in addition to intimidating her undergraduate students at Connecticut College for Women, now Connecticut College and coeducational. By her own admission she served the Men, by which, of course, she meant the Poets. In rapid succession she held a Fulbright in Aarhus, Denmark, followed by a year at Harvard, and one term at Princeton. Among her students at Harvard were Helen Vendler, David Kalstone, Paul Alpers, and Stephen Orgel, who told me at the recent *Comus* festival at the Folger Library that the first paper he wrote for her was returned to him with a single, short comment: "Boy scout, build a fire."

She was a marvel, almost six feet tall, from the pillbox hat on her head, always awry, always asserted by a no. 2 pencil for instant note-taking, to the black suede number 11s on her feet. She was magical, aloof, and cutesy down-to-earth in rapid succession. She was very churchy, any church. She had her two bourbons before dinner while the potato and two hot dogs boiled away. She was the only teacher I know who could get away with a weekly assignment: "Read Drayton." She never opened a classroom door because she was burdened with twenty or thirty books. We knew that she was there because she would kick the door. At the time of her great peregrination she was at work on what became *Allegorical Imagery*, with those interminable sets of seven virtues and vices from Macrobius, Guillaume de Conches, Alanus and the rest. It was a little like hearing the Parson's Tale with all those fingers of this and that sin. Roz paid great heed to Frances Yates's *Art of Memory* and prided herself on having as her memory place the bridges on the Merritt Parkway from New Haven to New York. Try it, if you are accident prone! And all the while that she was trying to instill in each of us our own memory place she had sitting in front of her a written-out version of all the sevens. When we offered to duplicate it for the class, she said it would defeat the purpose of education, and that was that.

I once arrived at the Houghton Library at the same time as she, and waited as she squinnied through the window. As this squinneying went on for fully five minutes, I asked what she was doing: "Trying to catch Helen White's eye so she'll make them let me in." I pointed to the buzzer on the side of the door: "Sakes, why weren't you here years ago?"

That might have been the beginning of the electronic age for Roz Tuve, but alas she died too early in the sixties to enjoy the new age of Spenser studies. She used a small Olivetti, the fifties version of the laptop, typed triple space so she could correct the untruths of what she was saying about her men, which goes far to explain the occasional lumpishness of her prose. She would have been grumpy about Deconstruction and New Historicism, as she was about New Criticism. I have in my possession a series of letters between Roz and William Empson, which encapsulates their differences on the subject of George Herbert's poem "The Sacrifice:" woman vs. man, American vs. British, scholar vs. critic, but by the end of the correspondence they had become friends. It is a fascinating view of a time when these oppositions had not become generic terms: Feminism, Postcolonialism, Theory.

I think that recent criticism of Renaissance poetry has neglected to learn from *Elizabethan and Metaphysical Imagery* and from *Allegorical Imagery* what might be very profitable for those of us who have thrown out Tillyard's *Elizabethan World Picture* and nearly every other hierarchical principle because we do not believe that the Renaissance behaved that way. Social sciences rear their generic heads, but I do not want to play the prophet. Even for me Roz's formulation of literary problems are a little dated, tagged to the errors of that current scene. But there is much to learn from her, much that she could not teach even to her own contemporaries. She once told me that she had never had a book accepted by the first press she had sent it to, this on the night I had invited her away from her potato and two hot dogs to celebrate *The Kindly Flame*'s acceptance. Enough to give the young me pause. Somewhat later I met Wimsatt in London, who asked me what I was reading, to which I replied Rosemond Tuve. His answer turned me from New Criticism: "A nice old duck, but not much for cerebration"—Goodby. Who reads Wimsatt's fallacy essays today, yet they were the foundation for Stanley Fish and a good many others who carried the principles of those essays to even more vertiginous logic, but Roz could not be used in that way. She did not do theory like Wimsatt; she did not do readings like the New Critics. She gave insights into imagery. She positioned us to poems but never talked nor took the picture. She never wrote the book on Spenser, but she knew his poem better than any Spenserian I have ever met. She is still worthwhile.

I really did not want to make this apologia for Tuve, but the more I tried to cut it out, the more it stuck, and I will let it stand. She is not the only Spenserian who has failed to gain the recognition deserved. I think especially of Alastair Fowler's *Spenser and the Numbers of Time*, a book that came out about the time of *The Kindly Flame*. It is a difficult book, but it presents an extraordinary new insight into the structure and meaning of Renaissance poetry. It has dropped out of sight critically because we do not want to admit his basic principle that number is the skeleton of poetry. As one who has played the numbers racket with poetry, I have felt the benign neglect served up to number people. Try Fowler again too.

I told Roland Greene that I would give a reminiscence of my memory of the fifties. I hope you will not think it too frivolous. It was my life, and I thought you might find it amusing to share with me the laughs I have had—which still amuse me. I look forward to listening to what you are going to do to amuse me in our continuing process of getting to know Spenser.

ELIZABETH D. HARVEY

Sensational Bodies, Consenting Organs: Helkiah Crooke's Incorporation of Spenser

This essay examines Helkiah Crooke's transposition of the body allegory in Book II of the *Faerie Queene* into his anatomical treatise, *Microcosmographia* (1615). The central point of contact between the texts that I explore is Spenser's elision of the genitals, his refusal to include the sexual and reproductive organs in the knights' tour through the Castle of Alma. I contextualize Crooke's negotiation with this elision, and my aim is to suggest not only the intricate intertextual exchange between these medical and poetic texts, but also to examine the way the allegorical and anatomical modes are intertwined. I propose that Crooke's incorporation of Spenser makes manifest principles of allegory that in turn come to underpin early modern medical understandings of the body. Crooke's explicit decision to include the genitals in his anatomy provides an interpretation that may allow us to glean more about the enigmatic relationship among the organs of generation, the passions, the senses, and the mental faculties in *The Faerie Queen*.

> Woman as womb, the unconscious womb of men's language: for her own part, she would have no relation to "her" unconscious except one that would be marked by an essential dispossession.
> In absence, ecstasy . . . and silence.
>
> —Luce Irigaray[1]

HELKIAH CROOKE, SEVENTEENTH-CENTURY PHYSICIAN and promoter of the dissemination of medical knowledge into the vernacular, used Spenser's *Faerie Queene* as a structural model for his influential anatomical treatise, the *Microcosmographia* (1615). This essay will examine the commerce between these two texts by considering Cooke's transposition of the body allegory in Book II of the *Faerie Queene* into his anatomical treatise. The central point of contact between the texts that I will be exploring here is Spenser's elision of the genitals, his refusal to include the sexual and reproductive organs in the knights' tour through the Castle of Alma. I will contextualize Crooke's negotiation with this elision, and my aim is to suggest not only the intricate intertextual exchange between these medical and poetic texts, but also to examine the way the allegorical and anatomical modes are intertwined. I propose that Crooke's incorporation of Spenser makes manifest principles of allegory that in turn come to underpin early modern medical understandings of the body. My consideration of these texts as reciprocal interpretations of the human body has, in other words, a great deal to tell us about how a younger contemporary of Spenser's understood him and how both writers imagined sexuality and reproduction.[1] Indeed, Crooke's explicit decision to include the genitals in his anatomy provides an interpretation that may allow us to glean more about the enigmatic relationship among the organs of generation, the passions, the senses, and the mental faculties in *The Faerie Queene*.

My epigraph, taken from Luce Irigaray's essay on female pleasure, "Così Fan Tutti," suggests some ways of thinking about the convergence of these relationships. Although Irigaray invokes a psychoanalytic tradition, her objections to Freudian and Lacanian ideas can be mapped onto the emergent anatomical tradition in which Crooke participates. Irigraray argues that psychoanalysis understands female sexuality through laws and models that were devised for male subjects (not unlike the Galenic homology), and that furthermore, because psychoanalysis takes discourse itself as the object of its analysis, the body is in a sense discarded in favour of the language that purports to describe it.[2] Women, especially sexualized women, are, however, resistant to the hegemony of this discursive reality; they escape "the existence of a language that is transcendent with respect to bodies" (89).Women are thus the bodily remainder, and in order to occupy this place, Irigaray contends, they must remain bodies "without organs"(90). They secure male erotic pleasure, yet they themselves do not have a discursive knowledge of this pleasure or the organs with which this erotic enjoyment is associated. Men, whose pleasure derives from the body of the Other, nevertheless articulate their enjoyment in relation to their own bodies. Female pleasure thus becomes "ek-static" (98), literally standing outside of the discursive realm, a "fault," a "gap," an "abyss" in language and knowledge. As we will see, both Spenser and Crooke are analogously preoccupied with female pleasure and with the sexual organs. For Spenser, the organs of sex and generation are quite literally a "gap" in his allegory of the body, and although Crooke includes them in his anatomy, they are associated with an intensity of pleasure that produces an ecstasy very much like the one Irigaray describes.

Crooke was born in 1576, 24 years after Spenser, and like the poet, Crooke was a sizar (the poorest category of student) at Cambridge.[3] Crooke apparently received a bachelor's degree in 1596, the same year in which the first six books of *The Faerie Queene* were published, and in the subsequent year he studied medicine in Leiden, where he wrote an anatomical thesis, *De corpore humano ejusque partibus princibus*. Crooke was steeped in the tradition of "moral anatomy" during this time, an engagement with the spiritual implications of dissection; the idea that the human body inevitably revealed God's larger design, which permeates Crooke's later defense of anatomy, may have been sown in Leiden.[4] He then returned to Cambridge, where he earned his bachelor's degree (this time in medicine) in 1599 and his degree of doctor of medicine in 1604.[5] Although Crooke probably never met Spenser, he would have known him by reputation at Cambridge, and he was intimately and demonstrably familiar with *The Faerie Queene*. In the preface to the twelfth book of the *Microcosmographia*, he makes the Spenserian architecture of his anatomy, which is visible in glimpses throughout the book, apparent:

> The glory and beauty of this stately Mansion of the *Soule* we declared in the first book. The outward walles we dismantled. The Cooke-roomes and sculleries with all the houses of Office and roomes of repast we survayed in the third. The Geniall bed and the Nursery we viewed in the fourth and fift. In the sixt we were ledde into the rich Parlor of pleasure, wherein we were entertained by a levy of Damozels; one *Modest* as Modesty it selfe; another *Shamefast*, another *Coy*, another *Iocond* and merry, another *Sad* and lumpish, and a world of such *Passions* we found inhabiting in the *Little world*, there also we saw the curious clocke of the heart mooved by a perpetuall motion; the Heralds of honor, those nimble and quicke Pursevants, those agile spirits whose presence gives life, whose pleasance gives cheere & refreshment whether soever they are sent. From

> thence wee ascended in the seventh Booke by staires of Ivory into the presence Chamber, where the *Soule* maketh her chief abode; there we saw the Counsell gathered, the Records opened, the Dispatches made and signed for the good government of the whole family. From thence in the eight Booke we clombe unto the battlements, and saw the watch of the senses set to discover and give warning of the approches of enemies or friends. In the ninth we observed the guard appointed to fetch in the provision from without, to entertain or give the repulse, to defend or offend as cause required. In the tenth we discovered the Materials which filled up the empty distances in the walles, and parted the rooms asunder. In the eleventh we followed the courses & conveyances, the enteries and Lobyes which leade throughout the whole edifice from chamber to chamber, out of one office into another. Now we are arived neare the principals of the building, where we may see how they are ioyned, how they are *fastened and bound together*, how they are covered and defended, how they are *interlaced and intertexed*. And finally, in the next and last booke wee shall with God to friend come unto the Principals themselves and to the very foundation & groundworke whereon the whole Frame is raysed (my emphasis).[6]

Crooke, as anatomist, guides his readers through a dissected body whose materiality is mediated and, as I will claim, veiled or deflected by means of Spenser's allegory. While the *Microcosmographia* is a synthesis of classical and continental medical and philosophical sources—Hippocrates, Aristotle, Galen, Gasper Bauhinus, Andreas Laurentius—and Crooke does occasionally refer to other poets, such as Virgil and du Bartas, Spenser's *Faerie Queene* provides the structural scaffolding for the treatise. It is fitting, then, that this extended description of Crooke's anatomical itinerary should appear at the beginning of his penultimate chapter, on the "gristles" or cartilage, since that chapter and the final one, on the bones, both treat the body's skeletal framework. Just as the body's foundation, the "principals" of the building, is its bony architecture, so does the Castle of Alma supply Crooke's anatomical structure. Appropriately, the most overt expression of Crooke's indebtedness is situated at the entrance to his discussion of cartilaginous connections, the materials that "interlace" and "intertext" the body and, by extension, his book.

Why should Spenser's body allegory have appealed so much to Crooke that he made it his central poetic intertext in the *Microcosmographia*? In his important explication of allegory, Gordon Teskey argues that at the heart of the word, from the Greek, *allo* and *agoreuin*, "other speaking," lies a rift that separates the categories of the material from the ideal. He suggests that the Platonic and Aristotelian metaphorics of insemination and parturition that subtend allegory mirror a struggle between the heterogeneity of the material other and the idealizing impulses to which it seeks to harness this matter.[7] Allegory casts a veil over its own workings, he contends, seeking to conceal the violent subjection of the female material to its expression of abstract ideas. Teskey claims that this forceful yoking is usually obscured in personification, but he provides a series of illustrative examples of prosopopeia that reveal allegory's struggle to contain the disorder upon which its powerful claims to order rest. Where Teskey focuses on feminine personification as the quintessential trope of allegory, I will examine by contrast the place of matter, the ways in which actual bodily processes, especially generation, are juxtaposed with the metaphorizing underpinnings of the allegorical mode.

That Spenser elides the generative organs in his body allegory is, I suggest, a manifestation of allegorical (or indeed, Irigaray's version of psychoanalytic) logic, a refusal not just to expose the inner workings of sexuality but also to reveal the material version of generation that sustains allegory's capture of the material.[8] Reading the Castle of Alma through Crooke's eyes allows us to consider it from the perspective of a physician who continually confronted the material and gendered nature of the cadaver he anatomized and the mortality he inevitably touched.[9] Yet although Crooke insists upon reintroducing the generative parts that Spenser suppresses, allegory becomes important to him precisely because it allows him to borrow the metaphorizing and idealizing mechanisms of allegory at the moment that he ostensibly exposes the secrets of the female body and the origins of life itself. His invocation of allegory provides a sense of ideal structure when he confronts the dissolution of the dissected body's wholeness into its constituent parts and into the chaos of dead matter. He furnishes an interpretation of Spenser's riddling geometrical stanza (II.ix.22) as he prepares to remove the cadaver's skin in the second book, for instance, an imposition of mathematical and allegorical form that will replace the bodily integrity lost through its flaying.

Allegory is vital for Crooke because, deep in the gristles and "scarfe-skin" of mortal corporeality as he is, he must continually insist upon the illusion of life, upon the active workings of the body that ultimately offer a rationale for the practice of anatomy. Hippocrates, Galen, and Vesalius enact the same fantasy of the life of the corpse, a vitality that is instilled in the corpse through both rhetorical and visual means.[10] Beyond this anatomical tropology lies Crooke's own conviction that the soul, though inaccessible to the eye and insensible to the anatomist's touch, is knowable as an extension of the body's parts and functions. He is thus most interested in the places where the body and soul are tied together, and nowhere is this more apparent than in the organs of reproduction, the organs through which souls are infused into new bodies. He calls these generative parts the "Geniall bed" (907), a metonymic phrase that simultaneously enfolds the domestic space of coupling into the body and evokes Genius, Spenser's porter with a double nature from the Garden of Adonis, who guides souls in and out of the garden.[11] Crooke names the corporeal location of the child's growth and nourishment the "nursery" (907), a place resonant of Plato's featureless receptacle in the *Timaeus*[12] and of Spenser's use of the word in the Proem to Book 6 of *The Faerie Queene*. There the "sacred noursery/Of vertue," like the womb, lies hidden "from the view of men," it is "deriu'd" from "heauenly seede," "long with carefull labour nurst," and, having grown to "ripeness," it "burst[s]" forth (VI.Proem.3). This depiction of the virtue of courtesy through conception and birth metaphors calls up a natural and vegetative lexicon reminiscent of the Garden of Adonis, the first "seminarie" of "all things"(III.vi.30).

Plato's nurse or chora, his "receptacle of becoming," is the space between the eternal forms and the changing copies, a place that although modelled on the analogy of human parenting, cannot correspond to the mother because it does not contribute characteristics to the offspring. As Irigaray puts it in "Così Fan Tutti": "The receptacle can reproduce everything, 'mime' everything, except itself. It is the womb of mimicry"(101). It is a featureless container, partaking neither of the forms nor of sensible matter. A kind of mechanism of translation, it is an intermediary whose ability to nourish or nurture defines what otherwise escapes explication. Elizabeth Grosz defines it this way: "The world of objects, material reality in all its complexity, is in fact infiltrated by the very term whose function is to leave no imprint, no trace. *Chora* is interwoven throughout the fabric of Plato's writing. It effectively intervenes into Plato's account of ontology, political rulership, the relations between heavenly bodies (his cosmology), and the organization of the human body—of all that makes up the world."[13] If Plato's chora left its imprint on his own depiction of the human body, it also impressed itself on medical and philosophical discussions of human generation that sought to explain conception, ensoulment, the place of parental contribution to offspring, and the questions about the relationship between spirit and matter that subtends human propagation. The Platonic legacy (probably mediated by Aristotle) is clear in Spenser's account of generation in the Garden of Adonis, where Chrysogone provides a narrative counterpart to the garden itself; although she produces twins, she is deprived of the agency and participation associated with conception and birth in early modern culture: "Vnwares she them conceiu'd, vnwares she bore:/ She bore withouten paine, that she conceiued/ Withouten pleasure"(III.vi.27). The topography of the garden corresponds to the anatomy of the female sexual organs, but generation in the garden is set in a kind of a paratactic relation to it. The planting and breeding of creatures is juxtaposed, in other words, with Spenser's gynecological landscape, but he offers no causal linkage between them. Human generation is subsumed into the Platonic fable of creation and represented through a literalization of the vegetative imagery that suffuses medical accounts of reproduction from Hippocrates forward, but rather than serving as a displaced account of the elided genitals in Alma's castle, the Garden of Adonis offers a different version of elision, an account of propagation in veiled, mystified terms.

In Spenser's allegory of the body, the knights are led into the kitchen, and having been given a tour of the premises, they are brought to the section where waste is by "secret wayes, that none might it espy" "auoided quite, and throwne out priuily" (2.9.32).[14] Alma then conducts them, their minds "fill" with "gazing wonder" and "rare delight" at the "goodly order" and "workmans skill" of the "Port Esquiline's" evacuative marvels, directly to the chamber of the heart, thus "avoiding," to recapitulate Spenser's pun, a tour of the reproductive organs.[15] Spenser's reluctance conforms to an established tradition in medical literature, one that was emphatically articulated in John Banister's 1578 English anatomical treatise, *The Historie of Man.*[16]

The structure of Alma's castle in fact closely mimics Banister's *Historie.* The sixth book of his treatise, the "Historie of the Generative Partes," is flanked by Banister's description of "the instrumentes serving to nourishment" in the fifth book (an anatomical analogue to Alma's tour of the kitchen and one that ends in a description of the bladder's excretive functions) and by the seventh book, "of the makying of the hart," which parallels the knights' visit to the heart's parlor in Alma's castle. In the chapter on the instruments of propagation, which lies between the discussions of the organs of nourishment and the heart, Banister describes the male reproductive organs in detail. He declines, however, to depict or explain the female generative parts. He argues that he is "from the begynnying perswaded, that, by lifting up the vayle of Natures secrets, in womens shapes, I shall commit more indecencie agaynst the office of *Decorum*, then yeld needfull instruction to the profite of the common sort" (88). Spenser, it would seem, exemplifies in his reluctance to image the genitals the medical tradition that replicates the inherent secrecy of the female body.

It is from this tradition that Helkiah Crooke explicitly departs. In his address to the Company of Barber Surgeons at the beginning of his treatise, he situates himself as heir to John Banister: "But because it is now a long time since your *Banister* (that good old man) first presented you with a service of this kinde, and no man hath seconded him; I have adventured to commit unto you these first fruites of my untainted fame." Like Banister, Crooke writes in English, a choice that he defends in his passionate statement about the importance of anatomical education for both physicians and surgeons. Just as Spenser had created an indigenous English literary tradition, partly through his "Englishing" of continental and classical sources and partly by fashioning an English literary genealogy with Chaucer as his authorial ancestor, so too does Crooke seek to construct an English medical ancestry with Banister as his fore-father. Crooke's insistence on writing in English situates him in opposition to the exclusive and privileged traditions of the College of Physicians, who object specifically to Crooke's providing a depiction of the organs of generation in the vernacular. Part of their disapproval was bound up with Crooke's refusal to use Latin, the linguistic sign of the physicians' knowledge and authority. Translating anatomical texts into English made them accessible to an audience, principally the barber surgeons, that would ordinarily have been excluded from this entitled group, and Crooke was thus eroding the boundary of a profession that sought to distinguish itself from the barber surgeons.[17] But his Englishing of these texts also compounded the affront to modesty by removing the veil of linguistic difference; that Crooke proposed to describe anatomical functions of the mother in the "mother tongue" was a kind of violation of propriety and the maternal body. The traces of Crooke's antagonism with the College are evident throughout his prefatory letter to the barber surgeons. He refers in particular to the accusation against him that the anatomical illustrations in the *Microcosmographia* were as obscene as Aretino's and that his inclusion of Books Four and Five on the parts of generation was shameful and inappropriate. Buried in these remarks is a short but tumultuous history of attempted censorship in which the College of Physicians attempted to stop the publication of the book, first with the help of the Bishop of London, then by intimidating the publisher and his wife, then by threats of book burning should it be published, and finally by radical emendation of the offending parts. None of these attempts was successful, and Crooke published the *Microcosmographia* in its original form.[18]

Why should describing or depicting the female sexual and reproductive organs in particular be so vigorously prohibited? One answer seems to be provided by nature itself: that women's generative organs are naturally cloaked within the body supports a tradition in medical and anatomical literature which continues and extends this secrecy. In the fourth book of Crooke's anatomy, "Naturall Parts belonging to generation, as well in Men as in Women," Crooke sets out to define the proportion of the male and female parts. As he frequently does, he begins by invoking Galen, in this case, the well-known Galenic homology: while women have organs of generation that are identical in shape to the male reproductive organs, men's appear "outward," and women's "for want of heat" are "retained" within the body. Crooke argues that this phenomenon is found in nature, for instance in the mole's eyes, an example he derives from Galen. Crooke elaborates on the simile: it is not that the mole is without eyes, he asserts, but rather that their eyes lie "deeper in their heads" and are "over-covered"(4.9). To support his gloss, he cites Virgil's *Georgics*: "aut oculis capti fodere cubilia talpe" (Or blood-winkt Moles have dig'd their Bowers).[19] The context in Virgil is a catalogue of underground life, a list of creatures (mice, toads, weevils, ants) who live surreptitiously, hidden from sight. Not only does Crooke thus elicit an invisible, secret world through his allusion, one that in the *Georgics* needs to be vigilantly controlled, but he goes on to suggest that women's organs are both veiled by nature and held captive, in restraint, or in bands. Just as matter is detained by the allegorical "poetics of capture,"[20] so in anatomical discourse are the female generative organs restrained by the absence of heat that would lift them out of their dark, interior world. The secrecy of the female generative organs is thus inherent in their interior positioning.

In the Preface to the fourth book, Crooke debates with himself about the wisdom of describing the generative organs, especially in his mother tongue: to reveyle the veyle of *Nature*, to prophane her mysteries" "seemeth a thing liable to hevy construction"(197). Invoking a legal context, however, he ponders the justice of arraigning "vertue at the barre of vice," and he argues that we must come upon the knowledge of "these secrets with pure eyes and eares" and not with "lewd and inordinate affections"(197). He says that he has endeavored "by honest wordes and circumlocutions to molifie the harshnesse of the Argument," and in a final gesture towards the conventions of reticence that govern these representations, he says "we have so plotted our busines, that he that listeth may separate this Booke from the rest and reserve it privately unto himselfe" (197). The putatively "obscene" parts of the book are positioned, in other words, in a kind of pull-out section, so that the history of the private parts can be read in solitary seclusion, a solution that allows Crooke both to publish and also to maintain the secrecy of the sexual organs. Despite providing his anatomy in a detachable section, Crooke nevertheless continues to justify his inclusion. With Spenser's sense of time, "eterne in mutabilitie"(3.6.47), as Muse, he defends sex and the reproductive organs as furnishing a perpetuity, not a speculative or imaginary eternity, but one that we may see with our eyes and feel with our hands because it is embodied in these organs (198). Having explained the divine impulse of reproduction, Crooke dilates upon the pleasure that attends the reproductive urge: "that there might bee mutuall longing desire betweene the sexes to communicate with one another, and to conferre their stockes together for the propagation of mankinde, beside the ardor and heate of the spirits conteyned in their seeds, the parts of generation are so formed, that there is not onely a naturall instinct of copulation, but an appetite and earnest desire thereunto, and therefore the obscoene parts are componded of particles of exquisite sense, that passion being added unto the will, their embracements might be to better purpose"(199). Crooke is eloquent is his description of the mutuality of sexual passion, but he was also cognizant of the difference between men and women.

While he subscribed to the Galenic homology in many respects, he also reserved a special fascination for the unique character of the female genitals.[21] This is especially apparent in one of the questions that Crooke includes in the fourth book: "The wonderfull consent between the wombe, and almost all the partes of womens bodies."[22] The etymology of the words he uses, sympathy and consent, is derived from the same the same root, meaning to feel together, to accord, and they thus suggest the way that the womb and the other parts of the body are bound together through sensation. The womb or matrix is, then, a feeling organ—it generates a powerful sympathy or consent with all the other parts of the body.

The knights in Alma's Castle turn from the kitchen to the heart's chamber, bypassing the genitals. David Lee Miller has argued that in this avoiding, sexuality is displaced through a process of sublimation into an allegorical coupling within the heart.[23] He suggests that the sublimation is both an allegorical movement, a purification or transmutation of fleshly contamination, and also a psychoanalytic refinement of libidinal energy, a channelling of instinct into social interaction. We might think of the relationship between the womb and the heart not as a relationship of displacement but as one of consent, Crooke's term for the heart-womb linkage. Crooke discusses the pathological consequences of this sympathy, which produce such symptoms as "light faintings," "desparate swoondings," "the cessastion of breathing"(239), a condition that sometimes counterfeits death so completely that it is difficult to tell if the woman is still alive. This state can be extreme enough that Crooke cautions using certain proofs of life lest the woman be buried while she is yet living. This senseless condition mimics Crooke's description of the sexual act itself, which he says is engendered by so "incredible a sting or rage of pleasure" that "we are transported for a time out of ourselves," an ecstatic state of forgetfulness that Hippocrates called a little epilepsy (199). These two bodily states, an affliction of the heart that is produced by uterine sympathy and the sensory intensity of sexual coupling, come together for Crooke in a moment of Spenserian allusion. In his book describing the anatomy of the heart, Crooke says that a blockage of a coronary artery produces a "dulnes" that turns the patient into a "senceles stocke" (40). This is, of course, the exact phrase that Spenser used to depict the transport of feeling in Amoret and Scudamore's hermaphroditic embrace in the 1590 ending to Book III: "But she faire Lady ouercommen quight/ Of huge affection, did in pleasure melt,/ And in sweete rauishment poured out her spright./ No word they spake, nor earthly thing they felt,/ But like two senceles stocks in long embracement dwelt" (III.xii.45a). This ecstatic coupling is consonant with Crooke's description of the ravishing pleasure of sex that produces an altered state, a little epilepsy. "Stock" is a word that Spenser often uses for the generational, whether in the genealogies Arthur and Guyon read in Alma's turret about "the antique stocke" (II.x.36), or in the Garden of Adonis, where "infinite shapes of creatures" are bred, and although they are daily sent forth into the world, their "stocke" is never diminished (III.vi.35). Crooke's own explication of the purpose of the generational ("to conferre their stockes together for the propagation of mankinde" [199]) together with his allusion to Spenser in the portrayal of cardiac obstruction binds the organs together in a union of sympathy, one shared not only by the figurative melding of the lovers but also by Crooke's incorporation of Spenser. This intertextual fusion thus functions not only to authorize and structure Crooke's anatomy but also to import sensation into it, to infuse the flayed, dissected, and partitioned cadaver with the poetic memory of its vital functions. In his preface to Book Twelve, Crooke reminds us that the heart is both a metaphoric place, the seat of the passions, a chamber occupied by personifications, and also an anatomical location where "the curious clocke of the heart [is] mooved by a perpetuall motion"(907). Shuttling back and forth between an imaginative, poetic account of corporeal structure and an anatomical explication, he fashions a body whose workings include social transactions, spiritual dimensions, and a pervasive awareness of the way life is implicated in mortality, and death always shadows the living.

If the heart houses the passions, the senses, what Crooke calls "intelligencers between the body and the soul"(6), are powerfully entangled in them. The hermaphroditic union that converts the lovers into "senceles stocks" results from an effusion of sensation so extreme that it paradoxically deprives them not just of feeling but of life itself. Abstracted from the very bodies that confer this intense pleasure, the lovers are outside themselves, ecstatic. This image is recapitulated in Amoret's adventures. Amoret, who is "conceiued/ Withouten pleasure" (III.vi.27) is nevertheless raised with Pleasure, the daughter of Cupid and Psyche, as her "companion" (III.vi.51) in the Garden of Adonis. Associated with sensual delight as she is, it is appropriate that, in a moment of convergence between the allegorical and anatomical modes in the House of Busirane, her heart is removed from her body where it lies in a silver basin, "transfixed with a deadly dart" (III.xii.21). One of the questions Crooke attempts to answer in the "Controversies" about the heart is whether the organ can endure grievous hurt and whether people or animals can survive the extraction of the heart. He cites several examples of beasts and men who continue to live even when their hearts are out of their bodies, and he concludes: "That a creature can walke and cry when his heart is out I beleeve well so long as the spirits last in his body which it receiveth from the heart" (419–20). As his description of the heart as a "rich Parlor of pleasure" and "a world of . . . *Passions*" (907) makes clear, the heart is, like the genitals, a feeling organ. It has a passionate life that is associated both with the senses and with the figurative sense of "feeling," and this emotional and sensory world is as important to extract from the corpse as the anatomical structure that harbors it.

Where the Castle of Alma is besieged by the externalized emblems of the five senses, Crooke is by contradistinction concerned to explain the complex imbrication of the senses with body and soul.[24] Following Aristotle, Crooke privileged vision, but he understood touch as the fundamental sense, the one associated with life itself. Aristotle in *De Sensu* wavers about whether to give primacy to the visual or the auditory sense, yet he also finds touch essential to being, calling it "the indispensable sense."[25] In *De Anima,* he asserts that "all animals whatsoever are observed to have the sense of touch," and therefore it must be the "primary form of sense."[26] Where all the senses are associated with sexuality, there is a rich iconographical and literary tradition that makes tactility the primary sense for sexuality.[27] Michael Drayton's sonnet XXIX "To the Senses" in *Idea*, for instance, captures the privileged positioning of touch in the early modern hierarchy of the senses.[28] The speaker's heart is besieged by "conqu'ering Love," and he thus summons the five senses to his aid, but one by one, each of them is overcome by Love's blandishments. Sight is corrupted by beauty, hearing is bribed with sweet harmony, Taste is delighted by the sweetness of the beloved's lips, Smell is vanquished by the "Spicerie" of her breath, and finally Touch remains as the solitary guardian of the heart's citadel. Figured as "The King of Senses, greater than the rest," Touch not only yields to Love, handing over the heart's keys, but he also persuasively addresses the other senses, endorsing Love's conquest and telling his companion senses that "they should be blest."

For Crooke, touch is linked through sexuality to the origins of life. The organs of generation are imbued with a "most exquisite sense of Touching," a ravishing pleasure that overcomes the disgust supposedly ordinarily evinced by the "filthy" procreative act. The ubiquitous linkage between sexuality and tactility that informs early modern representations of touch is here subsumed into (and celebrated as) a reproductive impulse, an urge for eternity.

This tradition is invoked and extended in Crooke's ligature of touch, sexuality, and maternity:

> For first, it is by the benefit of Touching that we are conceived and formed in the fertile Garden of our Mothers wombe. For our wise and provident Nature ayming at Eternity, hath endued the partes of generation with a most exquisite sense of Touching, for the conservation of the Species or kindred creatures, so that the creatures beeing ravished with an incredible kind of pleasure, doe more readily apply themselves to venereall embracements, (otherwise a thing filthy and abhominable) and endeavor the procreation of their owne kindes. When the Infant in the wombe yet liveth onely a vegetative life, hee is first of all

> endued with the sense of Touching; whereby hee is cherished, nourished, and encreased, and is at length perfected; for so long as he is in the prison of the wombe, he neither seeth, nor heareth, nor smelleth, nor tasteth any thing, but yet hath absolute necessity of the sense of Touching, that he may be able to avoyde imminent dangers. (648)

In this passage, which seems almost to be an anatomical gloss on the Garden of Adonis, Crooke depicts tactility's primacy as possessing both an originary and generative power. Touch is the "root" sense because it informs sexual pleasure, which in turn engenders life. Crooke's syntax implicitly removes human agency and resituates the generative principle in the personification of Touch, and the child that is so conceived and formed in the "garden" of the maternal womb is thus appropriately entirely governed and furthermore rendered secure by its sense of tactility. Crooke imaginatively enters this chora, this haven of embryonic unfolding, asserting that the developing fetus is effectively blind and deaf, incapable of tasting and smelling, and thus entirely dependent on its sense of touch. The growing child is doubly contained: within the flesh of the mother's body and within the envelope of its own skin.

As Crooke tells us elsewhere, the womb itself is a web of muscular and sensory fibers (217–28). The matrix communicates with the other organs through a network of nerves and membranes, and the manifestation of the connections is sensory, a sympathy often expressed in pain or a disorder of feeling. This web becomes startlingly visible in Crooke's account of conception in the Fifth book, where the History of the infant is described: "We begin with the seed which is like the *Chaos*. Upon which . . . the Formative spirit broodeth it first. After as a Spider in the center of her Lawnie canopy with admirable skil weaveth her Cipresse web, first hanging it by slender Ties to the roofe, and after knitting her enter braided yarn into a curious net: so the spirit first fasteneth the seed to the wombe with membranes and ligaments, after distinguisheth it into certaine spermaticall threds which we call *Stamina corporis*, the warpe of the bodie" (257). Crooke's explication of conception turns the matrix into a kind of chora, a place where the spirit weaves itself into the body's "warpe." This "fertile Garden of our Mothers wombe" (648) bears the imprint of Spenser's Garden of Adonis, where in that "wide wombe of the world" a generative "huge eternall *Chaos*" supplies nature's progeny. Crooke borrows the mythic resonance of Spenser's formulation, but "chaos" is resituated within the human seed and the development of child is replanted within the garden of the maternal body.

Crooke's spider image contains, however, a cautionary notes about perils of an effusion of sensation, which while capable of generating life, must be tempered. When Alma's castle is attacked by the assailants of the five senses, the adversaries of tactility's bulwark include spiders:

But the fift troupe most horrible of hew,
And fierce of force, was dreadfull to report:
But some like Snailes, some did like spyders shew,
And some like vgly Vrchins thicke and short:
Cruelly they assayled that fift Fort,
Armed with darts of sensuall delight,
With stings of carnall lust, and strong effort
Of feeling pleasures, with which day and night
Against that same fift bulwarke they continued fight.
(II.xi.13)

We can see the danger of these "stings of carnall lust" and "darts of sensuall delight" in narrative form in the Bower of Bliss, where Acrasia lies on her bed of roses. Verdant's "sleepie head" disposed in her "lap," the enchantress is "arayd, or rather disarayd" in a veil that Spenser describes thus: "More subtile web *Arachne* can not spin,/ Nor the fine nets, which oft we wouen see/ Of scorched deaw, do not in th'aire more lightly flee"(II.xii.77). Arachne's tapestry in Ovid's *Metamorphoses* imaged the sexual transgressions of the gods, and she thus figures by extension a sexual licentiousness that is expressed in Acrasia's subsequent capture in Guyon's restraining net. If Acrasia's "lap" holds the sexual instruments of pleasure (Crooke's Chapter XVI is entitled "Of the Lap or Privity" and it treats external female parts, the nymphae, the clitoris, the lips, and the "mount of Venus" [228–30]), the translucent veil that dis-covers her is linked not only to tactility and its dangers, but for Crooke, to a ravishing pleasure that leads us back to the Garden of Adonis, to the mysteries of conception.[28]

Crooke attempts in the *Microcosmographia* to image the genitals that Spenser elides in his allegory of the body, and in doing so, he gathers within his portrayal the parts of sexuality and generation that Spenser scattered into narrative moments: the hermaphroditic embrace, the Garden of Adonis, and the Bower of Bliss. His anatomy thus enters the spaces veiled by the cultural imperatives of modesty, and they provide, as I have argued, not just medical descriptions, but representations that draw on a cultural imaginary. In a limited way, Crooke anticipates Luce Irigaray's call to portray the elision of Western metaphysics, which includes not only the maternal space of the womb, but the multiplicity of the sexual and reproductive parts, and the diverse pleasures associated within them. She suggests that the " '*elsewhere' of female pleasure* might rather be sought in the place where it sustains ek-stasy in the transcendental," a place, in her words, that is outside the logic of a phallocratic economy.[29] The style or discourse in which this rediscovery will ideally take place involves a style that, rather than privileging sight, relies on the tactile.[30] As Irigaray says in an aphoristic gloss on *Speculum*: "Surely man favors the visual because it marks his exit from the life in the womb?"[31] She contends that Western philosophy's occultation of the maternal contributes to a metaphysics of visibility (which in turn nourishes the hierarchical ordering of sexual difference), and her re-conception of philosophy, which has political, epistemological, psychoanalytic, and ethical implications, involves re-incorporating the feminine-maternal body and its "language" of tactility.[32] While Irigaray's resistance to the tyranny of the scopic regime defines *Speculum of the Other Woman*, her elaboration of an opposing theory, what we might call her metaphysics of touch, nevertheless undergirds it and achieves a fuller expression a decade later in *An Ethics of Sexual Difference* and in a lecture printed in *Sexes and Genealogies*:

> If we look seriously at this composite and provisional incarnation of man and woman we are brought back to the sense that underlies all the other four senses, that exists or insists in them all, our first sense and the one that constitutes all our living space, all our environment: the sense of *touch*. This is the sense that travels with us from the time of our material conception to the height of our celestial grace, lightness, or glory. We have to return to touch if we are to comprehend where touch became frozen in its passage from the most elemental to the most sophisticated part of its evolution. This will mean that we need to stay both firm and mobile in our cathexes, always faithful, that is, to the dimension of touch.[33]

Crooke's portrayal of a sexual ecstasy derived from tactile pleasure, of touch as a ravishing delight that moves beyond language, and of an encompassing touch that defines the maternal chora, feeds his subsequent explication of the organs, especially the female and maternal parts. Even though he sought to establish himself as an anatomist, with its attendant gestures of medical colonization, his observations often seem to resist the emergent visuality of anatomical discourse because of his emphasis on the senses, especially touch. As the mediators between body and soul, the senses serve simultaneously as conduits out of the body (ecstatic movements) and also to anchor the soul within the materiality of its bodily refuge.

NOTES

1. Walter R. Davis says that Kenelm Digby provided the "earliest extended commentary on a single stanza of *The Faerie Queene*" in 1624, but I will argue that Helkiah Crooke makes this stanza central to the explication of the body furnished by his *Microcosmographia*. ("Castle of Alma," *The Spenser Encyclopedia,* ed. A. C. Hamilton et al. Toronto: University of Toronto Press; London: Routledge, 1990:24–5).

2. "Così Fan Tutti," p. 87. Subsequent page references appear in the text of my essay.

3. Where Spenser was a fellow at Pembroke Hall (now Pembroke College), Crooke was awarded a scholarship at St. Johns's College. My information about Crooke's life is taken primarily from the biographical portrait that C. D. O'Malley provides in "Helkiah Crooke, M.D., F.R.C.P., 1576–1648," *Bulletin of the History of Medicine*, XLII, 1 (1968): 1–18. While the details of Crooke's life that he supplies are immensely useful, O'Malley's interpretation of the records and fragmentary bits of evidence portray Crooke as a relentlessly ambitious, often unethical opportunist. O'Malley's characterization exactly replicates, and indeed amplifies, the perspective of the College of Physicians, which objected not only to Crooke's behavior with respect to litigations and his failure to pay his College dues, but also to his desire to disseminate anatomical learning in the vernacular. That Crooke appealed directly to the Company of Barber Surgeons in his highly successful *Microcosmographia* (which the College tried to suppress) and criticized the physicians in the prefatory address suggests not only the rivalrous tensions among the emergent parts of the medical profession but also that Crooke may well have been seen as an agent of change, a figure who threatened the hegemony of the physicians. I am grateful to James Broaddus for conversations about Crooke and the censorship of books four and five of the *Microcosmographia.*

4. Jonathan Sawday's *The Body Emblazoned: Dissection and the Human Body in Renaissance Culture* (London and New York: Routledge, 1995), 110, 167. Sawday says that Crooke took a medical degree in Leiden in 1597, but C. D. O'Malley notes that Crooke's thesis was an exercise in disputation, not a fulfillment of the requirements for the medical degree (O'Malley, 3).

5. O'Malley, 2–3.

6. Helkiah Crooke, M I K R O K O S M O G R A P H I A. *A Description of the Body of Man. Together with the Controversies thereto Belonging. Collected and Translated*

out of all the Best Authors of Anatomy, Especially out of Gasper Bauhinus and Andreas Laurentius (London: William Jaggard, 1615), 907. All subsequent references are to this edition and will be cited in the text.

7. Gordon Teskey, "Allegory, Materialism, Violence," *The Production of English Renaissance Culture*, ed. David Lee Miller, Sharon O'Dair, and Harold Weber (Ithaca: Cornell University Press, 1994), 293–318, 293–4

8. There is, of course, some discussion about the gender of the body in Spenser's allegory. Although I do not assume that the body is unequivocally feminine, I nevertheless concentrate on the female body parts because those were the parts most frequently censored in medical texts (such as Banister's *Historie of Man*), and the debates around the decorum of representing the female genitals were much fiercer and more pervasive.

9. Valerie Traub has explored in revealing ways the confrontation between the anatomist and abjected cadaver he dissects ("Gendering Mortality in Early Modern Anatomies" in *Feminist Readings of Early Modern Culture: Emerging Subjects*, ed. Valerie Traub, M. Lindsay Kaplan and Dympna Callaghan [Cambridge University Press, 1996], 44–92). In her examination of anatomical illustrations, she contends that anxieties about death and the dead body that the anatomist touches (and with which he may be identified) contribute to the gendering of knowledge. As she says, "early modern anatomical illustrations demonstrate the extent to which gender is reciprocally *manufactured* in order to defend against the vulnerability to mortality that all bodies share"(45). As we will see, this gendering of embodiment in anatomical representation is shared by allegorical theory, for both displace anxieties about the abjected, mortal, and material body onto a female principle.

10. See Andrea Carlino's analysis of anatomical iconography in *Books of the Body: Anatomical Ritual and Renaissance Learning* (originally published in 1994, trans. John Tedeschi and Anne C. Tedeschi (Chicago: University of Chicago Press, 1999), Traub, "Gendering Mortality," and Sawday, *The Body Emblazoned.*

11. David Lee Miller discusses the relationship between the Castle of Alma and the Garden of Adonis in *The Poem's Two Bodies: The Poetics of the 1590 Faerie Queene* (Princeton: Princeton University Press, 1988). See in particular his comparison of spatial patterns of descent (222–24) and gateways and anatomical zones (266–72); these discussions suggest the way that the erasure of the sexual organs in the Castle of Alma is recuperated in the Garden of Adonis.

12. *Plato's Cosmology: The* Timaeus *of Plato*, trans. Francis MacDonald Cornford (Indianpolis and New York: Bobbs-Merrill, 1957), 177–96.

13. Elizabeth Grosz, "Women, *Chora*, Dwelling," in her *Space, Time, and Perversion: Essays on the Politics of Bodies* (New York and London: Routledge, 1995),117–18.

14. Spenser, Edmund. *The Faerie Queene*, ed. Thomas P. Roche. New Haven and London: Yale University Press, 1981.

15. David Lee Miller, *The Poem's Two Bodies,* 180.

16. Iohn Banister, *The historie of man sucked from the sappe of the most approued anathomistes, in this present age, compiled in most compendious fourme, and now published in English, for the vtilitie of all godly chirurgians, within this realme* (London: Iohn Day, 1978).

17. Midwives were also the beneficiaries, as is evident in the degree to which Jane Sharp depends on Crooke. See my essay, "Anatomies of Rapture: Clitoral Politics/

Medical Blazons," *Signs: Journal of Women in Culture and Society,* 27.2:315–46 and Elaine Hobby's introduction to her edition of Jane Sharp, *The Midwives Book, Or the Whole Art of Midwifry Discovered* (New York and London: Oxford University Press, 1999).

18. O'Malley provides a useful description of Crooke's battle with the College over censorship (8–11).

19. Virgil, *Georgics,* Book I: 182; Crooke, 212.

20. Teskey, 307.

21. Janet Adelman questions the extent to which Crooke adhered to the Galenic model. See her essay, "Making Defect Perfection: Shakespeare and the One-Sex Model." In *Enacting Gender on the English Renaissance Stage,* ed. Viviana Comensoli and Anne Russell (Urbana and Chicago: University of Illinois Press, 1999), 23–52. I respond to her in some depth in "Anatomies of Rapture."

22. Where Crooke's anatomical descriptions of the body's parts and organs adhere to the established decorum of his classical and continental sources, his Prefaces and especially the sections called the "Controversies" which follow each book engage in speculation and debate. It is in the "Controversies" that Crooke introduces the most pressing medical puzzles of the early seventeenth century, where he questions Galenic authority, and where he confronts some of the questions that circulate among anatomists, physicians, and even in the popular imagination. The Controversies are thus the space of change, where competing opinions jostle each other and where the new anatomical knowledge encounters the tenacious inherited, accreted, often fantastical "truths" about the body.

23. Miller, *The Poem's Two Bodies,* 174–183, esp. 170, 174, 178.

24. We can glimpse Crooke's fascination with the senses in the number of questions he generates in the "Controversies" following Book Eight, on the senses. Where the second highest number of questions, thirty-three, is appended to Book Five, on generation, Book Eight almost doubles that by offering sixty-four controversies.

25. Aristotle, *De Sensu* (*On Sense and Sensible Objects*), trans. W. S. Hett, *Aristotle,* Vol. VIII, Loeb Classical Library (Cambridge, Mass.: Harvard University Press, 1936), 436b.

26. Aristotle, *De Anima. The Basic Works of Aristotle,* ed. Richard McKeon (New York: Random House, 1941), 533–603, 413b.

27. Neoplatonic thought, for example, relegated touch (along with taste and smell) to the lower, more bodily senses. The sense of touch frequently evokes the erotic and seductive, and early modern depictions of the Five Senses sometimes portray Touch through lascivious or pornographic scenes. See Louise Vinge, *The Five Senses: Studies in a Literary Tradition* (Lund, Sweden: Royal Society of Letters at Lund, 1975); Carl Nordenfalk, "The Five Senses in Late Medieval and Renaissance Art," *Journal of the Warburg and Courtauld Institutes,* 48 (1985). 1–22; Gino Casagrande and Christopher Kleinhenz, "Literary and Philosophical Perspectives on the Wheel of the Five Senses in Longthorpe Tower," *Traditio,* XLI (1985), 311–327.

28. For a fuller analysis of touch, spider imagery, and the Bower of Bliss, see my essay, "The 'Sense of All Senses' " in *Sensible Flesh: On Touch in Early Modern Culture,* ed. Elizabeth D. Harvey (Philadelphia: University of Pennsylvania Press, 2002).

29. "The Power of Discourse,"*This Sex Which Is Not One* (*Ce Sexe qui n'est pas un*, Editions de Minuit, 1977), trans. Catherine Porter (Ithaca, New York: Cornell University Press, 1985), 77–8.
30. "The Power of Discourse,"79.
31. *Sexes and Genealogies*, trans. Gillian C. Gill, (Paris, Les Éditions de Minuit, 1987; New York: Columbia University Press, 1993), 59. Irigaray has, of course, been charged with essentialism for statements like these, and it is thus important to read her in the contexts of her overarching project, which sets out to expose patriarchy's structures and operations. Her central target is Western philosophical thought, or, as Margaret Whitford puts it, the "*passional foundations of reason*" (*Luce Irigaray: Philosophy in the Feminine* [London and New York: Routledge, 1991], 10).
32. She asks in *An Ethics of Sexual Difference* whether sensation is not for Merleau-Ponty structured like language; see *Ethics*, trans. Carolyn Burke and Gillian C. Gill (1984, Paris: Les Éditions de Minuit, 1984; Ithaca: Cornell University Press, 1993), 158. For a brilliant treatment of the complexities of Irigaray's endeavor, see Margaret Whitford, *Luce Irigaray*, especially the chapters "Feminism and Utopia" and "Woman and/in the Social Contract."
33. *Ethics of Sexual Difference*; *Sexes and Genealogies*, 59.

THERESA KRIER

Daemonic Allegory: The Elements in Late Spenser, Late Shakespeare, and Irigaray

Luce Irigaray reactivates for postmodern philosophy terms from the presocratics on the elements and elemental motion. After considering what this move allows her to think, this essay turns to an Irigarayan notion of elemental motion in relation to *Mutabilitie* and Shakespeare's *Tempest*—for the playwright has read the 1609 *Faerie Queene* closely, and responds to it. All three writers think out implications of personification allegory in relation to temporality, narrative sequence, and the theme of justice. Spenser's mythic allegory deploys ancient Stoic allegory, by which the vitality and superabundant will of deities is transformed into a physics taking the cosmos as pervaded by divine energies; *The Tempest* chooses this as mythic allegory's most attractive form of survival. It is precisely elemental motion as the daemonic that Shakespeare brings into drama from Spenser. So some allegory is daemonic, not in Angus Fletcher's sense of representing fixity of character, but in an almost opposite sense of structuring a fluid, Irigarayan movement-between. The essay concludes with some speculations on Irigaray's work on the mediating function of the placenta, and the maternal in *The Tempest*.

> We should also think about the fact that all philosophers—except for the most recent ones? and why is this so?—have always been physicists and have always supported or accompanied their metaphysical research with cosmological research.
> (Luce Irigaray, "Wonder: A Reading of Descartes, *The Passions of the Soul*," 72)

The elements—earth, air, fire, water, sometimes wood, sometimes stone—arouse intense interest among creators of poetic and dramatic forms in the last years of the sixteenth century and the first couple of decades of the seventeenth. This happens for various reasons, among them developments in science and the history of philosophy. But in this essay I am concerned with what the elements might allow writers to think, and I look at the work done by the elements in passages from Spenser's *Mutabilitie Cantos*, first published in 1609, and Shakespeare's *The Tempest* (1610–11), which rethinks a good many issues of Spenser's poem as its great precursor and sometimes its antithesis, in light of Luce Irigaray's work on the elements. As is often the case in his plays, Shakespeare in *The Tempest* is articulating a space for himself not only within drama but also within a specifically poetic history, and works out through his response to *Mutabilitie* some implications of personification allegory in relation to time, narrative sequence, and the theme of justice. In this essay I emphasize how often Spenser and Shakespeare use elemental movement to carry literary thinking. Through their materialism, especially their plotting of elemental motions and transitions, characters change, ethics emerge, literary resources develop.

Irigaray in the 1970s often wrote dense, passionate, and critical readings of the heroic tradition of philosophers. But since the 1980s she's also written in lyric vein, turning to pre-Enlightenment sources for concepts that she would trope in strange and provoking ways. She went, for instance, to the elements of the presocratic philosophers, and to the ancients' physics of motion and space. She used them extensively to open up and critique unarticulated assumptions about matter held by particular philosophers. Assumptions about matter are, in the nature of things, assumptions about origins; hence, for Irigaray, unacknowledged assumptions about the maternal. She wrote an entire book called *The Forgetting of Air in Martin Heidegger*—and she means this as a charge against him, a charge that carries force because Heidegger works the element of earth so intensively, in his figures of world, rift, clearing, gathering, and so on. She says, "Perhaps one must remove from Heidegger that earth on which he so loved to walk. To take away from him this solid ground, to rid him of the 'illusion' of a path that holds up under his step . . . and to bring him back . . . to the world of the pre-Socratics"—where she will ask him to think about air as the gift provided first by the mother.[1] In fact she takes all of metaphysics since Plato as a forgetting of the elements of air, fire, and water, as it searches for firm *grounds* on which to construct theory. Another of Irigaray's books is called *Marine Lover of Friedrich Nietzsche,* the philosopher whom it addresses and whose privileging of fire suggests to Irigaray a concomitant disavowal of all that water can signify:

> And what presumption is this to claim that you raise all the deep seas up to your heights? Did you ever reach their heights? And when you aver that the seas wish to become mountain tops and light, isn't this the talk of a man of *ressentiment* who says, "As long as the sea remains sea, some movement resists my will. Some path of light is hidden from me in the sea."
>
> And if the sun, in the innocent and impatient ardor of his rising, comes first to the sea to drink, why interpret this as the sea's will to become air so that she can rise up after him?[2]

Irigaray works from presocratic implications, and more recent philosophers' unintentional demonstrations, that any one element, left to itself, would dominate and thus annihilate the world, which requires variety and balance of elements. Thus thinking about the elements becomes thinking about justice. Anaximander is said to have insisted that the essence of beings is not any one element, but the infinite, which nonetheless makes room for the "mutual imperialism" of the elements. The infinite is "that from which there is, for beings, generation; in it destruction also takes place, according to what must be; for beings render justice and reparation to one another, from their mutual injustice, according to the summons of Time."[3]

In books like those on Heidegger and Nietzsche and in her championing of flows and flux, Irigaray wants to make explicit a dynamic of matter that remains latent, or even repressed, in what became the canon of philosophers, most explicitly in her work on philosophers concerned with the elements in creative ways: Nietzsche, Bachelard, Levinas, Heidegger. In essays from the 1970s like "The 'Mechanics' of Fluids," "Volume without Contours," and "Is the Subject of Science Sexed?" she argues that classical science cannot think adequately about either matter or bodily life if, as it has at key moments, it privileges solids, substances, and objects of a self-contained unity which are defined by closing out all that is non-identical and much that should be taken not as unity but as multiples. As in Anaximander, then, Irigaray's thinking about the elements is in part a way to think about justice within time. And as if to think out the temporal in its most elemental forms, Irigaray takes to scientific articulations that emphasize process, event, mobility, the overlap or meeting of fields of energy, passage, interval; articulations of "gradation, shadows, flows and intensive magnitudes."[4] In short, mobility and multiplicity pervade all Irigaray's work on the elements.

Movement is also her central figure for a social future in which she can hope. She uses the elements to create models that give lyrical voice to her hopes for transformations of cultures and of individuals' experience, for new visions of old texts and the ways that they open into our incalculable futures:

> Once we have left the *waters* of the womb, we have to construct a space for ourselves in the *air* for the rest of our time on earth—air in which we breathe and sing freely, in which we can perform and move at will. Once we were fishes. It seems that we are destined to become birds. None of this is possible unless the air opens up freely to our movements.
>
> To construct and inhabit our airy space is essential. It is the space of bodily autonomy, of free breath, free speech and song, of performing on the stage of life.[5]

It should be emphasized that Irigaray never privileges random, chaotic movement or restlessness. There are at least two kinds of movement that she does foster in her work on social possibilities. One—in a voice utopian, exhortatory, arguing for the agency and freedom of the subject—is motion from confinement into the freedom of air, as in the passage above. Like other philosophical, didactic writers from Lucretius through Freud, she always recognizes the obstacles to this process of becoming, how much gathering of energies it requires, and her tones combine fierceness with compassion for being struggling toward such mobility. The second sort of movement creates an interval between two beings facing one another and making an intersubjective, generative space between themselves. Movement here creates not rigid but elastic or fluid boundaries of that interval, a constantly shifting interplay of nearness-to and distance-from each other. I infer that she works out this kind of fluxional materialism of multiples specifically as an alternative to Julia Kristeva's notion of the maternal chora, at once a space and a unitary mass, which Kristeva reworks from Plato's *Timaeus*. Irigaray perhaps wants to counter this Kristevan notion because it implies a kind of materialism that lends itself with fatal ease to a traditional binarism of passive, feminine matter and active, masculine form. Irigaray can thus offer readers of Renaissance writing useful ways of thinking about matter and material in poetry, and about allegory, outside that powerful but restrictive binarism.[6]

Of course a vitalism of the elements, its complications of any simple dichotomy of matter and form, celebration of natural process and movement—none of these things will be new to readers of

Spenser or Shakespeare, and one could just say that there are plenty of parallels between Irigaray's and the poets' affinity for the primal elements. There is Spenser's attention to earthy substrata and fertile gardens, his many waters, his angels and dragons cleaving the tender air, his vignettes of light in motion. Shakespeare scatters with generous hand his green worlds, gardens, woods, desolate heaths, tempestuous winds, oceans and shores and sea-storms; Shakespeare's speakers often articulate their sense of fragmentation, inner rending and torment with topoi of the elements, as in *Lear* and *Macbeth* and Sonnets 44 and 45; characters' responses to human amplitude and recoils from imaginings of degradation rely equally on a kind of intimacy with the elements, as in Vernon's great description of Hal tranformed in *1 Henry IV,* or the terms with which all the characters speak of Caliban in *The Tempest.*[7] But Spenser and Shakespeare, like Irigaray, also use the elements as instruments of thought, and keeps thought in motion—keeps *movement* going—by distinct passages and transitions from one element to another.

Irigarayan delineations of elemental mobility focus a problem that often presents itself in comments on Spenserian allegory. Angus Fletcher, brilliantly linking personification with the notion of the daemonic, argues authoritatively that allegorical agents "compartmentalize function. If we were to meet an allegorical character in real life, we would say of him that he was obsessed with only one idea, or that he had an absolutely one-track mind, or that his life was patterned according to absolutely rigid habits from which he never allowed himself to vary."[8] Such a subject, if met in real life, would be enslaved to an *idée fixe,* a repetition compulsion, even to the death drive; in another metaphysic, he would be possessed. The sense of a phenomenal deadness within many personifications is evident throughout Spenser's work. Kenneth Gross observes that allegory often has a "sense of something killing within its animations," and he discusses exemplary figures of Envy in the House of Pride, Maleger, Malbecco—figures whose life *is* deadness, or conveys a commitment to death, in one way or another.[9] Such reflections on a link between compulsion, a death drive, and personification create one productive way to think about how Spenser transforms personification poetry and drama composed from late antiquity through the fifteenth century. In Fletcher, the account of a sense of deadness arises from the influence of a mid-twentieth-century Freudianism that fits neatly with psychomachic allegory from Prudentius to Spenser, with its focus on the parts of the dramatically suffering individual who seeks harmony among them.[10] But it is easy to see that personification in *The Faerie Queene* is of many kinds, not psychomachic only, and amenable to infinite modulations and gradations, including a capacity not to represent deadness but to endow intensified life to a character. Then how might we describe and account for the sense of vitality and animation conveyed, for example, by the great structural opposite to the pageant of the Seven Deadly Sins, Mutabilitie's procession of the seasons, the months, and the elements? Spring and Fall, July and September, in *Mutabilitie* manifest joy in their animation, not rigidity, grotesquerie, or deadness. But why?

I suggest that Spenser wishes to find alternatives specifically to the phenomenal deadness in some fictions of virtues and vices and in the ubiquitous moralized interpretation of ancient epic, and that he finds such an alternative precisely in the elements, especially in elemental motion, and their potential relationships to character. Such a move would have been accessible to him in part because of his career-long meditation on visual motifs in calendars, probably in larger part because of his Ovidian/Lucretian sense that these temporal changes are precisely metamorphoses of the elements: combinations, dissolutions, and recombinations.

Both the iconographical and the poetic traditions in turn owe their allegorical vitality to the long-lived influence of ancient Stoic exegesis of myth, in which allegory works otherwise than in Fletcher's influential account. Stoic interpretation transforms myth, and especially ancient deities, into principles of physics, as Jon Whitman's work demonstrates.[11] Thus Diogenes Laertius reports that for the Stoics, God is

> the father of all, both in general and in that particular part of him pervading all things, and which is called by many names according to its powers. They give him the name Dia, through whom *(di' hon)* are all things . . . Hera, because of his suffusion of the air (*aera*); Hephaestus, because of his spreading to the craftsmanlike fire (*tekhnikon pyr*); Poseidon, because of his saturation of the water; and Demeter, because of his permeation of the earth. (cited in Whitman, 32).

Or again, Stoics suggest that in Homer's reference to Zeus' going off to Ocean to feast, "Zeus" means "sun," because the exhalations of the ocean nourish the sun.[12] As Whitman notes, in this kind of exegesis, "The gods lose their personalities in the interests of science, but bequeath to the world that survives them their personal energy and dynamism" (32–33).

Spenser refigures this mythopoeic physics into thinking about narrative: in *Mutabilitie,* recurring to intractable issues of justice and dominion, he proposes a freshly conceived temporality with which to endow his ancient and medieval personified figures, and a concomitant move from moral allegory.[13] Literary history in the middle of the twentieth century tended to find physical allegory the most trivial and eccentric of its possible levels of signification, but Irigaray's work and much recent work on the writing of science makes it possible for us to see a point to physical allegory within personification. Thus, for Spenser, the turn to elements and elemental motion in *Mutabilitie* means that he uses the elements and elemental motion to think about (a) how to make a personified character lively; (b) what it would mean for a character to commit to a temporal trajectory toward life rather than death; (c) how and why one literary element leads into another in a narrative; (d) for the last time in his career, the difficult relationship between narrative temporality and justice.

Here I consider these questions through a moment of transition: Mutabilitie's strongly forensic speech on the restless flux of the elements (*FQ* VII.vii.17–26), and its relation to the ebullient, lyrical pageant of personified months that follows it (VII.vii.27–46). Her speech on the flux of the elements includes passages like these:

> Ne is the water in more constant case [than earth];
> Whether those same on high, or these below.
> For th'Ocean moveth still, from place to place;
> And every River still doth ebb and flow.
>
> (VII.vii.20)
>
> So likewise are all watry liuing wights
> Still tost, and turned, with continuall change,
> Neuer abyding in their stedfast plights.
>
> (VII.vii.21)
>
> Therein the changes infinite beholde,
> Which to her creatures euery minute chaunce;
> Now, boyling hot: streight, friezing deadly cold:
> Now, faire sun shine, that makes all skip and daunce:
> Streight, bitter storms and balefull countenance,
> That makes them all to shiuer and to shake.
>
> (VII.vii.23)

All her arguments on elemental motion take this tack: flux is constant, in spite of material bodies' possible wishes for stasis, and the general affect evoked is hopelessness, through the trivializing of universal flux and cheapening of the elements. But this is an odd feeling tone in a philosophical poem's discourse on the elements. When Ovid, one of Mutabilitie's major precursors in philosophical poetry, speaks of universal flux through Pythagoras, the affect governing his lines is clearly that of wonder, reinforced by compassion for his auditors (*Metamorphoses* XV). When Lucretius, her greatest predecessor, represents the flux of atoms in its alarming randomness, his contemplative wonder, and his desire to free his hearers from the terrors of death, lift and warm the philosophic verse (*De rerum natura*). When Irigaray, Mutabilitie's great successor in philosophical poetic writing, speaks of the elements, she is motivated by passion for a new world in which philosophers would not so easily make Woman the unacknowledged prop of their metaphysics, a world in which women would not be oppressed, mutilated, or buried alive, in which we could figure out what justice would mean in terms of sexed or sexuate rights.

Mutabilitie, although she does not exactly lie, distorts emphasis and neglects certain facts about the elements and about creaturely life within the elements, as these occur in poetry, cosmology, encyclopedias and other kinds of writing on the natural world. When speaking of waterfowl, for instance, she leaves out facts about the nesting habits and dwellings and stable rearing of their young, well-known details of topoi concerning water and birds, and argues instead for their random restlessness: "Ne have the watry fowls a certain grange,/ Where to rest, ne in one stead do tarry;/But flitting still do fly, and still their places vary" (VII.vii.21). Mutabilitie's forensic purposes here lead her to appropriate the natural phenomena of the world to serve her own desire. Compassion for the fluxional, passionate, suffering world—a major topic of philosophical poetry—simply fails to arise. She also rejects the familiar association of mythic deities with particular elements; for her their complex associations and identifications reduce to the question of who can best Jove and the other Olympians:

So, in them all raignes *Mutabilitie;*
How-euer these, that Gods themselues do call,
Of them doe claime the rule and souerainty:
As, *Vesta*, of the fire æthereall;
Vulcan, of this, with vs so vsuall;
Ops, of the earth; and *Iuno* of the Ayre;
Neptune, of Seas; and Nymphes, of Riuers all.

For all those Riuers to me subiect are:
And all the rest, which they vsurp, be all my share. (VII.vii.26)

* * *

Mutabilitie also neglects discussion of the tempos and temporal intervals within which changes comes about, as if casting change as universal flux obviates any need for attention to temporal causation and shape. In this she differs from Irigaray and the poets alike, who understand temporality as crucial to their undertakings in cosmological and justitial speculation. A temporal interval might be the length of a few stanzas within which new and unforeseeable futures arise; a temporal interval might be the split second between dancing among masquers and its sudden disruption by a magician. Intervals like these in narrative and dramatic works always invite interpretation because they function as a gap. This sense of interval is essential also to Irigaray's sense of the subject as a process, in her work on elemental motility and on movement more generally, in her vivid evocations of relationships in which two people *vis-à-vis* honor a space between, which they traverse in an unending choreography, and in her descriptions of angels as figures for movement or the beyond or intimacy.[14] More explicitly, she talks about interval in comments on tempo from her essay on wonder in Descartes:

> It matters for "man" to find a vital speed, a growth speed that is compatible with all his senses and meanings, and for him to know how to stop in order to rest, to leave an interval between himself and the other, to look toward, to contemplate—*to wonder.* Wonder being an action that is both active and passive. The ground or inner secret of genesis, of creation? The place of the union or the alliance of power and act . . . . This first passion is indispensable not only to life but also or still to the creation of an ethics . . . . [The] other . . . should *surprise* us again and again, appear to us as *new, very different* from what we knew or what we thought he or she should be.[15]

Irigaray resurrects wonder in her readings of Plato's *Symposium* and of Descartes, but when she asks, "Is [wonder] the passion that Freud forgot?" ("Wonder," 80), she addresses herself to Freud and Lacan as well, trying to find a new temporal model of the event as an interval in which persons encounter each other, a model which could also be a model for justice. As Krzysztof Ziarek says, "she situates [psychoanalytic] desire in the context of will, intention, and teleology"—in desire we're driven to appropriate another, to fill a lack, to master the lost object—but wonder occurs in an event or advent of meeting an other, "a non-appropriative and transformative relation to the other."[16] This much might not be a surprise to readers of ancient and medieval philosophers on contemplation. More oddly, in *An Ethics of Sexual Difference* Irigaray says that "Wonder is the motivating force behind mobility in all its dimensions" (73); in encounters or meetings characterized by wonder, we experience "the point of passage between two . . . space-times or two others" (75). Wonder keeps us on the move in relation to that which is new in any encounter with an other, even an other long familiar or a non-human other, like Spenser's months and seasons.

How might we sustain the temporal phenomenon of wonder rather than desire for an object? Partly by the ceaselessness of thinking, since, for Irigaray as for writers on wonder since antiquity, wonder is an intellectual as well as an affective event. Irigaray licenses us to find in this temporality a sense of surprise—a word she uses often—as an experience of love not based on desire as Freud or Lacan would put it. She suggests that desire debases the event by turning that which is met into an object; this is what Mutabilitie does with her desire.[17] As Ziarek writes, an oedipal logic of absence-vs.-presence of a lost object "already marks a certain forgetting of the temporality of being;" desire is put into motion by a (mis)reading of being in terms of possession and lack—a logic that substantializes and objectifies the . . . temporality of being" (K. Ziarek, ¶17). The alternative form of love is wonder, which spurs mobility, and for Irigaray this is tantamount to hope in a future—a temporal phenomenon. The surprise within wonder is, for Irigaray, not an abrupt or sudden thing, but an open, sustained moment of contemplation—an event. The months *are* this kind of event temporality. The seasons and months are transformative conditions within which we dwell as the space-time of the zodiac turns. Mutabilitie wishes not to point this out when she describes the motions of the elements, but the pageant seems to assure us of the fact. One couldn't say that the objects carried by July or September, or the condensation of their energies in these human forms, are debasements of being; nor do they exude deadness. Rather they unfold the energies of mythic beings into a physics and a lexicon of the elements; they manifest the nature of the month as an *event* in which we find ourselves. Perhaps what we are given in the pageant is a generative tension between the motivating force of elemental mobility and its manifestation in emblematic objects. The poetic actions of the pageant fill up time with their mobility, and space with their personifications and objects, in a dynamic tension—the internal logic of the zodiacal calendar and of Stoic interpretation.

Mutabilitie's self-interested, unwondering exposition of elemental flux as chaotic movement and her wishful deposition of the gods of earth, air, fire, and water constitute a crucial temporal interval in which readers discover within themselves some kind of dissatisfaction, a hankering for another sense of time than the one she articulates. More exactly, the topos of elemental flux, in Mutabilitie's fashioning of it, suspends us in a brief moment of alarm or anxious fatigue at the chaotic randomness of the elements, which I think is the opposite of Irigaray's sense of surprise.[18] The forensic description of elemental motion works on its audience differently than its speaker hopes, creates a different succession of literary and justitial events. Then the arrival of the pageant functions for the reader as a reprieve from the randomness for which she argues; it allows us breathing space, what a poet might think of as expansive breathing time or caesura, for wonder. The pageant would come as the answer to a desire that Mutabilitie's stanzas on elemental flux have accidentally awakened. Retrospectively, Mutabilitie's stanzas on elemental flux become a disappointment to the reader, and the pageant an awakening of hope in a future of dwelling in the elements in some way transformed from Mutabilitie's advocacy of "changes infinite . . . / Which to her [the Earth's] creatures euery minute chaunce" (VII.-vii.23). The pageant figures do not seek stasis in any denial of the constant animating activity of the four elements; they do not represent the obsessiveness of which Angus Fletcher speaks or the phenomenal deadness of which Kenneth Gross speaks; its personifications participate in no historical tradition of psychomachic allegory with narrative pressure to unify and harmonize personified bits of a character. The pageant does provide the reader with a relief from Mutabilitie's forensic pressure, with an interval for wonder, with rectifications of her speech's assertions about the elements.

Thus of fire, Mutabilitie—who borrows from Spenser's depiction of Malbecco turned into Gealosie in a complex moral and psychomachic allegory in *The Faerie Queene* III.x—argues that although it can never be quenched, every day

> Wee see his parts, so soone as they do seuer,

To lose their heat, and shortly to decay;
So, makes himself his owne consuming pray.
Ne any liuing creatures doth he breed:
But all, that are of others bredd, doth slay;
And, with their death, his cruell life dooth feed;
Nought leauing, but their barren ashes, without seede.

(VII.vii.24)

Mutabilitie here echoes the ancients who speculated on the rage for sovereignty within any one element; she thus raises a question of justice, but it is one that she has no intention of righting, because it serves her own purpose, again unlike the great and compassionate writers on elemental strife in all centuries. But when fire appears in the pageant of months, it is understood as a force that retains its vigor yet is harnessed by a Vergilian sense of georgic labor that makes possible a human dwelling within the elements:

Then came hot *Iuly* like to fire,
That all his garments he had cast away:
Vpon a Lyon raging yet with ire
He boldly rode and made him to obay:
It was the beast that whylome did forray
The Nemæan forrest, till th'*Amphytrionide*
Him slew, and with his hide did him array;
Behinde his back a sithe, and by his side
Vnder his belt he bore a sickle circling wide.

(VII.vii.36)

The dynamic combination of fire's rage and fire's contribution to human well-being, theatrically presented, ought to arouse wonder in the reader, and is not unlike the wonder that Ariel takes delight in creating when he describes his own performance as fire and then as proffer of air and earth: "Now in the waist, the deck, in every cabin,/ I flamed amazement. Sometime I'd divide/And burn in many places; on the topmast,/The yards and bowsprit would I flame distinctly,/ Then meet and join" (1.2.197–201); then "The King's son have I landed by himself,/Whom I left cooling of the air with sighs" (1.2.221–22).[19]

It is this contemplative wonder, an experience of possible love in the meeting between oneself and the months personified, that rescues the reader from the desolating, cheapening, and uncompassionate view of Mutabilitie on elemental flux. After her speech, the pageant of months is a happy turn. Its archaism and ordered energies are made a surprise in Irigaray's sense precisely by its following upon an exhausting vision of absolute randomness. The energies of each personification make them avatars of a time, an event, and so no matter how familiar each one is, our reading encounter with it is always new.

* * *

Shakespeare's most intensive and sustained deployment of the elements occurs in the four late plays examining his work's relationship to the mythological, allegorical, and romance discourses from antiquity, the Middle Ages, and Elizabethan England: *Pericles, Cymbeline, The Winter's Tale, The Tempest.* Indeed it is largely his late-career searching of those discourses, within the early seventeenth-century sense that possibilities for mythopoeic romance are fading, and a commitment to discovering what can be preserved from earlier poetic and narrative modes during this period of nostalgia, that *cause* Shakespeare's turn to ancient philosophy's structuring of the elements and elemental motion.[20] The 1609 publication of *The Faerie Queene,* which included *Two Cantos of Mutabilitie* for the first time in print, fuels this nostalgia and instigates specific meditations from dramatists and poets. Here I take *The Tempest* as a response to the 1609 *Faerie Queene,* especially as Shakespeare read retrospectively in the light of the *Mutabilitie Cantos.* That Shakespeare read Spenser intensively, and worked Spenserian poems hard, can no longer be doubted (see note 20 below). But since *The Tempest*'s relationship to Spenser is the least articulated of his relationships to the many texts relevant to the play, it is worth mentioning here some shared elements that suggest Shakespeare uses the 1609 *Faerie Queene* as an occasion to situate himself in a specifically poetic history.

Both poem and play treat of a witch-mother with an uncouth son; Spenser's Book IV ends with cantos celebrating the world's many waters and set in the sea, which attracts to itself many marine figures and motifs—sea-nymphs, music, shape-shifting powers, numinous beings working out strategies to bring about a successful outcome for young lovers—reworked intensively in the play, where the elements of air and water come to be not only the material simples of which all things are compounded but pervasive atmospheres in which characters live and undergo mysterious changes. The titular virtue of

Spenser's Book V is Justice; its chief protagonist, like Prospero, struggles to impose repentance and social harmony on intractable populations, with the aid of a servant with superhuman powers (indeed Talus, man of iron, unsubtle, violent, remorseless, and heavy, might have served as antithetical inspiration for Ariel); its episodes, like the play, treat explicitly the difficulties of including mercy and forgiveness in the creation of justice. Both Spenser and Shakespeare consider the possibilities and difficulties of enfranchising to themselves or otherwise ordering unruly beings of an island in servitude. *Mutabilitie*'s chief story is also about justice, specifically about a possible usurpation and what judicial court would be adequate to evaluate claims to dominion, topics that Spenser weighs in Book V's trial of Duessa (another witch-mother, if we link the witch Duessa to the historical and problematically maternal Mary, Queen of Scots).

Both poets create characters who move from one element to another, characters with other than natural lineages and capacities, and freely adapt Graeco-Roman myth to this end. Mutabilitie's forensic speech, as we've seen, relies heavily on elemental flux as the basis of its claims, and this kind of temporality undergoes transformation in her subsequent pageant, which nevertheless retains a lexicon of the elements. That pageant stands between ancient and medieval static, visual representations of the seasons and months, and Jacobean masque, and in both the writers are thinking about wonder within dramatic form; Shakespeare's representation of a masque in *The Tempest* is the most explicit index to his transformation of Spenserian personification allegory.[21] Shakespeare's masque, composed with an ear to Spenser's *Mutabilitie* pageant, reverses the relationship between pageant of seasons and temporality. In Spenser, the arrival of the seasons provides wonder, relief, and the possibility of the new after Mutabilitie's devastating and alarming speech about elemental flux. In Shakespeare, the wonder awakened by the masque only partially embraces Prospero; for him wonder is a stage device, out of which he is abruptly tumbled when thought returns him to the unpredictable, unfolding history of real encounters opening before him. Wonder becomes *opposed* to the surprise of what's to come.

The Tempest famously unfolds within elements of air and water but attends as well to earth, fire, wood, all capable of marking the kind of freezing of agency that Fletcher allows us to perceive as a phenomenal deadness (Ariel pent in a cloven pine) as well as marking excesses of human agency—Prospero's exorbitant anger and abuses of power, Ariel's ravishing capacity for flight, Caliban's stubborn dedication to what he understands as his earthy essence. Once again I turn to the ways that the writer searches out the animations of personification, temporality and sequence, and the difficult relationship between narrative temporality and justice.[22]

If *The Tempest* has long provoked critics to try out various allegorical schemes, mostly unsatisfactory, this is because the play is in fact involved with allegory. But it is not, or not only, a set of layered univocal allegories, either religious or topical. Rather, it thinks out its relationship to historically specific sites of allegorical fiction and interpretation—most relevant here, the Odyssean romance-epic and its mythopoeic avatars in Spenser's romance-epic, Drayton's satires, and mythopoeic masques. It chooses as mythic allegory's most attractive form of survival not moralizing allegory and not psychomachic allegory but ancient Stoic allegory, by which the vitality and superabundant will of deities is transformed into a physics which takes the cosmos as pervaded by divine energies. This is also to say that in *The Tempest* Shakespeare plays out possibilities less like those of the allegorical life of the Red Crosse Knight and the pageant of the Seven Deadly Sins in *The Faerie Queene* I than like the mobile exuberance of Mutabilitie's pageant. Shakespeare considers, in creating *The Tempest*, how to play out in dramatic character and event the buoyant energies of Spenser's elements and their configurations in seasons, months, and days. Thus, for example, Spenser's July stanza, cited earlier, rectifies the injustice in Mutabilitie's words on fire, but July is not, as a character, engaged in any narrative action vis-à-vis another character; the characters of *The Tempest*, infused with an elemental-allegorical energy and temporality, do inhabit such a world, as Ariel does when he flames amazement at the start of Prospero's justitial action. Shakespeare must be conducting a thought experiment about what would happen if an element became a character, with an elemental impulse to expand agency everywhere, thus transforming agency like Ariel's into a drive toward dominion like Prospero's.

One of Shakespeare's answers is that such a character has encounters, every one of which involves choices about justice. It might be useful to say that what Spenser presents to the reader as an event in an Irigarayan sense becomes, in *The Tempest*, an encounter, in Roland Greene's sense:

> An encounter is discontinuous in time, inolving by implication two distinct phases . . . . Encounters are two-staged events: something happens, and then it is counted, recounted, interpreted. Further, 'encounters' have a palpable investment in alterity because the first sense of the term, going back to its vernacular

> roots in Old French, is adversarial: at its most basic level an encounter happens between and a subject and an another who are, and go, against one another.[23]

From this point of view, Spenser's months and seasons begin to look less like representations of change and more like a brilliant series of present instants; they do not in themselves face toward what Irigaray would call "the advent of a meeting" (*Forgetting of Air* 18). This is the very point of wonder, which is "the bridge, the stasis, the moment of *in-stance* . . . . Where I am no longer in the past and not yet in the future" (*Ethics* 75). The elements' relevance to justice remains insofar as they are witnesses in the contest between Mutabilitie and Jove, and insofar as details of their descriptions resolve thematic knots from earlier sites in the epic; but Shakespeare transforms them in his play by attributing agency and desire to them. Thus Prospero is roughly analogous to the *Dia* or god of ancient Stoic allegorical interpretation, and he would like to extend his powers over others; but he finds his will circumscribed and partially thwarted by the characters with whom he has encounters, characters who have agency and will of their own, like the elements that hold one another's powers in check and so thwart his hopes for what would count as a different kind of justitial resolution, that is, his own dominion. If all the humans did repent, and if Caliban were transformed into what Prospero would think a civilized being, and if Ariel would stay with him and love him, we might have something more recognizable as a moral or psychomachic allegory. Shakespeare's choosing precisely not those resolutions is, among other things, a choice about what to retain from earlier traditions of allegory, a choice that conserves the issues of temporality and justice implicit in Stoic elemental allegory, when it is inflected by the possibility of encounters between beings. Shakespeare's own encounter with *Mutabilitie* would amount to the difference between, on the one hand, Spenser's brilliant procession of discrete months and seasons, which taken all together form a cyclic temporality; and on the other hand the tensions and improvisations of act and feeling between Ariel and Prospero, or among Iris, Ceres, Juno in the masque, encounters that open history to a creative, undetermined future. In both Spenser and Shakespeare, the unpredictability or surprise of event and encounter makes justice by denying the will to power, the specific culminations that the pageant-summoners, Mutabilitie and Prospero, hope to institute.[24]

Elemental mobility, of which Irigaray and Spenser make so much, is central to *The Tempest* too, most obviously but not solely in the figure of Ariel; in this context I return to Angus Fletcher on the daemonic. For Fletcher, the daemonic becomes invariably a fixity of character, the daemonic agent hardly an agent at all. Thus even when he does turn to ethical issues I've linked here with a tradition growing from Stoic allegorical interpretation, Fletcher sees them as diminishments of an *a priori* complex humanity:

> Pride, strength, and the struggle for power . . . comprise a unity of concerns that frequently demonstrate in the clearest possible way the daemonic character of allegorical agency. How many modern allegories take up the problem of political power directly . . . . In none of these is the element of the miraculous far from the surface. They dramatize the tyrannical spellbinder's absolute hold over the common man. An unnatural Faustian energy drives their heroes and villains. (54–55)

Or again, "The daemon of a man is his fate, his Moira, his fortune, his lot, whatever is specifically divided up and allotted to *him*. Through the working of destiny he is narrowed to the function represented by his daemon" (59–60). There is a logical problem in thinking this way *necessarily* about the characters of any allegory, since it seems to imply that a character starts out by inviting us to think of her as a person with psychic complexity and temporality—as a subject—then turns out to be a reduced person, analogous to an obsessive or compulsive or a possessed person. But here I pursue a different path, about the daemonic as a principle of movement-between, rather than a unitary reductive force within an individual person.

It is a commonplace of work on Irigaray to say that her activation of the presocratic elements allows her to propose a new materialism in relation to gender; but for readers of fictions her focus on elemental mobility is a form of the daemonic that differs usefully from Fletcher's.[25] Indeed it is almost contrary to Fletcher's. Irigaray figures in dozens of ways the value, the freedom, the potential of movement, so extensively that we might think Hermes her tutelary deity, Ariel her good genius. She highlights the ethical relevance of the space traversed in movement, especially when it is an intersubjective space of two beings vis-à-vis. She thinks about the space of the airy and watery elements, the kinds of motion possible and suitable to each. She speaks much of angels as mediators: "The angel is that which unceasingly *passes through the envelope(s) or container(s)*, goes from one side to the other, reworking every deadline, changing every decision, thwarting all repetition."[26] Daemons, as David Farrell Krell reminds us in his work on Homer, are mediators between heaven and earth; they are uncanny and cunning; they reveal what has been concealed, what perhaps ought to remain concealed, like figures in allegory. Homer figures them sometimes with veils, for example, the veils that Calypso and Ino use in their relations with Odysseus.[27] A report from Aetius says that there are *daemons* or powers in all the elements, and John Sallis speculates that this must be "precisely what makes it possible for things to come forth in their manifestness."[28] It is certainly the case that philosophers from the ancients through Heidegger and Irigaray take air as that element which most perfectly enables things to come forth, a point brought home in Shakespeare's masque. (This fact about air must also underwrite all epic descents from heaven, beginning with those of Hermes, and including Hal's airborne horsemanship which creates an interval of wonder in Vernon.) Spenser's Mutabilitie is daemonic insofar as she moves between earth and heaven, making encounters happen. Less surprisingly, Spenser's veiled goddess Nature, before whom Mutabilitie argues her case, is a daemon, mediating between earth and heaven and their respective temporalities of flux and eternity. Daemons, as the example of Nature can remind us, thus mediate between shapes of time as well as between one place and another.

It is precisely elemental motion as the daemonic that Shakespeare brings into drama from Spenser. Ariel is, above all, clearly daemonic in all Irigaray's and Krell's senses. He moves among air, water, earth, and fire; he brings about encounters; he loves to awaken wonder in the audiences for whom he performs, including himself; he makes possible Prospero's melioration of a Jovian rancor; he craves the freedom of agency for which Irigaray's figure is motion in air; he perhaps sends the Italians home with his "auspicious gales" (5.1.314), as Calypso had sent Odysseus in another poem of the sea and of what Roland Greene calls 'island logic;' he is uncanny and cunning. (These are exactly the aspects in which he differs from Shakespeare's earlier avatar of the fleet spirit of motion, Puck.) Perhaps we ought to think of allegory in *The Tempest* as a daemonic, elemental process of metamorphosis to which the characters are exposed on the island, event or encounters that happen between or to characters, rather than trying to instantiate allegory in a character who is solid; to do the latter would be to transform event and wonder into mere object and desire.[29] Then Ariel's flights and songs (sweet airs, as Caliban calls them), and performances and winds would figure such encounters, offering all whom he touches—not just wicked brothers but Prospero himself—occasions for acknowledging their parts in creating justice within the temporal unfolding of elemental life. Prospero as Medea-like magician thinks of his powers as daemonic.[30] If the daemonic is understood in the Irigarayan sense rather than Fletcher's sense, then it is not too much to imagine that Caliban in his elemental hybridity, and even Sycorax, need to be refigured, especially by Prospero, not as monster but as daemon, a power which he may never understand in itself but in relation to which holds his future. (The 'monstrous,' Irigaray suggests, is "that which hampers the possibility of a new age" ["Sexual Difference," 15].) In the words "This thing of darkness I/Acknowledge mine" (5.1.275–76) and his concomitant release of Ariel "to the elements," Prospero commits himself to a riskier, more transformative future than he seems to have planned, by loosing his command over air itself to a sense of commitment to a daemon of another and heavier element.

The functions of the daemonic in this play coalesce in the betrothal masque of 4.1, where Ariel, one daemon of air and water, in his capacity as stage manager, summons or brings into manifestation Iris, another daemon of the same elements, to summon and bestow blessings from maternal goddesses on the young lovers. Shakespeare's Iris, "many-coloured messenger" of Juno (4.1.76), is daemonic in both Homeric and Irigarayan senses; she is also, as Stephen Orgel and John Gillies remind us, daughter of Thaumas or Wonder, wife to Zephyrus, one of the Winds (*Tempestates*, related to *tempus*, time or temporality, and *tempestas,* weather), and sister to the harpies, whom Hesiod and Homer associate with wind and storm: a strong family among elemental motions.[31] Socrates had observed, as Plato tells, that "he [i.e., Hesiod] was a good genealogist who made Iris the daughter of Thaumas."[32] And in *The Faerie Queene* V.iii.25, Spenser describes Iris in a simile about the power of the true Florimell to inspire wonder, "As when the daughter of *Thaumantes* faire,/Hath in a watry cloud displayd wide/Her goodly bow, which paints the liquid ayre;/That all men wonder at her colours pride." All these feminine marine daemons owe their force in the Renaissance to maternal sea-nymphs who stage scenes of instruction, most notably Homer's and Statius' Thetis and Virgil's Cyrene, in *Georgics* 4.[33]

I said above that some daemons mediate experiences of temporality, like the air in which things come into being or manifest themselves; we might now add to air the water of *The Tempest*, salty medium of transformation, in which things come into being but keep themselves undisclosed, like Ferdinand's father in "Full fathom five," or like the bliss within the clouds ready to drop riches, which haunt

Caliban. I think this is why some daemonic moments involve maternal presences, as when Odysseus is reborn from the sea, salt-encrusted and naked, with the help of the veil of Ino, the sea-nymph who stands in for Calypso, or when it is fitting that an august but nonetheless maternal Dame Nature judge between Mutabilitie and Jove. Shakespeare picks up this Spenserian temporal link between elemental daemonic motion and elemental maternity in his late plays. In light of Hermione's maternal blessing on Perdita near the end of *The Winter's Tale,* in light of the amniotic gestation amidst the uncanny sounds of the ocean that Pericles imagines for Thaisa ("belching whale/And humming water," 3.1.62–3) from *Pericles*, in light of the knowledge that these plays come just after 1608, when Shakespeare's own mother died—I cannot help hearing in the songs of the maternal spirits' songs in *The Tempest* traces of a benign maternal presence. Now much has been made of the ways that the presence of Sycorax, monstrous mother, pervades the play. Janet Adelman beautifully demonstrates how often Prospero incorporates the maternal body in order to control maternal functions of birth, gestation, origination.[34] In this he is not unlike the Zeus who swallows wives and children because he fears their future power, or the *Dia* of the Stoics, who pervades all things and can therefore claim the names even of Hera and Demeter. Ted Hughes and Marina Warner hear in the roars, curses, howls, confused noise, and sea-churning of the play testimony to the fact that the island has all along belonged to Sycorax.[35]

Such comments on the ghostly demarcations of the lost Sycorax are among the most moving and convincing aspects of work on *The Tempest*, but they comprise only part of the story about absent mothers; I think that the masculine/feminine Ariel, Iris and the figures of Juno and Ceres sing the wishes of that figure who, as Stephen Orgel suggested, keeps slipping from view in the play: Miranda's mother, "Prospero's Wife."[36] It was Miranda's mother, says Prospero, who assured him that the child she was carrying was his own: "Thy mother was a piece of virtue, and/She said thou wast my daughter" (1.2.55–6); later in the same scene, Miranda defends her grandmother, Prospero's own mother, in the same way, after hearing about Prospero's wicked brother: "I should sin/To think but nobly of my grandmother:/Good wombs have borne bad sons" (1.2.118–20). Years after the deaths of these two maternal figures, an air of some benign, and not only malevolent, maternal intention hovers over the island. Caliban senses them: perhaps "the sounds and sweet airs" that "give delight and hurt not," sounds whose source must be Ariel, are a way for Shakespeare to suggest that it is not only water but also air, or water combined with air, that make a maternal element; Caliban's exquisite apprehension of maternal presence in those airs may just as well be from Miranda's mother and grandmother as from his own mother. The sounds and clouds and riches that Caliban senses or dreams, all around him like an atmosphere but not his to command, elicit his wonder as a relationship to knowledge which does not involve mastery. It is both the elemental nature of the percept (atmosphere, noise, clouds) and the necessary space between Caliban and percept (it is not an *object* toward which he can move, which he can grasp or reel in) that make his response one of wonder. So it is not accidental that thoughts of a benign maternal presence can lead to the airy daemonic spirits of *The Tempest.* Thus Caliban's most famous speech, the one in which he speaks of these airs and the clouds that promise riches, begins with the words of biblical angels, the daemons of another myth: "Be not afeard" (3.2.133–41); later, as Iris, Ariel will say, "Of her society [i.e., that of Venus]/Be not afraid" (4.1.91–2); Ariel can sing of transformation by the amniotic waters of the sea, giving a painful knowledge to Ferdinand in mysteriously consoling form. As Thomas Bishop says, "it is the self's relation to the origins, force, and significance of its knowledge of the world that is at stake in these moments [of wonder evoked by theatrical spectacle]."[37]

This sense of a world of apprehension within which the subject dwells but which cannot be known directly either as another subject or as an object, is precisely what Irigaray elaborates when she considers the psychic structures elicited by *in utero* life:

> Within her womb, an amnion and a placenta, a whole world with its layers, its circuits, its vessels, its nourishing pathways, etc., a whole world of invisible relations that adheres to her womb, that takes place in her womb . . . . But this world is not to be confused with her . . . . they have never really met each other face to face, as if their mouth-to-mouth, mouth-to-ear were still mediated by an umbilicus.[38]

In the same essay, Irigaray carries forward the sense of the placenta as a mediating veil (it mediates nourishment and waste, for example, in a literal pregnancy) in order to work toward the idea of angels (what I've been calling, in this context discussing literary allegory, the daemonic) as mediators, thus something of the mother as making possible the imagining of mediating figures:

> Yet the whiteness of angels, their semitransparence, their lightness, the question of their sex, their purity (in the Rilkean sense: as pure as animals), could all these attributes not be a reappearance or recollection of that [i.e. the placenta] by which and thanks to which messages from the beyond are transmitted? Beyond what? The ultimate veil. Whence they would emerge. Always coming from beyond the horizon. And yet the element traversed would not be opaque or very colored, but rather airy, allowing free passage—like the angel. Who is sent, or comes, from heaven, on a mission, to do a job. ("Belief Itself," 35–36)

Of course many times throughout her career, Irigaray has spoken of fluids, especially water, as a mediating element associated with the maternal. In this context it seems entirely appropriate that two of Homer's daemons from the *Odyssey*, Calypso and Ino, use veils in their dealings with Odysseus, especially in their sending him through water to rebirth. Ariel too has been a water-nymph early in his mission—Prospero commands him, "Go, make thyself like a nymph o'th'sea" (1.2.301)—in order that he may sing to Ferdinand "Come unto these yellow sands" and "Full fathom five" (1.2.374–405), and water nymphs are summoned in the masque to dance with the reapers, in one of its many figures of harmonizing the elements. All of these moments mark, to my mind, a trace of the benign maternal, a counter-weight to the split-off malevolence of Sycorax circulating like a contagious air through the island.

But if Ariel obliquely figures a mother, what happens to our other sense that Ariel forms part of Prospero's reconstituted family, as a child along with Miranda and Caliban?[39] Even if Ariel *could* be played to show a protomaternal tenderness toward the suffering creatures on the isle, he is more often played to show sibling rivalry. But what if making Ariel his child is one aspect of Prospero's mistaking of his nature, as he mistakes or simply cannot find the right terms for Caliban's nature? Then Ariel could bespeak Miranda's mother and grandmother; for Prospero, Ariel might be the feminine presence he could not master or save earlier, in the persons of his mother and his wife. Then *Prospero* could be the child in a *fort-da* game, hoping to hang on to his omnipotence or believe in his own magical mastery, by sending Ariel beyond, up and out, then summoning him back, again and again. But Ariel is not an object of desire, in the reifying way of which Irigaray has spoken; he finally insists on being a subject—not of desire, but of wonder. I think this means, in the context of *Mutabilitie* and *The Tempest*, that Ariel insists on being a character not in a moralized allegory, nor even in the neoplatonic allegory that characterized real court masques, but a character in an elemental allegory of the kind envisaged by the Stoics.[40] The elements and elemental movement remain fluid and unpredictable even to Prospero (the masque content may even have been composed by Ariel), and his disgruntlement and interruption of the dance point us toward his new, open-ended future.

Irigaray links the maternal to angelic motion and veils through intensive engagements with Freud's *Beyond the Pleasure Principle* and Derrida's reading of Freud in *The Post Card*. For our purposes, it is enough to open the possibility that the child experiences a metamorphosis from one kind of temporality to another through the changing relationship to the mother in birth. This would make the maternal just one instance of the daemonic, within allegory and fiction, as the moving agency from one form of temporality to another.

NOTES

1. Luce Irigaray, *The Forgetting of Air in Martin Heidegger*, trans. Mary Beth Mader (Austin: University of Texas Press, 1999), 2.

2. Luce Irigaray, *Marine Lover of Friedrich Nietzsche*, trans. Gillian C. Gill (New York: Columbia University Press, 1991), 13–14.

3. This fragment is cited by Theophrastus in *The Opinions of the Physicists*, Fragment A2, which is in turn preserved by Simplicius in his *Commentary on Aristotle's Physics*. See also Michel Serres, from whom I borrow the phrase "mutual imperialism" and the citation from Anaximander, "Anaximander: A Founding Name in History," trans. Roxanne Lapidus, in David C. Jacobs, ed., *The Presocratics after Heidegger* (Albany: SUNY Press, 1999), 135–44, and for a careful discussion of the steps of Anaximander's argument, Jonathan Barnes, *The Presocratic Philosophers* (London and New York: Routledge, 1979), 19–37.

4. Christine Battersby, *The Phenomenal Woman: Feminist Metaphysics and the Patterns of Identity* (London: Routledge, 1998), 99.

5. Irigaray, "Divine Women," (1984), in *Sexes and Genealogies*, trans. Gillian C. Gill (New York: Columbia University Press, 1993), 66.

6. Gordon Teskey makes use of this dichotomy of matter and form in his argument about allegory, e.g. in his chapter about Spenser's *Mutabilitie Cantos*; see *Allegory and Violence* (Ithaca: Cornell University Press, 1996), 168–88. Teskey's book focuses on and generalizes from neoplatonic traditions of dualistic thinking about matter, but does not much address earlier kinds of allegorical thinking, as he now observes (in correspondence).

7. In this passage on the newly daemonic Hal like the daemonic god Mercury, Shakespeare draws from Spenser's description, in *The Faerie Queene* I.xi, of the Redcrosse Knight's resurrection after immersion in healing waters, during his battle

with the dragon. Shakespeare's Vernon says "I saw young Harry, with his beaver on,/His cuisses on his thighs, gallantly armed,/Rise from he ground like feathered Mercury,/And vaulted with such ease into his seat/As if an angel dropped down from the clouds" (4.1.104–08; cited from David Bevington's edition *The Complete Works of Shakespeare*, 4th ed. [Chicago: University of Chicago Press, 1997]; below I cite *Pericles* from the same edition). See also Philippa Berry's book on vitalism in Shakespeare, *Shakespeare's Feminine Endings: Disfiguring Death in the Tragedies* (London: Routledge, 1999); Catherine Gimelli Martin, *The Ruins of Allegory: "Paradise Lost" and the Metamorphosis of Epic Convention* (Durham: Duke University Press, 1998).

8. Angus Fletcher, *Allegory: The Theory of a Symbolic Mode* (Ithaca: Cornell University Press, 1964), 40.

9. Kenneth Gross, "The Postures of Allegory," in *Edmund Spenser: Essays on Culture and Allegory*, ed. Jennifer Klein Morrison and Matthew Greenfield (Aldershot, England: Ashgate, 2000), 169.

10. Thus Freud: "The projected creations of primitive men resemble the personifications constructed by creative writers; for the latter externalise in the form of separate individuals the opposing instinctual impulses struggling within them" (*Totem and Taboo*, trans. James Strachey [London: Pelican, 1955], 121n.3). Julia Kristeva cites this passage in her own discussion of personification as a form of projection, developing ideas of Melanie Klein's, in *Powers of Horror: An Essay on Abjection*, trans. Leon S. Roudiez (New York: Columbia University Press, 1982), 60–61.

Fletcher's sense of allegorical personification is also shaped by his acute mid-century awareness of the consolidation of political power in the hands of tyrants and demagogues (whose analogues we shall see when we consider Mutabilitie's and Prospero's drive to power), whose susceptibility to obsession, compulsion, and something spookily like possession would have been strikingly apparent through radio and television. He is also influenced by what the Romantics and various kinds of Gothic writers made of premodern allegory, as conversation with John Watkins leads me to think.

11. I owe my understanding of Stoic exegesis to Jon Whitman, *Allegory: The Dynamics of an Ancient and Medieval Technique* (Cambridge, Mass.: Harvard University Press, 1987), 31–46 and passim; Robert Lamberton, *Homer the Theologian: Neoplatonic Allegorical Reading and the Growth of the Epic Tradition* (Berkeley: University of California Press, 1986); Michael Murrin's wonderful chapter "The Goddess of Air" (on Hera) in his *The Allegorical Epic: Essays in Its Rise and Decline* (Chicago: University of Chicago Press, 1980), 3–25; Félix Buffière, *Les mythes d'Homère et la pensée grecque* (Paris: Les Belles Lettres, 1956), 79–186 and *passim*. Don Cameron Allen gives an enormous amount of useful publication history and paraphrase of interpreters available to Renaissance readers, but does not quite know what to do with the materialism of allegorical physics, in *Mysteriously Meant: The Rediscovery of Pagan Symbolism and Allegorical Interpretation in the Renaissance* (Baltimore: Johns Hopkins Press, 1970), for example, 85, 201–3. In the latter pages he discusses the Renaissance print history and popularity of Cicero's *De natura deorum*, which both Spenser and Shakespeare could easily have known and which vividly describes the Stoic understanding of the relationship between divinity and physics.

12. Lamberton, *Homer the Theologian*, 265.

13. Literary-historical and intellectual-historical treatments of value for their synopses of elemental systems from the ancients and descriptions of instances in Spenser's epic include Jon Quitslund's recent *Spenser's Supreme Fiction: Platonic Natural Philosophy and "The Faerie Queene"* (Toronto: University of Toronto Press, 2001), especially 162–76; S. K. Heninger, *Touches of Sweet Harmony: Pythagorean Cosmology and Renaissance Poetics* (San Marino, CA: Huntington Library, 1974), which focuses on the mathematics and geometry of the elements; James Nohrnberg, *The Analogy of "The Faerie Queene"* (Princeton: Princeton University Press, 1976), 583–86 and passim; Patrick Grant, entry for "elements" in *The Spenser Encyclopedia* (Toronto: University of Toronto Press, 1990); James Carscallen, "The Goodly Frame of Temperance: The Metaphor of Cosmos in *The Faerie Queene*, Book II," in *Essential Articles for the Study of Edmund Spenser*, ed. A. C. Hamilton (Hamden, CT: Archon Books, 1972), 347–65.

14. See, for example, her essay "Place, Interval: A Reading of Aristotle, *Physics* IV," in *An Ethics of Sexual Difference*, trans. Carolyn Burke and Gillian C. Gill (Ithaca: Cornell University Press, 1993), 34–55, and "Belief Itself," in *Sexes and Genealogies*, 23–53.

15. Irigaray, "Wonder: A Reading of Descartes, *The Passions of the Soul*," in *Ethics*, 73–74. To Irigaray's discussion should be added T. G. Bishop's analysis of wonder in Descartes, Plato, Aristotle, and Longinus, in *Shakespeare and the Theatre of Wonder* (Cambridge: Cambridge University Press, 1996), 1–12, 17–41.

16. Krzysztof Ziarek, "Love and the Debasement of Being: Irigaray's Revisions of Lacan and Heidegger," *Postmodern Culture* 10, 1 (1999), ¶ 16. URL: http://www.muse.jhu.edu/journals/pmc/v010/10.1ziarek.html.

17. Turning a person into an object or into matter and then debasing it is what Teskey argues that allegory *tout court* does; see his moving chapter from *Allegory and Violence*, "Personification and Capture: Francesca da Rimini" (1–31).

18. On wonder, surprise, and temporality, see Ewa Plonowska Ziarek, "Toward a Radical Female Imaginary: Temporality and Embodiment in Irigaray's Ethics," *Diacritics* 28, 1 (1998): 60–75.

19. Citations come from *The Tempest*, ed. Stephen Orgel (Oxford: Oxford University Press, 1987).

20. For a rationale on linking these four plays in a chronological arc that ends with *The Tempest*, see Simon Palfrey, *Late Shakespeare: A New World of Words* (Oxford: Clarendon Press, 1997), 31–32, 138–68; on early seventeenth-century drama's nostalgia for late medieval and Elizabethan romance, see Richard Hillman, *Intertextuality and Romance in Renaissance Drama: The Staging of Nostalgia* (New York: St. Martin's Press, 1992, and Margaret Tudeau-Clayton, *Jonson, Shakespeare, and Early Modern Virgil* [Cambridge: Cambridge University Press, 1998). On nostalgia in seventeenth-century Spenserians, see Michelle O'Callaghan, *The "Shepheard's Nation": Jacobean Spenserians and Early Stuart Political Culture, 1612–1625* (Oxford: Clarendon Press, 2000).

21. Shakespeare also thinks about personification, and enables later discourses to think about the politics of personification, in his engagement with texts on the new world, especially their personification tropes of her. See John Gillies, "The Figure of the New World in *The Tempest*," in *"The Tempest" and Its Travels*, 180–200.

22. In the thick of so much recent work on Shakespeare as a man of the theatre, see arguments about his purposive situating of himself as a poet, for example, Julia Lupton, *Afterlives of the Saints: Hagiography, Typology and Renaissance Literature* (Stanford: Stanford University Press, 1996), 197–206; Theresa Krier, *Birth Passages: Maternity and Nostalgia, Antiquity to Shakespeare* (Ithaca: Cornell University Press, 2001), 139–64; Patrick Cheney, "Shakespeare's Sonnet 106, Spenser's National Epic, and Counter-Petrarchism," *English Literary Renaissance* 31, 3 (2001): 331–64, especially 332 n.3, for a survey of studies on the relationship between Spenser and Shakespeare's work; Cheney, book in progress, *Shakespeare's Scattered Poems: The Un-Making of the National Poet-Playwright, 1593–1640*; Colin Burrow, "Life and Work in Shakespeare's Poems," *Proceedings of the British Academy* 97 (1998):15–50, and his Introduction to Shakespeare's *Complete Sonnets and Poems* (Oxford: Oxford University Press, 2002), esp. 1–5. Before these, A. Kent Hieatt argued for the importance of Shakespeare's sense of himself as a poet in relation to Spenser, in "The Genesis of Shakespeare's *Sonnets*: Spenser's *Ruines of Rome: by Bellay*," *PMLA* 98 (1983): 800–14, and "*Cymbeline* and the Intrusion of Lyric into Romance Narrative: *Sonnets*, "A Lover's Complaint, Spenser's *Ruins of Rome*," in *Unfolded Tales: Essays on Renaissance Romance*, ed. George M. Logan and Gordon Teskey (Ithaca: Cornell University Press, 1989), 998–118; and before Hieatt, W. B. C. Watkins, *Shakespeare and Spenser* (Princeton: Princeton University Press, 1950).

23. Roland Greene, "Island Logic," in "*The Tempest*" *and its Travels*, ed. Peter Hulme and William H. Sherman (Philadelphia: University of Pennsylvania Press, 2000), 139. On "island logic" in a different register, see Palfrey, *Late Shakespeare*, 138–45.

24. On the will to mastery see Tudeau-Clayton, *Jonson, Shakespeare and Early Modern Virgil*, 194–244 and passim.

25. To my knowledge, Irigaray speaks of the daemonic in its Greek context only in "Sorcerer Love: A Reading of Plato, *Symposium*, 'Diotima's Speech,' " in *Ethics*, 20–33. Elsewhere she uses not Diotima's example of Eros, but biblical images of angel and spirit. I discuss Diotima's famous words on Eros as daemon in "Psychic Deadness in Allegory: Spenser's House of Mammon and Attacks on Linking," in *Imagining Death in Spenser and Milton*, ed. Elizabeth Jane Bellamy, Patrick Cheney, and Michael Schoenfeldt (Palgrave, 2003).

26. Irigaray, "Sexual Difference," in *Ethics*, 15.

27. David Farrell Krell, "Kalypso: Homeric Concealments after Nietzsche, Heidegger, Derrida, and Lacan," in *The Presocratics after Heidegger*, ed. David C. Jacobs (Albany: SUNY Press, 1999), 101–34.

28. John Sallis, "Doubles of Anaximenes," in *The Presocratics after Heidegger*, 151.

29. Still, it would be possible to take a personification as consolidating processes rather than objects. Thus Palfrey suggests of Caliban that in him "Shakespeare refines the analogical processes which, in all the romances, allow single moments or characters to stand for a complex community or cultural transformation. Caliban embodies the processes . . . that are narrated as having preceded him: he makes tangible the engagement of political discourse with origins" (*Late Shakespeare*, 155). If we followed this line of thought, we would also have to work out how or whether multiples—of historical processes, or of many peoples—are condensed in a unitary

being in a way that doesn't create more problems than it solves. Spenser's Irena presents us with this problem; she is a unitary embodiment of a nation only in a hopeful sense, or a way that displays the failure of her kind of personification. Does this nonce formation of Irish peoples, histories, regions, and issues illuminate or obscure the problems that Spenser addresses in his book of Justice? Irena perhaps fails as a personification of a multiple (and may be meant to fail), precisely because her human boundary or outline is so firm; Caliban succeeds as coalescence of a multiple precisely because of the role of the elements in his constitution as a character. Elizabeth Fowler's work on social person as defined in legal and political discourses offers new ways to consider the work of personification. See "The Rhetoric of Political Forms: Social Person and the Criterion of Fit in Colonial Law, *Macbeth*, and *The Irish Masqve at Covrt*," in *Form and Reform in Renaissance England: Essays in Honor of Barbara Lewalski*, ed. Amy Boesky and Mary Thomas Crane (London and Cranbury, NJ: Associated University Presses, 2000): "one motive of ethnographic writing in the period is the project of making a coherent *collective person* . . . out of populations in order to constitute a unified object of study" (76). But Caliban is also a screen for the actions and projections of other characters; this makes him both allegorical constellation and suffering subject. "Like an embodied roar," Palfrey says, "Caliban is always a process, simultaneously, of becoming, ending, suffering, and punishing, agent and object symbiotically, with all the violence such collapsing binaries can muster" (155).

30. This point comes from Stephen Orgel's introduction to his edition, 47–48.

31. Orgel's introduction to the play, 47–48; Gillies, "Shakespeare's Virginian Masque," *English Literary History* 53 (1986), 673–707, here 686–89; see other strong discussions of the play's masque in Tudeau-Clayton, *Jonson, Shakespeare*, and Palfrey, *Late Shakespeare*, 250–64.

32. Plato, *Theaetetus* 155d, trans. F. M. Cornford, in *Plato: The Collected Dialogues*, ed. Edith Hamilton and Huntington Cairns (Princeton: Princeton University Press, 1961), 860.

33. For general discussion of these figures, though not in the direction of maternity nor the daemonic that I suggest here, see Laura M. Slatkin, *The Power of Thetis: Allusion and Interpretation in the Iliad* (Berkeley: University of California Press, 1991); Andrew Wallace, "Placement, Gender, Pedagogy: Virgil's Fourth Georgic in Print," forthcoming in *Renaissance Quarterly*.

34. Janet Adelman, *Suffocating Mothers: Fantasies of Maternal Origin in Shakespeare's Plays, "Hamlet" to "The Tempest"* (London: Routledge, 1992), 237–38.

35. Ted Hughes, *Shakespeare and the Goddess of Complete Being* (New York: Farrar Straus Giroux,1992), 382: "Sycorax . . . is still everywhere, like the natural pressure of the island's atmosphere. Prospero's statement that she died is little more than a figure of speech: the island . . . is hers." Warner cites this passage in her own essay " 'The foul witch' and Her 'freckled whelp': Circean Muations in the New World," in *"The Tempest" and Its Travels*, 97–113.

36. Stephen Orgel, "Prospero's Wife," *Representations* 8 (1984): 1–13, rpt. in *Representing the English Renaissance*, ed. Stephen Greenblatt (Berkeley: University of California Press, 1988), 217–30.

37. Bishop, *Shakespeare's Theatre of Wonder*, 31. See also Irigaray, "Wonder" and "Belief Itself," in *Sexes and Genalogies*, trans. Gillian C. Gill (New York: Columbia University Press, 1993).

38. Luce Irigaray, "Belief Itself," 33–34.
39. Orgel describes this family vividly: "the witch Sycorax and her monster child Caliban, who is so often and so disturbingly like the other wicked child, the usurping young brother Antonio; the good child-wife Miranda, the obedient Ariel, the adolescent and libidinous Ferdinand" (18).
40. Thomas Bishop, *Shakespeare's Theatre of Wonder*, notes that masques, so often based on a neoplatonic metaphysic, created a "clarity of image that smoothes the surface and points recognition all one way" (176), but that in *The Tempest* masque, "the smooth annunciation of image [Prospero] desires is revealed not as a hierophantic transparency, but as a figurative recompense covering the intuition of a basic flaw" (177).

GORDON TESKEY

"And therefore as a stranger give it welcome": Courtesy and Thinking

This essay uses Hamlet's and his companions' first encounter with the Ghost as a model for thinking, and traces its implications for allegorical thinking, chiefly in *The Faerie Queene* VI, through Heidegger's work on thinking. As in Spenserian Courtesy, thinking in Heidegger does not seize the object or dive into its center: it moves into nearness with the otherness of the stranger. The model of the unknown to which thought is directed is not the physical object, like a tool, the union of matter with form: the model of the unknown to which thought is directed is a person. The first claim of this essay about *The Faerie Queene* is that Spenser is not primarily a narrative poet but a poet whose concern is to think. Spenser thinks in subtle, allusive, indirect, and intuitive ways about problems too complex to be dealt with in the isolating, linear fashion with which human problems are usually met. The second claim of the essay, therefore, is that for Spenser thinking is an encounter with the strange to which courtesy is the key.

THE WORDS IN MY TITLE, "And therefore as a stranger give it welcome," are spoken in the last scene of the first act of *Hamlet.* The time is shortly before dawn—"the glow-worm scents the matin to be near" (90)—and the ghost, having observed this, has just gone to ground, leaving the Prince of Denmark with the injunction to remember and revenge.[1] Hamlet rejoins his companions and swears them to secrecy. Not content with a merely verbal oath, he demands that they swear on his sword. Marcellus is offended: "We have sworn, my Lord, already" (147). But Hamlet insists and the ghost, whom they—and, indeed, we—think has departed, startlingly reinforces this demand, crying from the earth, "Swear by his *sword*!" (161; my emphasis). At this, an astonished Horatio utters the gentlemanly oath, "O day and night but this is wondrous strange!" (164), to which Hamlet replies, "And therefore as a stranger give it welcome." With his usual practice of arresting others' words, Hamlet torments a predicate adjective into a personal noun: what Horatio vaguely designates as *strange* becomes on Hamlet's lips a *stranger*. It is a mild reproof, reflecting the prince's instinctive regard for the otherness of others: treat the ghost as a person, not as a thing: "as a stranger give it welcome." It is a courtesy to do so.

The verses Hamlet speaks immediately following this are better known: "There are more things in heaven and earth, Horatio,/Than are dreamt of in your philosophy." This remark invites us to place the comment on strangeness and strangers in the context of philosophy, or rather, more broadly, in the context of thinking. Thinking is not to be restricted to the calculative grasping of things. Nor is thinking to be understood as *theoria*, the accurate representation of what stands before the eye of the mind. Thinking is to be understood as an encounter with the strange as a stranger. Such an encounter will be different from the traditional scene of thinking, in which the solitary subject grasps, handles, and manipulates conceptual objects. The language of the *concept*—L. *conceptum*, past participle of *concipio* "to take or lay hold of, to take in, to take to oneself, to receive, etc.," Lewis and Short; cf. Gr. *prosecheia*; Ger. *Begriff*—is a metaphorics of grasping. Instead, thinking is to be understood on a different metaphorical scene: that in which one moves into the presence of the unknown as if the unknown were not an object but rather another subject, a stranger. On this scene, accordingly, the metaphorical model for thought is no longer the grasping of a thing but the exercising of courtesy. Such courtesy does not take possession, nor does it invade the object to discover what it is in its essence, so that a definition, an imposing of limits, can be formed. Courtesy invites a partial disclosure and opens itself in turn to attention from the other, showing a welcoming openness to the strange. Courtesy does not seize the object or dive into its center: it moves into nearness with the otherness of the stranger. The model of the unknown to which thought is directed is not the physical object, like a tool, the union of matter with form: the model of the unknown to which thought is directed is a person.

This model of going near to an unknown and yet attentive other is a significant change of perspective when we reflect on the thought-character of allegory as a literary form that represents concepts as persons. For the allegorical personification, like the structure of the person on which it is metaphorically based, discloses some meaning while always holding more in reserve—this reserve being, ultimately, the truth of the system as a whole. We read *The Faerie Queene* with a patient openness that allows for this reserve, not seeking to grasp the truth of the whole or to penetrate to the heart of the meaning of any single part. For these very acts of grasping and penetrating leave us, especially when we read *The Faerie Queene*, empty-handed or in an empty place. The poem has receded and eluded us, as if offended, like the ghost in *Hamlet*. We are compelled, therefore, to relinquish the traditional thought-models of grasping and penetrating and to read instead with courtesy, with a relaxed openness to the strange that allows the poem to disclose itself to us of its own accord and in its own time.[2] The most ancient forms of courtesy, as we see in Homer, allow the stranger to remain strange—that is, to some extent hidden—even as the stranger is welcomed.

We might at first suppose that the burden of the meaning of Hamlet's remark rests on the word *more*: there are more things to study. Philosophy—in the broad, Renaissance sense of the term as *scientia*—is the open project of explaining the *things* of this world. Many of the things of this world have not been explained; but they will be explained, or at least theoretically they can be explained, in the future. Keep an open mind about supernatural phenomena, such as ghosts. One day we will know all about them, including whether they are illusory or real.

But to suppose that this is what Hamlet intends is to misapprehend the radical force of his remark. That force emerges in the second verse, where Hamlet characterizes the entire project of philosophy as a kind of dreaming. In particular, he characterizes the philosophical concept of the *thing* as a dream. (I hear Hamlet's ironical stress on that word: "There are more *things* in heaven and earth, Horatio.") Philosophy reduces the flux of existence, and the flux of our consciousnesses inside existence, to a gigantic array of hard-surfaced things. It is an array of phenomena, of "appearances to consciousness," as the word *phenomena* implies, phenomena that are also "thrown against" consciousness, which is why we call them *objects*. As the flux of existence is reduced to an array of things, so is the flux of consciousnesses reduced to the solitary, contemplating subject. This subject grasps the phenomena as if they were things, or as if they were tools—useful things—for adjusting and manipulating other things.

The concept of the thing opens the way for the mathematical category of the unit. By the abstraction of flux into units, all things are subject to enumeration and measurement. With mathematics as a tool, all the interactions of the phenomena, all the events in our world, can be analyzed as the outcome of the physical laws governing things. Hamlet is calling the project of scientific and philosophical understanding into question—actually, he is being scornful of it in Horatio—when he speaks of philosophy as dreaming. The methodological point is that when we encounter the unknown and seek to make it known we should take care not to assume inadvertently that the unknown already belongs to the known as a thing. To assume the thingly character of the unknown is to make it likely that we will miss it completely, taking hold instead on a thing, like the *eidolon* of Helen, that reflects our presuppositions. Yet that is what we do: we assume that the strange is a thing. For it is impossible not to make this assumption if we are to "think" in the familiar philosophical way, according to the rules. But the assumption of the thingliness of the strange puts us off the track from the start. The result is that we are not really thinking. We are instead dreaming the philosophical dream, in which a solitary, conscious subject confronts a world of unconscious things. To do otherwise—to assume the unknown may be looking back into us as we look into it—is to be unscientific, superstitious, or religious. Yet that is what Hamlet invites us to do: to move into the presence of the stranger without taking hold, allowing the stranger to remain in some essential way hidden. Hamlet invites us not just to consider the strange theoretically but to welcome the strange as a stranger. Such hospitality—a word which in the Indo-European languages enfolds aggression (hostility) as well as welcome—declines to take hold of the stranger, the guest, as if the stranger were an object or a tool, even though that is what the traditional model of thinking demands: the grasping hold. The hospitality, or, to use the word which will dominate in this essay, the courtesy which one shows to the ghost allows the ghost to have an advantage of us too, to look at us, to assess us, to anticipate us, even as we look toward him.

★ ★ ★

Readers will recognize in these remarks on *Hamlet*, and in particular on the characterization of philosophy as a kind of dreaming, the influence of Martin Heidegger's claim that the task of thinking lies ahead of us still, that we have not yet begun to think and need to find out what thinking is before we can do it.[3] But surely this is an outrageous claim. We have a proud tradition of philosophical thinking more than two and a half thousand years old. And philosophers are precisely those who are professionally concerned with the nature, the reliability, and the limits of thinking as such. With what right—more importantly, with what evidence—does Heidegger malign philosophy thoughtless? To understand this claim of Heidegger's it is important to recognize at the outset what it does not mean. Heidegger's claim that we have not yet begun to think does not mean that no one today is engaged in intellectual activity of a high order, some of it—particularly in the natural sciences—of the highest order ever attained. Likewise, Heidegger's claim does not mean that philosophy as it has been practiced since antiquity, and as it is practiced in the modern world since Descartes, is of no intellectual value: on the contrary. The intense study of the history of philosophy—and few great philosophers have been so preoccupied with the history of philosophy—is necessary if we are to find out how to understand and escape the limits within which that history subtly but powerfully encloses us. Nor does Heidegger's claim mean that no one has ever thought. The poets have thought. The entire philosophical tradition has been the playing-out of the consequences of some original, poetical thoughts, which are no longer visible from within that tradition. Heidegger says that the poets, or some of them, have thought in the past and that some of them are doing so now. We must once again go to the poets to find out about thinking. Because it is a craft rather than a calculation, and because it is open to the otherness of the unknown, asking not "what is it?" but "what does it say?", poetry is more nearly allied than philosophy is to what Heidegger understands by *thinking*. That is the proposition that Heidegger aims to explore in his later work on thinking.

I have a much more limited aim, which is to find out about thinking in Spenser, and particularly in *The Faerie Queene*, a poem which, as a "continued allegory or darke conceit," comes closer to thinking—to speculative reasoning about the human—than any other work of literature known to me. I have two claims to advance in respect of this poem. The first is that Spenser is not primarily a narrative poet but a poet whose concern is to think. Spenser thinks in subtle, allusive, indirect, and intuitive ways about problems too complex to be dealt with in the isolating, linear fashion with which human problems are usually met.[4] Romance narrative, the conventions and iconography of allegorical expression, the deployment of episodes and characters, are all for Spenser instruments of thinking, of questioning in regions that are only indicated by the terms with which he begins: holiness, temperance, and so on. This point can be made more directly, and more polemically: in *The Faerie Queene* thinking actually happens. *The Faerie Queene* is not a *representation* of what has already been thought, cloudily enwrapped in allegorical devices. There is nothing secondary about it. Instead, *The Faerie Queene* is thinking enacted as a creative, a poetic event. This event of thinking does not occur on the model of what would become the classic situation for early modern philosophy, in which the subject contemplates a surrounding world of unconscious objects. The event of thinking in *The Faerie Queene* is instead an encounter between persons, or, as we call them, personifications. The place of the subject, of thinking consciousness, is not in the author, or not exclusively in the author. There is a circulation of conscious energy, a noetic circulation, which passes through the author into the work and through the work back into the author as the work of composition proceeds. A similar process of noetic circulation occurs in the process of reading. But the main point is this: that thinking in *The Faerie Queene* is not a thinking about objects, a conscious reflection directed towards unconscious things. Thinking in *The Faerie Queene* is an intersubjective encounter between persons, where one mind engages with and responds to another, and neither mind achieves a "grasp" of the situation in its totality. Instead of "grasping" a thought or a problem, the model of thinking we encounter in Spenser is an approach to the other which yet leaves the other alone, in its own space. For such encounters the model of tool-grasping is no longer adequate to the nature of thought. We are in need of something like the model of courtesy, of the encounter with the stranger who is welcomed.

The second claim I advance, therefore, is that for Spenser thinking is an encounter with the strange to which courtesy is the key. Courtesy, the virtue of book six of *The Faerie Queene*, partly because it comes last, is usually regarded as the least profound of the virtues with which the poet contends intellectually in the course of his poem. Holiness and Justice, for example, will seem to us deeper, more fundamental virtues than Courtesy. Courtesy is usually thought of, in C. S. Lewis's exact phrase, as a "supervenient perfection."[5] Both words in this phrase tell: courtesy is *supervenient* becomes it comes from above and is laid on at the end; and courtesy is a *perfection*, in the sense of that word as a completion, because it is the last stage, the *telos*, of moral development. By courtesy the completed moral subject is given its finishing gloss. Understood in these terms, courtesy is attractive and graceful, but it is superficial too, having been laid on at the end. Small wonder the Legend of Courtesy comes last in the books Spenser completed, after Justice and Friendship, which are surely more important social principles than it.

Yet because of the way Spenser thinks it is dangerous to assume that that which comes last is that which is least fundamental. The opposite is more often true. In traditional, constructive, propositional thinking, which works according to method, the remotest conclusions are implied in, and follow necessarily from, the original premises. That at least is the ideal. But it is an ideal of absolute closure and reversibility. This aesthetically pleasing effect of philosophical method is captured, for example, in *Paradise Lost*, when, at the end, Adam's response to the angel Michael's narrative, "Henceforth I learn that to obey is best" (12. 561) follows from the poem's opening line, "Of Man's first disobedience." And the last verses of Milton's epic—"They hand in hand with wand'ring steps and slow/Through Eden took their solitary way"—owe much of their force to our feeling that they complete on an emotional level what the poet, at the outset, said he would do: "justify the ways of God to men" (1. 26). In *Paradise Lost*, as in a philosophical treatise such as Hegel's *Phenomenology*, it seems as if the entire arc of thought is contained *in nuce* in the opening moves. It seems, in short, as if the work is a representation of thinking that has already been done, and as if the work itself, as a structure of thought, is reversible.

In contrast to this, each book of *The Faerie Queene* begins, or places near the beginning, episodes that set forth the subject of the book in the most traditional, formulaic, and even, on occasion, hackneyed way. Only as the poet proceeds, as the complications of his narrative open unexpected resources and vistas, does original thinking begin. The conclusions—or, rather, the open places the poet gets to by the end of each book—are not reversible. That is, we cannot work back from those open places to the opening moves and see how the conclusions have been developed necessarily from origins. The opening moves seem like earlier, more naïve stages in the thought, unrelated to the thought at the end. They seem so because they are. As he works to fill out a thought by means of narrative Spenser almost inadvertently explores the thought more deeply. But rather than saying "inadvertently" it is better to say that while the poet is concentrating on various deliberate mental actions—among which is the complex, Spenserian stanza—he is moving instinctively, though on purpose, deeper into the problems he raises. And where he gets to is unanticipated in his first thoughts.

* * *

In this respect, as in so many others, Spenser stands in contrast to

Milton. When we read through the arc of Milton's epic achievement, from *Paradise Lost* to *Paradise Regained* and *Samson Agonistes*, we feel that everything pertaining to the thought, the *dianoia* of these poems, has been worked out in advance. Before *Paradise Lost* Milton wrote discursively on church government, on marriage, on the state and its relation to citizens, on intellectual freedom, on civil power, on logic, and on theology. He was about fifty-seven years old when he completed *Paradise Lost*, having begun the poem in his late forties, when he had worked out all the fundamental structures of his thought. Artistic discoveries and choices are made in the course of Milton's great poems, but their thought contains nothing the poet had not said before. In this sense, Milton's poems are brilliantly didactic achievements. They do not think: they teach what has already been thought.

Spenser does not have Milton's capacious, grasping, essentially discursive, conceptual power. He is an intuitive and, more importantly, an instinctively conservative thinker who proceeds by wandering, non-deliberate procedures into original, and often radical thoughts. Spenser begins with commonplace formulations and ideas, commits them to the impulsive course of his narrative, introduces new iconographical material where it seems artistically appropriate to do so, and in effect allows those ideas to complicate and develop on their own before intervening again. By this process, which I have called noetic circulation, the poet is led into strange and unexplored areas of thought. If Milton could see farther than Spenser into any given issue—and the "givenness" of the issue is important—Spenser can take us into areas of thought of which Milton could not have suspected the existence. Milton is the poet of the will as a rational project, grasping the truth and setting it forth with unmistakable clarity and irresistible force. Spenser is the poet of *Gelassenheit*, of composure and calm, but also of "releasement," or "letting go," whereby the very relaxation of effort and of mental tension gives to his project an experimental character, allowing unexpected structures of thinking to emerge. In *The Faerie Queene* Spenser does not represent thinking that has already been done. He is thinking, so to speak, right in front of us, in very course of writing the poem. Milton had to figure everything out. Spenser wanted to find something out.

* * *

To find something out is Spenser's aim in the Legend of Courtesy.

The virtue of courtesy, to which Spenser comes at the end, is the most indispensable, the most deeply-rooted of all. He seems to sense this as the book opens, asking the muses to reveal to him "the sacred noursery/Of vertue" (*FQ* VI proem 3) which the gods planted in the earth and carefully tended there, having brought the seeds from heaven:

Revele to me the sacred noursery
  Of vertue, which with you doth there remaine,
  Where it in silver bowre does hidden ly
  From view of men, and wicked worlds disdaine.
  Since it at first was by the Gods with paine
  Planted in earth, being deriv'd at furst
  From heavenly seedes of bounty soveraine,
  And by them long with carefull labour nurst,
Till it to ripenesse grew, and forth to honour burst.

Amongst them all growes not a fayrer flowre,
  Then is the bloosme of comely courtesie,
  Which though it on a lowly stalke doe bowre,
  Yet brancheth forth in brave nobilitie,
  And spreds itself through all civilitie:
  Of which though present age doe plenteous seeme,
  Yet being matcht with plaine Antiquitie,
  Ye will them all but fayned showes esteeme,
Which carry colours faire, that feeble eies misdeeme.
(*The Faerie Queene* VI.Proem.3–4)

We note that the earth-rooted inculcation and growth of something derived from the stars is more fundamental than the image from the previous book. Justice, Astraea, returns to the earth, in the person of her deputy, Artegal, but Justice is not grown in the earth. Justice is the imposition of abstract principle on whatever circumstances it finds on the ground. Justice is tempered by mercy, but not by sympathy for or knowledge of the other. Although it is derived from the heavens, like Justice, Courtesy grows up out of the ground. Justice is theory, courtesy is habitual practice. Justice must be learned, courtesy is bred. What we learn in official institutions, when we are older, and must pay for the knowledge, will seem more important to civil society than what is bred in us at home. Reflecting this initial, low estimation of courtesy, Spenser shows the flower of courtesy growing from a "lowly stalke" because it does not at first seem so exalted or important as justice. Yet even as its lowliness is acknowledged in this passage courtesy branches out dramatically, spreading itself into "all civilitie," that is, into every region of human community. I repeat here the most relevant verses from the passage above:

> Amongst them all [the flowers of virtue] growes not a fayrer flower,
> Then is the bloosme of comely courtesie,
> Which though it on a lowly stalke doe bowre,
> Yet brancheth forth in brave nobilitie,
> And spreds it selfe through all civilitie.
> (*The Faerie Queene* VI.Proem.4)

It is possible to read this passage as saying that courtesy merely accompanies and lends grace to all the other virtues, and in so doing deserves to share in the "brave nobilitie" of them all. The most superficial of the virtues must be given equal status with the rest, once the book on it begins, if only out of courtesy. But Spenser's point here is deeper: it is to contrast an initial estimation—that courtesy grows on a lower stalk than, for example, justice, or holiness—and a later, better judgment: that society, and indeed justice and holiness themselves, can exist nowhere without courtesy. Society can exist without justice—there are societies which are fundamentally unjust, and society can exist without holiness—there are idolatrous societies aplenty. But no society can exist without courtesy. The point is more apparent, perhaps, if we recognize that much of what we currently mean by *culture*, in the anthropological sense of the term, is embraced by what Spenser meant by *courtesy*. The episode of Briana and Crudor, for example, fully anticipates the argument of Claude Lévi-Strauss's *The Raw and the Cooked*: the same distinction is explored by Spenser as the foundation of courtesy. I would put this in more active terms, defining courtesy as, and establishing its ground in, the fundamental desire for community.

Of course, the grammar of the statement—"and spreds it selfe through all civilitie"—does suggest that there was civil society first and courtesy after. But in this image Spenser is not so much representing the way things are as he is manifesting the process of *thinking* about the way things are. He is disclosing the order of assumptions by which he thinks about civil society: first, he sees its more evident structures, say, of holiness in churches, or of law in the courts, and then, gradually, he recognizes that courtesy is indispensable to civil society. Courtesy is less obvious because it is not a formal institution of civil society. Courtesy therefore does not initially appear before the eye of the mind. But when one reflects more deeply on the conditions necessary to civil society it grows upon one, like a thought branching forth through one's earlier thoughts, that courtesy is the most fundamental of these conditions. Courtesy is the most fundamental of the conditions necessary to civil society because the ground of courtesy, unlike any of the other virtues, is *the will to community*. This is the thought that in Spenser's mind "spreds it selfe through all civilitie."

I now summarize what happens in the passage from the proem to the sixth book of *The Faerie Queene*. The poet asks the muses to reveal to him what he then reveals to us: the garden, or "sacred noursery" of the virtues, which has been planted in the earth with much effort ("with paine") by the gods, from seeds which they have brought from heaven. Carefully nursed by the gods, the entire garden grows to maturity and blossoms in "honour," achieving that fulfillment of the virtues by which they, the virtues, become conspicuous as the flowering of an ideal social order: " . . . And by them [the gods] long with careful labour nurst,/Till it [the "sacred noursery"] to ripeness grew, and forth to honour burst" (VI proem 3). The garden in flower becomes the image of the ideal of civil society. What is revealed next is the flower of *courtesy*, which I have said is rooted in the fundamental will to community. Courtesy is revealed as a blossom which, though on a "lowly stalke," and therefore closer to the ground than the others, branches forth among them and rises to their height. No flower, we are told, is fairer than it, and no flower rises to a greater height of honor and "brave nobilitie." But for all its exaltation, courtesy begins lower to the ground, sheltering itself there—I take that to be the sense of the verb *bowre*—and taking its strength from the earth. At first, courtesy appears simply to be low to the ground, making an attractive carpet against which the more striking flowers are seen rising above it and "bursting forth to honor." Yet as the poet thinks about courtesy through this image of it as a bed of blossoms, the image grows in his mind. The floral carpet is his initial mental image of courtesy, an enameled mead beneath the soaring flowers of the higher virtues, giving to those flowers a beautiful ground. But the floral ground suddenly rises up and engulfs the higher flowers, branching and spreading "though all civilitie" until no other blossom can surpass that of courtesy in nobility and honor.

I take this subtle but remarkable effect, which is so typical of Spenser's hallucinogenic art, and so unique to him, as an occasion to repeat my major claim. By means of the complicated, dynamic image of the garden of the virtues, in which a lower carpet of flowers suddenly rises up among the highest, Spenser is not representing his thought about courtesy: he is not representing thinking that has already been done. Spenser is showing us the process of his thinking as it develops. The referent of the garden image is not civil society and the place of courtesy in civil society. The referent is instead the process of thinking about civil society and of discovering, by noetic circulation, the fundamental importance of courtesy in civil society. The "spreading" and "branching" to which Spenser refers, the rising up of the carpet of blossoms to become entangled in the flowers to which they were formerly a background, is the spreading, branching, and rising of Spenser's thought. We are seeing Spenser thinking. But we are seeing Spenser's thinking occurring not in his head but in the otherness of his poetic enterprise. Spenser is not grasping at the essence of courtesy but moving into nearness with the problem of courtesy, treating the problem itself in a courteous way by allowing it to disclose itself (and no more of itself than it wants to disclose) in its own time. In his proem to the book of Courtesy, Spenser is welcoming that virtue, which is as yet strange, as a stranger. It is a stranger that reveals itself to the poet as he writes, and to which he will respond as he presses on with his tale. We must remember, however, that although much is revealed in this passage about courtesy—its unobvious but foundational importance for civil society—the blossoms of courtesy hold much more in reserve, remaining fundamentally strange. In this passage, courtesy and thinking about courtesy are one and the same.

⋆ ⋆ ⋆

How does Spenser arrive at the thought of courtesy? He does so by a process of thought similar, though on a much larger scale, to what we have observed in the nursery image. The poet arrives at the thought of courtesy by thinking about the failure of his Legend of Justice. The failure of the Legend of Justice to be a theory of justice (notice, that I do not say, the failure of Book Five, which is a success) results from a failure to find an adequate ground for the theory. As I mentioned earlier, Spenser begins with an Astraean theory of justice: justice descends from the stars, like the starry goddess Astraea returning to earth. This justice is imposed on whatever circumstances it may find on the ground. In other words, the circumstances on the ground are not taken into account or allowed for. The result of this blind imposition of abstract justice on circumstances of which it is wholly ignorant—-the English plantations in Ireland are never far from Spenser's thoughts in this book—can be predicted: the ceaseless, mechanical bloodletting for which Talus becomes the symbol. Spenser's solution in the end, which comes after Book Five, was not better reconnoitering and sterner repression but an exploration of the will to community. It was the writing of Book Five that taught Spenser that there can be no justice where there is no underlying will to community. Only where the subjects of justice desire to live together, and to maintain order together, can justice, which is protection against those who reject what the community assents to, begin to be established. Spenser's word for this desire is, as I have also said, courtesy. Courtesy is for Spenser the most fundamental of the virtues, the basis on which all the other virtues stand. Spenser did not think this at the outset of his writing *The Faerie Queene*: at the outset he thought Holiness was the foundational virtue. The Puritans (if we are to accept Ben Jonson's interpretation of the Blattant Beast) made him think otherwise.

Earlier, Spenser appears to have supposed what most of us would suppose at the start. Before one can worry about cultivating mere courtesy, the more necessary virtues must be established in the self, for example, Temperance, or self-control with respect to one's appetites, Chastity, or self-control with respect to other's appetites, and Friendship, a balancing of concern for the self and the other. Courtesy, it is supposed, comes later in one's breeding, being reserved chiefly, though by no means exclusively, for strangers. Yet when we think of child rearing we see that courtesy begins at home and actually comes first among the virtues. Courtesy is the basis on which the other virtues are raised. To resume Spenser's terms, Temperance, Friendship, and even Justice, are impossible without courtesy; and Holiness and Chastity are disgusting without courtesy.

* * *

In what I have said so far the reader will discern the influence of Martin Heidegger's thought about thinking, especially in *What is Called Thinking? Was heisst Denken?* (1954). But it is in the small, occasional book on thinking, *Gelassenheit* (English trans. *Discourse on Thinking*) which we see the early development of Heidegger's radically non-metaphysical and non-scientific exploration of thinking.

The first part of the book is the essay entitled *Gelassenheit* ("calmness," "composure," in modern German, but also a mystical "letting go," or "releasement"), which is a memorial address on the composer Conradin Kreutzer, delivered in Heidegger's home town, Messkirch, on October 30, 1955. The second, and principal part of the book dates back to notes taken in 1944–45. It is a dialogue between a Scholar, a Scientist, and a Teacher, which takes place as they walk on a country path, and which breaks off, incomplete, as they draw near to "human habitation."

This discussion is meant to be, and it is, the esoteric portion of the book, although it begins with the unexamined assumption that thinking is the distinguishing mark of the essence of human nature. Alluding to an earlier discussion, the Scientist asks the Teacher what is meant by the proposition that man's nature is to be found by looking away from man. The Teacher replies that if thinking is the essence of man's nature, then thinking itself can be seen only when we look away from thinking.

Clearly, two senses of *thinking* are intended in this statement: on the one hand, thinking as re-presenting and calculating, on the other hand, thinking in the sense to be explored in the dialogue. But there is also a subtler, methodological point to the apparent paradox of looking away from thinking in order to see thinking, a point indicated in the setting of the dialogue as a walk on a country path away from human habitation. To think about thinking is to proceed on assumptions about thinking which are themselves to be put into question. To find thinking, therefore, one must wander away from thinking itself, as one wanders on a country path away from human habitation. One must relax and wander at ease—hence, *Gelassenheit*—if one is to release one's grasp on former certainties.

A critical moment comes at the end of the dialogue when the Scholar mentions that there is a single, Greek word, which has often come to his mind in their discussion about thinking. But each time he was about to propose this word it seemed to fit less well with what drew near to them, as they wandered, as the nature of thinking ("was sich uns als das Wesen des Denkens näherte."[6] This is one of those interesting moments in the dialogue in which the speakers, who have gone out into the country to find thinking, have the feeling that something which *they* would call the nature, or the essence of thinking, but which far exceeds that particular naming, is stalking them. In the camouflage, as it were, of "the Nature of Thinking," something draws near to them, unseen, in the forest. In any event, the Scientist observes that even if this single word, which the Scholar is withholding, is no longer suitable, the Scholar might as well reveal it, since they are approaching human habitation and must break off their discussion. The single word is all that remains of Heraclitus' fragment 122, αγχιβασίη (*anchibasie*), "near-going," or "moving into nearness," "*in-die-Nähe-gehen.*" This allows one of the speakers to propose "*In-die-Nähe-hinein-sich-einlassen,*" "letting-oneself-into-nearness," a relaxed self-surrender, which allows one to approach without seizing, and to think by being open to what reveals itself of its own accord. [7]

We see this in Spenser: the poet asks if he may receive from the other the disclosure of what was unknown: "Revele to me the sacred noursery . . . ." To whom is he speaking? He tells us he speaks to the muses, the "sacred imps, that on *Parnasso* dwell." But it is also they who are stalking him, drawing near to him, in the forest of romance; and they are in the camouflage of thought. We note that the muses must be courted, courteously invoked. We note too that the poet, in thinking, does not think directly toward the thing, the object of thought. The poet moves into nearness with the revealing muses who are moving into nearness with him. He moves into a personal relationship, in the hope that they will disclose some of their wisdom to him. But he hopes this without expecting that they will, or that they could, disclose all. Moreover, he hopes the muses will disclose some of their wisdom to him without expecting that the wisdom will be something he can grasp and apply to the world, as a thing final in itself. The wisdom will instead be something he will take into himself only to send it out again into—into what? Into the poem, that is, into the developing project of *The Faerie Queene*, which is not a poem at all, if by the noun *poem* we mean to designate an object, an artifact. *The Faerie Queene* is instead a project, a throwing forward and a releasing of the self into thinking, a very long, unimaginably complex, heroically sustained, yet delicate, courteous probing of the unknown. *The Faerie Queene* is Spenser's actual thinking, which occurs in noetic circulation through the project in which he is engaged. *The Faerie Queene* is therefore an intellectual action: a poetic releasement of the self for moving into nearness with wisdom.

NOTES

1. *The Riverside Shakespeare*, 2nd ed., ed. G. Blakemore Evans et al. (Boston: Houghton Mifflin, 1977). Quotations from Spenser are from *The Faerie Queene*, 2nd. ed, edited by A. C. Hamilton; text edited by Hiroshi Yamashita and Toshiyuki Suzuki (London: Longman, 2001).

2. The subject of thinking in literature has received remarkably little useful attention, apart from one book, which in its conjectural and exploratory approach has opened an entire field. I refer to Angus Fletcher's *Colors of the Mind: Conjectures on Thinking in Literature* (Cambridge: Harvard University Press, 1991). Using an analysis of literary metaphor in the light of Wittgenstein's discussion of truth in language-games, Fletcher explores "the range of literary and artistic representations" of what he calls, in a chapter so named, "Iconographies of Thought" (34, and 15–34). The discussion of thresholds of thought in Fletcher's book on Spenser, *The Prophetic Moment: An Essay on Spenser* (Chicago: University of Chicago Press, 1971), anticipates what he refers to in *Colors of the Mind* as "the extreme situation" (244), the moment where figuration presses at the boundaries of the conceivable. Another significant book on thinking is Sean Kane's study of how Spenser manages to think outside the traditional models of intellectual mastery and power. It is by striving to escape the divide-and-rule logic of binary oppositions on a flattened conceptual plane that Spenser discovers an ecological thinking responsive to patterns of relationship in the thought-world. See *Spenser's Moral Allegory* (Toronto: University of Toronto Press, 1989).

3. Martin Heidegger, *What is Called Thinking?,* trans. J. Glenn Gray (New York: Harper and Row, 1968), 3, a translation of *Was Heisst Denken?* published in 1954. See also the following: *Discourse on Thinking*, trans. John M. Anderson and E. Hans Freund (New York: Harper and Row, 1966), a translation of *Gelassenheit*, 1959, based on notes dating from 1944–45; *The Question Concerning Technology and Other Essays*, trans. William Lovitt (New York: Harper and Row, 1977), the title essay, based on a lecture given in 1955, appears in *Die Technik und die Kehre* and *Vorträge und Aufsätze*. Relevant discussion also occurs in *Basic Questions of Philosophy: Selected "Problems" of "Logic"*, trans. Richard Rojcewicz and Andre Schuwer (Bloomington and Indianapolis: Indiana University Press, 1994), a translation of *Grundfragen der Philosophie: Ausgewählte "Probleme" der "logic,"* published in 1984 and based on lectures given in 1937–38.

4. I say this in "Spenser's *Mutabilitie* and the Authority of Forms," in *Allegory and Violence* (Ithaca: Cornell University Press, 1996), esp. pp. 174–76.

5. C. S. Lewis, *The Allegory of Love* (Oxford: Oxford University Press, 1936), 351–52. Cited with useful discussion in A.C. Hamilton, ed. *The Faerie Queene*, 2nd ed. London: Longman, 2001), 14. In the first edition (1977) Hamilton, in a discussion of criticism of book six, notes a consensus that Spenser is no longer concerned with "abstract moral, philosophical, or historical argument" but instead with romance, where "manifold, mysterious meanings [are] conveyed in a 'poetic' context" (621). The placement of *poetic* in quotation marks indicates a nervousness with that designation as well. The book is neither philosophical thinking nor pure poetry, if by "poetry" we mean that which remains outside thought. Instead, a kind of poetic thinking occurs, or rather, thinking is disturbingly identified with the poetic. Hamilton cites Kathleen Williams, who notes that the mythical quality of the book makes "commentary feel itself absurd" (strange reflexive pronoun). Hamilton also cites Humphrey Tonkin, who speaks of allegory merging into myth. Yet Hamilton is unwilling to go along with the suggestion, which lurks behind these and Lewis's remarks, that book six is intellectually lightweight. Instead, he emphasizes that the

allegory is "especially fine and subtle" (622). In seeking to capture how this fineness and subtlety works, Hamilton asserts that in the Legend of Courtesy the "darke conceit" is "displayed on the literal surface of the romantic fiction" (622). The particular value of this observation, in my judgment, is that it separates the thinking that occurs in this book from the object-centered notion of "concepts" hidden beneath the surface, demanding that the interpreter reach for them, and grasp them. Critics experience frustration and perplexity with Book 6 because the traditional models of thought, and of the mediation of thought by interpretation, are relinquished in this book for a model of thought as sociable, courteous movement toward the unknown, a movement into nearness that only appears to be intellectually easier because it does not involve grasping, conceiving, mastering the unknown.

6. Martin Heidegger, *Gelassenheit* (Stuttgart: Neske, 1959), 68. *Discourse on Thinking*, trans. John M. Anderson and E. Hans Freund (New York: Harper and Row, 1966), 87.

7. *Ibid.*, Ger. text p. 70; Engl. trans. P. 89.

Index